ART AND PHILOSOPHY

ART
and
PHILOSOPHY

by

JOSEPH MARGOLIS

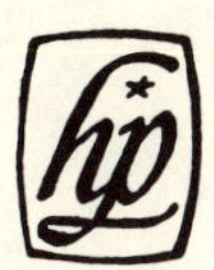

HUMANITIES PRESS
Atlantic Highlands, N.J.

First published in the United States of America
in 1980 by Humanities Press Inc.
Atlantic Highlands, N.J. 07716
Copyright © 1980 by Humanities Press Inc.

Library of Congress Cataloging in Publication Data

Margolis, Joseph Zalman, 1924—
   Art and philosophy.

   Includes bibliographical references and index.
   1. Art—Philosophy. I. Title.
N70.M34 1976   701   76-19063
ISBN 0-391-00645-2

Contents

Introduction

Part One. The Work of Art

Part Two. Criticism and Appreciation

Part Three. The Literary Arts

For Meyer Schapiro and Michael Lekakis,
masters of art

Acknowledgements

Portions of several chapters in this book have been published earlier, in somewhat different form: "Mr. Weitz and the Definition of Art," *Philosophical Studies,* IX (1958); "The Problem of Relevance in Esthetic Criticism," *Bucknell Review,* VII (1958); "The Identity of a Work of Art," *Mind,* LXVII (1959); "Aesthetic Perception," *Journal of Aesthetics and Art Criticism,* XIX (1960); "Describing and Interpreting Works of Art," *Philosophy and Phenomenological Research,* XXII (1961); "On Disputes about the Ontological Status of a Work of Art," *British Journal of Aesthetics,* VIII (1968); "Numerical Identity and Reference in the Arts," *British Journal of Aesthetics,* X (1970); review of E.D. Hirsch, *Validity in Interpretation, Shakespeare Studies,* IV (1970); "Critics and Literature, *British Journal of Aesthetics,* XI (1971); "Art as Language," *The Monist,* LVIII (1974); "Works of Art as Physically Embodied and Culturally Emergent Entities," *British Journal of Aesthetics,* XIV (1974); "Robust Relativism," *Journal of Aesthetics and Art Criticism,* XXXV (1976); "The Ontological Peculiarity of Works of Art," *Journal of Aesthetics and Art Criticism,* XXXVI (1977); "Strategy for a Philosophy of Art," *Journal of Aesthetics and Art Criticism,* XXXVII (1979); "Literature and Speech Acts," *Philosophy and Literature,* III (1979). They are reproduced with the permission of the publishers.

Preface

This book has gone through a great many vicissitudes and I am enormously relieved to see it in finished form. The young Danish aesthetician, Lars Aagaard-Mogensen, urged me four years or so ago to reprint an earlier book of mine, *The Language of Art and Art Criticism* (Detroit: Wayne State University Press, 1965). I began to recast that book, incorporating what I thought was the best of the earlier material with my current views. But the effort led to an enormously unwieldy manuscript that I grudgingly came to see was not very well formed at all. Somewhat more than two years ago, the Danish publishing company which originally commissioned the book experienced such financial troubles about halfway through the page proofs that, on their plea, I withdrew the manuscript altogether. Fortunately, Simon Silverman, of the Humanities Press, was prepared to undertake its publication. In the meantime I was able to complete and publish *Persons and Minds* (Dordrecht: D. Reidel, 1978), which, as I now see, enabled me to formulate the theory of persons and cultural entities on which my entire effort in aesthetics has always, however inchoately, depended. I have, therefore, been able to rework in a fresh and more fundamental way my theories regarding criticism and the arts.

I should also say that I have come to see a unity in aesthetics that I was not able to detect at all fifteen years ago; perhaps more accurately, there were no signs in the then-current literature of any kind of compelling unity. The essential themes that now unify my views, and that I find genuinely promising in a larger sense, are a sympathy for the widest application of a moderate relativism (that escapes incoherence), and a commitment to a nonreductive materialism specifically designed to accommodate the emergence of cultural phenomena. I know of no sustained effort to advance these views elsewhere in the philosophical literature. And

I am persuaded that aesthetics is the most strategically placed philosophical discipline of our time, for it provides an ineliminable foundation of the most detailed sort for a fresh inquiry into the relationship between the physical and non-cultural disciplines and those studies—variously termed social, historical, and behavioral—that center on the analysis of language and the characteristic work and conduct of ourselves, creatures that form and are informed by the contingent cultural context that we alone can grasp.

I have tried to confine the contents of this book to the special concerns of aesthetics. But I find myself already pursuing implications for what might be called a philosophical anthropology and for the methodological issues of the cultural sciences. I think I have always construed aesthetics as providing paradigms for the theory of human history, action, even perception and knowledge; this book completed, I can now turn to explore whether the notion is actually as fruitful as it still seems. In any case, most of the best-known work in Anglo-American aesthetics has been all but indifferent to the ontological and methodological implications of viewing art and its appreciation as fully cultural phenomena. I hope this book will suggest something of the full force of that admission—both in terms of correcting a now-obvious distortion, and of identifying a larger conceptual unity that ought to affect our picture of what a science is. I press the point, I suppose, in order to wear my philosophical heart on my printed sleeve.

I have benefited from exchanges with too many people to name here. I hope my friends will see where they have helped me. But I should like particularly to thank Ruth Bray and Grace Stuart, who, as so often in the past, have put my work into readable form, and Donald Callen, who has improved the text by numerous suggestions.

August 1978   J.M.

INTRODUCTION

1. Initial Strategy for a Philosophy of Art

In theorizing about the fine arts, one is invariably fascinated by local details. Just recently, for example, an unusual report—possibly the first such report—has been published of an autistic girl who produced an extraordinary body of drawings by the age of six (Selfe, [1978]). The psychiatrists and teachers who worked with her finally managed to train her to speak a few words; but as a result of their success, she simply stopped the amazing flow of fresh creations that had apparently replaced speech. Many have theorized that the kind of genius certain very young prodigies exhibit must exclude the skills of the plastic arts, since the maturation of these skills—unlike, say, mathematical and musical gifts—has been thought to be peculiarly dependent on cultural influences. Karl Bühler, in fact, is reported by Nigel Dennis [1978] to have held that the early learning of speech comes to dominate early graphic ability and eventually "swallow[s] it up completely." Thinking of Nadia, the prodigy in question, we cannot fail to ask ourselves about the difference between what we take to be ordinary perception and the gifted perception of those who, in an apparently effortless way, transform what they see into what they draw. An enormous number of similar cases arrest our attention, demanding to be explained. Confronting the evidence, we realize, of course, that we know remarkably little about the acquisition of language and culture by the young; although we see the success of the process manifested in pertinent behavior. All the artistic creations that fascinate our eye and ear quite baffle the understanding—Blake's illustrations as much as those of our autistic child, Couperin's choral music as much as the chants of children. We certainly cannot claim to have analyzed the work of the creative mind. Hence, especially in the arts, we rummage among its collecting deposits.

But in theorizing about the arts, as in so much else, the power of a conception lies not so much in illuminating selected details—though it must do that much—as it does in defining closer, convincing unities among large domains of inquiry previously felt to be linked in spite of the incapacity of prevailing schemes of thought to match our intuitions. What, for example, is the connection among artworks, speech, human history, and the deliberate actions of intelligent persons? One is inclined to say that they are all culturally significant, culturally emergent phenomena. To grant the point seems easy enough. And yet, this concession implies, in part, the much less obvious idea that a theory of art will be compelling to the extent that the domain it organizes may be seen to be systematically related to all the other salient features of the cultural life of man. With the promise of such a theory, it is even possible to trade academically reinforced internal plausibilities for potential gains in linking art with the rest of human culture, provided we allow our intuitions sufficient time to adjust to findings and discount, in stages, any excessive distortion of the relationship between art and other cultural phenomena. Conceptual change works in this way; but to say so is not to deny the necessary overlap, diachronically, between earlier and later phases of the language in which even discontinuous theories are formulated (*contra* Feyerabend [1975] and Kuhn [1970]). In effect, this means that the proposal of a new conception of the arts must be integrated with a running dispute of the most compelling alternative conceptions. Doubtless, there are many ways in which to press such a theory—some of which will not seem too much of an academic exercise. The debates of aestheticians will eventually be measured against the interests of the rest of the art community and even of the world at large. But ultimately, our theories must be appraised by other informed professional theorists. Therefore, it is just as well to meet the question head on.

An apparent, but only apparent, aside will suggest the force of emphasizing the common cultural status of art, human history, action, language, and persons. In his well-known *Individuals* [1959], a book which seemed bold and fresh when it first appeared, coming after a sustained avoidance of ontology in analytic philosophical circles, P.F. Strawson identified both persons and physical bodies as what he called "basic particulars," that is, a "distinguishable class or category of particulars such that, as things are, it would not be possible to make all the identifying references which we do make to particulars of other classes, unless we make identifying references to particulars of that class, whereas it would be possible to make all the identifying references we do make to particulars of that class without making identifying reference to particulars of other classes." As is known, Strawson refused to countenance a Cartesian dualism regarding persons and insisted that *both* persons and bodies were basic. In Strawson's view, therefore, on pain of contradiction, persons and bodies could not be treated as one and the same, and physical bodies could not form the proper parts of persons. Persons were said to be distinguished from physical bodies in that both P- and M- ("personal" and "material") attributes could be ascribed to them, whereas only M-attributes could be ascribed to physical bodies.

Strawson's account was confronted by certain problems which he has apparently not yet resolved. For instance, his "persons" prove to be merely sentient creatures, hardly persons in any full-blooded sense; he has never explained the relationship between persons and bodies, in virtue of which a person may have precisely the same attributes as an associated physical body said not to be part of that person; two distinct entities not parts of one another must, contrary to Strawson's original intention, be admitted to occupy precisely one and the same place; and so on. This is not to discount Strawson's striking and reasonable claim that persons cannot be reduced to physical bodies; it is only to say that *if* his proposal is to be defended at all, it had better be defended in an entirely different way.

What is extraordinarily suggestive about Strawson's maneuver, as far as the philosophy of art is concerned, is simply that it is a consequence of Strawson's theory that *persons and physical bodies cannot be distinguished from one another in any purely perceptual way*: whatever properties a physical body has that may be discriminated by means of the senses cannot, according to the theory, distinguish that body from a person said (in some way not explained by Strawson, but capable of being explained) to be (nondualistically) "affiliated" with that body. Once we grasp this point, we see that it is an easy matter to hold—in fact, the thesis may be even more obvious—that *words and sentences cannot be identical with the sounds and marks with which they are* (in some sense to be explained) *"affiliated," though they cannot be distinguished from those sounds and marks by any purely perceptual means.* *If* we entertain the possibility that all cultural phenomena exhibit this characteristic, namely, that they are in some sense (nondualistically and nonreductively) affiliated with physical bodies or material entities of some sort, then we are directly led to suppose that the pattern is exhibited as well by artworks.

This is a remarkably economical way of outflanking a great many of the best-known theories of art in the twentieth century and of welcoming some of the more interesting newer theories that have surfaced in recent years. It is not, of course, a complete argument, only a sketch of the strategy of an argument. The reason for pursuing it is its initial simplicity and its promised scope. It rests on intuitions that are at least worth considering, analogies that are at least plausible, and a conceptual thread that draws us back to our opening concern with the linkage among the various sub-domains of the cultural world. Much of the charm of our approach lies in its not having to prejudge—except in terms of resisting an extreme reductionism—the actual ontology of art and in its ability to proceed, at least dialectically, against certain claims and admissions by those who have already formed a focused theory of art. A few specimen cases will show at a stroke the surprising power of this modest beginning.

In one of the most suggestive recent papers bearing on the ontology and appreciation of art, "The Artworld" [1964], Arthur Danto offers a number of intriguing claims that he has still to make fully systematic and explicit. These claims include at least the following: (i) artworks are related to, and distinguished from, "real [physical] objects" by "the *is* of artistic identification," that is, they are not identical with those objects but possess physical properties or incorporate physical parts of such objects in virtue of which they are identified as, and are, the entities they are; (ii) artworks are easily mistaken for real objects when they are (in the sense of "the *is* of artistic identification") just those real objects; (iii) artworks are specimens of entities that "enjoy a double citizenship," apparently belonging to the real world (of physical objects) and to what Danto terms the "artworld"; (iv) it is the theory of art, to which we subscribe in some sense, "that takes [an object] up into the world of art, and keeps it from collapsing into the real object which it is (in a sense of *is* other than that of artistic identification)"; (v) two different but perceptually indiscernible artworks may be identical with (in the sense of the *is* of artistic identification) one and the same real physical object, which is thereby "contain[ed] . . . as part of itself"; (vi) construing physical objects, via some theory of the artworld, in terms of the *is* of artistic identification "*constitutes* it a work of art"; (vii) "To see something as art requires something the eye cannot descry—an atmosphere of artistic theory, a knowledge of the history of art: an artworld," that is, a knowledge of the causal and historical conditions relevant to the production of artworks, informed by a theory of how real objects are related (by the *is* of artistic identification) to artworks.

There are, however, certain telltale weaknesses in this intriguing set of claims. First of all, there is a clear equivocation (doubtless intended but nevertheless not entirely resolved) in holding that *there is* one object, one and the same, that is both a purely physical object and also an artwork. If the "is" of artistic identification is not the "is" of ordinary identity (as must be true), then *one and the same* object cannot possess dual citizenship, as Danto claims. Secondly, if Danto favors the analogy with Strawson's case, which he mentions sympathetically, then he cannot hold that the *parts* of a physical object can as such be the parts of an artwork; and if he does hold that the parts of the one may be the parts of the other, then he cannot (so it would seem) maintain that the "is" of artistic identification is not the same as the "is" of identity. Finally, if he holds to the parts thesis unequivocally, then it looks as if he cannot hold that the identification of an artwork depends on considerations of a nonperceptual sort.

Clearly, we are invited to refine Danto's account by virtue of the convincing instances that Danto himself adduces: for instance, his analysis of two (fictitious) frescoes, *Newton's First Law* and *Newton's Third Law,* which look for all the world like identical white vertical rectangles nearly divided into equal squares by a horizontal black line, deliciously confirms the ease with which perceptual indiscernibility can be demonstrated. It is quite important to bear in mind that Danto wishes to press two quite different but related theses about perceptual distinction: (a) that it is possible to identify as numerically distinct two works of art, having quite different properties, that are *perceptually* indistinguishable; and (b) that to identify an object as an artwork is to rely on *nonperceptual,* causal and historical, grounds informed by our theorizing about the artworld. More recently, Danto [unpublished] has sketched a very pretty and amusing account of how to construe the Manhattan telephone directory as both a kind of novel and a kind of sculpture. The plausibility of his illustrations and the general drift of his account, together with the existence of an enormous body of artworks that require a theory rather along the lines he suggests, undermine completely all versions of the theory that artworks are essentially (or in some alternative sense, characteristically) *perceptual objects.* To grasp the force of Danto's thesis—admitting the weaknesses noticed—is to defeat at a stroke such well-known and extremely influential theories as the one defended for so many years by Monroe Beardsley.

Let us be clear about the strategy of the argument before applying it in detail. We begin with a general intuition that cultural phenomena—persons, artworks, words and sentences, and actions that form the body of human history—share certain distinctive properties, precisely those that mark such phenomena as culturally emergent. The essential clue lies with the fact that some kind of functional and nonperceptual distinction is required to sort persons from mere bodies, words and sentences from mere marks and sounds, human actions from mere bodily movements, *and,* in all likelihood, works of art from the physical materials in which they are somehow manifested. Strawson provides an incompletely worked-out suggestion along these lines, with respect to persons; hardly anyone disputes the point, with regard to language; and Danto presses just such a thesis with regard to art. The supporting analysis of cultural phenomena is lacking, of course (*see* Margolis [1978a]). But the thesis functions dialectically to cast considerable doubt on theories that treat artworks exhaustively, essentially, characteristically, or distinctively in terms of perceptual qualities. Part of the plausibility of pressing the thesis lies with the ready availability of specimens that cannot be suitably sorted in perceptual terms: this obtains among artworks as well as among other kinds of items, and it obtains even among the so-called visual arts (as opposed to, say, literature, the most recalcitrant of the arts in this respect)—for example, in Rauschenberg's "Erased DeKooning Drawing" and Duchamp's *L.H.O.O.Q. Shaved* (Binkley [1977]). Its plausibility also derives from not depending on any particular theory of culture, that is, on any theory that might be thought to be merely ad hoc. Of course, the provision of a suitable theory would be decisive; but such a theory would be bound to accommodate or to explain away the importance of just the nonperceptual considerations mentioned. There is, therefore, a certain prima facie weight in favor of the thesis, so that any version of the counterthesis may be judged suspect to the extent that it fails to address itself effectively or at all to the apparent discrepancy within the cultural domain. It is very easy, particularly on the strength of specimen cases, to suppose, for instance, that cultural phenomena must be distinguished in intentional, causal or productive, functional, or historical terms. But of course to admit that much is to admit that artworks must be identified in nonperceptual terms.

Thus, for example, Frank Sibley's [1959a] well-known theory, that the discrimination of aesthetic qualities is a form of *perceptual* taste, becomes immediately vulnerable merely by being made to focus, as Sibley intends, on the appreciation of art. Sibley's view of the logical peculiarity of aesthetic concepts is undermined precisely because the thesis *requires* that the concepts in question be essentially perceptual in nature. Admit distinctions involving aesthetic taste that are not perceptual: you will have admitted distinctions that Sibley's theory *cannot* accommodate. Similarly, the argument condemning the so-called Intentional Fallacy, developed by William Wimsatt and Monroe Beardsley [1954a], may be seen to be particularly contrary to the very nature of art itself; it appears that (if art is admitted to be a cultural phenomenon) it is quite impossible to deny the relevance of intentional considerations. These are mere sketches of arguments, of course. But precisely for that reason, they show the remarkable economy and promise of the strategy being considered.

As it happens, that strategy is double-edged. Not only does it oblige us to disqualify theories that hold artworks to be merely perceptual objects; it obliges us to clarify the relationship between physical and cultural phenomena as one other than that of identity. Hence, not only must Sibley's and Beardsley's theories fall; but Danto's and Strawson's must fall as well, at least to the extent that each contradicts the very distinction on which it rests. Strawson's does so, by implicitly admitting that two numerically distinct things may occupy the same place, even though occupying a place is central to Strawson's formulation of the very notion of numerical identity. And Danto's does so (more pertinently to our issue), by implicitly claiming that a work of art is both a physical object and an object different from any (mere) physical object.

The uneasy ambiguity of Danto's position becomes, ironically, more significant precisely insofar as, favoring the spirit of Danto's own account, we review his analysis of other cultural phenomena. Without doubt, his theory of action is the most instructive in this regard. There (Danto [1973a]), he explains, "I want to isolate those bare, neutral actions before they are colored by the sorts of meanings they are shown to have on the Arena walls and in common life . . . *basic* actions, as I shall term them . . ." On the other hand, he also says: "Actions we do but not *through* any distinct thing which we also do . . . I shall call *basic,* and mediated ones [those in which a man does . . . something *through* some other thing that he does] are accordingly nonbasic" (cf. Brand [1968]; Stoutland [1968]). Danto treats a basic action, therefore, as a "component" of a mediated action. (In this, he differs from Donald Davidson [1971], who is inclined to treat any seemingly mediated action in terms of alternative descriptions of one and the same "primitive action.") Hence, Danto regards mediated actions as not identical with basic actions. Furthermore, mediated actions are distinguished as "more human and more social . . . taken up into the fabric of communication, and deposited as part of human history . . . described in human or cultural terms." But, says Danto, a basic action "is identical . . . with a physiological series [of movements]," which of course reinforces (at a price) his point that basic actions are not identical with mediated actions. Still, one would have expected that the relationship between a basic action and a mediated action would form an appropriate (cultural) analogue of the relationship between a physical object and an artwork—that is, a construction parallel to the *is* of artistic identification. Such a theory would have been a very trim revision of our original intuition about the common features of different kinds of cultural phenomena. *But the parallel could not obtain in the same sense in the case of human basic actions, since, on Danto's own theory, it is "I," one and the same person, who performs both kinds of action.* Hence, it is quite impossible that a basic action be strictly identical with a set of physiological movements; and, in the sense in which, by parallel to the *is* of artistic identification, a basic action *is* (culturally) identical with a series of physiological movements, it *cannot* be the "bare, neutral," colorless action that Danto originally posited. This follows, of course, directly from the admission that it is one and the same culturally informed agent who performs both sorts of action. This seeming aside is instructive about Danto's theory of art because it helps, precisely, to clarify (and challenge) the thesis that one and the same object, the artwork, enjoys "dual citizenship" as both a physical object and a work of art. We see here, therefore, the need to clarify the ontology of art in a way that explicitly escapes the temptation toward reductionism.

In his comprehensive survey of the field of aesthetics, Beardsley [1958] says very little directly about the nature of a work of art. The Index of his *Aesthetics* shows only a few entries under the heading "work of art"; none under "art" and none related to the definition or ontology of art; the entries he does provide refer, suggestively, to the heading "aesthetic object." Since his important overview of the literature, Beardsley has rarely turned to examine the nature of artworks. When he has, his primary concern has been to oppose two theses about art: (i) that, against Danto, he says he is "not yet convinced that all works of art must be about something" [1976]; and (ii) that, against T.J. Diffey [1969] and George Dickie [1974], the thesis of "art-status-conferrable kinds of object" is circular and would be unconvincing even if it were not [1976].

Now, the key to understanding Beardsley's view rests within his notion of an aesthetic object. But, in the context of what has gone before, we may approach the issue once again by way of a seeming tangent. First of all, Beardsley presses the point that "we may easily agree . . . that the possession of aesthetic qualities (in Frank Sibley's sense) is normal to artworks. If, therefore, the possession of such qualities could be shown to depend directly on the existence of an institution, art would be essentially institutional by [reference to the condition: 'If the existence of some institution is included among the truth-conditions of "this artwork has property P," where P is a normal property of artworks, then artworks are essentially institutional objects'].'' Beardsley's strategy, therefore, is to hold fast to a version of the thesis that art is essentially perceptual; if, then, the institutional thesis could be made to accommodate the perceptual, Beardsley would be prepared to accede to it.

Secondly, Beardsley actually touches on the general problem of cultural emergence. He takes note of the notion of the "is" of embodiment (Margolis [1974a]); acknowledges the analogy between persons and artworks; and draws attention to an intended further analogy between artworks and human actions. Of three descriptions of.what is putatively one *event* or one *action* (the point is not clearly resolved)—viz. "The man's arm's moving"; "The man's raising his arm"; "The man's signalling"—Beardsley says: "On my view, they all describe the same event . . . There is no need to talk of 'embodiment' . . . It has not been proved, I think, that the arm-movement *cannot* be the same event as the signalling; it occurs at the same time and place . . . Granted that apart from human society there is no such act as signalling; but surely there may be such an act as raising one's arm—*that* is not dependent on society or culture." But if signalling *is* "dependent on . . . culture" and if the raising of the arm is one and the same action as the signalling, then, on the hypothesis Beardsley himself adopts, it is quite impossible that the action in question, raising the arm, is not dependent on culture. Beardsley claims further that the *action* is identical with the mere physical *event* of "the man's arm's moving," but he does not show this. Here, we may simply observe that he fails to come to grips with the very difficulty that Danto himself failed to resolve previously; and he compounds the puzzle by neglecting to show that no relationship other than strict identity is required (the "is" of artistic identification, the "is" of embodiment, or some suitable analogue) in order to account for the peculiarities of our discourse about cultural phenomena. In particular, *if* Beardsley concedes that signalling is culture-dependent, then he *has* conceded that that action can be identified only on nonperceptual—that is, on intentional, historical, selected causal—grounds. If, further, he holds that the physical *event* of the man's arm moving can be identified on perceptual grounds (which seems entirely reasonable), then it is quite impossible that the *action* be identical with the event. Consequently, *if,* as seems to be his intention, Beardsley concedes that the analysis of persons, artworks, and human actions ought to yield to a common rubric in the relevant respect, then he cannot but have undermined his own theory that works of art (or their appropriate surrogates, in the context of his account) are perceptual objects. Once again, then, we see the advantage of canvassing the issues in a setting larger than that afforded by the philosophy of art.

Beardsley's quarrel with Danto, that works of art need not exhibit "aboutness," or intentionality (in Brentano's sense [1973]), is entirely fair—but, unfortunately, it misses the point of Danto's claim. It is true that Danto appears, in "The Artworld" [1964], to hold that all artworks exhibit intentionality. But his more considered view is that questions of aboutness are always and necessarily pertinent to artworks—as opposed to mere physical objects—even if it is the case that a particular artwork is not "about" anything. In short, the discovery that a given work is not about anything rests on nonperceptual considerations. So Beardsley's objection, ironically, confirms the more important claim.

Beardsley's objection against Dickie is also double-edged. Although Dickie's thesis, that artworks are what they are by virtue of some sort of institutional conferring of artwork-status, seems either preposterous or vacuous (cf. Margolis [1975a]), Beardsley does not show that artworks are not what they are by virtue of the institutional life of a culture; he does not even challenge the claim. But if he were to concede it, then, on the foregoing considerations, he would have to concede further that artworks are identified on nonperceptual grounds, for reasons paralleling what has already been said about the distinction between actions and physical events and between persons and physical bodies. Dickie's maneuver, then, is in general accord with the more promising approach to cultural phenomena; but somehow, apart from the weakness of his thesis about an actual conferring act, he utterly neglects to explain the nature either of artifacts or of institutions. He clearly borrows Danto's conception of an artworld, by which he means to stress that the distinguishing marks of art are "nonexhibited propert[ies]" which (in Danto's phrase) the eye "cannot descry." He rightly finds the remark to be "in need of elucidation," but he does not supply what is needed. He merely announces that the artworld is "an institution" or "an established practice" that provides "a framework for the *presenting* of particular works of art."

However, Dickie does emphasize and argue for the thesis that "there is no reason to think that there is a special kind of aesthetic consciousness, attention, or perception." This is precisely what Beardsley is at pains to resist; but his argument is a little obscure because, in a recent account of the aesthetic situation, he [1970a] substitutes the notion of "experience" for that of "perception." In context, however, it is reasonably clear that Beardsley does not wish to deny his earlier thesis, that what we are interested in aesthetically is what we perceive as directly presented; possibly (as in speaking of literature) he finds the term "experience" broader and thus more satisfactory than the term "perception." In fact, his intention is simply to concede that our interest in literature cannot be merely perceptual in the sense proper to the plastic and musical arts; he does *not* concede that, in the latter arts, our interest is *not* restricted to the perceptual. In his most recent version of the issue [1978b], Beardsley speaks of our interest in "perceptual and intentional" values; but "intentional" is clearly meant to range over what, in the aesthetic experience of literature, is merely the analogue of what is aesthetically perceived in the plastic and musical arts.

A few of Beardsley's remarks will make his position clear. "The aesthetic value of an object," he says, "is the value it possesses in virtue of its capacity to provide aesthetic gratification"; and "Gratification is aesthetic, when it is obtained primarily from attention to the formal unity and/or the regional qualities of a complex whole, and when its magnitude is a function of the degree of formal unity and/or the intensity of regional quality." The relevant clues to understanding his view of aesthetic values, then, are these: (i) they are objectively found in objects, are possessed by them; (ii) they are discriminated by means of perception or experience, particularly "when *correctly experienced*"; (iii) they are a function of properties of formal unity and regional quality, which Beardsley has always construed explicitly as perceptual. In fact, Beardsley's position bearing on plural "presentations" of "the same aesthetic object" [1958] holds, that: "In our descriptions of aesthetic objects we are interested in the perceivable properties [of such objects], for which we shall reserve the word 'qualities.' Thus when I speak of the regional qualities of a complex, I mean its perceptual regional properties." Similarly, he holds that unity applies "to the phenomenally objective presentations in the experience" of an object; by "phenomenally objective presentations," he clearly means "all that one is aware of, or conscious of, at a given time"—as in "visual, auditory, or verbal" phenomena, explicitly excluding "knowledge of . . . causal conditions . . . the physical basis, the physical processes of creation, and the biographical background [of whoever produced the object]."

Nevertheless, in the very context in which he advances this well-known thesis, Beardsley concedes that "a work of art is certainly something deliberately fashioned by human effort—it is a *work,* it is the product of art, or skill, at least in the traditional sense of the term." This would seem utterly to undermine the restrictions that Beardsley imposes on "aesthetic objects." For, though he does not wish to treat "work of art" and "aesthetic object" as equivalent notions, he does say [1958] that, having so far "sedulously avoided . . . the term 'work of art,' " we might (once admitting that non-art may be aesthetically appreciated), try "to sort out works of art from all perceptual objects that are not works of art." So Beardsley seems to be disposed at one and the same time to treat artworks as *perceptual* objects and to admit that they must be distinguished as art by reason of their having been produced by some culturally informed human effort—which cannot be perceptually discriminated and which is explicitly excluded from the aesthetic domain. Consequently, Beardsley is caught in the dilemma that the very objects he invites us to appreciate aesthetically cannot be identified as such under the conditions which are to restrict our relevant appreciative attention. This is surely a *reductio.* All the other well-known difficulties of Beardsley's position bearing on plural "presentations" of "the same aesthetic object" (no longer, puzzlingly, of the same artwork) depend on his having overlooked this essential dilemma (*see* Margolis [1965]).

One final reference may serve to round out our general strategy. Nelson Goodman [1968] was greatly responsible for advancing a theory of art in terms of which it proved quite impossible to treat artworks merely as perceptual objects. Goodman demonstrated this in detail in his analysis of representation, symbolic function, forgery, and notationality. But Goodman's explanation of the symbolic function of art is noticeably defective; its essential weakness concerns the range of attributes that may be directly ascribed to, or "found in," artworks. Hence, as in our examination of Danto's account, an examination of Goodman's may be expected to reveal some difficulties either with the attributes of art or its conditions of identity or both. On the second count, nothing need be said here, except that Goodman's constraints on the reidentification of a work of art are neither convincing nor necessary. (We shall return to the issue.) For our present purposes, it is Goodman's account of the properties of works of art that is instructive.

Now, Goodman holds that works of art are "symbol systems . . . of a particular kind." He needs to show, therefore, that every work of art, *qua* work of art, has some assignable symbolic function. Apparently, works of art always or characteristically possess expressive properties, even if they fail to possess any other kind of symbolic property. Here, his claim is that "what is expressed is metaphorically exemplified"; "whereas almost anything can denote or even represent almost anything else, a thing can express only what belongs but did not originally belong to it." We may press Goodman's thesis at two points: (a) why should the possession of expressive qualities entail exemplification? and (b) why should expressive qualities be construed metaphorically? The same considerations intrinsic to Goodman's thesis dissolve both questions.

Goodman explains exemplification thus: "Exemplification is possession plus reference. To have without symbolizing is merely to possess . . . [A] swatch [of cloth] exemplifies only those properties that it both has and refers to." If, therefore, works of art merely possess properties—in particular, expressive properties—without exemplifying them, we should have provided a strong basis on which to deny that (in Goodman's terms) works of art are symbol systems. The argument is straightforward. First of all, it is clear, even in terms of Goodman's example, that an object may possess a great many properties (for instance, perceivable properties) that it does not exemplify; a piece of blue cloth may not be a *sample* of blue cloth or of a certain blue even though it possesses the color in question. We may not *choose* to treat it as a sample. Goodman's argument would be entirely unconvincing if it did not maintain that *expressive* properties must be treated in a distinctive way—that is, metaphorically. The second step of the argument, then, is this: even if an expressive property is first ascribed metaphorically, it does not follow that, in possessing that property, an object *exemplifies* the property; it is logically quite possible, say, that we ascribe "being a toad" to some particularly disagreeable person without claiming, implicitly or explicitly, that that person thereby exemplifies "being a toad." There seems to be no difference here between literal and metaphorical ascription—though there is, also, no reason as yet to construe expressive ascriptions metaphorically. The third step of the argument, then, is this: in order to hold that, in possessing an expressive property, an object must exemplify that property, Goodman is obliged to hold that artworks are of such a sort that they can never merely possess (without exemplifying) such a property. Goodman nowhere provides the argument.

On the face of it, there is only one possible way of construing the *objects* to which we are to ascribe expressive properties so as to render Goodman's claim manageable—even if not defensible. That adjustment would force us to treat artworks as mere perceptual objects—which of course Goodman resists. Concede, for the sake of the argument, that to speak of artworks is to speak of the distinctive functioning of physical objects. Construe certain objects as physical objects *possessing* perceivable properties, and hold that only by treating them as entities *exemplifying* expressive properties can they be treated as possessing those properties—and, therefore, as functioning as artworks. That is, *if* possessing expressive properties is what justifies us in treating an object as an artwork, then its identification depends on nonperceptual grounds—because, on Goodman's thesis, such possession itself presupposes that the object has a symbolic function, exemplification. Hence, *if* expressive properties do not depend on exemplification, then, on an adjustment of Goodman's thesis, they would be ascribable to objects first identifiable in perceptual terms. But then, the conceptual distinction of artworks would be entirely lost.

The trouble is that Goodman had already compellingly shown that artworks were not perceptual objects; that is, he had shown that they were not objects that (i) could be properly identified or reidentified in purely perceptual terms, or (ii) could be ascribed relevant properties exclusively of a perceptual sort. *If,* however, artworks were admitted to be cultural or culturally emergent entities, then *there would and could be no antecedent reason for denying:* (1) that artworks *literally* possess expressive properties, and (2) that artworks possess them without exemplifying them. This would not show that artworks do not possess symbolic functions essentially or characteristically, only that they could not be said to do so on Goodman's grounds. In short, his entire maneuver appears to be self-serving: first, claim that artworks possess a symbolic function; then, assign a superfluous symbolic function (exemplification) in order to demonstrate that whatever important (expressive) properties artworks possess, they possess in virtue of the symbolic function assigned. The arbitrariness of the maneuver becomes particularly clear in Goodman's account of style [1975]. "Style," he maintains, "has to do exclusively with the symbolic function of a work of art as such"; in fact, it has to do with a work's exemplifying the style it possesses. But this is most uneconomical—and entirely unnecessary—for the reasons already adduced. Hence, Goodman's account gains much of its seeming plausibility by an implicit appeal to paradigms of actual objects (physical objects, for instance) unsuited to the kind of ascription literally required in the artworld. Furthermore, rejecting Goodman's thesis, we are bound to find another basis for distinguishing artworks.

We may break off our account at this point. It was, after all, intended as an initial dialectical exercise to demonstrate the philosophical force of testing the most debated theories of art against conceptual uniformities among the salient phenomena of the various sub-domains of culture. If the foregoing considerations are indeed reasonably telling, we may claim that the strategy both economically exposes the essential weakness of the most influential theories current in Anglo-American aesthetics, and directs us to the key puzzles that a more satisfactory philosophy of art may be expected to resolve.

2. The Ontological Peculiarity of Works of Art

In the context of discussing the nature of artistic creativity, Jack Glickman [1976] offers the intriguing comment, "particulars are made, types created." The remark is strategic, but either false or misleading; and its adjustment illuminates in a most economical way some of the complexities of the creative process and of the ontology of art. As an instance of the distinction he has in mind, Glickman offers the following: "If the chef created a new soup, he created a new kind of soup, a new recipe; he may not have made the soup [that is, some particular pot of soup]." *If,* by "kind," Glickman means to signify a universal of some sort, then, since universals are not created (or destroyed), it could not be the case that the chef "created" a new soup, a new kind of soup (*contra* Wolterstorff [1975b]). It must be the case that the chef, in making a particular (new) soup, "created" a kind of soup; otherwise, of course, that the chef created a new (kind of) soup may be evidenced by his having formulated a relevant recipe (which locution, in its own turn, shows the same ambiguity between type and token).

What is important here may not be immediately evident. But if the chef can be said to create (invent) a new (kind of) soup, and if universals cannot be created or destroyed, then, in creating a kind of soup, a chef must be creating something other than a universal. The odd thing is that a kind of soup thus created is thought to be individuated among related creations; hence, it appears to be a particular of some sort. But it also seems to be an abstract entity if it is a particular at all. Hence, although it may be possible to admit abstract particulars in principle (*see* Goodman [1966]), it is difficult to concede that what the chef created is an abstract particular *if* one may be said to have *tasted* what the chef created. The analogy with art is plain. If, in painting *Les Demoiselles d'Avignon,* Picasso created a new kind of painting, it would appear that he could not have done so *by using oils.*

There is only one solution *if* we mean to speak in this way. It must be possible to instantiate particulars (of a certain kind or of certain kinds) as well as to instantiate universals or properties. I suggest that the term "type"—in all contexts in which the type/token ambiguity arises—signifies abstract particulars of a kind that can be instantiated. Let me offer a specimen instance. Printings properly pulled from Dürer's etching plate for *Melancholia I* are instances of *that* etching; but *bona fide* instances of *Melancholia I* need not share all relevant properties, since plural printings, printings that follow a touching up of the plate, or printings that are themselves touched up may be genuine instances of *Melancholia I* and still differ markedly from one another—at least to the sensitive eye. Nothing, however, can instantiate a property without actually instantiating that property. So to think of types as particulars (of a distinctive kind) accommodates the facts that we individuate works of art in various ways—performances of the same music, printings of the same etching, copies of the same novel—and that works of art may be created and destroyed. If we further grant that in creating a new soup, a chef stirred the ingredients in his pot, and that in creating a new kind of painting with *Les Demoiselles,* Picasso applied paint to canvas, we see that it is at least normally the case that one does not create a new kind of soup or a new kind of painting without (in Glickman's words) making a particular soup or a particular painting.

A great many questions intrude on Glickman's ingenious thesis at this point. For example, Glickman wishes to say that, though driftwood may be construed as a creation of "beach art," it remains true that driftwood was *made* by no one and is in fact a natural object, and hence it is also true that "the condition of artifactuality" so often claimed to be a necessary condition of being a work of art, is simply "superfluous." "I see no conclusive conceptual block," says Glickman, "to allowing that the artwork [may] be a natural object." Correspondingly, Duchamp's "readymades" are created out of artifacts which the artist did not actually make. Glickman's thesis depends on the tenability of his distinction between making and creating; and as we have just seen, one does not, in the normal case at least, create a new kind of art (type) without making a particular work of that kind (that is, an instance of that abstract particular—the type, not merely an instance of that kind—the universal). In other words, when an artist *creates* (in Glickman's terms) "beach art," a new kind of art, the artist *makes* a particular instance (or token) of a particular type—*this unique token of this driftwood composition.* The artist cannot create the universals that are newly instantiated, since universals cannot be created; he can create a new type-particular (a particular of the

composition of art using the driftwood. If the bottlerack were said to be identical with Duchamp's *Bottlerack* (the token or the type), we should be contradicting ourselves; the same would be true of the driftwood case. Hence, in spite of appearances, there must be an ontological difference between tokens of artwork-types and such physical objects as bottleracks and driftwood that can serve as the materials out of which they are made.

My own suggestion is that token works of art are *embodied* in physical objects, not identical with them. I should argue, though this is not the place for it, that persons, similarly, are embodied in physical bodies but not identical with them (*see* Margolis [1978a]). The idea is that not only can one particular instantiate another particular in a certain way (tokens of types) but one particular can embody or be embodied in another particular with which it is (necessarily) not identical. The important point is that the principle of identity cannot work in the anomalous cases here considered (nor in the usual cases of art) and that what would otherwise be related by way of identity are, obviously, particulars. Furthermore, the embodiment relationship does not invite dualism, though it does require a distinction among kinds of things and the kinds of properties of things of such kinds. For example, a particular printing of Dürer's *Melancholia I* has the property of being a particular token of *Melancholia I* (the artwork-type), but the physical paper and print do not, on any familiar view, have the property of being a token of a type. Only objects having such intentional properties as that of "being created" or, as with words, having meaning, can have the property of being a token of a type (*see* Peirce [1939], IV, §537).

To say that one particular is embodied in another means that: (i) the two particulars are not identical; (ii) the existence of the embodied particular presupposes the existence of the embodying particular; (iii) the embodied particular possesses some of the properties of the embodying particular; (iv) the embodied particular possesses properties that the embodying particular does not possess; (v) the embodied particular possesses properties of a kind that the embodying particular cannot possess; (vi) the individuation of the embodied particular presupposes the individuation of the embodying particular. The "is" of embodiment, then, like the "is" of identity and the "is" of composition (Wiggins [1967]), has a logically distinctive use. On this theory, a particular physical object will be taken to embody a particular object of another kind in such a way that a certain systematic relationship will hold between them. Thus, for instance, a sculptor will be said to make a particular sculpture by cutting a block of marble: Michelangelo's *Pietà* will exhibit certain of the physical properties of the marble as well as certain representational and purposive properties; it will also have the property of being a unique token of the creation *Pietà*. The reason for theorizing thus is, quite simply, that works of art are the products of culturally informed labor and physical objects are not. So seen, works of art must possess properties that physical objects, *qua* physical objects, do not and cannot possess. Furthermore, the concept of embodiment promises to facilitate, without dualistic assumptions, a nonreductive account of the relationship between physical nature and human culture. This suggests that the so-called mind/body problem is essentially a special form of a more general culture/nature problem. But that is another story (*see* Margolis [1978a]).

We must be careful here. The "is" of embodiment is invoked in cultural contexts to facilitate our discourse about cultural particulars. Speaking thus, we mean to say: (i) artworks, persons, words and sentences, and the like exist, are real; (ii) are constituted as such in some cultural "space"; (iii) are recognized as such by persons suitably informed regarding the cultural context in which they are thus constituted. Hence, we may notice the doubtful features of Danto's so-called "*is* of artistic identification." First of all, Danto speaks of mistaking "an artwork for a real object" (which it may be, by virtue of the *is* of artistic identification). That "is," he says, "has near-relatives in marginal and mythical pronouncements" (as in holding that someone *is* Quetzalcoatl, or that those formations *are* the Pillars of Hercules). But artworks *are* real; they are simply not identical with equally real physical objects. Secondly, Danto speaks of his philistine (Testadura) who may not see a painting as a painting: "*all he sees is paint.*" Here, Danto holds that we cannot help him "until he has mastered the *is of artistic identification* and so *constitutes* it a work of art." But the artwork is already constituted in its cultural space; a particular viewer may discover it there—he hardly constitutes it as such. In effect, Danto has confused (ii) and (iii), above; alternatively, he has confused the psychological with the hermeneutic (cf. Habermas [1971]; Gadamer [1975]).

A work of art, then, is a particular. It cannot be a universal because it is created and can be destroyed; and because it possesses physical and perceptual properties. But it is a peculiar sort of particular because unlike physical bodies, (i) it can (and must) instantiate another particular; and (ii) it can (and must) be embodied in another particular. The suggestion here is that all, and only, culturally emergent or culturally produced entities exhibit these traits. The ontological characteristics assigned are no more than the most generic characteristics of art; its distinctive nature remains unanalyzed. Nevertheless, we can discern an important difference between these two properties. The first property, that of being able to instantiate another particular, has to do only with individuating works of art and whatever may, contingently, depend upon that; the second property has to do with the ontologically dependent nature of actual works of art. Thus we may speak of type artworks as particulars because they are heuristically introduced for purposes of individuation, but cannot exist except in the sense in which particular tokens of particular type artworks exist. So, we can never properly *compare* the properties of a token work and a type work (*contra* Wolterstorff [1975b] and Wollheim [1968]). What we may compare are alternative tokens of the same type—different printings of the same etching or different performances of the same sonata. In short, every work of art is a token-of-a-type; there are no tokens or types *tout court*. To say that an artist has created a new type is an ellipsis for saying that a certain set of particulars constitute tokens of a type, and that the artist is credited with so working with the properties of things, instantiated by the members of that set, that they are construed as tokens of a particular type.

The dependencies of the two ontological traits mentioned are quite different. There are no types that are separable from tokens because there are no tokens except tokens-of-a-type. The very process of individuating tokens entails individuating types; that is, it entails individuating different sets of particulars as the sets of alternative tokens of this or that type. The only apparent problem with this theory is in relation to the concept of different tokens of the same type, which, in the arts, is intended to accommodate the fact that the often aesthetically decisive differences among tokens of the same type (alternative performances of a sonata, for instance) need not matter as far as the individuation of the (type) work is concerned (*contra* Goodman [1968]). But particular works of art cannot exist except as embodied in physical objects. This is simply another way of saying that works of art are culturally emergent entities; that is, they exhibit properties that physical objects cannot, but do not depend on the presence of any substance other than what may be ascribed to purely physical objects. Broadly speaking, those properties are what may be characterized as functional or intentional and include design, expressiveness, symbolism, representation, meaning, style, and the like. Without prejudice to the nature of either art or persons, this way of viewing art suggests a very convenient linkup with the functional theory of mental traits (*see* Putnam [1960] and Fodor [1968]).

A reasonable theory of art could hold that when physical materials are worked in accord with a certain artistic craft there emerges, culturally, an object embodied in the physical materials that possesses a certain orderly array of functional properties of the kind just mentioned. Any object so produced may be treated as an artifact. Hence, works of art exist as fully as physical objects but their existence depends on the independent existence of some physical object. Works of art, then, are culturally emergent entities, tokens-of-a-type that exist embodied in physical objects.

PART ONE

The Work of Art

3. The Cultural Nature of Art

It is clear that one's account of the nature of criticism and of the nature of an artwork is conceptually linked in the most intimate way. What we indicate we are talking about and what we may justifiably say of it depend on what it is; and what it is will, in turn, be conceded by considering how it may be fixed and identified, and what may be said of it. I believe that the problem of identifying and fixing the reference of an artwork and the concession of admissible critical remarks can be managed without deciding the precise ontological nature of an artwork; in fact, a premature solution of that problem is bound to do violence to the concessions that must be made. It will suffice to avoid both an excessive idealism that finds nothing in the public world that would count as a work of art, and an excessive (or reductive) materialism that denies that anything exists that is not merely and entirely physical. Critics and historians of the arts readily confuse the logical status of their own comments because of their confusion and prejudice about the nature of what they are commenting upon. The problem is a general one affecting all phenomena thought to appear exclusively in a cultural context—artworks, persons, words and sentences, institutions, practices, and conventional actions. The reason is simply that our theory of such phenomena is attracted in opposing directions by the relative economies of acknowledging only physical objects and the need to provide a suitable locus for the peculiar sorts of properties that must be ascribed. We should be able to formulate, however, an explicit theory of the actual ontological standing of a work of art that is fully congruent and sympathetic with the special problems of reference and characterization (particularly, interpretation) in the arts and, at the same time, responsive to the requirements of an informed account of the ontology of other kinds of entities. But first, consider the extremes to be avoided and a sketch of the reasons for doing so.

There is a familiar directness in the well-worn question of the so-called "mode of existence" of a work of art. The phrase appears, notably, in Wellek and Warren's *Theory of Literature* [1956]. I hold that whatever we may hope to clarify regarding critical relevance and the identity of a given artwork, by answering the question of a work of art's mode of existence, we may clarify more effectively by answering a set of related questions; also, there are assignable reasons for thinking that the usual answers lead invariably to paradox and mystification. I cite Wellek and Warren's own solution as a dreadful warning to future enthusiasts:

> The work of art . . . appears as an object of knowledge *sui generis* which has a special ontological status. It is neither real (like a statue) nor mental (like the experience of light or pain) nor ideal (like a triangle). It is a system of norms of ideal concepts which are intersubjective. They must be assumed to exist in collective ideology, changing with it, accessible only through individual mental experiences, based on the sound-structure of its sentences.

In general, speculation about the mode of existence of a work of art has, like speculation about so many other cognate questions, oscillated between the poles of materialism and idealism. The alternatives appear in one of the most focused accounts in the English language, Collingwood's *The Principles of Art* [1938], as the views of art as craft and of art as imagination. Without subscribing to Collingwood's own thesis and argument, I think we do quite readily concede what it is he insists on, in declaring that: "The work of art proper is something not seen or heard, but something imagined." For he does not by this wish to deny (a paradox he avoids) that one does listen to music, and hear the sounds that comprise music; he wishes to insist only that "there is something else which he must do as well."

Collingwood's interest of course is to amplify his own theory of imagination; but independently of this I think we all agree that the appreciation of a work of art is relatively "remote . . . from the specialism of its sensuous basis" (cf. Hospers [1956]). Materialism founders because the developed range of comments that we allow in our discourse about works of art simply cannot be construed coherently as comments *about* material objects (that is, about artworks construed as nothing more than material objects). This is not to say that reference to material objects is not crucial to our discourse about art; it is only to say that an artwork is not simply a kind of material object. The issue is both subtle and complex, and quite impossible to settle by mentioning a few examples. Generally speaking, however, the most promising strategies require either positing entities whose nature permits the direct ascription of properties of the kinds in question or construing the intended ascriptions as applying to physical objects by way of some enabling relationship or intervening role or the like. For instance, if in speaking of a certain painting I must address myself to symbols that are (said to be) in the painting, then although I cannot of course ignore its colored pigments, either I cannot construe the painting—which contains symbols in some irreducible or ineliminable way—as a mere physical object, or else I must be able to explain what special circumstances permit me to associate a symbol or symbolic function with a physical object. The latter alternative clearly obliges me to suppose that it is at least in virtue of a relationship between a human person and a physical object—a relationship, for instance, of taking an interest in that object in terms of certain historical and cultural concerns proper to human beings—that, under determinable circumstances, a physical object may be said to be, or function as, a symbol.

I have deliberately sketched the issue in the broadest possible terms, because: (i) it is not peculiar to artworks but applies to all cultural phenomena uniformly; and (ii) I shall not attempt to construct a conclusive argument in favor of the first of the two alternative strategies mentioned, though I mean to favor it. Still, a very short argument can be given against the second alternative, which suggests that a decisive argument can be mounted as well. Notice that, on the second alternative, all questions about ascribing symbolic, representational, expressive, stylistic, and similar properties are made to depend on a relationship between a physical object and an entity (person) about which precisely the same kinds of questions arise; the properties of persons—formulated in terms of intentions, meanings, reasons, purposes, and the like—cannot readily be specified in terms of relationships between mere physical objects. Hence, only if persons could be successfully reduced to physical objects, and their cultural properties satisfactorily accounted for in terms of their physical properties, would there be any prospect of an ontological economy in attempting to treat artworks as mere physical objects. Since that is extremely unlikely—perhaps even impossible in principle or in terms of managing discourse in real time (*see* Margolis [1978a])—we may safely dismiss the second strategy as most unpromising. In doing so, we have not even mentioned problems more local to discourse about art—for instance, regarding the fact that works of art are public objects whose distinctive properties are regularly described, debated, appraised, and appreciated. To characterize our options somewhat more formally, then, we may say that our usual habit of speaking of artworks permits us to ascribe certain *monadic* properties directly to them, that include not only those normally ascribed to physical objects (color, pitch, and texture, for instance) but others that are peculiarly cultural in nature as well (symbolic, representational, and expressive properties); whereas, on the second strategy, we are obliged to treat culturally significant properties as dyadic or *polyadic* and ascribable only in virtue of some determinate relationship involving a particular person, or persons. The difficulty, in terms of the second strategy, of accounting for apparently spontaneous attention to, and objective exchange about, the properties of artworks testifies to the force of our first strategy.

This illustrates the permanent hold that idealists have over materialists in theorizing about the mode of existence of a work of art. On the other hand, returning to Collingwood, we must admit that we do talk *about* works of art and in doing so are emphatically not talking about anyone's mind, either that of the artist or of whoever appreciates the work of art. Collingwood, in countering the theory that art is craft, held that a composer may, for example, sing or play or write his music down in order to "make it possible for others to get into their heads the same thing which he has in his." He meant by this that the real work of art (being a work of imagination) is made in the mind and exists in the mind, and may exist in the mind of the listener just as it does in the mind of the composer. But it seems anomalous to hold that in talking about a work of art we are somehow talking about something in the mind of the artist or in the mind of the listener. The difficulty is compounded when, say, we find a musical score that has never been played. We want to say that the composer did indeed create the music, and we are tempted to say that the music was in his mind—since the score is not the actual music and since, if it were played, possibly no particular performance would capture what we mean by the music. But this is a difficulty that can be managed without the expensive solution suggested.

We want to hold that in talking about a work of art we are talking about a public object; and our paradigms of public objects are, precisely, material objects. This illustrates the permanent hold that materialists have over idealists in theorizing about the mode of existence of a work of art. But to say this is not to suppose that a theory of art can convincingly avoid reference to the work of our imagination—as if it were something other than the work of art, something that stands in an external relationship to the work of art. For instance, when we speak of an interpretation of an artwork, we are not speaking of something *added* to an artwork—intact, so to say, without an interpretation; we are speaking, rather, of what often must be supplied in order to be able to speak of a work of art at all, that is, to give a reasonably adequate account of its properties. Similarly, R.K. Elliott [1966-1967] observes, searching aspects of aesthetic appreciation closer to perception but hardly reducible to it: "The emotion expressed in a lyric poem may be 'there for me in the speaker of the poem,' even if the speaker is a fiction and even if the emotion was never experienced by the historical poet." The point of admitting interpretation, the play of imagination, the understanding of meanings, and the like as *cognitively* pertinent to appreciating artworks is simply that it entails that artworks must be entities quite distinct from mere physical objects or objects accessible merely through sensory perception.

As I see the matter, then, the difficulty in construing artworks as material objects is simply that much of what we say about them—as, in some important sense, descriptive of, or very nearly or in substantial part descriptive of, them—could not coherently be said about material objects. Correspondingly, the difficulty in construing artworks as ideal objects of some sort is simply that we do wish to speak of them as public objects and address ourselves to public properties—for instance, with respect to paintings, to their actual colored pigments, which are in no one's head, and which cannot be (as Collingwood holds) "accessories of the real work." The upshot is a stalemate that is not resolvable in terms of the extreme alternatives mentioned. Richard Wollheim [1968], while conceding that *Ulysses* and *Der Rosenkavalier* cannot be mere physical objects, insists that "the *Donna Velata* and Donatello's *St. George* most certainly are." Wollheim recognizes the objection that "there is an incompatibility of property between works of art and physical objects"—usually stressing representational and expressive properties—but he claims that these are actually compatible with construing an artwork as a physical object. In defending his thesis, Wollheim manages to ignore the difference between an artist's *intending* to use certain physical lines, colors or the like in representing this or that, and the work's actually *possessing* the intentional property of representing this or that. He does not opt for the full physicalist theory, because he finds that literature and music cannot be thus favorably analyzed. But his preferred view of painting and sculpture corresponds rather neatly to the counterpart view of those who hold that, though language poses the problem of intentionality—which cannot be managed in materialist terms—the admission of persons does not as such constitute a serious threat to the prospects of a reductive materialism (Sellars for instance [1963]; *see* Margolis [1978a]). *That* doctrine fails to accommodate the essential fact that if the intentional nature of language is irreducible in physical terms, then the linguistic *ability* distinctive of persons confirms that persons cannot be mere physical objects. Hence, if Wollheim concedes that representation is inherently intentional, he has in effect conceded (against his explicit claim) that paintings that *have* representational properties cannot be mere physical objects.

But if we consider more carefully *why* we speak of an artwork as a kind of *object* which, having the curious properties that we must assign to it, must therefore have a curious "mode of existence," we find that we can usually forestall this way of speaking without any philosophical losses whatsoever. I do not mean to say by this that examination will show that an artwork is not an object of some sort (but something else). I should say that the principal reasons we speak about artworks as objects, in the aesthetic context, are to facilitate our critical and appreciative exchanges. Here there seem to be at least two distinct concerns to be serviced. One bears on reference or identification—on what it is we are speaking about; the other bears on justification or defense—on whether what we are saying about a particular work is true or plausible. Now I claim that a philosophical account of both these considerations may be satisfactorily provided without invoking the problem of the mode of existence of a work of art; and that, on the contrary, any interest we may have in answering the ontological question ought to be guided by our resolution of these two issues. So I am not denying that artworks are objects, or are as reasonably taken to be objects as any that we normally admit; the conveniences of co-predication and reference entirely support so construing them. What I insist on, for reasons that will gradually become clear, is only that we should not fall at once into the clichés of the ordinary way of speaking of physical objects, or into the conceptual traps of certain venerable theories of the nature of art. These pitfalls are not, it seems, easily avoided. It may, therefore, prove useful to maintain that works of art are "utterances" of some sort, not necessarily verbal and not necessarily analyzable in terms of some version of a speech-act model, construed in a way that marks the culturally relevant similarities between speech and art.

The relationship between the two issues mentioned, the reference and the justification of critical comments, is itself instructive. For although our critical comments will understandably range over whatever we take to be aesthetically relevant to artworks, the way in which we secure the identification and reidentification of what it is we are talking about need not itself be particularly responsive to aesthetic considerations. For example, it is altogether reasonable to identify the sculpture we are talking about (Michelangelo's *David,* for instance) by identifying the block of marble it was cut from, or the block of marble about which speaking in a certain way counts as talk about the sculpture in question. But we need not suppose that locating the marble block in some physical space is itself aesthetically relevant in any way to a discussion of the properties or merit of the sculpture. On the contrary, it is reassuring in a certain sense that we can identify that with which we may be engaged in critical controversy in a manner relatively independent of such controversy. If, for example, *what* we are speaking about may depend in a crucial way on *which* interpretation or assessment we subscribe to, we should find ourselves in a hopeless muddle respecting questions of defense and justification—and, in fact, respecting questions of taste altogether. This type of confusion marks a fatal weakness in views like that of Wellek and Warren (cf. Wellek [1963]; Matejka and Pomorsky [1971]), that emphasize a certain ideal intersubjective system; also, in views like Roman Ingarden's [1973a, 1973b], that fail to specify explicitly the bearing of interpretive contributions on the determinate integrity of a work of art and on its individuation. Thus, Ingarden perceptively identifies the separate "strata" of an artwork, but he says nothing about how they are ontically linked (cf. Dufrenne [1973]; Graff and Krzemién-Ojak [1975]).

Consistently with the distinction between the two issues of reference and judgment and employing the type/token distinction already introduced, we can specify conditions on which we identify the particular works of art we are speaking about. We identify instances among the different arts in quite different ways—for example (quite roughly speaking), we identify a musical composition by reference to a musical score, although no one supposes that music (in an aesthetically relevant sense) is merely a musical score; and we identify a painting by identifying a certain piece of canvas, although no one supposes that the properties that serve to identify that canvas must be relevant to an aesthetic appreciation of the painting itself. In fact, the advantage of this way of securing the reference or identification of the particular work of art about which we are disputing is not merely that our dispute is thereby referentially grounded, but also that we do not foreclose on disputes within the *theory* of criticism, that is, on what may be claimed to be relevant aesthetic considerations in the discussion of fine art. Also, of course, if the account of reference or identity is allowed to stand (even if it is adjusted along comparable lines), we should have serviced one of the most important questions respecting works of art and critical discourse about them without directly considering (and without needing to consider) what kind of object an artwork is or what mode of existence such an object might be said to have.

Having secured the reference of critical comments, we still face the questions of what sorts of comments are aesthetically eligible, and of how such comments are defended and justified. While I do not wish to deny that theories about the nature of fine art are relevant here, a reasoned account of what sorts of remarks are eligible—for instance descriptions, analyses, comparisons, interpretations, expressions of preference, appraisals, value judgments, verdicts—may be provided without first raising the issue of what kind of entity an artwork is, or what mode of existence may be ascribed to it. We attribute properties to a work of art and interpret, appreciate, and evaluate works of art; we relate all of these critical activities *to* the work, but (as we have seen) we secure the identity of a particular work by securing the identity of something (a block of stone or a musical score, say) on which the work in question depends in a determinate way. Artworks are, so to say, the logical subjects of aesthetically relevant comments, but in any sense in which we refer to them ostensively (as opposed to merely grammatically) we refer to objects like blocks of stone and musical scores, normally without attempting to settle the ontological issue.

Let me make the force of this reasoning a little clearer. Imagine that we read a puzzling novel, Camus's *L'Etranger,* for instance, in which we readily comprehend the literal meaning of what we are reading, and yet ask ourselves what it all means. What we request is an interpretation, a way of plausibly construing the action of the novel, such that what we have read may be said to have a certain significance and coherence that compares favorably with the organization of more explicit stories. It is clear that we often feel called on to attempt to interpret novels in this way. For our present purposes, we need to consider that the question of whether to allow or disallow interpretation as being aesthetically relevant may be treated quite independently of what has been called the mode of existence of works of art. An examination of the critical literature, for instance, might persuade us that we cannot draw a very sharp line between those statements that merely describe works of art and those statements that interpret them (however reasonably) beyond the limit of their describable features. Also, we *may* be persuaded that if one comprehensive and satisfactory interpretation is provided for a given work—the alleged work being more fully understood or appreciated *as* a work of art with such interpretative invention—we cannot, in principle, foreclose on the possibility of alternative and even incompatible interpretations of the same work. For example, the possibility clearly arose in the early reception of Camus's novel (Brée [1959]; Luppé [1960]; Champigny [1959]; W. Lewis [1952]; Cruickshank [1959]). But if the coherence imputed cannot straightforwardly be said to be *found* in these works in a sense in which they may merely be described (or, in some simple sensory sense, perceived), if an artwork cannot be fully seen as such without being assigned such coherence, and if alternative and even incompatible accounts of such coherence may defensibly be given of the same work, what, we may ask, is the ontological status of an artwork?

It is, of course, conceivable that if it were antecedently determined that an artwork had this or that kind of ontological status, it would be inappropriate to entertain certain sorts of critical comments; for example, if it were taken to be an independent and intact entity of some readily discernible sort, so-called interpretations of the work (construed now as overt descriptions) would, to the extent that they were supposed to be true (however incomplete they might be), converge toward some ideally comprehensive and internally coherent interpretation of that work. Monroe Beardsley [1958], for instance, speaking about an "aesthetic object," offers as a critical postulate: "If two presentations of the same aesthetic object have incompatible characteristics, at least one of them is illusory." Beardsley means by "presentation" the aesthetic object "as experienced by a particular person on a particular occasion," and in the context of his discussion he intends the term to apply to aesthetic objects that "are visual, auditory, or verbal." The result, we may suppose, is that incompatible musical interpretations, as well as incompatible interpretations of a given piece of literature, cannot be jointly defended as true of the same "aesthetic object." Beardsley is drawn to conclude that though Toscanini's and Furtwängler's performances of Beethoven's *D Minor Symphony* are performances *of the same symphony,* answers to a question about the length of the symphony's first movement, based on the two performances, "cannot be true of the same aesthetic object, even if they are true of the same *symphony*"; it follows, for Beardsley, that "the name of a symphony is not the name of a single aesthetic object."

But the question of whether (in Beardsley's terms) the performances provide us with "true" accounts of, or the "veridical" properties of, the work remains unresolved; the question is disallowed merely because of an ontological analogy—already challenged by the admission that artworks are cultural objects of some sort—supposed to hold between artworks and so-called "perceptual objects." Beardsley is also prepared to speak of "the class of presentations of a particular work of art [aesthetic objects]" which, he says, "seems to be definable in terms of exposure to a particular physical stimulus; it is that stimulus, or vehicle, which remains constant, as a condition of each presentation, however the presentations themselves may differ." But even this is not true, say, for slightly varying printings of a Dürer etching, or for performances of the *Brandenburg Concerti* on period instruments as opposed to contemporary instruments, and it is arguably not even true for the Toscanini and Furtwängler performances of the first movement of the *D Minor Symphony*. Physical stimuli will be inadequate, therefore, to fix the common object (the work of art) of which either the "aesthetic objects" are members or the "presentations" are presentations. Beardsley loses, therefore, the individuation of artworks.

Beardsley actually speaks of presentations both of works of art *and* of aesthetic objects, and clearly the same account cannot be given of both usages. The first is apparently to be fixed by physical stimuli; the second, by the way in which a certain "perceptual object" is "experienced by a particular person on a particular occasion." But the concept (and the individuation) of a perceptual object is not entirely clear, and it is, as we have already seen, quite doubtful that a work of art—or what about a work of art we are interested in aesthetically—may be captured by confining our attention to perceptual objects, or to the perceptual aspects of given objects. In what sense, for instance, is a poem a perceptual object? And do perceptual objects permit non-converging interpretations to be jointly defensible? These two questions profoundly challenge Beardsley's replacement of talk about works of art with talk about "'aesthetic objects," and his insistence that aesthetic appreciation is somehow confined to "perceptual" considerations. In any case, the subtlety of the ontological issue and the ease with which distinctions intended to be helpful may prove to be tendentious are perfectly clear. Beardsley's critical postulate may well be false if interpretation is distinguished from description—relative to what he calls aesthetic objects; and it may well be uninformative about artworks proper if the relationship between aesthetic objects and artworks cannot plausibly be viewed as one of class inclusion. A trim way of resolving the issue is to concede that reference to physical objects (or notations) facilitates the reference and numerical identity of artworks but that their appreciation must be grounded in *their* actual properties, not in the properties of alleged "stimuli" objects nor in the properties of alleged "perceptual" objects (or the inner mental life of aesthetic percipients). On the argument, the properties of artworks cannot be restricted to properties accessible to sensory perception alone.

If we allowed as aesthetically relevant the question of the defensibility of incompatible musical and literary interpretations (without supposing that these are interpretations of quite the same sort), we should have to dismiss all ontological models that, like Beardsley's, rule out the question, solely on the grounds of remaining consistent with the model. If we scan critical practice, therefore, we may address ourselves to the various kinds of judgments that are made by considering the methodological features of their defense; but if we proceed by constructing antecedent ontological models of the kind of entity an artwork is, we may be forced to rule against otherwise aesthetically admissible judgments, and may be forced to adopt some critical postulate like the one Beardsley himself puts forward. For on no view of the descriptive characterization of an *entity* are we going to be able to hold that incompatible descriptions may be jointly defended as valid or true characterizations of the same entity. Theorists like Beardsley proceed by asking: If works of art are such and such sort of entity, what kinds of critical claims are admissible? I, on the other hand, am proposing—and insist on emphasizing that in doing philosophy this way I am *recommending* how to construe artworks, not claiming to have discovered what they are—that priority be given to the analysis of standard critical comments and judgments rather than to a would-be frontal analysis of the ontic nature of art. Initially at least, a theory about the mode of existence of a work of art will collect our antecedent findings about the practice of the criticism and appreciation of art.

I must also stress the often fatal difficulty involved in construing an artwork as an entity of some ontologically distinct sort. *If* what has been said about the interpretation of an artwork holds—that, in principle, incompatible interpretations may be defended and that often, because of the puzzling nature of particular works, we cannot even characterize an artwork as such without reference to some interpretation by means of which its very structure *as* an artwork may be exhibited—then the properties or features that interpretations impute or ascribe to artworks cannot be construed as the native, *describable* properties or features of such works. And if we are nevertheless characterizing (and often must characterize) particular works in this way, we cannot speak of them as *entities* in quite the same way in which we speak of physical entities and the like.

But, of course, what appears to be a fatal flaw is often no more than a conditional difficulty. The enabling clue is, I think, an intriguing one. Admitting that they are different, I believe we treat *artworks* and *persons* as entities of a similar sort and speak about them in somewhat similar ways. Artworks, of course, characteristically lack minds; although when we think (however metaphorically) of man made in the image of God, of Pygmalion's art, and of the possibility of intelligent robots, even this contrast begins to fade. Both artworks and persons (not, by the way, merely human persons, if it turns out that there are persons in interstellar space or that dolphins should prove to be persons) are culturally emergent entities. Both are accorded a measure of rationality below which they cannot fall, on pain of failing to be an artwork or a person. The schemata employed in our discourse in order to make this clear about artworks are decidedly varied. But we may take it as a rough approximation that Kant's [1952] "purposiveness without purpose" (generously construed, for instance, as allowing buildings to be directed to an external purpose and as allowing "found art" to be imputed purposiveness in terms of an appreciative tradition) fixes the form of rationality that may be minimally assigned to anything construed as an artwork—which hints at least at the strategic importance of the question of interpretation. Correspondingly for persons, rationality or coherence—for instance, regarding intention, belief, desire and action—cannot be absent in any creature thought to function as a person. (One cannot for instance be said to intend to do what one is said to believe oneself incapable of doing, and one cannot be said to perform actions that are utterly incongruent with what one is said to want and desire and believe). We begin to realize that we impose as necessary conditions of artworks and persons constraints utterly unlike those that may obtain for purely physical objects. Furthermore, since the existence of artworks is at least causally dependent on the culturally informed work of persons, the identification of artworks is conceptually parasitic on the identification of persons and their cultural milieux.

Works of art and persons are, as I have already argued, *embodied* in physical bodies (or marks or movements, in the case of some works) and, as emergent entities, exhibit emergent properties. These two considerations, embodiment and emergence, serve as the foci of any relevant ontological proposal and must be properly understood. But embodiment—however appropriately construed—enables us to answer questions about how we refer to and identify artworks and persons, as well as questions about the prospects of a program such as that of a consistent materialism; and emergence—however appropriately construed—enables us to answer questions about the propriety of ascribing attributes of given sorts to entities of given sorts, as well as questions about the prospects of a program such as that of resisting reductionism. What is interesting, then, is that precisely the same puzzles and maneuvers obtain whether we speak of artworks or of persons and that these are just the classical puzzles and maneuvers available elsewhere in the metaphysical enterprise (Margolis [1976a]). Here, we need stress only the properties and nature of an artwork.

If an artwork is "embodied" in a physical object, then whatever convenience of reference and identity may be claimed for a physical object may be claimed for an artwork, in spite of the fact that to be embodied in an object is not to be identical with it. So embodiment provides a basis for speaking of emergence without losing the advantages of reference and identity—as do certain extreme forms of idealist views that somehow locate works of art in plural minds or in some vaguely specified "space" of intersubjective ideology (cf. Wellek and Warren [1956]). Thus Michelangelo's *David* may be identified and referred to as a sculpture embodied in a particular block of marble; and thus identified, we may refer to it and attribute properties to it. Physical objects have the advantage of being identifiable in exclusively extensional terms: the block of marble in which the *David* is embodied may validly be ascribed physical properties regardless of the description under which it is identified. Any tampering with this thesis, regardless of puzzles about the cultural provision of, and diachronic changes among, descriptive categories (the putatively benign problem of an epistemically centered transcendental idealism) is a move in the direction of ontic idealism (Putnam [1978]). What is true of purely physical objects, *qua* physical objects, is true regardless of how we may replace, in sentential contexts, the identifying expressions by which they are denoted or referred to; codesignative descriptions may be substituted in otherwise extensional contexts, *salva veritate*. But this is not true of *culturally* emergent entities (though it may be true of simple emergent entities, for instance of plants with respect to an inanimate world); hence it is not true of artworks (or of persons, or even of conventional actions ascribed to persons).

To say that a work of art is *embodied* in a physical object is to say that its identity is necessarily linked to the identity of the physical object in which it is embodied, though to identify the one is not to identify the other; also, that, *qua* embodied, a work of art must possess properties other than those ascribed to the physical object in which it is embodied, though it may be said to possess (where relevant) the properties of that physical object as well. Also, if in being embodied works of art are emergent entities, then the properties that a work of art possesses will include properties *of a kind* that cannot appropriately be ascribed to the object in which it is embodied: there is a measure of adequation that needs to be acknowledged between entities *of a certain kind* and the *kind* of attributes ascribable to them as being of that kind. Finally, if works of art are *culturally* emergent entities, then they will exhibit culturally significant properties (for instance, representational, symbolic, and expressive properties) that cannot in the same sense be ascribed to merely physical objects; as such, identifying references to artworks will exhibit whatever limitations obtain on the ascription of such properties.

To say that artworks (and persons) are culturally emergent entities is to say that though they are identifiable insofar as they are embodied, *they* can be identified only as the emergent entities they are. And that means that there is nothing *to be* identified as embodied apart from what would rightly be said to be thus embodied. The point is simply that artworks cannot be identified as such except in a cultural context; only if we understand how, say, words can be culturally construed as embodied in sounds or marks or how the steps of José Limon's *Moor's Pavanne* are embodied in physical movements, can we even admit that there is anything to be identified.

Artworks are identified extensionally only because, once we are clear about the kind of thing they are, we know that their identity can be linked with the identity of the physical objects in which they are embodied. But to locate or specify something as an artwork requires reference as well to the artistic and appreciative traditions of a given culture. Nowhere is this more strikingly clear than when we speak of "found art"; for unless a person is suitably sensitized, he will not even see that there is an artwork *to be* identified. In this sense, all art is found art—whether driftwood and smooth stones, or Duchamp's assemblages or constructions or readymades, or Michelangelo's *David.* To be aware of the presence of an artwork is, I am suggesting, to be aware of an object that (roughly, in the Kantian sense) exhibits purposiveness without purpose; and that to be aware of such an object is to construe physical objects or marks as supporting a certain culturally emergent object. So, works of art are said to be the particular objects they are, in *intensional* contexts, although they may be identified, by the linkage of embodiment, through the identity of what may be reliably specified in *extensional* contexts. Works of art are identified extensionally in the sense that their identity (whatever their nature) is controlled by the identity of what they are embodied in; but to identify them *as* what they are is accomplished only intensionally (by reference to the very cultural tradition in which they may actually be discriminated) (cf. Wollheim [1974]; Ingarden [1975]; Danto [1973b], [1974]).

It is *essential,* in speaking of works of art, *to attribute* to them certain patterns of purposiveness and it is essential to materialism to hold "that physical phenomena have none but purely physical explanations" (D. Lewis [1966]). On a materialist view, then, the relationship between physical phenomena and the phenomena regarding the purposiveness of art is either one of identity (which is problematic, given the intensional constraints on identifying works of art), or else it is of another sort, like embodiment, that both is compatible with materialism and accommodates the peculiarly emergent nature of art. To treat artworks as purposive is to concede: (a) that their existence depends on the work of persons; (b) that their properties, construed purposively, are informed by the cultural traditions in which human persons work purposively; and (c) that, therefore, those properties need not be construed in either narrowly biographical or metaphorical terms.

The artistic and appreciative traditions of a culture prepare both would-be artists and would-be audiences to construe ordered physical materials as artistic *media.* Here, a useful equivocation arises; for in mentioning media, we mean to speak at one and the same time of the physical medium in which an artwork is embodied, and of the artistic medium in which the emergent work is actually formed. Thus, a painting is embodied in the medium of colored pigments applied to canvas; but, also, a painting emerges as a purposive system of brush-strokes—that is, *placed* or "intended" colors and forms. Similarly, a dance is embodied in physical movements but it is itself a system of articulated dance steps. Artistic media may themselves be construed as embodied (by way of particular brush-strokes, dance steps, words and phrases, and the like) in physical media. The crucial point to remark is that, in so speaking, we make an automatic *ontological* adjustment: we shift from reference to a purely physical medium whose properties yield, in the relevant sense, to "purely physical explanations" to reference to the art object essentially composed of *dance steps, brush-strokes,* or the like—compositional ingredients that are themselves informed by the purposiveness of the entire work. Briefly, artworks exhibit purposiveness essentially in being composed of elements of some artistic medium, whereas physical objects are composed entirely of physical parts (which, relative to some embodied art, may serve as its physical medium).

These simple observations support certain extremely large distinctions. Artworks are Intentional objects of a culturally emergent sort and, because they are, they can only be identified as such intensionally. To say that they are Intentional is merely to say, in the Kantian manner, that they exhibit an interior purposiveness; they are composed of strokes, steps, phrases, or the like. (The sense in which "Intentional" is here used as a term of art relates directly to the concept of the rule-like. By contrast, "intentional" applies also to non-linguistically endowed creatures, though it is explicated, heuristically, only by reference to the Intentional [(Margolis [1978a])]. For convenience, we may drop the orthographic distinction.) This is not to say that artworks are *about* anything at all (cf. Danto [1964]), although novels and poems are, characteristically, intentional in this sense as well; architecture, music, landscape gardening, and carpets are normally not. Also, of course, the Kantian formula is to be construed in the most generous sense supportable: no antecedent canons of purposiveness need be applied (*see* Taylor [1964]).

A work of art, then, can be identified as such only relative to a culture with respect to the traditions of which it actually exists. I do not mean by this that works produced in one culture cannot be appreciated in another, or cannot be appreciated in another in terms of the distinctions favored in the generating culture (*contra* Osborne [1974]; *see* Jarvie [1970]). But works of art exhibit a further ontological complication. They often cannot themselves be ascribed a coherent design—an internal purposiveness—without imputing, by way of interpretation, properties that yield a plausible and suitably complete purposiveness. Think, for instance, of interpreting a puzzling painting like Leonardo's *Last Supper*. Is the representation of Leonardo's fresco to be construed in terms of Judas's betrayal or in terms of the institution of the Eucharist? And is the scene to be construed in terms of a pregnant moment of natural time, or in terms of the timeless import of all relevant moments of the story? It is not simply that the ascription of certain properties to an object logically depends on the ascription of other properties—for instance, that being a square entails being a rectangle—but rather that the ascription of properties of certain sorts and the appraisals of works of art themselves depend on the identification of the work *under a certain description* (or interpretation); that is, they are intensionally qualified. For it is logically possible to identify one and the same work under alternative and incompatible interpretations (each interpretation compatible with the minimally describable features of the work in question), where the truth value of further characterizations and appraisals of given works will be affected by such intensional identification. Isabel Hungerland [1955], it may be remarked, once advocated that we accept "that interpretation which does the best for the work, i.e., which results in the highest rating in the order of worth." But she did not consider that the nature of the work is not first fixed and then interpreted; she also did not consider that the work is itself identified *for* relevant description and appraisal *when* it is interpreted (that is, when the embodying medium may, by way of interpretation, be plausibly construed to embody a work of a given design). This is also the reason that Chekhov objected to Stanislavsky's portrayal of his plays as tragedies; the intensional characterization under which the plays were thus identified precluded certain further characterizations and appraisals *of the plays*.

We see, then, that discourse about works of art behaves intensionally in at least two distinct ways: first, in that they are identified intensionally relative to cultural contexts in which they may be said to be embodied in a physical medium; second, in that characterizations and appraisals of them are relativized to plausible interpretations. It is precisely the physical embodiment of a work of art that minimizes the threat of losing common reference and common grounds for interpretive and appraisive dispute; for by linking the work of art to its embodying medium we minimize intensional considerations.

What shall we understand, then, by physical embodiment and cultural emergence? First of all, we must admit a logically distinctive use of "is," the "is" of embodiment, which is not to be collapsed into the "is" of identity; the two differ in somewhat the same sense in which the "is" of composition is different from that of identity (Wiggins [1967]). Michelangelo's *David* is that block of marble (or, that block of marble *is* the *David*) only in the sense that the *David* is embodied in it. Second, to hold that one entity is embodied in another is simply to subscribe to a theory regarding different kinds of entities and the attributes properly ascribable to them, such that reference can be made jointly to embodying and embodied entities. Embodied entities must be emergent in some sense, though the issue of embodiment concerns only the matter of the (ontological) adequation between entities and their attributes. Since everything there is is of one kind or another, being of a kind sets constraints on what may properly be ascribed (whether truly or falsely) to any putative entity. In admitting entities of different kinds we implicitly admit the possibility of entities of one kind being embodied in entities of another—persons in sentient bodies, or works of art in physical objects and movements. So embodiment is essentially a question of reference and attribution, ontologically construed. Consequently it raises no questions whatsoever of dualistic substances—no more than does the question of composition. Emergence with regard to entities, on the other hand, is concerned with the question of the circumstances under which entities of given kinds can first exist, relative to a backdrop of entities of other sorts (cf. Feigl [1967]). Emergent entities need not, of course, be embodied entities—though, prominently, they are. Perhaps plants may be construed as emergent entities though they are not, in any clear sense, *embodied* in any other entity, even if they are *composed* of other entities (for instance, micro-theoretical entities). But culturally emergent entities—notably, persons and works of art—must be embodied entities; for, in speaking of such entities, we mean to say that within—and only within—the context of a cultural tradition can we identify certain entities that possess both certain distinctive intentional attributes and certain physical attributes. Also, the admission of emergent entities—accounted for either in terms of an artist's craft or in terms of an audience's tradition of appreciation—is made at the expense of reductionism, simply because of the intensional constraints on reference and attribution that are thereupon admitted to obtain.

Monroe Beardsley [1976] has attacked this theory of mine. But there are two essential weaknesses in his account. First, he conflates the thesis of cultural embodiment with the "institutional" theories developed by Danto [1964] and Dickie [1974], which I expressly do not favor. Second, Beardsley himself favors an identity theory—as between physical events and human actions, works of art and the material objects they are formed from, and presumably between persons and human bodies as well—but he does so without adequate attention to the anomalies that result. Regarding the first issue, I should stress that art presupposes cultural traditions and institutions, not that works of art are institutional objects as such—unless the formulations be taken to be equivalent. They are not equivalent, of course, in Dickie's view (which Beardsley opposes); but that obliges Dickie, implausibly, to hold that art is a status actually conferred on artifacts (nowhere characterized) by some explicit ceremony (cf. Margolis [1975a]). Beardsley does not share Dickie's view, for he asks, fairly, *what* institution is it that makes a work of art a work of art? Nevertheless, the objection is not effective against Danto's account or my own. In different ways, we emphasize that there must be a network of cultural traditions and institutions *in order for* a work of art as such to be specified at all. Since this is not true for physical objects, the identities Beardsley favors still need to be defended. Danto, as we have already noted, introduces a distinctive sense of "is," the "is of artistic identification," though he fails to analyze it. A characteristic anomaly that Beardsley's account cannot handle is this: *if* physical movements are numerically identical with human actions, then why is it (i) that a physical movement that is qualitatively identical—in physical respects—with another movement (that, on the thesis, *is* an action) may not be an action? Why is it (ii) that physical movements of quite different sorts may be instances of the same (type) action? And why is it (iii) that the same physical movement may be, or convey, several different actions? For example, an arm moving through space in precisely the same arc exhibited by an arm that actually is signalling may not be signalling at all; also, in certain contexts, one may signal inadvertently. And one may play chess in quite a variety of ways, and make a *move* (type) in any number of different ways; hence the physical features of a movement do not set decisive constraints (either necessary or sufficient conditions) on an action, though an action is physically embodied. These puzzles cannot be resolved by the identity theory (Margolis [1978a], [1974b]). The argument that holds for actions holds, with even more obvious force, for works of art and persons (cf. Bunge [1977a, 1977b]; Margolis [1978b]).

To speak of works of art as physically embodied and culturally emergent proves to be remarkably economical, at the same time that it is hospitable to certain particularly puzzling features of the world of art. Provisionally, some form of nonreductive materialism may be taken to be entirely compatible with the admission of the intentionality of works of art and the intensionality of reference to them, and of appraisals based on the interpretation of works of art—always the most troublesome problems confronting ontological speculations about art.

Having said this much, we need to refine our theory. First of all, we must clarify the concept of a cultural context. "Cultural" signifies the property of any system in virtue of which certain entities emerge and exist, a system in which *both* persons *and* what they may produce—*a fortiori,* works of art—exist or once existed. Such a system is at once rule-governed, in that what is typically produced is intelligible only in terms of rule-like regularities (traditions, customs, practices, institutions), and rule-following, in that persons (as distinct from Homo sapiens) are essentially capable of using language, and of intentionally acting in accord with rules which they understand and are able to violate. These considerations straightforwardly point to the conceptual dependence of a theory of art on a theory of persons: the rule-like properties of art are ascribable only in a context in which creatures capable of acting in accord with rules (and therefore of informing things with rule-like properties) are already admitted to exist. Also, the anomalies of found art, driftwood, the dabbling of chimpanzees, and the like are all clearly resolvable in terms of the dependence of an appreciative tradition on some corresponding active tradition of actual craft work; to construe a sunset as a painting, for instance, is to presuppose painting; there can be no extension of the range of what may pass as art without reference to the distinctions of an institutionalized craft. This points, by the way, to an easy resolution of the vexed problem of defining art, and also, to the indisputable sense in which so-called conceptual art cannot but be parasitic on crafted work (*see* Lippard [1973]).

But all discourse about rule-governed and rule-following phenomena and, in a fair sense, the phenomena themselves are intensional. Consider that rule-like regularities provide for the distinction between such paired categories (ranging inevitably far beyond the purview of aesthetics) as "appropriate"/"inappropriate," "legitimate"/"illegitimate," "right"/"wrong," "beautiful"/"ugly," and a host of others including, prominently, distinctions of period styles and of kinds of artistic excellence. Now, nothing can be ascribed such attributes, except under a description in accord with the postulated criteria by which, precisely, such attributes are rightly ascribed. The intensional, therefore, is at once essentially linguistic (or dependent on language) and cultural; only a creature capable of construing something *under one description rather than another* could possibly be said to understand the nature of a rule and to follow it intentionally. It is in this sense that the cultural is sometimes said to concern the "significant" (cf. Gadamer [1951]), and it is also in this sense that rule-following behavior is said to be either incipiently linguistic or to presuppose linguistic ability (Margolis [1978a]). Hence, too, cultural entities may be said to exist only intentionally, in the sense that rule-following capacities (of persons) or rule-governed attributes (of machines, artifacts, words and sentences, works of art) are properly ascribable. Since the intensional is a distinctly linguistic—*a fortiori,* a cultural—phenomenon, there is no way to reduce the cultural to the physical. In that sense, the thesis that cultural entities are embodied in, and not identical with, physical bodies (or physical marks or movements—distinguishing, say, sculpture, poetry, and dance) must appear promising. Also of course, more pointedly with regard to persons than works of art, the thesis of embodiment provides a distinct alternative to dualism, since material composition is nowhere denied or displaced. Having conceded this much, we may relax the notion of rules as much as we care. Certainly, as far as language is concerned, there is no known way in which to show that speakers of natural languages subscribe to one determinate set of rules rather than another—where rules are thought to be formulable; or that adequate rules corresponding to actual linguistic competence are formulable at all (Quine [1960]; Ziff [1960]).

Turning to embodiment, we may say the following: it is sufficient for embodiment to obtain if, for some set of physical objects, (1) we postulate entities having certain essential rule-governed or rule-following attributes; (2) we ascribe to such entities, individually, some of the properties of the individual physical objects admitted; and (3) we hold the identity of individual entities having rule-like properties to be necessarily dependent upon the identity of those individual physical objects whose very properties they may possess. These conditions are sufficiently general to permit an interesting variety of puzzles to be explored—for instance about the numerical identity of works of art (and of persons) involving type/token distinctions—but we need not pursue these here. (The "is" of embodiment clearly differs from that of identity, since the first but not the second is asymmetrical and non-reflexive.) The conditions stipulated may be taken as both necessary and sufficient for cultural entities, but whether there is a useful sense in which we may speak further of embodied entities that are not of a cultural kind—for instance, bee swarms or sponges or, even more curiously, social amoeba (cf. Bonner [1969])—is an arguable matter; in any case, the question has been left open. The principal, if not the exclusive, use of the concept obtains in cultural contexts; and there, it permits us to locate persons and other cultural entities extensionally, in some spatio-temporal field, at the same time we acknowledge that such entities possess traits essentially different from those of physical objects, which are the paradigms of extensional location.

Cultural entities, then, are emergent not in the sense that a novel substance mysteriously evolves out of a physical substratum, but in the sense that, in familiar contexts of discourse, we admit novel particulars that possess properties essentially lacking in purely physical objects. Since those properties are merely intentional, rule-like, functional, it is particularly appropriate to specify a relationship between such entities and physical bodies that precludes identity, permits the ascription of both cultural and physical properties to selected entities, and obviates dualism. On the face of it, only the concept of embodiment can accommodate these objectives. We may, then, account for the emergence of persons, works of art, and other cultural entities by tracing the causal influences on physical objects and sentient creatures that produce the various sorts of cultural entities we acknowledge; but such causes *cannot* be restricted to those supplied in purely physical explanations, and they must be intentionally qualified as well. What, otherwise, are the causal forces acting on a sound, or acting on the physical processes that produce a sound, that serve to produce a word? And what were the original causes that acted on a certain block of marble that served to produce the *David*?

Finally, rules and rule-like phenomena are themselves essentially cultural. Rules must be instituted or at least develop in some recognizably social way; they must be capable of being viably replaced by alternative systems of rules; they must be capable of being followed and violated by beings themselves capable of recognizing that rules obtain, and that rules are followed or violated; and they must be capable of being conformed to, and reformed or revised, for reasons to which the beings affected subscribe (Shwayder [1965]; D. Lewis [1969]). Conceivably, some relevantly weak qualification under these conditions would count as rule-following behavior or rule-like phenomena. But a theory of rules is inseparable from a theory of societal life in which common norms and purposes, criteria for discriminating conforming and non-conforming behavior (and what may be produced thereby), may be specified. The very idea of rules—of grounds for distinguishing between legitimate and illegitimate, correct and incorrect, and the like—implies that the works of artists and the significance of what they produce obtain only in *intensional contexts*.

Works of art, then, may be said to exist only relative to a tradition, that is, relative to a system of rule-like regularities (and their extension and alteration), in which the craft endeavors of suitably informed persons produce objects that, in their turn, essentially possess congruent rule-like properties. That context is the intensional context of culture, within which works of art exist as intentionally emergent entities. The idea is that works of art essentially exhibit such distinctive features that—in order to preserve a viable form of materialism consistent with the admission that works of art (and persons) are actual entities—the relationship of embodiment must be conceded. Once again, these features include: (a) that works of art exist only in cultural contexts, as intentional entities; (b) that, therefore, they can be identified as such only intensionally; (c) that they are essentially distinguished as inherently purposive; (d) that they are thus distinguished in virtue of the rule-like or rule-governed order of their compositional elements; (e) that these elements sometimes cannot be completely discerned except by way of an interpretive imputation; (f) that they exist as a result of the artist's craft or the appreciative traditions of actual persons.

The concept of embodiment, however, serves to distinguish the entire range of cultural phenomena. It suggests a new way of construing the unity of all of our explanatory endeavors. The strategic importance of discourse about art, therefore, lies in the fact that there is absolutely no way in which to understand either the nature of art, or the nature of criticism, without attention to intensional considerations. That this is also true of discourse about persons, their linguistic ability, their institutions and history argues the need for a closer conceptual connection between the problems of aesthetics and the central puzzles of philosophy, particularly those that bear on the methodology of the social sciences.

4. The Identity and Individuation of Works of Art

We have characterized artworks as tokens-of-types, culturally emergent and physically embodied. But what are the advantages of having done so? The answer requires some care. First of all, we do not yet know what the nature of a work of art is in contrast to other cultural entities that are also generically tokens-of-types. Secondly, we do not yet know how to identify different tokens as tokens of the same artwork-type, in virtue of which we may fix the common reference of critical comments. What we require, therefore, is a clear conception of the congruence between our theory of art and the characteristic effort of professionals and amateurs to focus on the aesthetic appreciation of artworks. As we shall soon see, this is a singularly complex matter. Let us begin naively, therefore, with familiar puzzles about the numerical identity of works of art.

We speak ordinarily of a translation of a poem, but are the poem and its translation the same or is the would-be translation a different poem, and if it is, what is its relation to the other? What is the relationship between the text of a play and the mounting of a play that employs that text, and what is the relationship between two performances that use different versions or abridgements of a common text? How is a change of key in a performance related to the original score? What is the relationship between two performances of a score, one in the original key or rhythm, the other altered? What is the relationship between two performances of a score, one with the instruments originally indicated, the other with altered instruments? Are two performances by the same dancer, ostensibly intended to be the same, really the same dance? What of performances by different dancers? What is the relation of a reproduction of a painting to the original? These questions can, of course, be multiplied without end. The basic concern, obviously, is how we individuate and identify works of art.

That we do not individuate works of art as we do physical objects is clear not only from the fact that we speak of the same play or sonata, even if it is performed in substantially *different* ways, but also from the fact that we allow seemingly incompatible accounts of a given work (the counterpart of the description of a physical object) to stand. A few typical remarks from a book review (Hadas [1957]) will suggest the familiarity of the practice:

> The central innovation in this stimulating study of Sophocles' tragedy is the suggestion that Oedipus is meant to represent Athens, not merely in a figurative sense as a text for a homily, but as a literal equation . . . Too bare a summary cannot do justice to the cogency of Mr. Knox's proofs or to his valuable incidental insights. His interpretations must be welcomed with thanks, provided we do not (as he would doubtless insist we should not) exclude other modes of interpretation.

The expression "other modes of interpretation" signifies the reviewer's conviction that there are a number of plausible interpretations of the *Oedipus* cycle, among which some, including Knox's new interpretation, are not reducible to, or subsumable under, other interpretations.

Granting that such interpretations accord with our aesthetic interest, it is precisely that interest that threatens our effort to identify a work of art as a public object. Were contrary descriptions of an ordinary natural object, for instance, an oak tree, regarded as confirmed, we should insist that the descriptions were true of two different objects. But evidently, we do not speak of works of art in this way. The only conceptual shift possible is to provide a model of confirmation other than that of simple truth and falsity. Let us at least conclude that although the aesthetically relevant properties of an artwork make it what it distinctively is, such properties cannot by themselves facilitate our speaking of a single work. The argument, as we have already seen, drives us to suppose works of art to be different in certain fundamental respects from natural or physical objects; and in the light of certain philosophical difficulties in aesthetic discourse, this is a welcome proposal (cf. Ziff [1954]; Macdonald [1954a]). This accommodates, for instance, our practice of speaking of significantly different recordings of Bach's *Brandenburg Concerti*. That these recordings show variant properties that are of aesthetic interest, and that they involve the use of different instruments, need not force us to deny that it is the same *Concerti* that are being interpreted. In the same spirit, common usage offers such comments as, "How differently Horowitz plays it from Rubenstein," and even, "You'll have to practice a lot if you want to play it as Horowitz does."

The issue at stake, then, is the denotation of an artwork. We may ignore here all the general difficulties concerning the denotative boundaries of ordinary objects in nature and the referential use of terms. In fact we may, as an economy, simply deploy the type/token distinction already introduced, thereby linking at a stroke our findings regarding the ontology of art with whatever may be required regarding the numerical identity of artworks. C.L. Stevenson [1957] has usefully applied Peirce's distinction between tokens and types [1939] to ambiguities arising when we speak about a poem—but he often speaks in a way that is indifferent to its status as an object of aesthetic interest (cf. also Rudner [1958]; Stevenson [1950]). For instance, he examines such remarks as, "there are many poems that are about classical mythology," and "each student was expected to write down the same poem that the teacher recited." As Stevenson himself concedes, we could easily substitute specimen remarks in which the same ambiguities arise and all reference to art disappears. I should, however, like to avail myself of Stevenson's version of the type/token ambiguity, because of its bearing on our ontological commitment, and because of certain anticipated advantages, but with important reservations to be detailed. Let us provisionally adopt the following phrasing, disregarding the full context in which the statements occur:

> Now when we want to speak of [token poems] we obviously have a number of other terms available; we have such terms as "manuscript of a poem," "copy of a poem," "recitation of a poem," and so on. It may seem, then, that we should reserve the term "poem" itself for the corresponding type . . . it would . . . preserve a clear sense in which the copies, and so on, are *of* the poem. They are *of* it in the sense in which various individuals are of a certain kind, the relation being that of membership in a class.

Peirce, it must be remembered, regarded tokens and types as signs; we shall want to remain neutral on the matter of the adequacy of a semiotic theory of art (cf. Stevenson [1958]; Hiż [1977]; Eco [1976]). Perhaps, as suggested earlier on, it is sufficient to construe types and tokens as obtaining exclusively among culturally emergent entities.

Addressing the question of translation, Stevenson interposes a third notion, "megatype":

Two tokens will belong to the same megatype if and only if they have approximately the same meaning; so it is not necessary that the tokens belong to the same language or that they have that similarity in shape or sound that makes them belong to the same type. Thus any token of "table" and any token of "mensa," though not of the same type, will nevertheless be of the same megatype. The distinction need not be restricted to individual words, of course, but can be extended to larger linguistic units, including poems.

Now, to remain neutral on the semiotic theory of art and to accommodate the ontological and cultural peculiarities of artworks as well as to anticipate further difficulties, let us make the following adjustments: (*a*) read, with appropriate grammatical alterations, "impute a design to" for "have the meaning of"; and (*b*) take it that two tokens belong to the same megatype if and only if they approximately share some design from the range of alternative, and even contrary, designs that may be defensibly imputed to each; or, if the designs of both, however different, can be defensibly imputed to some token of the megatype signified by an art notation. (Here, "design" is a term of art meant to accommodate the greatest flexibility regarding what we take to be aesthetically relevant in the appreciation of artworks. It remains undefined, but it catches up the Kantian-like theme of the internal purposiveness of a work of art, sets no constraints on what may be aesthetically relevant, and remains hospitable to the possibility of plural, non-converging interpretations.) Furthermore, paraphrasing Peirce [1939] but misusing his terms as semiotically neutral, we may say: "in order that a type or megatype may be used, it has to be embodied in a token; such a token is an *instance* of the type or megatype." It should perhaps also be said that the apparatus proposed is just that—an apparatus. It has a heuristic use in that it permits us to formulate, in a relatively uniform way, all the alternative conditions for identifying a work of art; it does so without explicitly invoking our ontological thesis. As will be seen, it is, in fact, quite awkward as an adjunct of natural language. Its advantage lies, precisely, in articulating the systematic distinctions underlying our ordinary way of speaking of the arts; it need never replace the existing idiom. It also permits us to assess quite effectively certain well-known views about the individuation of works of art—for instance Nelson Goodman's [1968] contrast between autographic and allographic arts—as well as the strong tendency to construe works of art as types or universals rather than as particulars of some sort (Wolterstorff [1975b]).

The apparatus is now very convenient. We normally wish to refer to a poem through the text of some critical manuscript; if we need to invent a term, we may call it not merely an instance of the poem, but the prime instance. This way of referring to the poem surely corresponds to the practice of historical and critical studies in poetry. Other printings, including variant versions and translations, may then serve as additional instances of the megatype. We may even speak of good and bad translations in a non-evaluative sense, if we agree on the prime instance of a poem; this simply calls for specifying a procedure for applying (*b*). We may not agree on a prime instance, as in collecting variations of folk songs, but the application of (*b*) will allow us to decide to what extent two token songs are instances of the same megatype.

The notion of the prime instance is of signal importance in the plastic arts also, but in a novel way. Reproductions correspond either to copy tokens, as in plural sculpture castings or etchings from the same plate, or to translation tokens, as in reduced-scale color lithographs of great paintings (cf. Wacker [1960]). In the case of sculpture casting, or etching, an adjustment may be made. We need not actually insist on a single prime instance; there is a causal factor that may be appealed to by which to designate a set of prime instances. We see here that an important difference develops. In the literary arts, the prime instance is used only as a device for controlling the enumeration of tokens for a given megatype. We are inclined to identify *the* poem with the megatype poem and *use* it in the form of an acceptable token. (This remark is provisional as far as the question of universal versus particular is concerned.) Even when we have before us the first quarto and first folio editions of Shakespeare's *King Lear,* that is, two different prime instances, we still speak in this way. To illustrate, let me quote from some expert remarks (Duthie [1949]) on the *Lear* manuscripts:

There are two substantive editions [i.e., editions "which are not derived as to essential character from any other extant edition"] of *King Lear*—the first quarto edition, published in 1608, and the first folio edition, published in 1623. In Chapter II of the introduction to my edition of the play I have argued that we must accept the view that F *Lear* was printed from a copy of Q which had been brought by a scribe into general agreement with an authentic playhouse manuscript, doubtless a promptbook And in Chapter II, section (i), I have argued that we must accept the view that at some stage the Q text was memorially transmitted, i.e., that it is a reported text. In any given case, then, in which Q and F have different readings, we must assume that the F reading is genuine and the Q reading corrupt, *unless there is in that particular case, a definite reason for supposing that this is not so.*

If we are considering a sculpture or a painting, we identify *the* work of art with the megatype sculpture or painting as it is actually instantiated in the prime instance; and even when we speak of original copies of an etching, we mean to preserve the usage just specified. Clearly, we do not identify a work of art in precisely the same way in the different arts. (Again, the issue of universal versus particular needs to be looked at more carefully.)

It is not sufficient to explain the difference between a painting and a play in terms of such considerations as market value, since a first quarto *Lear* may prove as valuable a piece of property as an original painting. The clue to the difference seems to lie with the relationship between tokens and megatypes. It is possible to view the printed poem as *a notation* for *the* poem; it is not possible to view an original painting as such a notation. This is not to say that a physical medium is not required by a poem; surely, a poem depends on what we may call sound or voice just as a painting depends on pigments (cf. Bosanquet [1915]; Macdonald [1952-1953]).

Even Benedetto Croce [1922], contrary to popular view, seems not to have intended to deny that the artist's imagination is a craft imagination, though he mistakenly thinks the artist's differs from ordinary imagination as a matter of degree. It is ironic that Joyce Cary, who, as author of *The Horse's Mouth* [1944], surely saw and even portrayed the distinction of the craft imagination of the artist—that is, the construing of things in terms of the materials of his craft: a scene as pigments arranged on a canvas or words spoken on an occasion—could not, as aesthetician [1958], formulate his insight except as an enlargement of Croce's error. For example, he says that Housman "had to go and find words, images, rhyme, which embodied his feeling about the tree"—insisting thus on two distinct moments in artistic creation separated by an unbridgeable gap. Samuel Alexander's account [1933] is even more subtly misleading. Though he sees that "the external work [is] an organic part of the creative process," he concludes: "Except for the features which make the artist's act creative, there is no difference in kind between the discovery of the tree by perception and the discovery of the Slave in the block or of Hamlet in the English language. The artist's creativeness conceals from us his real passivity'' (cf. Kubie [1958]). What these theorists fail to understand are the implications of *craft imagination,* that is, of thinking in terms of an *artistic medium* (dance steps, brush strokes, musical phrases, words) rather than in terms merely of what is perceivable as a *physical medium.*

Returning to the difference between literature and painting, the pigments of the painting can be seen only as constitutive, whereas the written words of a page of poetry may be ambivalently taken to be constitutive of a poem, as in an actual token poem, or merely as a notation of what would be constitutive of any instance. In literary art, we *refer* to a prime instance in order to determine other instances of, say, a megatype poem. But in painting and sculpture, we *mean* by a painting *only* the megatype painting as it obtains in the prime instance; nothing else will do. I think our ordinary language bears this out. A student may be assigned the task of reading a poem, and he will do so by consulting at random any of a very large number of alternative printings—sometimes, as in Shakespeare, even variant editions; it is not at all appropriate to say he consults a likeness of the poem. But we have any number of locutions designed to caution against identifying a reproduction of a painting with the painting itself—for example, ''Let me show you a slide of Van Gogh's *Sunflowers*; it's not quite like the original, there's too much lemon and not enough orange in the petals,'' or ''You can get an idea of the painting from this postcard picture.'' The point—certainly an important one in the appreciation of art—is that the skill we prize in the poet's work is the arrangement of words that will sustain interesting aesthetic designs, not some peculiarly accidental physical notation of the poem. In painting and sculpture, it is the artist's execution *in* pigment and stone that counts.

The distinction may be summarized in this way: we use a poem in an aesthetically relevant way by locating instances of it, but we can use a painting only by locating prime instances of the painting. I speak here of *identifying* a work of art, *locating* and *using instances* of a work of art and *denoting* and *pointing* to the physical medium on which any instance depends. These are all, of course, distinctions in denotation intended to facilitate—but not to force—whatever ontic qualifications we require.

The distinction between poems and paintings allows us to accommodate translations and lithograph likenesses, which may be tokens of megatype art objects but not of type art objects. In a painting (I am addressing myself here to the proposals Stevenson has made regarding poems), we require that tokens be of the same type as well as megatype to be said to be instances of the same painting; usually, there will be a unique object. However, that requirement does not quite apply to poetry. And because of that, even when translations fail to provide for portions of the design of the megatype poem, we continue to speak of English translations, say, of the *Odyssey* as instances of the poem just as we would of versions in the original Greek.

It is easy to be misled here. The fact that language, generally speaking, is translatable and informal habits of aesthetic interest in literary art attend primarily to the translatable aspects of poetic language inclines us to speak about translations as we have just done. But if we share, with the New Criticism, an interest in the "texture" (Elton [1953] on the "texture" of the poem: "the quality of the poem beyond the merely paraphrasable rational content; the heterogeneous detail of the situation, including metaphor and meter"), we must revise our account of the location of an instance of a poem by revising our view of the elements in the design of a poem. A difference still remains between painting and poetry, though now the execution of the poet is conceived not only in terms of words but also in terms of physical sounds and rhythms. The difference we now see, which has suggestive implications for other arts, is this: the poet, because he chiefly composes with words, may be said (roughly) to *select* his materials from an antecedently well-defined and well-ordered fund (of language); his creativity chiefly relates to the *arrangement* of these materials, though in writing a poem he may well alter some of the elements of language itself, as by enlarging the metaphoric possibilities of given phrases. On the other hand, a painter cannot point to such a well-ordered fund—his creativity relates to the original *preparation* of the very materials he finally arranges.

There is, of course, a sense in which paintings, drawings, etchings, and even sculptures may be viewed as notations. A Cézanne watercolor frequently serves as a preparatory sketch for an oil; a Munch woodcut, for one of his oils; a drawing by Henry Moore, for a sculpture; a few pen strokes with the names of colors appended, for a Van Gogh. The relationships involved here, however, are fundamentally of a different sort from that, say, of a group of paintings by El Greco (the various versions for example of *Christ Driving the Money-changers from the Temple*). El Greco's composition may improve from painting to painting; but each version is, nevertheless, viewed as a complete painting and not as a notation. When a piece of plastic art is viewed as a notation, it must thereby cease to be viewed as a work of art; hence our question does not arise. However, a sketch by Frank Lloyd Wright of a building to be erected may of course attract our attention as a work of art; in that case, we no longer view it as a mere notation for some *other* work of art. The contrast with poetry is clear. The issue bears also on a large range of further distinctions—parallels, sketches, copies, paraphrases, allusions, borrowings, models, sources, influences, and forgeries (Hermerén [1975]).

In architectural construction, where direct invention in materials holds our attention, as in medieval cathedrals, we are inclined to treat the buildings much as we do paintings and sculpture, emphasizing prime instances. But in much of modern architecture, where mechanical execution has largely superseded direct invention, we are prepared to view different buildings as instances of the same megatype; in this latter case, architectural notations tend to be complete notations; and, correspondingly, the execution of any token building points to the artist's *arrangement* of antecedently well-ordered materials (cf. Abbot Suger [1947]; Giedion [1948]). The resemblance between individuating such architecture and individuating poetry is striking. There is also a parallel with so-called multiples, a form of sculpture in which blueprints usually play a decisive role.

An odd consequence follows for music. In the history of aesthetics, music has been frequently taken to be the fine art *par excellence,* because of the complete integrity of form and content, and because of its untranslatability (the view, for instance, of Walter Pater [1917]). In this regard, we should be inclined to suppose that we identify a piece of music more as we do a painting than as we do a poem. But the barest reflection shows that, at least in part, the contrary practice prevails. Normally, in concert music we cannot speak of a prime instance. All we have is a score; and a score, in contrast to a poem, is unequivocally a notation. Our individuation of a piece of music, as of a poem, presupposes an antecedent, well-defined, and well-ordered fund of materials. Because a music score is a notation, a sign of a work of art and not a work of art itself, and because our admiration for the composer refers (normally) to his *arrangement* of antecedently defined and ordered notes—think, however, of John Cage's compositions and of electronic music (cf. L. Meyer [1973])—any token performance of the megatype composition noted in the score will serve as an acceptable instance of the music. We need not deny that some music cannot be scored at all—for example, electronically produced music composed by cutting and splicing sound tapes. But such music is individuated much as sculpture and etchings are; the lack of a keyboard is decisive. In conventional music, just as in poetry, we use the musical composition instantiated in any random token, say, a recording or a live performance; we are inclined therefore, to identify a musical composition in the same way as a poem, in contrast to the way in which we identify painting and sculpture. We may say that, in music, we typically lack a prime instance and have instead a prime notation for possible tokens.

Music is, however, somewhat more complicated than we have allowed. The reason has already been given: typically, we have only a score to point to; we do not have an actual musical composition. (This consideration, in fact, has strongly encouraged the thesis that works of art are *kinds*—an issue to which we shall return shortly.) Even if we had a prime instance performance and no score, we would ordinarily be inclined to construct a prime score from it and prefer it even to the performance of the composer himself. An interesting point to observe is that precisely the same attitude is to be found in the dance, where a notational system (labanotation) has now emerged (Hutchinson [1954]), and in dramatic art. (Dance notation, of course, lacks the inherent interest of musical scores.) Even when intricate ballets were not scored but merely passed on by authoritative members of a company, and even when it was realized that different dancers could not help interpreting a given dance in terms of the idiosyncrasies of their bodies and temperaments, the idea persisted that all such performances were, however distinctive, performances of the same dance. Even though, to be sure, the fundamental movements of some old ballets are hopelessly lost, so that recent productions that have preserved the same name and some gross features of a remembered ballet are really new dances, the intention at least is clear; individuation was conceived in notational terms.

Now, these arts are more distinctly performing arts than poetry, fiction, painting, and sculpture. Given a prime instance of a poem, we can judge whether any other token poem, variant or translation, is (and to what extent it is) an instance of the same megatype poem. But given a token musical performance, dance, or a dramatic performance, we face further difficulties. We seem disinclined even to speak of a prime instance in the case of these performing arts; hence, we may suspect some important differences between them and literary art. (I again make an exception of electronic music, which, in an important sense, is not capable of being performed.) The fact is that when we are able, in any art, to start with a prime instance, we are in a position to decide whether any other token belongs to the same megatype; we have only to determine all the designs that may be imputed to the prime instance. And should a translation of a poem permit of a distinctive design, we have only to inquire whether and to what extent that design may be imputed as well to the prime instance. When we start with a prime notation only, and even disallow prime instances, we cannot control the identity of the work of art in the same way.

The important clue here is the contribution of the performing artist; it is clearly much more significant in the arts of music, dance, and drama than in the others already considered. We recognize that the performer *adds* in a distinctive way to the compositions sketched in the score or notation; at the same time, we wish to preserve the sense in which, for example, two performances of *Macbeth* are instances of the same megatype. That is, even though the performer *adds to* an artistic creation, we wish to preserve the sense in which significantly different performances may be instances of the same megatype. (That performers *add* something—variably—to a composition need not lead us to conclude that the work the artist composes is somehow inherently incomplete. The same holds for interpretive additions. The point is easily misunderstood and has led to unnecessary complaints. We shall return to consider it more closely.) Our effort, however, to identify an artwork need not correspond with our interest in it—we may, for example, be interested in the originality of the performer alone. Hence, in the performing arts, the ease with which we may locate a token performance as an instance of a given megatype depends on the ease with which we can identify that to which it adds its own distinctive contribution. In fact, where the individuation of compositions for the performing arts is closely governed by a notational device, notations necessarily fail to specify at least some of the properties of a performance that are normally of aesthetic interest; it is also open to dispute whether, and to what extent, what *is* notationally specified actually provides a necessary condition to be satisfied in confirming the identity of a putative token of some work. For instance, directors of George Bernard Shaw's plays often suppose that Shaw's stage directions (in the text) are recommendations and not necessary constraints on admissible tokens of his plays.

Drama is in a privileged position among these arts because it enjoys all the precision of identity that accrues to the literary composition on which it depends. Regardless of the differences among dramatic performances, if an individual performance can be looked upon as an instance of the megatype literary composition, all of its dramatic innovations will be discounted. That is, they will be discounted denotatively, in the sense that widely variant dramatic innovations will not disqualify performances from being tokens of the same drama; they will *not* be discounted in the sense that these innovations enable us to speak of a drama. Hence the importance of conceiving a written text as a score when we have drama in mind. In a dramatic performance, the staging and acting attract us primarily, but Orson Welles's modern dress *Julius Caesar* is no less an instance of the megatype drama than a performance of the Old Vic, regardless of which we may prefer; and the Old Vic's is no less an instance than the Globe Theatre performance, which must surely have been quite different. However, since we usually possess a prime instance of the literary composition in drama, we can be more detailed on the question of the extent to which two token plays are instances of the same megatype. We can always decide the extent to which two performances share peculiar dramatic features; we may determine, that is, not merely that two performances are instances of the same megatype drama but that they are instances, say, of the Old Vic megatype performance of the megatype drama.

Now, it is important to notice that when a literary composition is regarded as a notation for a drama, we are inclined to take an extremely relaxed view of stage instructions and the like—at least as far as numerical identity is concerned. This liberty reinforces the observation that it is sufficient to view a token performance as an instance of the literary megatype. The objective is to give the greatest latitude to the ingenuity of those who are to mount an actual performance. We have no difficulty, therefore, in viewing Laurence Olivier's film versions of Shakespeare's plays as instances of those plays although, as films, further puzzles about individuation arise.

In music and in the dance, however, we lack the prime instance that drama often possesses in virtue of being dependent on literary art. (Art forms like pantomine will of course resemble dance in the details under consideration.) The result is that we are left merely with a prime notation at best. If we have no prime notation, as is usual in folk music and folk dance, we can only determine the extent to which two performances are instances of the same megatype. Herein lies the difference, for example, between identifying a prelude by Rachmaninoff and identifying the folk song ''Barb'ry Allen.'' The same limitations that apply to folk art very frequently apply to even more formalized balletic and modern dance performances.

We may perhaps fix the distinction between music and dance if we consider the following contrast between a dramatic performance and a dance performance. Usually, the dance employs music; but, though we can identify a drama by reference to its literary text, we cannot identify a dance by reference to its accompanying music. Two different dances may be composed for the same musical composition, as has been done, for example, with some of Purcell's music; we would not, however, speak in this manner even of such different performances as Stanislavski seems to have provided of Chekhov's plays and of such as would accord with Chekhov's interpretation of his own plays. The medium of literary drama *includes* the medium of its corrsponding literature; the medium of music does not include the medium of the dance, nor does the medium of the dance include that of music. The dance and music share types of physical properties, rhythm for instance, in virtue of which they may *accompany* each other. We are even prepared to speak of an unaccompanied dance as an instance of the same megatype as a musically accompanied dance. Nothing comparable appears in drama, unless it is a pantomine version of a drama, which we identify in the same way we identify a dance and not in the way we identify a poem.

In the concert dance and in folk music, as has already been suggested, it is not uncommon to lack both a prime instance and a prime notation. It is even conceivable that two anonymous token poems of the classical Greek period may be discovered, which, though they appeared in different dialects, would be judged to be instances of the same megatype. Here, too, we might lack a prime instance and a prime notation; but we should have little difficulty, in accord with our discussion earlier, in deciding that the token poems are instances of the same megatype. In the drama, as we have seen, two performances that do not share a design in common may nevertheless be said to be instances of the same megatype if their respective designs may be imputed to the literary composition on which they depend. The element of performance, it must be remembered, adds to the composition. In the dance, invention in bodily movements tends to make each performance distinctive. Were the dance like painting and sculpture, we should merely say that each dance is a unique work of art; but dancing is a performing art in a sense that distinguishes it from these other arts. Even though the direct execution of each performer is what interests us in the dance, we are always inclined to think of dance performances as, at least potentially, performances based on a score or notation.

Since a dance notation is now available, we may expect, increasingly, that a prime notation may be provided for particular dances; in that case, the identification of a concert dance will very much resemble that of a musical composition. Short of this, it is still possible to speak, when we wish, of different token performances as instances of the same megatype dance. *If,* however, we wish to hold that two performances are instances of the same megatype dance, we must be prepared to formulate a dance notation for which either performance will be a plausible token. The relation then will be much like that holding among alternative musical performances.

To see how distinctive the performing arts are in this respect, we have only to consider that it is altogether possible to formulate a notation for which the three versions of El Greco's *Christ Driving the Moneychangers from the Temple* would be plausible tokens; it would seem possible to attempt something of the same sort for various paintings of the De Stijl school, or even for Picasso's *Ma Jolie* and Braque's *Man with a Guitar*. Nevertheless, we resist altogether this way of individuating paintings and sculptures. But in the dance, we sometimes have an option; there are, ordinarily, reasons of weight for preferring to treat particular performances as instances of a common megatype rather than as prime instances of their own distinctive megatypes. In drama, we have seen that a common text suffices for individuation; in the concert dance, the presence of a repertory company or some such consideration may be enough. In films, the production of a film tape of some sort is decisive; films, in fact, are construed rather like performances (recordings), whether they depend on the actual enactment of a dramatic piece via plural "takes" and splicing or whether, as in some of Norman MacLaren's animated cartoons, they do not. Certainly, the intrinsic complexity of the tokens that resemble one another and the distinctive way in which we typically identify works of this or that general kind of art will be contributing factors.

To recapitulate briefly: we do not always identify artworks in the same way. Sometimes (as, typically, in the plastic arts) we identify a work by identifying a megatype as actually instanced in a prime instance. It is interesting to speculate that if we could actually reproduce a fully accurate copy of a painting by some mechanical process, we would probably identify paintings somewhat more as we do poems or etchings. In fact, Richard Rudner [1972] cites the report of the almost perfect reproduction technique of a certain Guenther Dietz, whose work led Theodore Rousseau of the Metropolitan Museum of New York to speak of a "Dietz duplication" as a "facsimile" rather than a "reproduction." Sometimes (as, typically, in the literary arts) we identify a work by identifying the megatype of a prime instance and use that megatype in any suitable instance. Sometimes (as, typically, in music) we identify a work by identifying the megatype signified by a prime notation and use that megatype in any suitable instance. At other times (as, typically, in drama) we identify a work by identifying the prime notation on which it depends and the megatype signified by that notation, and use the megatype in any suitable instance which exhibits the general properties of the kind of art (type) to which the work in question is said to belong (for example, drama, dance, music, poetry). At still other times (as, typically, in the dance and in folk art) we identify a work by constructing a notation, the megatype it signifies being such as will permit us to use given tokens as instances of that megatype; the identification therefore is relatively loose.

It is important, after cataloguing the various ways in which we individuate artworks, that we understand describing, interpreting, and evaluating artworks as altogether independent critical enterprises. We have, with a view to those matters, simply accommodated a source of possible puzzlement (individuation) that may affect our handling of incompatible judgments. We have not really described the actual ways in which we individuate works of art; we have, rather, constructed an alternative (but hardly more convenient) language for individuating, a language that parallels our actual usage, and exhibits its logical features more clearly. The truth is that when we speak of a translation of a poem, of the numbered copies of an etching, and of the performances of a musical composition, such expressions fix the individuating distinctions we require. Nevertheless, they do not lend themselves conveniently to a systematic array in terms of which we may see at a glance the inherent variety of the individuating rules we employ for the different arts. The scheme we have applied has the triple advantage of clarifying usage in terms of the type/token distinction, both with respect to the numerical identity and the ontology of art, and of providing a basis for anticipating the problem of ambiguity, with which we must come to grips in describing, interpreting, and evaluating artworks.

I suggested, earlier, some additional puzzles about identity. One is raised in a systematic way by Nelson Goodman [1968], in applying his own concept of "notationality" to the identity of a work of art. The merits of the concept of strict notationality (the full details of which we need not here pursue) presumably appear to best advantage in the setting of a unified account of all imaginable symbol systems; Goodman construes the requirements it imposes on notational systems as imposing corresponding requirements on the identity of allographic works of art, that is, on works whose identity depends in some essential respect on a notational scheme. Thus, for instance, Goodman defines a score as "a character in a notational system" and, though "even in musical notation not every character is a score," he is prepared to count as a score "every character that may have compliants," that is, that may have an extension or denotata. Nevertheless, he says that "the verbal language of tempos is not notational [and] tempo words cannot be integral parts of a score insofar as the score serves the function of identifying a work from performance to performance" in spite of the fact that "the verbal language of tempos" *does* have compliants. I quite agree (granting with Goodman the transitivity of identity) that the compliance-classs of any notational system (that is, any "system" that is to meet his rigorous conditions of notationality) "must be disjoint" and not allow for ambiguous characters of intersecting compliance-classes. But this is not to say either that musical notations—scores—are correctly construed as belonging to notational *systems* (as opposed to notational *schemes,* which, like all natural languages, apparently may fail in just the ways indicated, by relaxing the semantic requirements of notationality), or that musical notations, *qua* notations, have the prime function of securing the identity of a work of art or of securing it by means congruent merely with notationality. (Scores may, for instance, function to provide instructions—never complete in terms of aesthetically interesting properties—for performing musicians [cf. L. Meyer ([1973])].) I agree entirely with Goodman that the purpose of a score is served "without captur[ing] all the [aesthetically relevant] subtlety and complexity of a performance." I am also prepared to agree (again in the spirit of the transitivity of identity) that *if* the identity of musical works is determined or determinable solely on a notational basis, then at least *some* sub-set of the characters of a given notation must meet Goodman's conditions of notationality; but this is not to say that a notation cannot tolerate ambiguity and intersecting compliance-classes (as, indeed, familiar notations do and must); nor is it to say that, even for putatively allographic works of art, identity is solely a function of notationality.

The quarrel may be given point if one recalls that, for Goodman, "full compliance with the specifications given [the score] is categorically required" in music; "the most miserable performance without actual mistake does count as [a genuine instance of a work] while the most brilliant performance with a single wrong note does not." "The innocent-seeming principle," he explains, "that performances differing by just one note are instances of the same work risks the consequence—in view of the transitivity of identity—that all performances whatsoever are of the same work. If we allow the least deviation, all assurance of work preservation and score-preservation is lost; for by a series of one-note errors of omission, addition, and modification, we can go all the way from Beethoven's *Fifth Symphony* to *Three Blind Mice*." But this is totally unconvincing, particularly when one takes a more generous view of what is included in a musical score and actual musical practice. I feel quite sure, for instance, that Goodman's own phrase "the most brilliant performance with a single wrong note" is an ellipsis for the phrase "the most brilliant performance *of the piece* with a single wrong note." Although I do not wish to be a stickler for actual usage, it is Goodman's own intention to deviate as little as possible, unless systematic advantages obtain, from the actual practice of fixing numerical identity among the arts. If I understand him correctly, this consideration in fact serves as the basis for distinguishing "real" definitions of musical works and for his resistance to attempting to determine the identity of paintings (autographic works of art) by reference to a notational system: "we cannot," he claims, speaking of paintings, "devise a notational system that will provide, for such works, definitions that are both real (consonant with antecedent practice) and independent of history of production [that is, the autographic consideration]." In any case, *if* strict notationality cannot be applied to music congruently with actual usage regarding individuation, and *if* some alternative form of "nominal" individuation is available, we may well ask why Goodman did not explore the properties of the alternative.

Although music is (primarily) an allographic art, the identity of musical performances depends to some extent on considerations normally critical for the autographic arts. In general, the different arts simply do not sort themselves out neatly—in respects relevant to identity—as autographic and allographic. The reason this is important is simply that the matter of the identity of a work of art need not presuppose either a strict notational system (which, on Goodman's account, does not seem to obtain in actual practice anyway) or the principle of strict notationality itself. In short, respecting musical performances, it seems reasonable and sufficient to hold that what Goodman terms "the history of production" (an autographic consideration) decides the identity of "the most brilliant performance with a single wrong note" and, therefore, permits us to restore notations of tempi and the like to the score and to tolerate ambiguity and intersecting compliance-classes without falling foul of the principle of identity. It appears, for instance, that if tempi fail to accord with notationality, then the relevant reasons will also preclude pitch as well (Webster [1971], [1974]). The history of musical notation shows conclusively that autographic considerations cannot be eliminated in speaking of the individuation of musical compositions, and such problems as those of temperament undermine Goodman's claims about notationality (Apel [1969], [1953]).

About painting, Goodman says, sensibly: "We are not as comfortable about identifying an architectural work with a design rather than a building as we are about identifying a musical work with a composition rather than a performance. In that architecture has a reasonably appropriate notational system and that some of its works are unmistakably allographic, the art is allographic . . . [otherwise it] is a mixed and transitional case." There is no doubt that architecture, *given its historical development,* sometimes appears as an autographic, sometimes as an allographic, art. But if we (rightly) distinguish, with Goodman, between the Taj Mahal and the plans for "Smith-Jones Split-Level #17," then there is no reason for not providing as well for a comparable distinction between one of Rembrandt's portraits of *Titus,* and the machine program for the "Kunin-Levitsky #86," which allows for the production of painting copies in a way that bridges the difference between architecture and etching and allows us to construe the original painting rather like a printing plate itself (cf. Rudner [1972]). In either of these cases, although painting is normally construed as autographic, allographic provisions bearing on the identity of particular works may be provided without the least neglect of the artist's ability or originality. Goodman himself observes that a notational system for painting may be trivially devised; for instance he says that "nothing precludes taking each [etching] plate itself as the unique inscription of a character having its impressions as its compliants." But he fails to draw the obvious consequence, that the concept of notationality cannot and need not be relevantly drawn from the domain of the arts.

Regarding literature, Goodman says, in the spirit of remarks already cited, that "a literary work . . . is not the compliance-class of a text but the text or script itself. All and only inscriptions and utterances of the text are instances of the work; and identification of the work from instance to instance is insured by the fact that the text is a character in a notational scheme—in a vocabulary of syntactically disjoint and differentiated symbols. Even replacement of a character in a text by another synonymous character (if any can be found in a discursive language) yields a different work . . . Both identity of language and syntactic identity within the languge are necessary conditions for identity of a literary work." This is helpful, but the fact remains that, even "as a phonetic character, with utterances as compliants, [the literary text] belongs to [only] an approximately notational system" and "as a character with objects as compliants, it belongs to a discursive language," that is, to a notational scheme only, to a scheme that fails to meet the conditions of notationality. Symptomatically, Goodman debates whether a linguistic character may be considered "to be a class of both [utterances and inscriptions]," which is tantamount to admitting an enormous range of ambiguity and uncertainty respecting compliance-classes. He also says nothing about variant versions of the same poem (Emily Dickinson's poems, for instance), though it is perfectly clear that—again, on autographic grounds—we tolerate what, on a purely notational basis, would be disastrous.

Corresponding difficulties arise as well for music, for Goodman holds that "specification of instrument is an integral part of any true score in standard musical notation; and a piano work and the violin version of it, for example, count strictly as different works." But if this is so, are we also bound to say that the substitution of a modern piano for an eighteenth-century piano, in putatively playing a Mozart composition, entails that we are *not* playing that composition? Actual practice regarding musical identification appears to have it that we are indeed playing that same composition. Here again, for purposes of identity, we must concede the importance for the so-called allographic arts of factors normally governing so-called autographic arts. These and similar considerations demonstrate that for none of the principal arts does identity depend upon, or require, adherence to the strict conditions of notationality. Notice, then, (i) that Goodman's insistence on the constraint of notationality accommodates no normal practice regarding plural tokens of the same type; (ii) that Goodman imposes a constraint which no natural language or natural notation actually approximates; (iii) that the plausibility of his thesis about numerical identity depends unconditionally on an exclusive division between allographic and autographic arts, which fails to obtain in actual practice; (iv) that the conditions for allographic identity are never met, on Goodman's own view, by the autographic arts, which nevertheless do support distinctive claims of identity; hence, (v) that the conditions for strict allographic identity (compliance with the constraints of notationality) may be completely replaced, without any loss of precision whatsoever, by a mixed compliance with natural notations and autographic considerations.

In fact, then, relaxing the requirements on identity and individuation (for example, the false-note case, musical transpositions, variant versions of literary pieces, and the like) need not, as such, fall foul of the principle of identity—as Goodman suggests. One is always able, given the unusual properties of works of art already conceded, to provide theoretical grounds for construing qualitatively different items as instances of the same work (just as we do, in quite other contexts, in holding that the Morning Star and the Evening Star are distinct phases of one and the same planet). Goodman's restrictions are unnecessarily severe on formal grounds; also, insofar as they are only idealizations of certain elements of actual practice, they clearly depart from such practice in unnecessary and unjustified ways. This enables us to tolerate notational ambiguity consistent with the principle of identity and it obliges us to admit, contrary to Goodman's view, that all works of art are to some extent autographic. The identification of all works of art depends, to some extent, on the conditions and history of production. Put another way, *if* Goodman has already conceded that the identification and reidentification of autographic art are possible, then there can be no purely logical objection to treating what he calls allographic art as autographic art, or as art exhibiting some autographic features.

A second puzzle regarding identity was briefly noted in introducing Stevenson's use of the type/token distinction. Stevenson held, it will be remembered, that tokens are of a type ("copies *of* the poem" for instance) "in the sense in which various individuals are *of* a certain kind, the relation being that of membership in a class." But of course "being of a kind" is not the same thing as "being a member of a class"; it is also reasonably clear that "being a token of a type" is not the same thing as "being a member of a class." It is true that for every instance in which something is said to be of a kind or a token of a type, a corresponding class can be constructed for which the given instance will also be a member of that class; but it is not the case that for every instance in which something can be said to be a member of a given class, that instance can also be said to be a token of an appropriate corresponding type, even if (trivially) it can be said to be an instance of a corresponding kind.

Richard Wollheim [1968] has attempted to formulate fairly precisely the distinction of types with respect to classes and universals ("kinds"). Wollheim holds that it is "a feature of types and their tokens, not merely that they may share properties, but that when they do, these properties may be transmitted [that is, 'when A and B are both f, f is shared by A and B ([but]) when A is f because B is f, or B is f because A if f, f is transmitted between A and B' (disregarding direction)]." Introducing the terms "generic entity" and "element" to cover the class/member, universal/instance, and type/token distinctions, Wollheim concerns himself chiefly with contrasting the latter two, since he takes the class relationship to be "the most external or extrinsic: for a class is merely made of, or constituted by, its members which are extensionally conjoined to form it." He then notes two differences between universals and types:

> In the first place, there is likely to be a far larger range of transmitted properties in the case of types than there is with universals. The second difference is this: that in the case of universals no property that an instance of a certain universal has necessarily, i.e., that it has in virtue of being an instance of that universal, can be transmitted to the universal. In the case of types, on the other hand, all and only those properties that a token of a certain type has necessarily, i.e., that it has in virtue of being a token of that type, will be transmitted to the type.

There is a certain telltale difficulty in Wollheim's account, for he says, "not merely is the type present in all its tokens like the universal in all its instances, but for much of the time we think and talk of the type as though it were itself a kind of token, though a peculiarly important or pre-eminent one. In many ways we treat the Red Flag as though it were a red flag (cf. 'We'll keep the Red Flag flying high')." Now, it is difficult to see how the type (the Red Flag) could actually "fly high" in the way in which a *token* red flag could, unless to say so is an elliptical way of saying that a token *of* the type is flying high. Type and token cannot share this property of flying and so it cannot be transmitted. But then, Wollheim cannot say that such properties of tokens can be predicated of types. It is not entirely clear what properties *can* be predicated of types (cf. Richards [1974]). Also, what Wollheim obviously means in saying that the type is often talked about as if it were a "peculiarly important" token is not that it is like a token, but only that we may *refer* to the type and not merely to the token—or that we may refer to the type manifest in some (or some set of) tokens. If, however—as we have already seen in connection with the performing arts—different performances of a certain musical composition may have divergent designs and yet be tokens of the type composition, then Wollheim must be mistaken in thinking that "all and only those properties that a token of a certain type has necessarily, i.e., that it has in virtue of being a token of that type, will be transmitted to the type"; for, the design that a particular token performance exhibits is just that "in virtue of" which it is a token of a certain type. To say of a performance that it is of a certain type is *not* to "transmit" its properties (such as design) to the type, but to designate it as such in virtue of that design's being defensible with respect to a *score* (that is in itself emphatically not a work of art at all, in the relevant sense). Furthermore, non-converging plural designs cannot all be properties of a particular token; tokens are *said to be* of the same type if (in the case of music) the score will tolerate any of a set of designs. (It may, incidentally, be conceded that although types are introduced heuristically, we may, for the sake of individuating works of art, refer to them. This is explained in part by the fact that we refer to a set of works as tokens-of-a-type, plural tokens of the same type. We need not deny [(*contra* Searle [1969]; cf. Margolis [1977])] that we can refer to types though they do not as such exist. (We shall return to the issue, in reference to fiction.)

It is useful to mention that Nicholas Wolterstorff [1975b] has pressed much the same point against Wollheim, though he put it by claiming that Wollheim goes astray in speaking of *sharing properties rather than sharing predicates.* "In many if not most cases," Wolterstorff says, "a sharing of a predicate does not have, underlying it, a sharing of a property for which the predicate stands. That property [for instance] which a grizzly possesses, of *being something that growls,* is not a property which the Grizzly [that is, the *kind*, the Grizzly] could possess. Once one sees this, it becomes clear that the formula has an extremely limited application. Cases of shared predicates are common. Cases in which those predicates stand for properties which can be shared are relatively uncommon . . . what the Grizzly's growling consists of cannot be identical with what a grizzly's growling consists of.'' Wolterstorff wishes to construe artworks of at least certain kinds as kinds themselves.

Wollheim had been motivated by the inadequacy of holding that all works of art are physical objects—or by the need to admit that "there are arts [operas, ballets, poems, etchings, etc.] where it is impossible to find physical objects that are even candidates for being identified with works of art.'' He therefore wished to consider (the phrasing is instructive) "any work of art that it is plausible to think of as a type," where "the hypothesis that all works of art are physical objects can be challenged.'' Obviously, Wollheim's resistance to the "physical-object hypothesis'' is entirely congenial with our own earlier ontological exploration. But having failed to formulate a satisfactory theory of the ontology of art, Wollheim is inclined to treat works of art (painting and sculpture, preeminently) as physical objects, wherever and to whatever extent possible. Thus he finds that the ascription of representational and expressive qualities to physical objects is entirely defensible; and he is inclined to treat works of art (performing arts and literature, preeminently) as types, wherever necessary—where type/token problems arise. But as we have already noted, Wollheim conflates the analysis of (an artist's) representation and expression with some object's actually *possessing* as a proper attribute of itself—not of a property merely assigned by some person—the property of representing or expressing something.

We do, it is true, credit a composer with having created an opera even if the opera has never been performed; and it is true that even then we speak of the properties of the opera. But our reason for doing so is to credit the composer in such a way that whatever performances properly comply with his *score* are taken to be performances of his music. This is emphatically not to say that *there is* a type entity to be distinguished from a token entity; it is to say only that works of art are tokens-of-a-type. There is no music, in the aesthetically relevant sense of what can be heard, if only an unperformed musical score obtains: all instances (tokens) of conventional music are performances; they are said to be *the same music* because we identify them by reference to their common score. Also, it is the possibility of performing "the music" in accord with the score that leads us to speak (elliptically) of unperformed music and of those minimal or characteristic properties that any performance would be bound to exhibit.

In fact, whenever one is tempted to speak of types without tokens, it will be noticed that scores or notations, or else causal arrangements (etched plates, for instance), are involved; none of these are, relevantly, artworks. One has only to notice Wollheim's remark that there are "properties that can pertain only to tokens (e.g., properties of location in space and time) and [properties] which pertain only to types (e.g., 'was invented by')." But of course, if only tokens can be located in space and time, *then how can allegedly type objects have spatial or temporal properties?* If a token etching, say, has thus-and-such spatial properties, how can *the* etching "share" or have "transmitted" to itself such properties? There is no coherent answer. We may, therefore, credit (as Wollheim suggests) someone with having invented "the Brigitte Bardot look" (the type), but that does not mean that there actually evolves a Brigitte Bardot look that has properties in common with its tokens. It means only that the type's tokens have certain related properties. And that, precisely, shows the economy of the type/token distinction (as well as its power when joined to the theory of embodied cultural entities).

Wolterstorff, it will be remembered, wished to substitute shared predicates for shared properties. This is an ingenious adjustment, which Wolterstorff clarifies by conceding at once that

predicates shared between art works and their examples do not function univocally when the sharing follows the general patterns we have uncovered. For what one means, in truthfully predicating "has 'no' as its third word" of some copy of *Sailing to Byzantium* is that the third word-*occurrence* is "no." But when one truthfully predicates "has 'no' as its third word" of *Sailing to Byzantium* itself, one cannot mean this. For the poem does not consist of word-occurrences. Similarly, what one means in truthfully predicating "has a G sharp in its seventh measure" of some performance of Bartok's *Fifth* is that in its seventh measure there was an *occurrence* of the G-sharp pitch. But the *Quartet* itself does not consist of sound-occurrences. I think it must be admitted that we have not discovered a systematic identity but only a systematic relation between the property designated by some predicate when it is truthfully predicated of some art examples and the property designated by that predicate when truthfully predicated of the art work. Our conclusion must be that the sharing of predicates between art works and their examples pervasively exhibits *analogical* predication.

The trouble with this way of speaking is patent: *What* is the *property* designated by the predicates given when predicated of the *artwork?* The only answer that Wolterstorff gives is neatly specified, once again, for the grizzly/Grizzly case: " 'Growls,' when truly predicated of the Grizzly, would seem to stand for the property of being *such that something cannot be a properly formed example of it unless it growls.*" Translated for the art context, the proposal yields the "suggestion that the concept of an art work is intimately connected with the concept of a correctly formed example of the work." There is no question that we *say,* "The Grizzly growls." But this is not enough to show that we hold that "growling" is somehow truly predicated of the Grizzly, just as growling is truly predicated of some particular grizzly. The concept of analogically sharing predicates is invented precisely because, as Wolterstorff claims, "art works are kinds" (and of course that there are other kinds) (cf. Wolterstorff [1970]). *If* artworks were not kinds, then the need to invoke analogically used predicates would be obviated.

Difficulties of at least two other sorts arise. For one thing, appeal to natural kinds does not provide an entirely suitable analogue of scored artworks or works for which a notation is available. The temptation to think of artworks as kinds is not strengthened by reference to the Grizzly or the like: there are no intentional considerations in virtue of which the properties of the Grizzly as opposed to the properties of grizzlies can be detected. (The Grizzly is introduced heuristically only.) Secondly, Wolterstorff's account requires that our knowledge of artworks as kinds provide criteria both for "correct" and admissible instances or "examples" of the work in question. But Wolterstorff nowhere supplies a sketch of such criteria, and familiar counterinstances to what he apparently favors are easily supplied. For example, Bernard Shaw's *Man and Superman* is normally produced omitting the Don Juan in Hell material; in the *pas de deux,* in the Black Swan scene in *Swan Lake,* the traditional thirty-two *fouettés* are often reduced to sixteen with alternative steps accommodating the ballerina's skill introduced to fill out the interval; Tchaikowski's "1812 Overture" is often not performed with a cannon. We seem neither inclined to deny that performances adjusted in these ways are "correct" nor to be clear about what departures from putatively standard practice yield either incorrect or inadmissible performances. (Consider, similarly, that an ungrowling grizzly is hardly an "incorrect" example of the Grizzly). In a word, notational considerations are invariably "interpreted" rather broadly within a practice and an appreciative tradition.

Now, the concept of being a token-of-a-type demonstrates that Wolterstorff's formula can be used without conceding that works of art are kinds. Also, the "token-of-a-type" formula has a demonstrable advantage: "Being such that something cannot be a properly formed example of the Grizzly unless it growls" does not entail or presuppose that the Grizzly "growls"; it merely entails that properly formed grizzlies growl. The same can be said of the token artworks of any type. That works of art are entities of such a kind that plural performances of a piece of music, or plural printings of an etching, may count as instances of the same work is not equivalent to Wolterstorff's formulation of "multiply perform*able*" or "multiply-object*ible*" entities (for instance, music or etchings construed as kinds). The essential difficulty of Wolterstorff's proposal is that we wish to say that we *hear* the music and *see* the sculpture, that the music *sounds sweet* and the sculpture *looks unbalanced;* in short, we wish *to attribute certain properties to the work itself* and, on Wolterstorff's view, we literally cannot. An extremely helpful counterconsideration is suggested by one of Wolterstorff's own remarks. As he says:

> Any one of the several objects of an object-work [the expression "object of an object-work" is meant to convey the example/kind relationship] can be destroyed without the object-work thereby being destroyed. I could, for example, perform the horrifying operation of burning my impression of Rouault's *Obedient unto Death,* but I would not thereby put the print itself out of existence. Nor could I put the print out of existence by destroying *any one* of the other impressions, nor even by destroying the original etched plate.

Here, Wolterstorff fails to notice that if I destroy *all* the authentic impressions made from the plate and destroy the plate, I will have destroyed the etching. Now, there seems to be no sense in holding that a *kind can be destroyed.* But on the illustration, Wolterstorff would be committed to that possibility. Clearly, sculpture, architecture, painting, and etching *can* be destroyed just as they can actually be seen; hence, they cannot be kinds. Music and literature cannot, in *this* sense, be destroyed, simply because their "properly formed examples" can be generated by reference to a notation *and* a notation is not a work of art. All the tokens of a notation may be destroyed, however, and the notation may cease to be remembered; in that sense, music and literature can be destroyed. Also, of course, it is clear they are actually invented. So the theory collapses. In effect, recalling our ontic commitments, our solution combines the advantages of the embodiment thesis—hence, of an emergent materialism—with the advantages of avoiding the extreme implausibility of platonism with respect to art. The type/token distinction need not be construed platonistically (cf. Hausman [1975]), and the actual properties of works of art preclude their being platonistic entities.

5. The Definition of Art

What is a work of art?

In contemporary aesthetics there is an impression that the correct definition of "work of art" has yet to be provided, or is an improper requirement if one is asking for the genus and difference of art (Osborne [1953]; Kahler [1959]; Macdonald [1952-1953]; Weitz [1956]). On the one hand, the traditional definitions of art or fine art are incredibly bad; on the other, the arguments against definition are hardly decisive. The expression "fine art" itself seems to be declining in popularity. There is a noticeable tendency to substitute such terms as "artwork" (Danto [1964]) or "piece" (of art) (Binkley [1977]) for "work of art," in an apparent effort either to neutralize the evaluative force of "fine art" or "work of art," or to suggest the informality or relativity or conventional footing of ascriptions of artistic status. Furthermore, it is not entirely clear what legitimate constraints may be called into play in seeking to define art "correctly." The paradigm for adjusting theoretical definitions occurs in the sciences, where congruence with causal explanation is decisive (cf. Putnam [1965]). But, in aesthetics, explanation is not primarily causal; it is couched in terms of justificatory reasons. Hence, the very status of the definition of art is bound to be regarded variably, depending on convictions about the objectivity of beauty or related values that the fine arts are said to manifest. In fact, there is so much dispute about *whether* would-be specimens of contemporary art are even eligible candidates that non-converging definitions cannot but be regarded as relatively inseparable from equally divergent parent theories—including, prominently, our ontic commitments, our view of aesthetic interest, our schemes of reference and individuation, and our practice within the scope of appreciation and criticism. This suggests that the definition of art is to some extent a reasoned proposal designed to accord closely with theories favored on independent grounds. The relative objectivity of a definition of art, then, depends on its accommodation of standard cases viewed within a reasonably defended larger theory. For example, to have demonstrated the importance and relevance of linking the ontology of artworks to that of other culturally emergent entities—particularly persons, language, and human action—is to have set a relatively objective constraint on competing definitions. In any case, it is quite impossible to test the adequacy of would-be definitions of art apart from the dialectical appraisal of the competing theories within which they function. But within such constraints, there seems to be no reason to suppose that definitions are either pointless or impossible. The effort has obviously occupied most persons concerned with questions of aesthetics.

I must single out Morris Weitz [1956] as the most outspoken and deliberate opponent of attempting "a true definition or set of necessary and sufficient properties of art" (cf. Osborne [1968]). If I understand his argument, he says: (i) that if, following Wittgenstein [1953], we "look and see," we shall find that what we call "art" exhibits "no common properties—only strands of similarities"; (ii) that "the very expansive, adventurous character of art, its ever-present changes and novel creations, make it logically impossible to ensure any set of defining properties"; and (iii) that the desired sort of definition "cannot occur with empirically-descriptive and normative concepts unless we arbitrarily close them by stipulating the range of their uses" (cf. Mandelbaum [1965]; Dickie [1973]; Sibley [1960]; G.E. Moore [1955]; Sclafani [1971]; Shafer [1971]). Weitz's charges need to be viewed in two ways—first on internal grounds, and then in terms of the theory of definition itself. Certainly, one sees that Weitz's claims depend on the (debatable) thesis that a valid or "true" definition must conform with the fixed essence of things; they also betray a distinct disinclination to accommodate diachronic changes in our theories. Alternatively put, accommodating such changes seems, on Weitz's view, to disallow definition.

The internal difficulties are easy enough to detail. In the first place, (i) and (iii) are incompatible, since (i) makes the question an empirical one—any proposed definition of "work of art" being, in Weitz's opinion, a *false* definition, and (iii) makes it a *logical* question—any claim of the required sort being *logically improper*; "arbitrarily" seems designed to signify that *any* extensional restriction would violate the logical distinction of "empirically-descriptive and normative concepts." In the second place, (i) and (ii) are incompatible, or at least arguing at cross purposes, since (i) holds that for any suitably large, *enumerated* set of items that we call "works of art" we shall find only "strands of similarities," and (ii) holds that any required definition for *such* an enumerated set will inevitably fail to apply to new items not included under that enumeration. In the third place, (i) is harmless, since it amounts merely to an admission of Weitz's own failure to discover more than "strands of similarities"; another might do better. And (ii) is also harmless, since Weitz can only pretend that any suitable definition for some enumerated set of items will be *logically* incapable of applying to future items. There is also no logical reason why a definition should "foreclose" on "creativity"; the definition of "living organism" need not "foreclose" on biological evolution. Again, Weitz would be oddly committed to the view that we could *recognize* a new object to be a work of art even if it did not share in the "common properties" discovered in some antecedent set of objects called "works of art"—we might here have to speak of a ruling rather than of a finding (cf. Abrams [1972]). And (iii) must be harmless, since it fails to do justice to the clear fact that we do have definitions by genus and difference in the "empirically-descriptive" domain, and that it makes no sense to say these definitions are *all* "arbitrary." To say so is misleading, since Weitz admits freely that "there are legitimate and serviceable closed concepts in art" for such definitions as "have been drawn for a special purpose." Aristotle's definition of "the extant Greek tragedies," for example, is *false*. But there seems to be no other way of proceeding to draw up a definition than to examine a set of items "for a special purpose"; the innuendo of (iii) is an idle one.

Wittgenstein, on whom Weitz depends, had been concerned to argue that concepts based on "family resemblances" are actually used in ordinary discourse. He sometimes exceeds his argument when he appears to claim that some concepts, "games" for instance, are usable *only* in terms of "family resemblances" (cf. Stevenson [1957]). Wittgenstein had already convincingly shown in an earlier study that questions very much like "Would you call this a work of art?" are misleadingly simple, unless a context is provided for directed answers—which, in effect, corresponds with the sense of Weitz's expression, "for a special purpose" (Wittgenstein [1958]). A particularly preposterous application of this otherwise sensible view appears in an account by John Ellis [1974]. Ellis offers as his *"definition* of literature: literary texts are defined as those that are used by the society in such a way that *the text is not taken as specifically relevant to the immediate context of its origin. "* His intention is to avoid the problems of what he terms "the reference theory of meaning" (which he associates with positivism), but his anxiety here brings him to an impossible view. First of all, a specification of what it is to be "used" as literature is never explicated on his account. Secondly, he obviously must equivocate on the necessary condition provided, since *some* literature undoubtedly originates as literature (whatever that may be). Thirdly, he does not supply sufficient conditions. His essential claim—not altogether unlike Dickie's [1974]—is reflected in the following: "It is the agreement of the community that makes them [that is, texts] into literature, in that the category is defined as those texts offered for that use" (cf. Silvers [1976]).

To return to Weitz, we may put the argument trimly by observing that unless one closes a concept extensionally, or provides for such closure, it makes no sense to say that some would-be definition in terms of genus and difference is *false,* and that *only* strands of similarity may be observed. To resist altogether closing a concept intensionally is simply not to entertain definitions at all. Furthermore, if we do not specify some "special purpose" for which a would-be definition is to be serviceable, it will be triflingly true that the best we can do is notice "family resemblances," since nearly any expression will have a variety of uses. A serviceable language does not require formal definitions; and it is clear that actual linguistic usage, bound as it is to be governed by the idiosyncrasies of individualized learning, cannot be expected to support the provision of necessary or sufficient conditions even for the most familiar objects. In particular, it is not obvious how to distinguish between differences in meaning and differences in belief in the context of actual usage (Donnellan [1962]; Putnam [1962], [1965], [1966]). On the other hand, providing a "special purpose" need not eliminate either logical possibility—genus and difference or "family resemblances." In effect, to close the extension of a term "for a special purpose" is to prepare to review the properties of a certain set of objects from the vantage point of a provisional theory. We "look and see" whether only "strands of similarity" may be found; and we must be prepared either to adjust our theory or to adjust the extension of a given term under the control of our theory. A definition, therefore, may fairly be regarded as a reasoned proposal, since even the acceptance of a certain extension as appropriately or defensibly restricted entails adherence to some provisional theory. Hence, confirming or disconfirming an "empirical" definition is an exceedingly complex matter; disconfirmation may rely entirely on internal evidence, but it is more likely to be the obverse side of an alternatively recommended extension controlled by an at least incipient theory. Here, debate tends to be almost completely dialectical though not without rigor, since the definition of art—as opposed, say, to the definition of living process or matter—cannot plausibly be supposed to be intended to fit into a larger body of relatively testable and causally unified science. But, as we have already observed, this suggests not that art cannot be defined but that it can be defined in a variety of ways. In effect, Weitz tends to confuse the implications of defining "empirically-descriptive" concepts with the viability of concepts that are not rigorously defined.

Still, we must be careful in drawing conclusions. Sometimes, when Wittgenstein speaks of "family resemblances," he is drawing attention to the fact that for a given concept there is no formulable rule for application to a new instance. On the other hand, he sometimes wishes, as when he speaks of "essences," to draw attention to the puzzling nature of rules themselves—asking what it is we appeal to in using a rule correctly (Wittgenstein [1956]). Weitz does not see Wittgenstein's larger concern when he says simply that "only in logic or mathematics" are concepts "completely defined." The point is that, for a special purpose, we may be able to construct a rule for using the concept "work of art," as we may for a mathematical concept, but that doing so leaves altogether unexplained how the rule is actually used. The question about the use of rules is the same for what Weitz has distinguished as empirically-descriptive and normative concepts, and for logical and mathematical concepts. More recently, Weitz has shifted ground somewhat, arguing that Wittgenstein's "basic contribution to aesthetics" lies in his "rejection of the doctrine that all concepts are and must be governed by sets of necessary and sufficient conditions or criteria" (Weitz [1973]). This is a decidedly weakened, however interesting, thesis, having the effect of conceding the propriety of definitional efforts of the most strenuous sort. Weitz holds that Wittgenstein is denying that it is a necessary condition of our use of language that there be an essence corresponding to our use of distinct terms. But even if there are no real essences, the concession does not preclude definition by necessary and sufficient conditions, simply because Weitz nowhere explains the conceptual relationship between *the definition of terms* and *our theory about the nature of things*. It is entirely possible for example that definitions yield (what may be called) nominal essences—formulations in terms of necessary and sufficient conditions linked to our theories and our systematic efforts to explain phenomena—without at all claiming to be discoveries of the real essences of things. Furthermore, *if* there are no real essences, it is obviously preposterous to construe definition as directed solely or even characteristically toward formulating the real essences of things.

Weitz's theory of definition has moved through a series of not altogether compatible stages. His most recent view [1977] champions the following theses: (a) that *not all* concepts are closed—"closed in the classical platonic sense of being governed by necessary and sufficient criteria"—that is, "there are concepts other than closed ones, of varying degrees of openness"; (b) that important open concepts obtain in the humanities as opposed to the sciences and that, therefore, the respectability of the humanities need not be "modeled on the precision and definitive sets of conditions governing scientific concepts"; (c) that he was mistaken in his original essay [1956]: concepts like "ancient Greek tragedy" (he now holds) are extensionally closed, but open in the sense that they are "perennially debatable"—any prevailing criteria may be rejected; concepts like "tragedy" are both "perennially debatable" and "perennially flexible"—"open-textured" in accommodating new cases; and concepts like "art" are said to be "perennially flexible" though not "perennially debatable" in spite of the fact that the criteria of art are not "necessary" (or "essential").

The difficulties with these adjustments are fairly straightforward. First of all, Weitz rejects essences, but seems obliged to claim knowledge of the essential properties of the *concepts* of ancient Greek tragedy, tragedy, and art; otherwise, how could he possibly know that they are constrained differentially in the way he says they are? A definition of tragedy now appears to be contrary to the very spirit of the concept. Secondly, insistence on "perennial flexibility" is, by itself, irrelevant to the adequacy of any definition, unless it can be shown that the mere appearance of new specimens of the kind of thing to be defined entails the inadequacy of a definition formed for any earlier set of specimens—which is patently false. Also, the insistence is tantamount merely to a warning that definitions may have to be altered under conditions of diachronic use—which is to say neither that definition is impossible nor that particular definitions are false or inadequate. Thirdly, Weitz characteristically insists on the admission of "indisputable examples" of open and open-textured concepts, but he does not explain the basis for their recognition, or for the recognition that criteria logically weaker than necessary or sufficient conditions are or are not open to dispute. This objection is particularly relevant since Weitz complains openly about "the insanity of modern art," that is, the pretense or madness of supposing that what is currently produced *is* art. The difficulty arises in somewhat different ways for "perennially flexible," "perennially debatable," and jointly "perennially flexible" and "perennially debatable" cases. Finally, and most decisively, Weitz never provides a theory of definition in virtue of which the validity of his particular charges may be supported. In fact, it is reasonably clear that Weitz believes that definitions are always intended only to capture the real essences of things. However, he demonstrates neither that it is true that tragedy and art have no essence, nor that definition is designed to formulate the essences of things, whether or not things have essences. The result is that Weitz's entire endeavor has a decidedly *ad hoc* quality about it.

More recent theories of definition (Putnam [1975a], [1975b]) show how it is possible to maintain consistently: (i) provisional extensional closure of "core" cases; (ii) diachronic revision of such closure in accord with the needs of a favored theory; (iii) definition in terms of necessary and sufficient conditions; (iv) denial that such definition is intended to formulate the real essence of the definiendum. In a word, one may close concepts without construing such closure and the resulting definitions in the "platonic manner." The point is all the more significant because Weitz himself criticizes Maurice Mandelbaum's review [1965] of his own position: Mandelbaum's "mistake," Weitz holds, "consists in confusing [the] conceptual truth about 'art' [that a study of its 'logical grammar' shows it to be used by way of 'disjunctive sets of nonnecessary, nonsufficient criteria'] with a factual [in fact, an essentialist] claim about art" (cf. also Abrams [1972]).

What needs to be emphasized is that *if* "theory *in* aesthetics" (or, for that matter, in any other domain) need not be "primarily—sometimes solely—the quest for real definitions," then the admission of paradigm cases (of artworks) does not require or entail that *further* instances satisfy the defining properties (necessary and sufficient conditions) for being of the kind defined. In Putnam's ([1975a], [1975b]) terms, the intension of the definiens need not determine the extension of the definiendum. This is why, though he is right in criticizing George Dickie's ([1974]) definition of art (because it is intended in the essentialist's sense), Weitz is mistaken in principle about definitions formulated in terms of necessary and sufficient conditions. He thinks that, if they are valid, definitions, "[whether] derived from present paradigms or not, must obtain across the board: to *all* works of art, not just the paradigmatic ones." The sense intended is that, in obtaining thus, new cases will and *must exhibit the defining properties of the core or paradigm cases.* But that is simply a mistake: we may continue to *believe* that new cases are instances (of art) though they cannot be paradigm instances (on the prevailing theory); and we may (when needed, diachronically) always redefine the "nature" of art by selecting a different set of paradigms. So it is not to the point to remark that "the disputed works of yesterday become the paradigms of today, just as the works of anti-art or non-art of today may become the respected and perhaps revered works of art of tomorrow." If, in fact, that phenomenon be admitted, it looks as if only an interest in nominal essences can accommodate our practice; the alternative is a kind of platonism *manqué*: individual cases (of art) are then what they are "indisputably," such, that we cannot fix their essential nature. This explains, also, why, *contra* Weitz, it is not in the least necessary to attempt to extend the sense of the artifactual (holding artifactuality, with Dickie, to be a necessary condition of art) in order to cover *all* cases. Granted that, as an essentialist, Dickie is bound to make the effort—with hopelessly implausible results: it is quite enough to define art in accord with the stereotypic features of the paradigms favored. No absurd consequences need obtain.

The point of these reflections is the propriety of attempting to define "work of art" or "artwork." As I have already suggested, the traditional definitions are remarkably poor. Weitz himself has advanced a radical thesis about the criteria of "work of art." He claims [1956]:

> None of the criteria of recognition is a defining one, either necessary or sufficient, because we can sometimes assert of something that it is a work of art and go on to deny any one of these conditions, even the one which has traditionally been taken to be basic, namely, that of being an artifact.

He offers in support: "This piece of driftwood is a lovely piece of sculpture." What he says is questionbegging, clearly open to *dispute,* and even, on the strength of a reasonably defended theory of art, false. Either the counterinstance on which it rests is irrelevant or Weitz is arbitrarily asserting that a piece of driftwood could be a sculpture (and therefore a work of art) without being an artifact. There is no question that ordinary language supplies us with such remarks; but we are not required to take every such remark as a literal statement of fact. For instance, a piece of driftwood might be termed "sculpture" in the spirit of a complimentary epithet (compare "She's an angel"). If anyone were pressed to explain it, he might of course say that the driftwood looks very much like a sculpture, that one could imagine the driftwood actually fashioned by a human sculptor. We need not, therefore, deny what is fairly taken by Weitz's opponent to be a necessary condition for an object's being a work of art, "namely, that of being an artifact." (Notice, of course, that in insisting that this is a necessary condition, nothing is implied *either* about real essences *or* about the analysis of what it is to be an artifact.)

Although I adhere to this view as I did when I first examined Weitz's claim, I now see that it needs to be clarified. Jack Glickman [1976] has usefully observed that the point in dispute between Weitz and myself may not have been one of whether a work of art must be an artifact but of "whether a work of art must have been made by someone." That is not quite accurate, but it is an extremely helpful way of focusing the issue. Glickman suggests that we might easily introduce the category "beach art" and include driftwood under that heading (or, perhaps, "beach-sculpture," which, by analogy with "guinea-pig," need not be a species of sculpture). He observes, quite rightly, of cases like driftwood (at least driftwood that is displayed in a certain way) and readymades like Duchamp's *Bottlerack,* that "an artist may create a work of art that no one has made." Unfortunately, Glickman takes the condition of artifactuality to be necessary *but* "superfluous." He is more concerned to stress (again, rightly) that works of art need not be made, in the sense of being produced or worked or manufactured (*objets trouvés*); they need not have been made by whoever creates art by displaying made objects in a certain way (readymades); they may have been produced by machines or chimpanzees; and the like. Glickman is wrong, I think, to take the condition of being an artifact as superfluous because he himself suggests that to be an artifact is to be a cultural object, an object that has a culturally specified function. Gary Iseminger [1973] offers a suggestion that is helpful here. He favors "an 'adverbial' theory of artifactuality. The basic notion is that of having properties artifactually, not having the property *being an artifact.*" This is not to deny the property of being an artifact, only to affirm the dependence of that property on another in virtue of which it is caused to obtain. A bottlerack, for instance, has, as a deliberately manufactured object, a certain culturally specified function, namely, to hold bottles. But, *as a readymade,* the bottlerack becomes an object displayed (roughly) as a manufactured-object-apt-for-viewing-in-whatever-terms-standard-works-of-art-may-be-viewed. In the spirit of this adjustment, Ursula Meyer [1972] observes that "Duchamp considered [his readymades] mainly a satiric gesture toward a dim-witted, elitist establishment. 'I threw the *urinoir* into their faces,' he wrote later, 'and now they come and admire it for its beauty.'" Stefan Morawski [1974] offers an opposed interpretation that nevertheless supports the same conclusion:

> The principal aim of dada is to suffuse ordinary life with art and to imbue ordinary objects with its attractions, rather than allowing our notions of art to be confined to the scarce 'works of art' owned

by a privileged few. Given this interpretation, John Cage or Marcel Duchamp should not be seen as the creators of new and astonishing para-artistic "gestures"—which, in turn, an art-starved and art-worshipping public may isolate and venerate—but as *provocateurs* whose aim has been to generate a heightened aesthetic alertness among the public and to direct this attitude onto socially perceptible data.

Even wood shavings that "serve no function" may be linked to a culturally specified function, as in the preparation of some other object. A stick thought to be magically endowed, Glickman observes, has a culturally specified function though it is neither made nor (very probably) viewed as a work of art. The driftwood case is ambiguous precisely because one might mean to say merely that driftwood is often *like* sculpture (but is not sculpture and, in that sense, not art); or one might mean that, displayed appropriately as an *objet trouvé*, it is "found art" (and, since not made, not sculpture). But the important point remains that something *is made* an *objet trouvé*: the properties of the *object* (in which it is embodied) are artifactually possessed by the *objet*. Recalling what has been said about the nature of definition, we are not at all obliged, in conceding this sense of artifactuality, to show that it applies to *all* cases of would-be art—for instance to Weitz's cases of living and dead trees [1977].

So-called conceptual art (wherever admissible) challenges our standard views even more strenuously, so much so, in fact, that it has encouraged Timothy Binkley [1975] to propose that "everything [is] art, (*x*) (*x* is an artwork)." Of course, distributively considered, it may well be that *"everything" could be viewed as* an *objet trouvé*, a readymade, an instance of conceptual art (Binkley's specimen: Robert Barry's piece, "All the things I know but of which I am not at the moment thinking—1:36 P.M.; 15 June 1969, New York"), or the like; that is, everything could be construed as an artifact—but then, everything thus construed could satisfy *what is* taken as a necessary condition of being a work of art. Binkley makes his proposal because he insists that the concept of art is "radically open, radically indefinable"; on his view, the concept "defeats the family resemblance account of art as perfunctorily as it defeats a definition proposing necessary and sufficient conditions." But he has only shown the potentially inclusive (though not vacuous) application of the concept of an artifact, not its inapplicability as a necessary condition. Furthermore, conceptual or informational or "idea" art is not sufficiently homogeneous to permit any generalizations at all. Also,

if one takes Lucy Lippard [1973] seriously, as when she favors the formula that "the concept or idea [is] more important than the visual results
of the system that generated the object [that is, the more conventional
'work of art']," then conceptual art is at best a kind of parasitic and
marginal art and at worst simply not art (cf. Rosenberg [1972]; Battcock
[1973]; Kirby [1965]; Henri [1974]; L. Meyer [1956], [1967]). One of the
first "pieces" of conceptual art she catalogues is *Two Exercises* (1961) by
George Brecht, associated with the Fluxus group. The instructions are as
follows:

> Consider an object. Call what is not the object "other." Add to the
> object from the "other," another object, to form a new object and
> a new "other." Repeat until there is no more "other." Take a part
> from the object and add it to the "other," to form a new object
> and a new "other." Repeat until there is no more object.

Most favorably construed, conceptual art (of this sort) is related to art in
a way analogous to that in which "mental acts" (or perhaps scores or instructions) are related to acts or actions: one may construe believing as a
mental act, as Peter Geach [1956] does, because of a certain formal
similarity with actual speech acts, but it is such by way of a certain
metaphor (believing is not actually "saying in one's heart"); similarly,
the event of thinking about something or other may be construed as a bit
of conceptual art, because the artist's thought informs his actual craft,
but to construe thinking in this way is to do so by means of an enormously attenuated metaphor (thought or conception is not a *medium* for
fashioning objects). The admission of conceptual art, in short, involves
an enormously tolerant extension (unless it is, frankly, a misnomer); but
it does not lead to an idealist theory of art. So the reason conceptual art
may be disallowed as art is quite unrelated to the reason anything (within
certain constraints) may be treated as an *objet trouvé*. Conceptual art
raises difficulties about the artistic medium; but whether anything (that
could, provisionally, be thought to involve a palpable medium) could be
construed as an *objet trouvé* depends on whether we may fairly defend
the *belief* that it is, in view of the properties of our core cases. Binkley
obviously supposes (with Weitz) that definition must capture the real
essence of art and, therefore, that he has produced a *reductio*. But he has
not, for two reasons: (i) because *if* (disallowing conceptual art)
everything can (reasonably) be viewed as an *objet trouvé*, the definition
need not be vacuous; and (ii) because in admitting the status of *objet
trouvé*, we are not obliged to extend its ascription beyond a use that accords with the theory by which its admission was originally governed.

I am saying, then, that the work of art is of the genus "artifact"; that to deny this, in any sense of the term's ordinary usage, is preposterous; and that Weitz is mistaken in his radical hypothesis regarding "the criteria of 'work of art.' " We still lack, of course, the differentia of artworks, and we must, in any case, remind ourselves of the extremely modest contribution to aesthetics any completed definition could possibly provide.

We have made some progress, however, because traditional definitions often fail to make provision even for the genus of art. Weitz himself [1950], in an earlier study, had proposed the following:

> Every work of art . . . is an organic complex, presented in a sensuous medium, which complex is composed of elements, their expressive characteristics and the relations obtaining among them. I hold that this is a *real* definition of art: i.e., an enumeration of the basic properties of art.

The "organicist" definition, apart from the difficulties of "organic complex," fails to rule out natural objects, as Margaret Macdonald [1951] has shown (cf. Osborne [1968]; Casey [1966]). In a curious way, the organicist limitation is to be found also in neo-Aristotelian definitions of art, which represent, surely, a continuation of the most venerable effort to answer the question. Elder Olson [1954], for example, states:

> The term "imitation" is used coextensively with "artificial"; it differentiates art from nature. Natural things have an internal principle of motion and rest, whereas artificial things—a chair or a table—have, *qua* products of art, no such principle; they change through potentialities not of their form but of their matter. Natural and artificial things alike are composites of forms and matter; but art imposes a form upon a matter which is not naturally disposed to assume, of itself, such a form. The acorn of itself grows into the oak; the stone does not of itself become a statue or tend to become a statue rather than a column.

Even granting the distinctions Olson makes here, we cannot fail to notice that he has overlooked those of his own master. Aristotle (*Metaphysics*) speaks not only of the natural and the artificial but also of the accidental, and the accidental occurs through what Olson calls "propensities . . . of matter." The accidental then shares with the artificial the distinction of lacking "an internal principle of action and rest." The verbal play of "propensities of matter" and "propensities of form" obscures the very issue at stake (cf. McKeon [1954]; Vivas [1961]; Stolnitz [1960]).

Now then, if being an artifact is fairly taken as the genus of artworks—in the sense of a useful nominal definition—we need to remind ourselves of what we have already said about the ontology of art and about our *aesthetic* interest in art. What we did was to deny that artworks could be construed as perceptual objects of some sort, and that our interest in them could be restricted to their perceptual properties. We were bound, it was argued, to admit the relevance of historical, causal, and intentional considerations; and we allowed, on a generous reading of Kant's well-known formula, that we were aesthetically interested in the internal purposiveness of artworks. We may give greater precision now to that particular notion, in an effort to provide the differentia of art. The required distinction between the generic and the specific has regularly—if somewhat awkwardly and even misleadingly—been noted in the standard literature. Thus, for instance, John Dewey [1934] notes the "difference between the art product (statue, painting, or whatever), and the *work* of art. The first is physical and potential; the latter is active and experienced." Stephen Pepper [1952] speaks of "the aesthetic work of art"; C. J. Ducasse [1948], of "aesthetic art"; and George Dickie [1974], of "the aesthetic object of a work of art."

A useful and reasonable definition suggests itself rather straightforwardly. In proposing it, however, I emphasize once again its small importance and its dependence on a competent, large, and independently defended theory of art. Furthermore, in putting it forward, I wish to stress that the key notions—"artifact" (already explored) and what will serve as the differentia—need to be articulated not only in terms of our theory, but also in terms of a reasonably settled collection of paradigm or "stereotypic" cases (Putnam [1975a]). Only thus can we hope to forestall the quite different but equally fatal impulses about testing definitions already encountered in Weitz, Mandelbaum, Binkley, and Dickie. Here, then, is a fair definition: *A work of art is an artifact considered with respect to its design.* ("Design" will be clarified shortly.) Critics of the various arts are, among other things, concerned to describe the design of particular works of art. But, precisely, it is describable works of art that may be evaluated; so we must define "work of art" or "artwork" in a value-neutral way to allow for speaking about evaluations of works of art—or at least in a way that is neutral to the range of intended evaluations. Henry Aiken [1955], it may be noted, insists that " 'work of art' is an expression of commendation" (cf. Ziff [1953];

Khatchadourian [1961]). But his view would make expressions like "That's a poor work of art" self-contradictory (cf. Barrett [1973]). Aiken, of course, is right in saying that "work of art" is actually used as an expression of commendation, but he is mistaken in thinking it is used only so; it is quite evidently used also in the sense of cataloguing certain objects eligible for aesthetic scrutiny. Terms like "artwork" (Danto [1964]) are intended for just that purpose.

Let us consider the thesis, then, *for central cases first;* then, we will liberalize conditions to accommodate whatever adjustments may be thought to be required. On the view of definition here favored, no disadvantage is likely to accrue. To say that an artwork is an artifact is (for the central cases) to say that some human being deliberately made it. He need not deliberately have made or selected every discriminable feature of the work; perhaps no one could do so. But he made it in the sense of applying his craft to the materials of his medium. Normally—in the least disputable cases—an artist works with wood, metals, paints, sounds, words, movements, voices, and the like. In working, he exercises a skill informed by a knowledge of the history and tradition of a given art; that is, he exercises one of the various crafts of sculpture, painting, music, dance, drama, poetry, or the like. He works either with physical materials (wood, stone, sound, or physical movement, say) or with culturally prepared materials already embodied in physical materials (words or dance gestures or the notes of a musical scale, say). In either case, the artist works with a *medium* embodied in physical materials.

In correspondence to the artist's engagement in his craft, the work of art or artwork he produces has some purpose. This is not to say that a biographical inquiry is necessary to discover the purpose of the work he produces—though that need not be precluded. Normally, the artist produces his work in some way that, to the informed audience, belongs within or extends, or departs from, a recognizable craft tradition. Thus, we speak of a painter's "brush strokes," of a poet's "choice of words and images," of a composer's "notation" and "instructions to performers" indicating "notes," "key," "tempi," and of a dancer's "movements" and "gestures." Here, the physical materials are construed (by the relation of embodiment) as the artist's medium; his work (in that medium) is detailed in terms of brush strokes, dance steps, musical phrases, sentences, or the like. The entire work exhibits, in the paradigm cases and in the minimal Kantian sense adopted, some internal purposiveness—that purposiveness we find in the systematic ordering of brush strokes, dance steps, musical phrases, sentences, or the like, in virtue of which we grasp the coherent *design* of the work. The various craft maneuvers that each artist has executed may fairly be taken to embed or manifest his principal *decisions or strokes* as an artist. A work of art, therefore, is an artifact in which the constitutive strokes of its manufacture (the exercise of the relevant craft) form a coherent design. The aesthetic appreciation of art, reduced in the barest way possible, is simply the appreciation of such designs.

We can liberalize the concept of an artifact along the lines suggested by conceding found art, readymades, anti-art, machine art, and animal art. The clue to doing so has already been provided: simply construe as an artifact any object that may be said to have a culturally specified function. In the sense relevant to the definition of art, artifacts are embodied entities, that is, entities having a culturally specified function in virtue of an artist's deliberate work. But, conceding the otherwise anomalous specimens already mentioned—or, to add an intriguing specimen, the Jericho Skull (c. 6000 B.C.), which became an image after death (cf. Gombrich [1960])—we must concede that the appreciation of the central instances of art evidently prepares a society to compose or create further artworks solely or chiefly by displaying selected natural objects (driftwood), accidental artifacts (the accumulated pattern of paint congealed on a pallette), or essential artifacts (Duchamp's urinal) as objects of aesthetic interest. So seen, the embodied/embodying relationship is invoked as an extension of its use in the central cases. To construe such objects as artifacts is to construe them in terms of their inherent design: that is (perhaps metaphorically), as composed of appropriate "strokes" or "decisions," by analogy with the central cases. This shows, incidentally, how inadequate it is to say that an object counts as a work of art when someone treats "an artifact as a candidate for appreciation" (Dickie [1974]). For that tells us neither what an artifact is nor what, respecting appreciation, confers on it the status of work of art (cf. Tatarkiewicz [1971]).

The definition of "artworks," then, specifies what is essential to a "normal" or "stereotypic" work of art, what accords with the central conception of a favored theory or favored set of competing theories. On the view that definitions provide only nominal essences, objects that deviate in one or another significant way from the normal case may, consistently, be admitted to be artworks. When developments invite or require a revision in the "core facts" regarding art, "artwork" will undergo a change in meaning and our definition will have to be replaced. But it will not be replaced because we will have *discovered a real work of art* that our definition fails to accommodate: our conception of the normal instances of art may have changed under the pressure of historical developments, and our theory will have to accommodate that fact (cf. Putnam [1975a], [1975b]).

The history of the definition of art is, it must be admitted, replete with the most extraordinary entries (cf. Kristeller [1951], [1952]; Panofsky [1938]; Tatarkiewicz [1963]). Even the most famous are often oddly narrow, partisan, bizarre, perverse, useless, incoherent, or flatly false—on any reasonable view. For example, Jacques Maritain [1930], proposing a neo-Thomist account of fine art, speaks of a work of beauty, which, by its distinction, "tends . . . to carry the soul beyond creation"; it embodies a transcendental property, "one of the divine attributes," that can be discerned in everything "in its own way." Sigmund Freud [1947] says, quite characteristically, that "the productions of the artist . . . give an outlet to his sexual desire." Freud seeks to inquire into the allegedly "organic bases" of artistic power, but he ends with an open admission that "the nature of artistic attainment is psychoanalytically inaccessible to us." Tolstoy [1938] is inevitably led to distinguish between "real art" and "its counterfeit"—the counterfeit including a really startling number of the prime instances of works of art. Clive Bell's view of art as "significant form" [1914] is either circular or saved by its own vacuity (cf. Weitz [1950]; Stolnitz [1960]). Susanne Langer [1953], viewing art as "the creation of forms symbolic of human feeling," finds it impossible, in principle, to specify what feelings the artistic symbol symbolizes (cf. Nagel [1943]; Langer [1942], [1957], [1962]). Jean-Paul Sartre [1963] holds flatly that "we can at once formulate the law that the work of art is an unreality . . . What is 'beautiful' is something which cannot be experienced as a perception and which, by its very nature, is out of the world" (cf. Bradley [1909]; Ingarden [1964]; Merleau-Ponty [1964]). C. E. M. Joad [1929] maintains: "A work of art is not a creation: it is the embodied memory of a discovery"—a discovery that turns out to be essentially Platonic.

There is at least one extremely widespread theory about the nature of art that calls for a sustained analysis. That is the doctrine that there are "languages of art," that works of art are somehow to be construed as utterances in a language. For instance, in a fairly early publication of contemporary aesthetics, T. M. Greene [1940] argued that a work of art, in expressing something about the world, could be taken as a proposition, whether or not linguistically paraphrasable. Interestingly enough, Greene did not linger to articulate the sense in which works of art could be said to be propositions; though in ascribing truth to them, in a respect proper to explicit statements, it is clear (despite difficulties in his own theory of truth) that he meant quite literally what he said. Similarly, Susanne Langer has failed to defend her much-debated thesis [1953] that

"Art is the creation of forms symbolic of human feeling." In a relatively late adjustment [1957], she concedes that "artistic import is *expressed,* somewhat as meaning is expressed in a genuine symbol, yet not exactly so. The analogy is strong enough to make it legitimate, even though easily misleading, to call the work of art the art symbol." What Langer's thesis comes to is the denial that works of art may be literally construed as linguistic utterances, or as symbolic utterances that behave in ways formally similar to the uses of language. The analogy between "art symbols" and "genuine" symbols may be conceded as benign, of course, once the ulterior philosophical claim is dismissed.

The elementary question posed by the thesis is just this: What are the minimal requirements of a language? Admittedly, the question is controversial—as may be seen in trying to decide whether Wittgenstein's sketches of seemingly minimal languages are viable and if so, what they entail. Be that as it may, there are some relatively indisputable features of a genuine language, which, once canvassed even informally, undermine the thesis. For example, languages are conventions of some sort: whatever the vehicles of meaning may be, they are said to have meaning, or to mean what they do, by virtue of rule-like or rule-governed conventions (cf. Grice [1957]). This consideration alone rules out the appealing thesis that art is "the languge of emotions," in the sense in which, because of natural causal connections, an artwork produces in an audience a sense of the emotional experience the artist originally thought as capable of being excited in himself and in others by the work he devised. There are variations on the thesis, but by and large it trades on some theory of "natural meanings" construed in causal terms. It was apparently the view held by Roger Fry [1933], and is variously described (and partially but not completely dismissed) by E. H. Gombrich [1962] as a theory of mere "natural resonance" or "emotional contagion" (cf. Wollheim [1968]).

To the extent that languages are conventional, their distinctive structures and processes are conventional as well. Any minimal language contains at least a vocabulary and a grammar and provides for selectively linking elements of a vocabulary and other morphemic components to form admissible sentences. We may be as generous as we please regarding surrogates of vocabularies, grammars, and well-formed sentences; but there can be no point to speaking of a *language* without some explicit attention to such features or to arguably suitable surrogates. It was, in fact, Langer's inability to specify a vocabulary—conventionally sorted, recognizable, and teachable—that finally washed out her otherwise interesting thesis (cf. Nagel [1943]). It is not necessary, it should be said, that the putative vocabulary of art be fixed in the manner of discursive languages; what *is* necessary is that there be designata for relevant symbols or symbolic forms. Even for what Langer calls "presentational" symbols, however, in terms of which, say, musical forms are said to be symbolic of the emotions with which they are isomorphic—or, "morphologically similar" [1942]—two essential difficulties remain: (i) that isomorphism is not a sufficient condition for anything to function symbolically; and (ii) that isomorphism (or even resemblance) cannot even be specified without the provision of a rule in terms of which relevant correspondences may be sorted. The point has been elaborately made by Nelson Goodman [1968] and, earlier, in a more informal way, by C. L. Stevenson [1958] (cf. also, Beardsley [1958]). In fact, as Stevenson very usefully implies, it is only by assuming the extraordinarily generous (but very nearly vacuous) sense of a "sign" that Charles Morris [1939] once favored, that the theory of presentational symbols (in the form sketched) has any prospect of being confirmed; his is the sense in which anything discriminated may be a sign (even an iconic sign) of itself, and the sense in which, in any "sign situation," *whatever* leads us to take account of something, existent or not, itself or something else, thereby functions as a sign.

Despite their obvious appreciation of the pitfalls of Langer's thesis, it is rather difficult to be sure that E. H. Gombrich [1960] and Ruth Saw [1962] have—in their respective efforts to support some version of the theory of art as language—actually managed to escape it. Gombrich, following C. E. Osgood's notion of "semantic space" [1957], confuses the difference between there being natural associations—say, gay and sad sensations and bright and dark colors—that may serve as the basis of a conventional idiom of emotions, and the specification of a vocabulary that conventionally exploits such associations. Ruth Saw seems to have followed Gombrich in neglecting this point as well.

It is, ironically, just the inventiveness of art forms that betrays the hopelessness of the thesis. For artworks are not simply novel expressions of some sort *in a language;* they institute new conventions that are not readily collected as admissible expressions formed from a relatively stable vocabulary and finite grammar. It is one of the firmest contributions of the new linguistics that a so-called natural language (that is, a language that is spontaneously learned by children growing up in a human society, from the fragmentary linguistic behavior they confront) must have a finite grammar capable of "generating" (in effect, describing or accounting for the grammatical structure of) an infinite set of eligible or well-formed sentences (cf. Chomsky [1972]). Nothing remotely like a finite and common grammar has ever been plausibly formulated for the various arts. (This, incidentally, points to the ineliminable weakness of structuralist aesthetics; cf. Barthes [1967b]; Culler [1975].) The best th. t we can do is specify the relatively *common properties* of any constellation of works of art that have been thought worth discussing together. Only if such common properties could be construed in terms of the features of a common language could the thesis in question conceivably be supported.

There are at least two sorts of confusion that infect the art language theory. One, already remarked, is the failure to distinguish between what a language might exploit among natural sequences, by way of a convention, and what conventionally is provided for in an actual language. To appreciate the point is to see at a stroke that the theory can hardly be supported merely by showing that conventional symbols are often used *in* works of art—for instance, to *represent* the Passion of Christ. Here, a rudimentary linguistic complex—or a complex that is a fair analogue of a linguistic element—has actually been incorporated into a work of art. No one would wish to deny this. But it does not support the theory that all works of art, even when they lack such representational functions, may properly be construed in terms of a vocabulary, a grammar, and determinate and well-formed sentences.

The other confusion is important because it goes to the heart of the issue of artistic expression. There is an understandable, but not for that reason defensible, tendency to construe the fact *that works of art have expressive qualities* as signifying or entailing *that works of art express* (that is, convey, as language meaningfully conveys) *utterances about some experience* or quality or the like. Here, the sensitive language theorist is likely to insist that this conception of art fails to do justice to the claim that art is the language of the emotions. Thus, Ruth Saw [1971] rightly insists: "A language of the emotions, then [that is, speaking of the fine arts] is not a language devised to convey information about emotions . . . What is decidedly and undoubtedly 'good enough' in the attempts of human beings to communicate their emotional states to one another is the whole world of poetry, plays, music, painting, dancing, and sculpture." She continues, searching for the correct formula:

> A communicates emotion B in these circumstances: A makes an object, visible or audible, that seems to him an appropriate expression of his emotional state, presents it to B who takes it as the appropriate correlate of the emotional state into which it causes him to pass. A and B each assumes that he is experiencing an emotion similar to the other's.

Saw sees quite clearly that to describe "art as communicating emotion" in this sense is not sufficient to entail that "art is language." But she apparently fails to see that she has not yet defended the thesis that art communicates emotion in a way that could lend support to the further thesis that art is language or symbol system. For, since there are no governing conventions to which A and B subscribe, they can only *discover* quite contingently that they have similar emotions under given conditions *and then decide* (in a way that parallels representation) to regard the work as signifying this or that emotion. So the work can be *made* to symbolize a given emotion and thus come to be used linguistically or quasi-linguistically; and a work of art may be said to "communicate" emotion if, in causing an emotion in one, it causes an emotion somehow appropriately similar to the emotion the artist intended to evoke—but that is the sense in which artists may, if they wish, exploit mere "natural signs." There seems, therefore, no way to recover the original claim in an interesting way.

Here, we may add the observation that, in construing works of art as expressive, we are doing no more than attributing to them *intentional properties* of a certain sort. In holding, for instance, that cats have a characteristic way of expressing annoyance, we are by no means holding that the expression is *conventional,* though of course it will be intentional in the sense that a certain bit of cat-behavior may rightly be said to express annoyance or have the property of expressing annoyance. Similarly, though perhaps unexpectedly, even a work of art, which essentially depends on exploiting conventions of various sorts, may conceivably have an expressive property that is *not* conventional. It seems perfectly possible, for example, that a given piece of music (if the theory of natural resonance has any plausibility at all) may exhibit a certain natural expressiveness—for instance, natural gaiety; it will do so because it organizes a pattern of sounds, but not necessarily because it possesses the property only conventionally. This shows, then, the important difference between conventionally representing emotions and being a natural sign of emotions—about which we regularly equivocate when we speak about expression. The theory of expressive qualities is not, as such, a theory about language at all, though it may (or may not) be a theory about communication; and the theory of the language of art is not, as such, a theory about properties in the usual sense, though it must be a theory about communication. For these reasons, it is quite possible that a work of art exhibit an expressive quality of a conventional sort without serving (*contra* Goodman [1968]) a linguistic or quasi-linguistic function in so doing. For instance, a dance step may exhibit a certain characteristic

romantic languor (may, since "romantic languor" is an intentional property, *express* languor) without *representing, referring to, exemplifying,*
or *symbolizing* such languor. Finally, a work of art may represent or
symbolize given expressive qualities or the like without *having* or *possessing* congruent expressive qualities. For example, a drama might well be a
representation of Christian piety without possessing the expressive quality of Christian piety (cf. Stevenson [1958]; Hermerén [1969]). Alan
Tormey [1971] offers a useful case: "Bernini's *David* . . . does not express [a concentrated and intense determination. It] *represents David-
expressing-intense-determination.*"

It is also important, in speaking of the minimal conditions of
language, to make provision for the performance of speech acts of
distinctive kinds—such as asserting, querying, commanding, and advis-
ing; and, consequently, to make provision for assigning truth values or
compliance values or the like to sentences or utterances used in performing such acts (cf. Austin [1962]; Alston [1964]). But there seems to be no
plausible sense in which the artist "uttering" his work of art straightforwardly performs a speech act or an act suitably analogous to a speech
act. In the context of a wide-ranging discussion of problems of meaning
in the arts, Göran Hermerén [1969], for one, is candidly puzzled by the
issue (cf. Margolis [1973a]). Thus Hermerén says:

> Personally, I am inclined to deny that an artist in a painting can
> state beliefs or promise to do things in the same sense of "state"
> and "promise" as he can state or promise to do things by uttering
> certain words in certain kinds of situations. However, this is a com-
> plex issue, and it cannot be discussed here . . . It is controversial
> how far the analogy between art and languages is illuminating, but
> the concepts of art, language, proposition, stating, etc., are still too
> unclear to permit a rational discussion of this problem at the pre-
> sent moment.

But, of course, apart from our intuitions, the very concept of a speech
act (that is, of illocutionary acts, of full-fledged speech acts that require
the use of language) presupposes that we have at our disposal sentences
formed from a lexicon of expressions and facilitating morphemes and the
like, in accord with a grammar; for, otherwise, there simply are no utterances to be used in performing any speech acts. This avenue of
defense, then, also proves to be a dead end. (The notion that the artist

"utters" his work has further implications bearing on the problem of intention, which we shall consider later.)

Another way of viewing the bearing of speech acts (or analogues of speech acts) on the analysis of works of art is to construe *expression* as the performance of some suitably characterized speech act by a speaker, and to construe a work of art as the *vehicle* of what the speaker expresses. Thus, for instance, on Ernest Jones's interpretation of *Hamlet* [1949], Shakespeare may be said to have expressed a good deal about his Oedipal feelings in writing *Hamlet.* On the thesis that the artist has expressed himself or his feelings or the like, to say that the *work* expresses the man or his feelings or the like justifies us in inferring from the properties of the work to the feelings of the artist. In that sense, the work may be said to "imply" what we properly infer. This is a vexed thesis that trades on G. E. Moore's well-known use of "imply" (cf. Schilpp [1942]); it also underlies John Hospers's thesis [1960] about implied truths in fiction and Morris Weitz's thesis [1950] about works of art embodying truth claims. The trouble, in a nutshell, is that the expressive function (no matter how it is articulated) is an ulterior function that may be assigned to works of art, that need not, *qua* art, exhibit such function. That is, works of art are not as such "utterances" used in performing speech acts or analogous acts; they are distinctive objects possessing what properties (including expressive qualities) that, on an ulterior theory (for instance, with a view to providing for an artist's intentions), we may construe as "utterances." Whatever the internal difficulties of accurate interpretation along these lines, the thesis does not show that works of art are essentially the vehicles of acts of expression; it shows only that, within limits, and for purposes bearing on the ascription of certain intentional properties, they may be so viewed. To admit this much is not to admit that art is language, only that a work of art may provide evidence about an artist's state of mind and that the relationship of evidence to inference may be reversed, *on an imposed theory,* and put in terms of the implications of initial acts of expression (cf. Tormey [1971]; Sircello [1972]).

Finally, we have already shown in another context that Nelson Goodman [1968] does not make good his claim that works of art are symbol systems of some sort. His error lies in conflating the possession and exemplification of properties—which is somewhat ironic, given his appreciation of Langer's errors. Failing to analyze the nature of artworks independently of his thesis about expressive and stylistic properties, he is led to theorize that the nature of art must be such that artworks can exhibit such properties only if they are symbol systems. But we have already seen that they may be so construed (as cultural entities) that they simply possess (non-metaphorically) expressive properties (cf. Urmson [1973]).

Goodman [1972] holds that "works of art characteristically function as symbols"; but he does not mean this in the sense one would suppose. For he goes on to say quite plainly that "a work need not unremittingly function as a symbol, and . . . some works, *by accident,* may not actually so function"; he adds that "when a work of art functions as such, it functions as a symbol. When it does not, it is inert not only as a symbol but as a work of art." More recently [1978a], Goodman has pressed his thesis in a way that suggests both that the question "What is art?" is "the wrong one" (it should perhaps be "When is art?") and that the essentialist view of art may be recovered if functionally construed. By "functionalist," Goodman means that "an object may be a work of art at some times and not at others . . . just by virtue of functioning as a symbol in a certain way does an object become, while so functioning, a work of art." With this ingenious recovery of essentialism—in the form of essential functions, *when* (as he says) an object is actually thus functioning—Goodman claims:

> Whoever looks for art without symbols, then, will find none—if all the ways that works symbolize are taken into account. Art without representation or expression or exemplification—yes; art without all three—*no.*

The argument is the one we have already reviewed. But in this late paper, Goodman makes it quite clear that the symbolic function of art pretty well depends on exemplification, since representation and expression are not universally ascribable to artworks, either conjointly or disjunctively. Here, Goodman's position rests entirely on a theory of samples. Admittedly, samples exemplify the properties they possess; hence, they symbolize and refer. But Goodman never explains *when* things exemplify. He says only: "The kind of property sampled differs from case to case . . . the sampled properties vary widely with context and circumstance." The normal view of samples is simply that *we,* in some communicative exchange, treat something possessing the properties it possesses as a sample of some of those properties; nothing is as such a sample, only treating it thus makes it one. If this is so, then Goodman has omitted to explain why we *always* treat artworks as samples of their own properties. Once we see that exemplification presupposes possession, the thesis is peculiarly easy to deny. But with its failure, the theory that art *qua* art functions symbolically falls as well.

This is perhaps a convenient place to add some remarks about representation, since Goodman's theory has occasioned a good bit of controversy on this matter. A recent paper by David Novitz [1975] inadvertently fixes the essential problem. Novitz makes the following claims (against Goodman and Kendall Walton [1970], [1971]), which are actually inconsistent:

> resemblance is a symmetrical relation and picturing is not

(True);

> visual resemblance is a necessary condition for picturing; and . . . recognition of such a resemblance is a necessary condition for determining what a picture is of

(The thesis under debate);

> the activity of depicting . . . is an intentional activity; so that a picture of a black horse, like the thought or story of Black Beauty, never requires the existence of the horse in question

(True). Part of Novitz's intent is to dispute Goodman's thesis [1968] that "denotation is the core of representation." But Goodman's thesis distinguishes quite clearly between representation (a two-term relation) and "_____-representation" or "representation-as" (a one-term characterization). When Goodman says, "Nor is resemblance *necessary* for reference; almost anything may stand for almost anything else," he is clearly considering the two-term relation of *representation* (not portraiture, for instance, or the picturing or depicting of some actual thing). More to the point, on Novitz's own view, resemblance is a two-term relation and symmetrical; but how can there be a resemblance, *an independently discernible resemblance,* between an actual object and an intentional, fictional, or imaginary object? Novitz says that "it is simply untrue that a picture cannot resemble a fictional entity. It can, provided that the entity in question has certain imaginary visual attributes. Of course anything which is entirely non-visual, no matter whether it is real or imaginary, cannot be pictured . . . "

The best that we can do with imaginary entities is to hold that they resemble actual entities because, and only in the sense that, their *descriptions* entail that we take them to resemble actual entities. But this is not to say that resemblance is a necessary condition for picturing. In fact, it is to say no more than that picturing may be construed as a one-term characterization; that entails that resemblance is *not* a necessary condition for picturing even if congruity with descriptions is a necessary condition. Where picturing, depicting, or portraying actual objects or persons is involved, a two-term relationship obtains: in such cases, resemblance (in some relevant respect) *is* a necessary condition. Goodman is not at all clear about this distinction (cf. Maynard [1972]; Wartofsky [1978]). Thus he remarks that "a Constable painting of Marlborough Castle is more like any other picture than it is like the Castle, yet it represents the Castle and not another picture . . . " Here, Goodman utterly fails to meet the objection that some respect or other may be specified in which the Constable perceptually resembles the Castle more than it resembles another picture. His (reasonable) emphasis on the conventionality of representation misleads him about the not completely conventional sense in which two-term picturing involves perceptual resemblance. There is an interesting distinction between one-term and two-term picturing, that tends to call Goodman's argument into serious question. If I have a picture (say, a photograph) of a particular horse, then it is quite possible that the picture may be unrecognizable as a horse-picture on any familiar view; for example, it may appear as a speck (cf. Novitz [1977]). But if I have a horse-picture (in the one-term sense), then there must be some assignable orientation—the representation-convention—in accord with which the picture perceptually resembles a horse. In this regard, picturing cannot be reduced to representing; and one-term picturing is an equivocal notion relative to existing or non-existing *kinds* of things.

But that is not to say that *representation* as a two-term relation requires resemblance. *Portraiture,* for instance, may be a species of two-term representation that, as such, requires resemblance. Novitz makes the additional observation, correctly, that "to represent something pictorially . . . is to use a picture to communicate information . . . about what is pictured . . . " But that is not to say that picturing requires either denoting or resemblance. What picturing (the one-term characterization) does require is that the ordered visual features of a picture be capable of being interpreted, fairly, as conforming to a description of "what is pictured"—where "what is pictured" is itself specified intentionally. Resemblance between pictures that putatively picture (allowing the equivocation) and actual X's inclines us to interpret a picture as picturing X's—whether they are thought to denote them or not—in virtue of postulating an intention to picture X's; otherwise, we have only resemblance without picturing. Where there are no actual X's, there is no actual resemblance, though we may, nevertheless, be justified in ascribing an intention to picture X's (or even a particular X). Representing, picturing, depicting, and portraying are uses to which pictures are put, paralleling rather nicely the sense in which the uses of language are specified as speech acts. But all are syntactically equivocal in that respect. Also, representation, even pictorial representation, does not require resemblance in either of the senses given; however, picturing, depicting, and portraying as two-term relations are normally taken in a sense in which relevant visual resemblances *are* necessary. Somewhat *contra* Walton [1970], [1971], Goodman does *not* deny that what represents and what is represented may resemble one another, only that representation does not as such logically depend on resemblance. A useful way of isolating Goodman's claim about the logical inadequacy of the resemblance conditions (already noted) is to point out that resemblance is symmetrical and representation is not (cf. Scruton [1974]; Dilham [1967]; Ishiguro [1967]; Goodman [1966]).

Still, there is no doubt that Goodman presses his thesis in a stronger way—for instance, with respect to realism in painting—and here, his claim appears both false and somewhat bizarre (cf. Manns [1971]). The issue may be pressed more forcefully. Although resemblance is symmetrical, the detection of resemblance may well exhibit certain asymmetries. For example, if it is said that a portrait of Wellington resembles Wellington, there will normally be certain constraints (jointly conventional and "natural") on viewing a two-dimensional canvas in virtue of which the resemblance to Wellington is reasonably affirmed; but the way in which Wellington himself would be viewed in order to affirm *his* resemblance to a painting need not proceed in the same way. This is why Goodman's purely formal account of resemblance has nothing to do with the perceptual conditions under which "natural" resemblances are recognized. Hence, contrary to what he says, the perception of resemblance *never* relevantly depends on trying to make what is pictured and the picture "deliver matching bundles of light rays to the eye." There are certain ways in which organisms like humans scan natural objects within their ecological space, within which resemblances will be duly noted; *and* there are appropriate ways, informed by a knowledge of artistic conventions, in which they will scan portraits and similar representations. Within the normal range of such paired practices, paintings will be readily recognized to resemble or not to resemble what they picture. The issue does not have to do with *mistaking* one thing for another (though it allows for this); it has to do with *matching* things as similar in accord with habits of viewing that have become natural to man in his cultural milieu. In this sense, Gombrich is right and Goodman is wrong—though Gombrich does not argue effectively for his own view.

It is entirely fair to hold that portraiture and realism are species of representation (in different senses)—requiring special constraints regarding resemblance. But merely to have explored these complications is to have shown that representational and symbolic functions cannot always be ascribed to works of art—hence, that works of art cannot be said to be language systems, in the essentialist spirit, in virtue of such functions.

There seems to be no other promising way in which to defend the claim that art is language or that works of art are linguistic or symbolic utterances of some sort—which is not to deny that works of art may be made to perform linguistic or symbolic functions, or that particular works may possess the property of serving some linguistic or symbolic function. We must conclude on the evidence, then, that the thesis is false. Nothing need be added regarding those arts that use language as a medium, simply because the medium is language: novels and poems are characters in symbol systems not because they are works of art, but because they are formed in and of language. Their existence complicates the analysis of the thesis but does not require adjustment on essentials.

PART TWO

Criticism and Appreciation

6. Describing and Interpreting Works of Art

Critics are teachers, fundamentally. Their comments are designed to influence, to instruct, to draw attention, to indicate, to suggest with tact, to remind, to correct, and a thousand other such functions. These uses of language deserve to be carefully catalogued. But it is as a more or less professional discipline, with its own appropriate techniques of inquiry and a distinct sense of making its judgments responsive to challenge, that it is open to correction and confirmation; criticism attracts philosophical interest chiefly because its judgments exhibit at times a certain novelty as well as the usual subtlety we have learned to associate with evaluative matters. In this respect, criticism admits of two complementary phases: giving an account of a work of art and evaluating its merit. There are those who insist, with T. M. Greene [1940] and Harold Osborne [1955], that the evaluative phase of criticism is either an inescapable part of the critic's work or the principal business of the critic properly so-called (cf. also, Arnold [1938] and Leavis [1945]). I see no profit in a quarrel about labels, but I should stress that the evaluation of artworks logically presupposes our ability to give an account of their properties. One must be able to designate the features of artworks in virtue of which their relative merit may be assigned, even if in practice critical language serves both functions at once. Disputes will arise about the relative importance of these functions. Hence, anticipating a complication, I find it economical to begin our discussion of criticism in a way more intimately related to the first, allegedly less important, phase than to the second.

Broadly speaking, the puzzles of criticism center on the objectivity of evaluation, the objectivity of interpretation, and the attempt to separate the two. Professional critics are characteristically persuaded that there are exclusive canons of objective interpretations, whether or not they hold evaluation to be objective as well. But the usual rationale is indecisive. For example, in a relatively recent exchange attempting to resolve the issue, a number of senior literary critics pretty well mangle any prospect of sorting descriptive, interpretive, and evaluative judgments. First, Murray Krieger [1968] says, "I have . . . been conceding the practical impossibility of keeping criticism inductive, of keeping taste out of it, once we first concede—in post-Kantian manner—the constitutive role of our categories of perception in conditioning all we experience." Krieger says the impossibility is "practical," which suggests that it need not be such in principle; but his reason, focused on the putatively constitutive categories of perception, is either irrelevant to the issue or, if relevant, would render the "impossibility" more than practical. Northrop Frye [1968] then avers, "It may be said—in fact it has been said by Mr. Krieger, and said very well—that it is not really possible to draw a line between interpretation and evaluation, and that the latter will always remain in criticism as a part of the general messiness of the human situation." Nevertheless, against this fatal concession, Frye hopes to save the "objectivity" of interpretation by intruding a naive contrast between facts and values: "There is a boundary line which in the course of time inexorably separates interpreting from evaluating. When a critic interprets, he is talking about the poet; when he evaluates, he is talking about himself, or, at most, about himself as a representative of his age." At the least, the very idea that interpretation is exclusively biographical and evaluation either autobiographical or (shall we say) historical is patently absurd, logically irrelevant, and contrary to the actual practice of critics (including Frye himself). E. D. Hirsch [1968] makes a similar concession and tries to save the "objectivity" of interpretation (or description) by appeal to what he takes to be Kant's "subjective universal" (cf. Kant [1952]): "1. The interpretation (description) of a literary work is necessarily correlative to the particular subjective stances which constitute its meanings. 2. Affects and value judgments necessarily subsist in the relationship between meanings and these correlative subjective stances. These value judgments are therefore inherent in literary description." The objectivity—or at least the universality—of such judgments (to avoid subjectivism or relativism) is presumably guaranteed by the "subjective universal": "The ascription of inherent value to a literary work of art is made possible by Kant's insight into the necessary subjective component that constitutes any shared cultural object." The desperate speculative extremes to which these otherwise lively critics are drawn attests to a rather widespread confusion.

Complication arises initially in the attempt to contrast interpretation with the description of a work of art. I would not say that the expressions "How would you describe that play?" and "How would you interpret that play?'' are never interchangeable. Nor would I say that internal complications within the first phase of criticism affect the problems of evaluation as such. They do not, though the relevance of particular value judgments will be affected. The point is somewhat obscured by Margaret Macdonald [1954a], who says, ''to judge a work of art . . . is to give a verdict on something to which the judge has contributed [by way of interpretation] and this also 'justifies' the verdict.'' Not all works evaluated are, however, interpreted in any significant sense; also, interpretation is not logically bound to have evaluative force. But it is relevant to notice that descriptive terms are frequently value-laden.

I am persuaded that the various arts differ in respects important for any theory of critical description and interpretation. Consequently, I shall not generalize for all the arts from illustrations drawn from any one or two; and I shall not suppose that critics, in any sense of ''description'' or ''interpretation,'' are doing the same sort of thing regarding different arts. In fact, they cannot do certain things in some of the arts that they can in others. But the distinctions needed concern what is internal to giving an account of the properties of artworks; value disputes may conceivably arise on the strength either of a description or an interpretation. We shall, therefore, preclude the use of ''interpretation'' in any value-laden sense. Actually, interpretations are thought to affect the assignment of values but not to be the equivalent of such assignment. ''That's just your interpretation,'' for example, suggests that, on the strength of a given interpretation, a markedly different value is to be assigned to some object than might otherwise have been assigned on another interpretation.

C. L. Stevenson [1950] has taken an opposing view. He supports an '' 'evaluative' or 'normative' conception of interpretation'' [1962]. By this he means that the activity of critics interpreting artworks implicitly raises the question of whether they are interpreting ''properly,'' or ''as they should.'' Nevertheless, he says,

> . . . the interpretation and evaluation of a poem are rarely separable steps in criticism. We do not *first* interpret it and then evaluate it, taking each step with finality. Rather, we test a tentative interpretation by considering the tentative evaluation of the poem to which it leads, progressively altering each in the light of the other.

There are several things to be noted here. First, Stevenson admits, in effect, that interpretation and evaluation are logically distinct. Second, since there is no logical reason why an interpretation should be altered in the light of the evaluation of the poem, Stevenson must be mistaken. A critic may reasonably insist on an interpretation pursued in accord with established practice, though it leads to devaluing a particular work; also, preferring an interpretation that yields a higher value entails its defensibility on independent grounds. Third, judging whether a critic's practice is professionally acceptable is logically distinct from judging whether any work that he interprets has merit or not. Judgment of the first sort is "normative" in the limited sense of assessing technical proficiency only; professional criticism need not be distinctive in this regard.

Stevenson insists that the "proper" group of readers "implicitly mentioned in an interpretive question, cannot be made explicit by means of factual terms alone, but must be indicated, in part, by means of evaluative terms." But if this is a professional question, it is "normative" only in the sense mentioned; it may, indeed, be treated as a factual question. And even if criticism were admitted to have normative features in this sense, it would not follow that critical judgments were imperatival (*contra* Stevenson [1944]; Hare [1952]; *see* Margolis [1971]; Casey [1966]). Judging professional competence is logically distinct from directing someone to act professionally. Also, the second may be justified (if at all) only if the first may be justified independently. Stevenson himself has recognized [1950], [1944] that the use of expressions like "X is red" implies "proper" conditions of viewing that are not normative; the existence of a professional context of criticism supports a strong analogy. Perhaps critical practice is not as stable or as regularized as testing perceptual judgments. But since public and professional canons are emerging, it cannot be said, on the grounds given, that interpretive statements are inherently persuasive. "Normative" criteria of truth and falsity must, in the various sciences, also gradually have emerged as the norms they are.

To return to our proposal, the shift from "description-" to "interpretation-" expressions will be taken to be significant. (If there are any critical contexts in which "interpret" and "describe" are genuinely and fully replaceable one by the other, they may be conceded. I shall not explore them, since we are interested primarily in distinctions among the ways in which we give an account of a work of art.) "How would you describe Matisse's *The Piano Lesson*?" and "How would you interpret The *Piano Lesson*?" may be taken by some to be equivalent. Beardsley [1970b] treats them as equivalent because he takes interpretation to be the disclosure of what is descriptively present but "hidden." Admittedly, if one substituted a painting by Grandma Moses, we should feel that "interpret" was a very strong term and probably inapplicable. In any case, in talking about critical descriptions, we must confine our attention largely to their informative rather than educative or affective aspects;

that is, we must confine our inquiry to those respects in which they may be accurate, comprehensive, detailed, or exact rather than shocking, startling, impressive, affected, or exaggerated (*see* Toulmin and Baier [1952]).

There are other activities, variously related to a critic's description, that may be independently assessed. For example, one speaks of analyzing a literary passage (or, even, of scanning a line of Latin verse). The emphasis is upon an apparent puzzle, on something not readily comprehensible, on what may be hidden but present. We sometimes speak of an analysis as an interpretation (cf. Stevenson [1962]), but nothing depends on this usage. An analysis, however, is not a description, though it may be ancillary to one. In giving an exhaustive description of a literary piece, one might include the findings of an analysis; one might even reformulate what was found by analysis for proper inclusion in a description. If description is aesthetically relevant, then so is analysis. Critics are also concerned to compare artworks; in doing so, they are not describing them, but they are trading necessarily on the describable features of what they are comparing. I am suggesting, in short, the strategic role of description. Adjustment may be needed for a variety of informative endeavors besides describing and interpreting works of art, but they are not more than adjustments.

Probably the most characteristic difference between describing and interpreting a work of art lies, so to speak, in the center of gravity of the two notions. "Describing" implies a stable, public, relatively well-defined object available for inspection; the effort of the describer calls for no special notice; differences in description are to be reconciled by a further examination of the object or the points of view from which it is described. "Interpreting," on the other hand, suggests a touch of virtuosity, an element of performance, a shift from a stable object whose properties are enumerable (however complex they may be) to an object whose properties pose something of a puzzle or challenge—with emphasis on the solution of the puzzle, on some inventive use of the materials present, on the added contribution of the interpreter, and on a certain openness toward possible alternative interpretations. In description, the emphasis is upon an object independent of any particular effort of description, an object that *has* or *has not* the properties attributed to it—with no antecedent restriction on what may be described (Toulmin and Baier [1952]; Austin [1952-1953]). (Macroscopic physical objects are the models here.) In interpretation, the emphasis is upon the critic's performance, on what is added beyond the mere materials provided. The *passage* from mere virtuosity to actual addition suggests the sense in which "interpretation" is used merely honorifically or as marking a logical distinction.

Obviously, the distinction between description and interpretation is essentially informed by the theory of art to which one subscribes, in virtue of which what is definitely *in* a work and what lies *outside* it may in principle be so marked. Monroe Beardsley [1970b] strenuously opposes the implied latitude regarding interpretation. "I find myself," he says, "rather severe with this line of thought [the suggestion 'that the literary interpreter, too (that is, like the performer of music) has a certain leeway, and does not merely 'report' on 'discovered meaning' . . . but puts something of his own into the work; so that different critics may produce different but equally legitimate interpretations, like two sopranos or two ingenues working from the same notations']." The implications of Beardsley's view are: (i) that interpretation behaves in logically different ways in literature and in music; (ii) that, in literature, there must be some ideally convergent interpretation to be supplied; and (iii) that literary interpretation is equivalent to the (perhaps difficult) discovery of what is descriptively present in the work. David Pole [1973] and E. D. Hirsch [1967], in rather different ways, favor (ii); they do not, however, reduce interpretation to description. Pole fails to demonstrate that "there exists . . . one right interpretation; ideally only one . . . . " Hirsch's account requires a closer examination (and will be supplied in due course).

There are difficulties in Beardsley's account. For one thing, though he subscribes to what he terms "the Principle of Independence" (that is, "that literary works exist as individuals and can be distinguished from other things"), he claims that what he terms "the Principle of Autonomy" (that is, "that literary works are self-sufficient entities, whose properties are decisive in checking interpretations and judgments") is a postulate "that is logically complementary to the first." But, as we have already seen, the numerical identity of an artwork can be managed without deciding the demarcation between description and interpretation. Only if one held a compelling theory about the nature and inherent properties of works of art, in addition to a theory about their individuation, could one hope to sustain the so-called Principle of Autonomy—by providing criteria for determining putatively internal properties to be or actually not to be internal. Beardsley, however, offers no such theory. He tends rather to construe artworks as physical objects, objects which afford no basis at all for ascribing culturally significant properties—hence, no basis for deciding matters of description and interpretation. He substitutes "perceptual objects" for artworks as the objects of aesthetic interest, but he fails to specify how the former are to be individuated or how they are related to artworks, hence, he fails to provide a reference for sorting descriptive and interpretive ascriptions. Furthermore, the usual questions of interpretive validity cannot even be formulated in exclusively perceptual terms. So the Principle of Independence is utterly neutral to our issue, and the Principle of Autonomy is vacuous or questionbegging.

Secondly, Beardsley cannot be sure that he has not misdescribed the "latitudinarian" view of interpretation: interpretation (in the sense he rejects) may not be simple "superimpositions," that is, interpretations that are merely "ways of *using* the work to illustrate a pre-existent system of thought [say, in taking the story of "Jack and the Beanstalk" as Freudian symbolism or as a Marxist fable]"; they may actually be needed precisely because there is no sharp demarcation line between what is internal and what is external to an artwork and because what is uncertain *in this respect may be important in terms of aesthetic appreciation.* Thirdly, the mere admission of so-called superimpositions would be a telling concession *if* (as is true) Beardsley has not provided the requisite theory in virtue of which superimpositions and "genuine" interpretations can be logically demarcated. Fourthly, the implied admission that there *is* a certain latitude in music and the other performing arts raises unresolved questions both about the tenability of the Principle of Autonomy in each of the arts, and about what may be the relevant differences between literature and the performing arts. Fifthly, in a context in which he opposes an extreme view ingeniously supported by Frank Cioffi [1963-1964] (cf. Hampshire [1966]), Beardsley himself concedes that

> Some things are definitely said in the poem and cannot be overlooked; others are suggested, as we find on careful reading; others are gently hinted, and whatever methods of literary interpretation we use, we can never establish them decisively as "in" or "out." Therefore whatever comes from without, but yet can be taken as an interesting extension of what is surely in, may be admissible. It merely makes a larger whole. But this concession will not justify extensive borrowings from biography.

I cannot see how this concession, generously advanced though it may be, can fail to undermine the Principle of Autonomy. Even the propriety of biographical reference and intentional interpretation (which Beardsley so strenuously opposes) surely becomes moot—which is not to say, of course, that critical interpretation lacks rigor altogether.

A sixth consideration (to which we shall return) concerns the nature of language itself, since Beardsley restricts himself here to literary interpretation. We shall argue on internal grounds chiefly. Beardsley rests his case primarily on the strength of the thesis that the interpretation of "textual meaning" as opposed to "authorial meaning"—in the sense proposed by E. D. Hirsch [1967]—is "the proper task of the literary interpreter" and that such meaning "lies momentarily hidden," say, in some poem but "really is something . . . that we are trying to dig out, though it is elusive." But Beardsley concedes that meanings may *accrue* to a literary text because of the historical conditions under which a living language is used. In his effort to contrast textual and authorial meaning, for instance, he says that "the meaning of a text can change after its author has died : . . . The *OED* furnishes abundant evidence that individual words and idioms acquire new meanings and lose old meanings as time passes; these changes can in turn produce changes of meaning in sentences in which the words appear." He offers the curious case of a phrase from Mark Akenside's "*The Pleasures of Imagination*" (1744): speaking about "the Sovereign Spirit of the world," the poem says that "He rais'd his plastic arm." Beardsley notes that the expression "plastic arm" "has acquired a new meaning in the twentieth century, and this is now its dominant one (though the older one has not disappeared). Consequently the line in which it occurs has also acquired a new meaning." He is even prepared to speak of "today's textual meaning of the line." But *if* he allows changing textual meanings (ignoring the question of the plausibility of his instance), then he *cannot* preclude the possibility of incompatible and non-converging literary interpretations in rendering a coherent account, unless he also maintains that there is an executive rule (unformulated) for determining which textual meaning to prefer; after all, large portions of an entire text may be subject to similar changes and may therefore support plural interpretations. Another reason Beardsley cannot, on his own principles, preclude the prospect of defending non-converging literary interpretations is that the theory of linguistic meaning to which he subscribes—William Alston's theory [1964] of "illocutionary act potentials" (regardless of its defensibility [*see* Margolis ([1973a])])—depends on speakers' intentions and cannot assign exclusively correct meanings to particular expressions.

Finally, the critic's interpretation is *not* restricted, as Beardsley claims, merely to ferreting out textual meanings; it is often concerned rather (as even the prospect of diachronic change in textual meaning confirms) with plausible ways in which the artistic *design* of a work (in the sense supplied) may be construed. Here, we cannot be certain of what is and what is not *in* the work. In fact, in the interesting case of competing interpretations of Wordsworth's "A Slumber Did My Spirit Seal" (which Beardsley discusses in the context of examining Hirsch's theory of authorial meaning), the principal question is not merely what the words mean textually (on Beardsley's own concession, this is no longer a matter that precludes plural readings), but what the poem "means," what coherent design may be imputed to the poem, or what it may be said to "disclose." Unfortunately, both Cleanth Brooks's and F. W. Bateson's interpretations (which Beardsley and Hirsch consider) are quite problematic. Bateson's pantheistic interpretation [1950], for instance, cannot be supported solely on the basis of the *textual meaning* (in Beardsley's sense or in any reasonably related sense) of the lines "No motion has she now, no force,/ She neither hears nor sees:/Rolled round in earth's diurnal course,/ With rocks, and stones, and trees" (cf. Beardsley [1970b]). And Brooks's interpretation [1951] (which, rightly understood, emphasizes the lover's shock—almost in a clinical sense—upon Lucy's death and consequent inertness) is careless about "textual meanings" in a way that does not vitiate the interpretation. The upshot is that Wordsworth's poem *does,* contrary to Beardsley's claim, appear to support two different interpretations of the poem's design, without even entailing different interpretations of the poem's textual meaning. There seems to be no way to preclude the possibility. The point is an important one because it shows at a stroke that interpretive divergence cannot be reduced to equivocation or textual vagueness: the language of the Lucy poem is strikingly explicit and semantically clear.

There is an instructive, well-worn disagreement about the role of the critic that rests on a failure to respect the difference between interpretation and description. The following passages (the first by G. S. Fraser [1955] and the second by T. S. Eliot [1932]) are quite representative of two conflicting views, both of which strike us as truisms:

> The reader gets from a great poem what he can bring to it; and though there are many kinds of poem in which it is important that the reader should bring an adroit responsiveness to verbal play, a dexterity on seizing nuances, it is always more important that he should bring what one can only call experience of life and openness to life, depth and humility.

> I have assumed as axiomatic that a creation, a work of art, is autotelic; and that criticism by definition is *about* something other

than itself. Hence you cannot fuse creation with criticism as you can fuse criticism with creation. The critical activity finds its highest, its true fulfillment in a kind of union with creation in the labor of the artist.

Actually, one of Eliot's more recent statements [1956], which finds him vigorously supporting a corollary of Fraser's position, threatens not only to replace his thesis of autotelism in art with the doctrine that art is inherently incomplete, but also to upset the simple subordination of criticism to artistic creation (cf. Wollheim [1968]). Current disputes within the hermeneutic tradition have, in a somewhat related way, oscillated between an emphasis on original "authorial intent" (Hirsch [1967]) and on a "reader response" (Fish [1972]; Bloom [1973]). It is not without interest to observe this gradual shift back to the views Oscar Wilde once expressed, albeit misleadingly, that criticism is even more creative than the production of fine art ("The Critic as Artist") and that contraries may be true in criticism ("The Truth of Masks"). This habit of speaking of art as inherently incomplete or defective and awaiting the interpretive critic's contribution to *finish* the work is admittedly unfortunate—but understandable. Clearly, artists sometimes produce works that inherently call for interpretation. What is initially defective or incomplete is our understanding, not the work; but for conceptual reasons, we cannot be certain that what is supplied by interpretation is really in principle descriptively available in the work itself. This is precisely what Beardsley ignores in replacing talk about the work of art with talk about the "aesthetic object." Also, of course, *if* valid interpretations need not be convergent or compatible (cf. Ingarden [1964]; Merleau-Ponty [1964]), it would be logically impossible to hold that interpretation and description were the same or equivalent endeavors. There is bound, therefore, to be a certain conceptual congruence between the admission of critical interpretation and our theory of the nature of artworks.

The performing aspect of interpretation is unquestionably clarified by the facts regarding the performing arts. In music, for instance, one actually speaks of a given piece (that is, of performing according to a given score) as an interpretation of that piece (score). "Do you prefer Elizabeth Schwartzkopf's or Kirsten Flagstad's interpretation of Beethoven's 'Ah Perfido?' " We should never use "description" in such a context. Of course, the question may be asked, "What has this use of 'interpretation' to do with aesthetic criticism?" It is true that the performing musician is not a critic as such, and it is true that the critic is not as such a performing musician. But there is a very marked similarity between the activities of the two.

Let us admit that the critic uses language in a characteristic way and that the musician plays his instrument; and let us admit that, in the context of aesthetic appreciation proper, the performance of the musician has a very clear priority over the efforts of a music critic. We may reasonably still view the musician's performance as a demonstration of his would-be interpretation of the score (in the critic's sense). The musician may not have the special skill to state his interpretation in the critic's language and his musicianship will obviously not suffer for the lack of it. But a music critic would be able to describe the essential features of the musician's interpretation. Here, the ambivalence of "interpretation" comes to our notice because the critic may be said to describe the musician's performance (that performance itself being an interpretation of the score or music) and a well-trained music critic may also provide us with a telling verbal interpretation of the same score. I am not equating the critic's interpretation with the musician's; they are different in quite important respects. I wish only to draw attention to the logical similarities between the two.

There is an important parallel here to the dramatic arts, in that drama critics frequently act as full interpretive critics even more than do music critics. Surely, the numerous interpretations of *Hamlet* (*see* Weitz [1964]) cannot all be construed as descriptions of actual dramatic performances; the critic has at times provided us with an interpretation that actors and directors, possessing altogether different skills, may or may not enact. I am drawing attention, in short, to a certain double use of "interpretation" in the performing arts—that use in which performing artists are said to interpret a score or text or, more elliptically, a particular work of art, and that in which a critic may discursively state an interpretation of such score or text or work without performing in the artist's manner. The critic is rather like a quasi-performer and the performing artist is rather like a quasi-critic. The former states his interpretation discursively though he may not demonstrate (perform) it; the latter performs (interprets) in his art, in effect demonstrating a would-be critical interpretation, which he need not state.

The reasonableness of linking these two senses of "interpretation" may perhaps be seen more persuasively in the attitudes of critics toward such difficult and controversial musicians as Arnold Schönberg. On the occasion of his death, in 1951, *Music and Letters* [1951] solicited, from some very well-known and competent musicians and critics, about twenty-five letters (some, extraordinarily revealing) of personal views of Schönberg's music. Here are some excerpts:

> Schönberg meant nothing to me—but as he has apparently meant a
> lot to other people I daresay it is all my fault.
>
> (*R. Vaughan Williams*)

> A few sentences of unresolved doubt are all I can contribute
> . . . Are his arbitrary sequences of notes supposed to be recog-
> nized, that is, remembered, by the listener? Or is their sole
> purpose the negative one of ensuring that there remain no traces of
> landmarks, tonal or otherwise, that is, nothing musically
> memorable at all? . . . can we ever find the criterion of
> Schönberg's "music sense"? . . . How many unsuccessful ex-
> humations are required before works are pronounced dead?
>
> (*Ivor Keys*)

Schönberg received, somewhat later, a rather spirited defense
(Neighbour [1952]; cf. also Sessions [1951]; Schönberg [1950]) against
these uncompromising letters—but a defense that ends with much the
same substantive conclusion:

> As far as I know, no one has yet succeeded in making the kind of
> analysis of Schönberg's later harmony of which I am sure it is
> capable in principle . . . In Schönberg's case one cannot hope to
> do more than draw attention to characteristics of the harmony
> which might eventually provide pointers toward a more complete
> explanation of its traditional basis.

Illustrations from the performing arts are important because we see
that, for those arts, it is extremely difficult to speak of describing a work
of art prior to any given performance (cf. Macdonald [1954a]). We have,
so to say, only a notation and certain general instructions about a work
(a score) or certain materials that are to be used in a characteristic way
(the sentences of a dramatic text). There is an obvious resemblance
between the notes of a musical composition and the words of a drama; as
with a drama, one may translate the notation and paraphrase the instructions of the score or interpret it. And though one may speak of describing the plot of a play, its style, its language, and similar features by in-
specting the text, much as one might speak of describing the melody and
harmony of a piece of music from the score, we are very clear that the
text must be used in a dramatic performance. Our dramatic interest lies
primarily in the way the play may be mounted and the parts interpreted,

precisely in what cannot be entirely foreseen from the text itself. There may, for similar reasons, be a subtle difference between a critic's describing a melodic line, without regard to any particular performance, and his interpreting the score. The crucial point is that a full description of a work of art—in music, drama, or dance—cannot be provided by a critic who merely studies score or text; only an actual performance of the work would allow for such a description. Hence we emphasize the basic difference between such arts as music, drama, and the dance and the arts of architecture, sculpture, and painting—and, correspondingly, the possible varieties of critical comments (*see* L. Meyer [1973]).

The interpretation of a performing artist, then, brings the work of art into full existence, in the sense in which the music is actually played, the drama enacted, the dance danced. The critic who wishes to interpret a score or text will not, by his effort, bring the work into such full existence but only indicate a way in which it may, at least in part, be performed. (No philosophical importance attaches to the expression "full existence"—nothing that might lead us to speculate, say, about the intermittent existence of a work of art. The issue bears on the force of the type/token distinction already discussed.) For this reason we distinguish the interpretation of a performing artist from that of the corresponding critic. It is important to emphasize their similarities as well, because we are helped thereby to see that a critic's remarks may be interpretive rather than descriptive, and could not then be said to be accurate or inaccurate; they might merely provide one account among an indefinite variety of admissible accounts. Also, the distinction of the performing arts provides us with an analogue of the claim that interpretive critics complete an otherwise incomplete work: the legitimate contribution of the performer suggests the logical distinction of the critic's contribution.

We see now why one speaks of a music critic's interpretation of a score and of a critic's description of a piece of music. (The same account holds for the critic of drama and the dance.) One may say the critic interprets the score (indicates a way of performing the music by analyzing the score), describes the music (that is, describes such features as the melodic line and harmony indicated by the notation itself, which every interpretation will have to accommodate), or else describes the actual performance—the interpretation—of some musician. So, to speak of the music critic's interpretation of the score or description of the music is to speak in a mixed way. On the first usage, we treat the critic as a quasi-musician; on the second, we treat him as an instructor of would-be musicians and musical audiences interested in faithfulness to the minimal constraints that scores impose (*contra* Goodman [1968]); and on the third usage, we treat the critic as a reporter of a musical interpretation.

I hasten to add, in order to sort out our views of the actual work of critics even within the performing arts, that music critics are usually less interpretive than descriptive, both in the sense of instructing would-be musicians and audiences in the minimal structure of some piece of music any performance would be obliged to accommodate, and in the sense of reporting some actual performance—in both of which endeavors evaluation is regularly expected. Drama critics are predominantly interpretive or only narrowly concerned with the description of an actual performance; only the second function clearly calls for a further evaluative effort on the critic's part. Dance critics are overwhelmingly inclined merely to describe performances, and therefore to assess these as well. The likeliest reasons for these preferences are not difficult to assign. Since music has little claim to a representational function, interpretive language is extremely vague and relatively unsatisfactory—or else decidedly technical. Full-fledged performances are considerably more instructive than discursive comments, except where the latter describe the formal structure of the music binding on all interpretations, which, for its complexity and formality, might escape detection. Where the conventions of performance, as in some contemporary music, are thought to be unclear, "analysis" will actually be interpretive. Interpreting speech and human behavior is well-developed outside the arts and we are all relatively skilled in the use of language in a way not to be found in music and dance; hence, there is less need to confine criticism to describing the structure of dramatic texts. The mere formal structure of a text is often thought not as complex as that of music nor nearly as adequate an object of interest; also, there is greater possible precision, and even economy, to be had in imagining dramas enacted along the interpretive lines specified by a critic. In the dance, the peculiarly personal and idiosyncratic nature of performance and the absence of any clearly ordered "keyboard" of movements makes dance notation rather more of an *ad hoc* device for preserving a rough sense of the structure of some dance than a score whose own internal subtleties require analysis.

We may also observe that where his effort is interpretive, we cannot judge the critic's remarks to be simply true or false (or at least not simply true, admitting an asymmetry between "true" and "false"), accurate or inaccurate. We can only judge whether his interpretation, like the performing artist's, is "plausible," "reasonable," "admissible," "indefensible," "not impossible," and the like. One may, for example, say, "I see how you might interpret the music (the score) that way." At any rate, even if we can judge an interpretation to be "false" in the sense that it is incompatible with what is admitted to be descriptively true, we cannot judge that it is true (cf. L. Meyer [1973]). The difference between a critic's interpretation and description centers then, as we have already suggested, on the virtuoso, performing aspect of the former; on the absence of any object prior to interpretation that may pass as the full work of art, in the sense proper to the performing arts; and on our familiar willingness, in the context of appreciation, to attend to alternative and even incompatible interpretations of a work of art. Beardsley [1958] of course opposes this view, holding it to be a basic postulate that "if two presentations of the same aesthetic object have incompatible characteristics, at least one of them is illusory." "A particular presentation of an aesthetic object," in his view, "is . . . that object as experienced by a particular person on a particular occasion." Though they may be partial, fragmentary, or differently focused, all of the relevant experiences of a company of aesthetic percipients will be ideally compatible, though there may not be an actually formulable ideal (cf. Hirsch [1967]). Nevertheless, Beardsley himself has noticed the incompatibility between Chekhov's conception of his plays and Stanislavski's conception; and this seems to be tantamount to admitting that there may well be incompatible presentations *of the same play,* neither of which is "illusory" (cf. Pepper [1955]). In any case, Beardsley has never shown us how to decide which, among competing interpretations, is illusory.

The plastic arts stand at the opposite end of the spectrum, with regard to description and interpretation, because sculpture and painting are not typically viewed as scores or texts of any sort to be used in a performance. The performing aspect of these arts (if any) is telescoped in the original effort of the artist; we ordinarily attend to the work produced in these arts and not to the production. (One can, however, imagine construing Picasso's virtuoso paintings on glass—which have been recorded on film—as constituting not mere painting but the exercise of a performing art, not unlike the dance, that uses the materials of painting in a certain distinctive way.) Consequently, the pigments on a canvas, the block of carved marble, the assembled building materials are viewed on the model of physical objects. (Though that they are not merely such poses, as we have seen, an uneasy problem in Wollheim's account [1968].)

Still, there are contexts in which one speaks of interpreting a particular painting or sculpture. There is hardly any use in asking for an interpretation, in an aesthetically restricted sense, of a Grandma Moses, a Currier and Ives print, the usual portraits of Matisse, rug designs, and the like. But what shall one say of Matisse's *The Piano Lesson*? I may point out to you the *witty* features of Matisse's painting: for example, the relations between the implicit movement of the metronome on the piano; the elimination of one of the boy's eyes by a diagonal, flesh-colored brush stroke—so that we understand his attention to be metronomically flicking back and forth between the open French windows and the piano keyboard; the slash of brilliant green color through the windows, that diagonally captures a part of the attention of the young pianist and confirms the field of play beyond; the window's being open in contrast to the imprisoning presence of the piano; the relaxed sensual sculpture by Matisse himself placed on a foreground table before the open windows, in contrast with an unfinished painting, also by Matisse, which is very angular and severe, and ambiguously placed behind the boy at the piano to suggest an unpleasantly enforced lesson. If I point out these features, which perhaps you had not considered or that might be relatively difficult to confirm decisively, you might concede that I had interpreted the painting satisfactorily; you might also, I admit, say that I had merely described the painting more accurately than another. Would there be a difference in speaking in these two ways?

It is important to notice that we suppose the painting and the sculpture to be intact objects, to be fully "there," to have been produced—as the work of art in the performing arts is not. If we exaggerate the interpretive contribution of the critic, we are inclined to reduce correspondingly the artist's achievement; we deprive the artist, in a way, of having put into his work (as in the case of Matisse) the relationships we have made out. Are we discovering these features in the painting or are we imputing them to the painting? If we prefer the first way of speaking, we shall speak of the critic's effort as descriptive; if the second, as interpretive. I do not see how we can deny that, in the plastic arts, there simply is no clear-cut agreement about what is actually in a painting and what is only plausibly imputed to it. There is no question about color and line and form and, ordinarily, representation. But not all of the comments about, say, *The Piano Lesson* are unambiguously comments about what is in the painting. The reason is that once we reject the view that artworks are merely physical objects—or, in some restricted sense, "perceptual objects"—once we construe artworks as culturally emergent, we cannot apply the usual criteria for demarcating what is and what is not "in" an object. Representation, significance, expressiveness, symbolic import, allusiveness, purposiveness, meaning, intentions, conventions, genres, historical context, and the like simply elude the usual boundaries of physical identification.

The issue may be made intuitively clearer if one poses questions about a painting rather than proposes an actual interpretation. Consider the following remarks (Lindsay and Huppé [1956]):

Frequently Brueghel seems to hide his meaning rather than reveal his meaning. For example in such paintings as "Christ Carrying the Cross" or the "Conversion of Saint Paul," we must search through masses of detail in order to find the iconographical center. In these paintings, the center of meaning, once discovered, is clear, but in such a painting as "Netherlandish Proverbs" the center of meaning is not clear. We gain an impression only of scattered images, yet the older title of the painting, the "Monde Renversé," seems to suggest thematic coherence. May the clue to the concealed meaning be found, not only in the upside-down sign hanging over the inn, but in the curious relation of sun to shadow, which appears to the eye after study? In the painting of "The Blind Leading the Blind," although the faces of the blind and their plight suggest poverty, yet their clothing seems to suggest something other than poverty. What clue is to be found which will explain an apparent discrepancy between vestment and status? In the "Fall of Icarus," why is our attention drawn from the titular center of the picture to the images of the ship which sails on obliviously, and of the peasants who toil on obliviously? Again, in the "Peasant Dance" what intention exists behind the pattern of the painting, which draws the eye, exactly as in the "Conversion of Saint Paul," through the color and the motion of the foreground, finally resting on the small figure at the center of the horizon with his back eloquently turned on the riotous scene in the foreground?

We compromise here, I believe. In simple works, we speak of description and of a critic's remarks as true or false, accurate or inaccurate, and so on. In difficult and puzzling works, we emphasize the virtuosity of the critic and speak of his interpretation; but our intention is initially more honorific than methodological, because we are inclined to view such comments as descriptive of, say, a painting—not interpretive, in the sense proper to the performing arts. Hence, there is no doubt that interpretation *sometimes* serves to convey a sense of virtuosity in fathoming what is hidden (but describable) in a work of art. Nevertheless, our own way of speaking has a methodological aspect, since, where we cannot point merely to colors and shapes and the like, we may be obliged to construe such physical marks in a certain way and our account of the painting will then be more clearly plausible or implausible than flatly true or false, accurate or inaccurate. Beardsley [1970b] discounts incompatible interpretations in accord with what he calls "the principle of 'the Intolerability of Incompatibles,' i.e., if two [interpretations] are logically incompatible, they cannot both be true (and they implicitly claim to be true)." "Indeed," he says, "I hold that *all* of the literary interpretations that deserve the name obey the principle."

The delicacy of the matter may be focused by a close examination of certain of Erwin Panofsky's views on criticism. Panofsky had reprinted [1955] the "Introductory" to his *Studies in Iconology* [1939] with modifications he himself did not regard as material but which, for our purposes, are revealing enough. The shift in the "Introductory," now titled "Iconography and Iconology," seems to be merely terminological, but it betrays an unresolved difficulty in Panofsky's thesis. What in the *Studies* are distinguished as "pre-iconographical description," "iconographical analysis in the narrower sense," and "iconographical interpretation in the deeper sense" become, in the altered reprint, "pre-iconographical description, iconographical analysis, and iconological interpretation." In the following, analysis of fine art appears to be restricted to the compositional and iconographical levels of attention:

> As long as we limit ourselves to stating that Leonardo da Vinci's famous fresco shows a group of thirteen men around a dinner table, and that this group of men represents the Last Supper, we deal with the work of art *as such,* and we interpret its compositional and iconographical features as *its own* properties or qualifications. But when we try to understand it as a document of Leonardo's personality, or of the civilization of the Italian High Renaissance, or of a peculiar religious attitude, we deal with the work of art as a *symptom of something else* which expresses itself in a countless variety of other symptoms, and we interpret its compositional and iconographical features as more particularized evidence of this "something else." The discovery and interpretation of these "symbolic" values (which are often unknown to the artist himself and may even emphatically differ from what he consciously intended to express) is the object of what we may call "iconology" as opposed to "iconography."

Yet, Panofsky does not remain consistent. "The intrinsic meaning or content [i.e., the iconological]," he says (italics added),

> is *essential* where the two other kinds of meaning, the primary or natural and the secondary or conventional (i.e., the pre-iconographical and the iconographical) are *phenomenal*. It may be defined as a unifying principle which underlies and explains both the visible event and its intelligible significance, and which *deter-*

mines even the form in which the visible event takes shape.

Elsewhere, however, Panofsky has no difficulty saying,

> And as the correct identification of motifs [i.e., the pre-iconographical materials] is the *prerequisite* of their correct iconographical analysis, so is the correct analysis of images, stories and allegories the *prerequisite* of their correct iconological interpretation . . .

The last stage of his maneuvers appears when he denies priority to any of the levels of attention:

> . . . we must bear in mind that the neatly differentiated categories, which . . . seem to indicate three independent spheres of meaning, refer in reality to aspects of one phenomenon, namely, the work of art as a whole. So that, in actual work, the methods of approach which here appear as three unrelated operations of research *merge* with each other into *one organic and indivisible process.*

The iconological approach now constitutes the effort of a "synthetic intuition" which seeks to apprehend the work of art as an organic whole; but even this view is subsequently made more tentative.

Aside from Panofsky's evident logical difficulties, the reasons for speaking of "interpretations" clearly shift as we turn from the performing arts to the plastic arts. In the first, the work may be performed and a critic may interpret score or text in lieu of an actual performance; in the second, the object is initially "there," produced, but we cannot say with precision what its boundaries are—neither in general for all the sorts of properties mentioned in talking about the plastic arts, nor sometimes for the particular properties ascribed to a particular work. Whenever we are so in doubt, we treat our account on the interpretive model rather than on the descriptive, falling back to those minimal elements that can with assurance be said to be described. This observation undercuts, I believe, the force of Paul Ziff's otherwise convincing challenge [1954] to S. Alexander's thesis [1939] that "the illusion is of the essence of the work of art." Ziff's attack is exclusively on the misuse of "illusion" and on the propriety of attributing such perceptual properties as "great depth" to a Cézanne, for instance (cf. Isenberg [1949a]). Ziff says nothing, however, about the indeterminacy we are speaking of here or of the need, at times, to interpret a work of art.

The literary arts (poetry and fiction, chiefly) lie somewhere between the performing arts proper and the plastic arts and share features more sharply assignable to these others. A critic's reading of a poem or novel is more like a musical or dramatic performance than like the description of a painting or sculpture; on the other hand, the poem and novel—because they are not strictly notations provided for a would-be performer and because of the intimate connection between written and spoken language—are viewed more in the manner of objects deposited and completed than as scores to be used in producing the artwork fully. But if we were to treat the literary critic's work primarily as descriptive, we should find magnified the peculiar difficulty of the plastic arts, namely, that of determining the boundaries of the work of art. Because the literary work is composed of words, not merely of sensorily discriminable materials, we are even more at a loss to decide cleanly between what we discover in a poem and what we impute to it. It is the failure of René Wellek and Austin Warren [1956] to make allowances of just this sort that reduces their earnest and penetrating study of "the mode of existence" of literature to what is very nearly nonsense. They survey all the puzzles about poetry and literature, coming to the conclusion that "the real poem must be conceived as a structure of norms, realized only partially in the actual experience of its many readers." But after assuring us that "we can distinguish between right and wrong readings of a poem, or between a recognition or a distortion of the norms implicit in a work of art," they concede that "the system of norms [itself] is growing and changing and will remain, in some sense, always incompletely and imperfectly realized." They then conclude, in a truly extraordinary burst, that

> The work of art . . . appears as an object of knowledge *sui generis* which has a special ontological status. It is neither real (like a statue) nor mental (like the experience of light or pain) nor ideal (like a triangle). It is a system of norms of ideal concepts which are intersubjective. They must be assumed to exist in collective ideology, changing with it, accessible only through individual mental experiences, based on the sound-structure of its sentences.

What they have obviously confused are the conditions for identifying an artwork and for defending what, within the diachronic practice of critics, may be said of it (cf. Vivas [1955]).

We do, as a matter of practice, attribute to a literary work much (in the descriptive sense) that might otherwise pass as interpretation; think, for instance, of the effect of James Joyce's having titled his remarkable novel *Ulysses.* The important point is that there need be no serious methodological complications. To speak of a critic's efforts as descriptive of music, or of painting, or of poetry, is, at least, to speak in an honorific way of the original genius of the creative artist; and to speak of the critic's interpretation is at least to emphasize his ingenuity without prejudice to assigning properties to the work he is commenting on. In all the arts, furthermore, there is a relatively indisputable range of comments that will be descriptive in the narrowest possible sense—in music and in dance, probably, the notes, melody, harmony, steps, positions, movements, style, and the like will be scored as a condition binding upon all interpreters, whether artistic performers or critics; in the plastic arts, line, color, texture, shapes, and, ordinarily, representations, genres, styles and the like will be describable; in the literary and dramatic arts, plot, action, characters, vocabulary, rhythm, rhyme, style of language, and the like are said to be described. (We shall, however, return to the question of style.)

Nevertheless, much that is decidedly interpretive rather than descriptive will also be found, particularly in literary criticism. A Freudian reading of *Alice in Wonderland,* a Marxist reading of the *Oresteia,* a proposal that Tennessee Williams's *A Streetcar Named Desire* inverts the Platonic Myth of the Cave are all taken to be interpretive proposals. Criticism is methodologically treated as interpretive, in the sense that any account will be viewed as plausible more than as true, once what is indisputably descriptive has been provided—and always with a caution that the work may be construed in alternative ways. There is absolutely no need here to fix once and for all—without attention to the peculiarities of particular works—what is descriptively assignable to any set of artworks. There is no minimal list. That is, the problem of interpretation is precisely what it is because there is no formal demarcation line between what is describably present in a work and what may be interpretively imputed to it. But this is not to say that we cannot specify what is (minimally) descriptively true of a particular work and what is (certainly) interpretively imputed to it. Also, it is not to say that the descriptive elements are of a certain uniform sort—for instance, physical features (cf. Reichert [1977]). (The logic of description and interpretation we may ignore for the time being.) The literary arts are troublesome because our firmest models of description concern what is narrowly accessible to sensory perception, and because language, the medium of literature, can hardly be explored without considering speakers' or writers' intentions and meanings as ascribed on the basis of associated background beliefs.

More radical views about the describable materials of literature are characteristically linked with radical views about interpreting the human condition itself. An emphasis, for instance, on the "historicity" of human nature, the impossibility of fixing the properties of human existence essentially rather than in terms of an ever-changing historical context, has, particularly in the hermeneutic tradition, been applied in such a way as to threaten to erase the distinction between description and interpretation, to encourage a radical relativism with respect to interpretation, and even to endorse the complete arbitrariness of the interpretive critic's response (cf. Heidegger [1962]; Gadamer [1975]; Derrida [1973]). The historicist theme has inevitably been applied to literary works themselves as well as to criticism, with the result that the properties of sentences in a text (notably, meanings) are no longer open to straightforward description (cf. Bloom [1973]; *see* Abrams [1976]). Derrida [1972] for instance holds that *"un texte reste d'ailleurs toujours imperceptible."* Taken literally, there can be no validity at all in critical interpretation, which seems preposterous (cf. Foucault [1965], [1972]); construed more generously, Derrida himself discloses textual meanings that criticism may defend as rigorously as any other (cf. Said [1978]).

The entire issue is nicely fixed by reflecting on the efforts of critics to eliminate all interpretations but "the" correct one—which, if possible, would justify treating interpretation as equivalent to description. But all such efforts can be shown to founder—for conceptual reasons—merely by scanning the views of prominent critics. This is nowhere more obvious or more challenging than in the attempts of so-called historical criticism.

In speaking of the historical criticism of literary texts, it is rarely noticed that all language users—even the participants in a casual conversation—are speaking and writing in a language that must be undergoing significant temporal changes all the time (different parts at different rates in different ways). No one can understand what is said in his own language without a grasp of its historical transformations even for contemporaneous intervals: slang makes this perfectly clear. There is, therefore, no literary or linguistic study that is not, at least implicitly, historically sensitized. To speak of historical criticism, then, as if the practice were opposed to standard literary criticism, is to risk utter incoherence. *If* the New Critics (*see* Wellek [1965]) ever wished to rid their work (which is not to say they ever did) of all historical orientation, they were attempting the impossible.

On the other hand, the advocates of historical criticism are devoted to a distinct project, which Robert Marsh [1967] for one has perspicuously characterized as follows: "to consider and eliminate, for a given work,

all reasonable interpretive possibilities but the one historically most probable . . . " Given that commitment, it is entirely possible to speak of
the relative opposition of historically oriented criticism and criticism
allegedly focused on the contemporary meaning and value of a "given"
work. The trouble is that *if* a work is "given" in any sense that bears on
the deliberate practice of critics, there cannot fail to be an interest in contemporary sensibilities *and* the historical refinement of those sensibilities. There must be some continuity and even, ultimately, a
systematic unity in these two apparently opposed approaches (*see*
Gadamer [1975]); otherwise, how to identify the relevant properties of a
"given" work *of which* a certain historical interpretation can be said
now to be "the most probable" becomes an insoluble puzzle (*contra*
Robertson [1969]).

One cannot pertinently attack or defend so-called historical criticism
without a theory of the nature of a literary work, of language itself, and
of human values. For example, *if* a literary work were "given" in any
sense comparable to that in which a physical object is given in perceptual
contexts, we should have strong grounds for objecting to, or for seriously
circumscribing, historical, biographical, and intentional considerations in
formulating an "objective" account of it. In fact, on such a view (never
mind the details, for the moment), the *interpretation* of a literary work
would be construed as uncovering, *finding* or discovering what is *hidden*
or embedded, but somehow present, *in the given work*: the distinction
between description and interpretation would dissolve and attention
would center on relatively unchanging perceptual qualities. It is probably
in this spirit that Wimsatt [1954] declares that "the verbal object will be
viewed by a critic in a kind of stereoscopic perspective which makes it
look somewhat like a physical object." On such a view, the work appears
to be given once and for all, so that historical considerations—*a fortiori,*
non-converging historical considerations—have little or no relevance (cf.
Beardsley [1958]).

But the sense in which a work is thus "given" is hardly obvious. Consider for example the following influential statement (Wimsatt [1954]):

> There is a difference between internal and external evidence for the
> meaning of a poem. And the paradox is only verbal and superficial
> that what is (1) internal is also public: it is discovered through the
> semantics and syntax of a poem, through our habitual knowledge
> of the language, through grammars, dictionaries, and all the
> literature which is the source of dictionaries, in general through all
> that makes a language and culture; while what is (2) external is

private or idiosyncratic; not a part of the work as a linguistic fact: it consists of revelations (in journals, for example, or letters or reported conversations) about how or why the poet wrote the poem—to what lady, while sitting on what lawn, or at the death of what friend, or brother. There is (3) an intermediate kind of evidence about the character of the author or about private or semi-private meanings attached to words or topics by an author or by a coterie of which he is a member. The meaning of words is the history of words, and the biography of an author, his use of a word, and the associations which the word has for *him,* are part of the word's history and meaning.

If I understand this passage correctly, "the meaning" of a poem is determined on "internal evidence" if it is fixed by reference to the history of the actual usage of the language, which *includes* now the author's own use and associations (provided only that that use be not "private"—in the sense I suppose of not being able to be reliably ascertained by public means). But if this be admitted, then there is *no* effective difference between internal and external evidence regarding the meaning of a poem: although an author's journal may be "external" as being "idiosyncratic" (though not necessarily "private"), it will be "internal" insofar as it forms part of the "history of words." Anomalously, also, what is "in" the poem will change with the changing career of language. Although this may be an allowable thing to say, the sense in which a literary work is "given" and the analogy between such a datum and the paradigms of perceptual contexts will become extremely problematic. If "external" means "unverifiable," then of course no one will favor external considerations; but if "external" merely means "idiosyncratic," then no grounds will have been advanced for precluding the relevance of intentional, biographical, psychological, or historical factors. How to determine relevance needs to be considered; but dogmas like the Intentional and Genetic Fallacies (Wimsatt [1954], [1968]) become utterly incapable of providing the least demarcation between what is internal or external to an artwork (cf. Wimsatt [1963]). An independent theory is required.

It is often not appreciated that a literary work, such as a poem, may be *identified*—for critical purposes—without determining the boundaries of what is internal or external to it, and without even deciding the defining characteristics of poems or other literary forms. To put the point sketchily, an uninterpreted authentic text may be fixed as a token instance of a poem; those who dispute about its interpretation can nevertheless agree that they are to construe the same text as a poem. The text will remain relatively constant through time, though the poem (whatever we may mean by "the poem") may have a significant history affected by changes in the language—including interim changes in the uses of the language—in which it was written. On the theory just examined, if the meaning of a poem depends on the history of the living language (cf. Eliot [1956]), then as the language changes—regardless of when the poem was originally "composed" (now a rather puzzling claim)—the poem itself, *a fortiori*, its meaning, will change. If so, then it will be extremely difficult to specify a sense—returning to Marsh's statement—in which the poem can be said to be *given*: the *text* will be given, but in what sense can the *poem* be said to be given? Furthermore, if artworks are identified as we have supposed, what should count as an admissible or inadmissible interpretation of a "given" work remains an entirely open question. Foreclosing on historical, biographical, psychological or intentional factors—in spite of the fact that such factors may be discerned in the public domain—will now be rightly seen to depend on a favored *theory* of poems (a particular theory of what is "given"), *not* on what is minimally needed to fix numerical identity. Also, if a grasp of linguistic meanings, even of contemporary language, requires some historical sensibility, and if collecting "internal evidence" entails reading a literary work in terms of the actual usage of the language, then—by a *reductio*—even a reading sensitized only by a grasp of contemporary usage, utterly ignorant of the usage of the moment of composition, will count as historical criticism! Historical criticism narrowly (and perhaps properly) so-called would then be no more than a restriction within a practice conceptually uniform for all literature. One might make this to be the sense, for instance, of René Wellek's much-quoted remark [1965]; "Literary theory without criticism or history, or criticism without theory or history, or history without theory and criticism [is inconceivable]." Again, if the claim is allowed, then admitting a contemporary sensibility and a sensibility attuned to usage at the moment of composition entails admitting a sensibility attuned to usage at any time between original composition and the present. If the meanings of the expressions of a living language may be accurately fixed for any given period, then it is simply a special interest that restricts interpretation along the lines preferred by strict historical critics (for example, Rosemund Tuve [1947]) or by those focused on contemporary sensibilities (for example, John Crowe Ransom [1941]). It would then be merely an accident that the profession failed to produce antiquarian champions ranging over intermediary periods and figures who, for instance, restrict their activities to formulating authentic Renaissance interpretations of ancient texts.

That the problem of "objective" criticism is muddled by the ablest theorists can be demonstrated at a stroke. René Wellek [1965], for instance, opposing the extreme relativism of some of his colleagues, holds that "literary study differs from historical study in having to deal not with documents but with *monuments.*" (One can hardly forget Wimsatt's image.) By this he means to congratulate the literary student who "can examine his object, the work itself," who can "isolate his object . . . the literary work of art . . . contemplate it intently . . . analyze . . . interpret, and finally . . . evaluate it by criteria derived from, verified by, buttressed by, as wide a knowledge, as close an observation, as keen a sensibility, as honest a judgment as we can command." The encouragement is gratifying. But when we turn to ask what Wellek understands by literature we learn that "the real poem must be conceived as a structure of norms, realized only partially in the actual experience of its many readers . . . [a] system of norms [that] is growing and changing and will remain, in some sense, always incompletely and imperfectly realized" (Wellek and Warren [1956]). Wellek's thesis does not seem to be entirely intelligible; but in whatever generous sense it may be read, it becomes quite impossible to speak of the critic's study of *monuments* in any sense analogous to speaking about physical objects "given" in perceptual contexts. Hence it is hopeless to take a stand on the bearing of historical, biographical, psychological or intentional factors in settling what is internal or external to a given work on the basis of such analogies. Wellek himself professes a sympathy for exploring just such factors. But, in a summary pronouncement, he manages to charge [1965] that "the work of art as an aesthetic unity is [often nowadays] broken up or ignored in favor of a study of attitudes, feelings, concepts, and philosophies of the poets." The blow is directed against Freudian, Marxist, Jungian, Existialist and related metacritical views, but theoretical justification is lacking and—if the passage cited is a fair sample of Wellek's views—impossible to provide.

Sometimes, a conception of the literary work yields to utter bafflement and suggests the impossibility of literary criticism itself. This is fairly explicit, for instance, in a well-known remark of Lionel Trilling's [1950a], not far removed from Wellek's view:

What is the real poem? Is it the poem we now perceive? Is it the poem the author consciously intended? Is it the poem the author and his first readers read? Well, it is all these things, depending on the state of our knowledge. But in addition the poem is the poem as

> it has existed in history, as it has lived its life from Then to Now, as
> it is a thing which submits itself to one kind of perception in one
> age and another kind of perception in another age, as it exerts in
> each age a different kind of power. This makes it a thing that we
> can never wholly understand—other things too, of course, help to
> make it that—and the mystery, the unreachable part of the poem, is
> one of its aesthetic elements.

The thesis, therefore, leads to the celebration of Babel (compare the exchanges between Leavis and Bateson and Leavis and Wellek: Leavis [1968]; Bentley [1948]). The principal difference between Wellek and Trilling is this: although they hold strikingly similar views of what a literary work *is,* Trilling inclines towards a radical relativism and Wellek explicitly opposes it. On the grounds given, Trilling tries to be the more consistent but Wellek is the more sensible.

One of the most arresting recent efforts to fix the object of critical interpretation in the flux of history has been made by E. D. Hirsch [1967] (also [1976]), whose views fall within the tradition of continental hermeneutics. His own statement seems admirably straightforward:

> As soon as anyone claims validity for his interpretation (and few
> would listen to a critic who did not), he is immediately caught in a
> web of logical necessity. If his claim to validity is to hold, he must
> be willing to measure his interpretation against a genuinely
> discriminating norm, and the only compelling normative principle
> that has ever been brought forward is the old-fashioned ideal of
> rightly understanding what the author meant . . . [I]t is the only
> kind of interpretation with a determinate object, and thus the only
> kind that can lay claim to validity in any straightforward and practicable sense of that term.

The difficulty, however, has merely been shifted. Hirsch construes interpretation (as opposed to criticism—which, more generously, concerns "intrinsic and extrinsic significance" [historically and personally variable significance], that may be imputed to particular works *once* their meaning is established) simply "as a re-cognition of the author's meaning"—nothing more, nothing less. The meaning of a text, for Hirsch, does not ever change for the author or for others; only its significance changes. "*Meaning,*" he says, "is that which is represented by a text; it is what the author meant by his use of a particular sign sequence; it is what the signs represent"—a formula which, in the tradition of Dilthey, seems to focus primarily on what the author *intended* by what he said rather than on the mere (but essential) *intentionality* of language itself. Wellek and Warren [1956], of course, hold the contrary view: "The meaning of a work of art is not exhausted by, or even equivalent to, its intention. As a system of values, it leads an independent life. The total meaning of a work of art cannot be defined merely in terms of its meaning for the author and his contemporaries. It is rather the result of a process of secretion, i.e., the history of its criticism by its many readers in many ages." (On merely internal grounds, however, this may well be incoherent.) Even Hirsch concedes that "there are usually components of an author's intended meaning that he is not conscious of"—by which caveat Hirsch hopes to avoid the psychologizing of meaning. It obviously threatens difficulties of its own.

For one thing, disagreements about the interpretation of a text usually depend, in Hirsch's view, on a disagreement about genre, on conventions governing types of utterances and the distinct purposes for which particular utterances are made. Criticism cannot go forward objectively unless there are such things as "intrinsic genres" and unless these genres are determinable. But the very concept of isolable "purposes" corresponding to "types" of discourse and defining "intrinsic genres" is both theoretically dubious and hedgingly advanced by Hirsch himself. He says, for instance, that he "departs from . . . Aristotle and the Neo-Aristotelians by [an] insistence on the entirely metaphorical character of an entelechy when that concept is applied to a form of speech. A verbal genre has no entelechy or will of its own . . . [its] purpose . . . is the communicable purpose of a particular speaker, nothing more nor less." The result is that the interpretation of a text and the validation of intrinsic verbal genres (one may substitute Wellek's "norms" with the same result) are simply two sides of the same enterprise; so the argument is circular. On the one hand, Hirsch admits that "at the level of history there is no real entity such as a genre . . . that can adequately define and subsume all the individuals that are called by the same generic name, such as ode, sonnet, command, prayer, or epic"; on the other, he says that "the larger genre concepts represent norms and conventions that were *actually* brought into play" [italics added]. These two statements cannot be reconciled in any way that can support the independent validation of critical judgments.

Secondly, Hirsch concedes that it is "an aspect of most texts" that "the author submits to the convention that his willed implications must go far beyond what he explicitly knows." Not only is this anomalous for any theory of unchanging authorial meaning but it makes radically impossible the distinction between a text's interpretation and the criticism of its "significance," between what is internal and external to the text itself. Hirsch himself supplies the evidence. Regarding the American Constitution, he speaks of valid interpretations of the law governing some "unknown and unforeseen state of affairs" and says that a valid extension is "implied" by the law—with no attention to historical and ideological conflicts generated by this sanguine approach (cf. Cardozo [1921]; Bickel [1975]). Of course, the text of all texts that, since Schleiermacher [1959], defies every such sanguine proposal is the Bible.

Finally, Hirsch's view of objective interpretation cannot, on conceptual grounds, be distinguished from interpretative criticism frankly committed to plausible and plural readings. Hirsch holds that "two disparate interpretations cannot both be correct"—which presupposes a determinate authorial meaning—and yet he concedes (with admirable honesty) that "every interpreter labors under the handicap of an inevitable circularity: all his internal evidence tends to support his hypothesis because much of it was constituted by his hypothesis" (the so-called hermeneutic circle). "Sometimes," he says, "the generic meanings implied by interpretations are disparate" (cf. Beardsley [1970b]). But this defeats the theory out of its own mouth. Hirsch's "genre" is designed at one and the same time to avoid being "a species concept that somehow defines and equates the members it subsumes"—it has "an indispensable heuristic function"—but Hirsch also says that it has "an inescapable constitutive function." It is at once a pragmatic hypothesis plausible in terms of our available information (and, one supposes, in terms of historical interest) and a probabilistic judgment that "refers to a reality that is partly unknown and which may . . . never be known with certainty."

More recently, Hirsch [1976] has modified his claims, though without effectively redeeming his thesis. He now distinguishes between "meaning" ("the determinate representation of a text for an interpreter") and "original meaning" ("authorial intent"). We are bound, he says, by the following "fundamental ethical maxim for interpretation": "Unless there is a powerful overriding value in disregarding an author's intention (i.e., original meaning), we who interpret as a vocation should not disregard it." Meaning, in either the narrow or broad sense, is still to be contrasted with "significance," that is, "meaning-as-related-to-something-else." Since Hirsch does not concern himself with specifying the nature and boundaries of the literary object, the distinction remains operatively idle; in effect, his is the literary counterpart of Panofsky's attempted distinction [1955] regarding the interpretation of painting. Hirsch cannot say when a linguistic expression is correctly interpreted (possibly departing from authorial intent) and when it is merely construed as significant beyond its context of use (involving contexts of application as opposed to contexts of use). The quibble is important because it is Hirsch's intention to forestall the relativists—particularly Heidegger and his associates (Heidegger [1962]; Gadamer [1976]; Derrida [1973]; Bultman [1955], [1962]). But the effort cannot succeed: Hirsch fails to show specifically how to overtake his opponents; he fails to grasp the full power of relativism, wrongly supposing that it precludes knowledge; and he fails to show how his own view (against his protestations) cannot be made to yield to a relativistic account. Radical relativism is incoherent, but Hirsch shows no way of resisting a more moderate—a "robust"—relativism. Symptomatically, he replaces the hermeneutic circle with a reliance on so-called "corrigible schemata" (of interpretation) —the expression is borrowed from Piaget.

Heidegger had shown an interesting way of construing the hermeneutic circle as yielding to relativism; and, as we have seen, Hirsch in effect concedes the point. But curiously, Hirsch offers no procedural clarification to confirm his "schemata"; he relies entirely on the effect of linking his own venture to the efforts of known non-relativists. Still, he makes a number of telling concessions. For example, he substantially qualifies the originally universal canon of interpretation postulated by Schleiermacher [1959]: "everything in a given text which requires fuller interpretation must be explained and determined exclusively from the linguistic domain common to the author and his original public." (The translation is Hirsch's [1976].) And he explicitly links the ethical responsibilities of interpretation to a recognition of the fact that "interpretation always implies ideology, and is thus never entirely removed from social action." But he has never shown how such concessions can escape effectively undermining his own attempted demarcation between meaning and significance.

The issue has been very actively debated in recent years, largely focused by the dispute between Hirsch and Hans-Georg Gadamer [1975]. Following Heidegger, Gadamer convincingly insists on the "historicity" of human existence and of the textual interpreter's position in particular. The very effort to recover authorial intent, the meaning of a text, the understanding of one's own outlook, depends on the work of a being who is historically "situated" (cf. Heidegger [1962]). One can understand a text—hence, interpret and appropriate it personally—only in terms of one's historically formed expectations regarding a text that has its own historical career. The text, Gadamer claims, links past and present interpreters in a real tradition; hence, by its effect (*Wirkung*) shifting from age to age, it is endowed with a history (*Wirkungsgeschichte*), which both shapes the characteristic way in which we understand a text (*wirkungsgeschichtlichen Bewusstseins:* "hermeneutical consciousness") and provides for the validity and critical correction of that understanding. Gadamer obviously wishes to avoid extreme relativism as well as the "objectivism" of Dilthey and Hirsch; also, the charge of "subjectivism" that Hirsch levels against him. But the fact remains that he never adequately accounts for the logical properties of interpretive judgments, the sense in which truth is preserved (cf. Heidegger [1971]), or the logical conditions of a valid method of hermeneutically informed judgment (*see* Riffaterre [1970]; Fish [1972]; Bloom [1973]; Hoy [1978]).

The Chicago School, rather like Hirsch, is committed in a similar spirit to a kind of pragmatic Aristotelianism, that is, to quasi-Aristotelian literary species and genera that are both useful—among plural systems of historical alternatives—and seemingly "real" (Olson [1952]). The hedging of the movement is well-known (Vivas [1963]; Wimsatt [1954]). But the genre problem remains essential for historical criticism. Whatever his early sympathies for a sort of Aristotelian essentialism, R. S. Crane [1967] has put the matter quite clearly:

> [The critic] must be a philosopher to the extent of possessing a general dialectical schematism appropriate to the discussion of any kind of discourse. This alone will enable him to give definition and compendency to his qualitative terms and will guide him in applying them to writers and works. An indefinite number of such schematisms is possible in criticism and literary history, since the structure of terms in any one of them is determined not by inductive investigation into the natures of works as particular kinds of concrete objects but by a logically prior analogizing of poetry to something else . . . The variety of available analogues for poetry (as for anything else) is without predictable limit, and thus there will always be a "new criticism" with every new generation if not with every new critic. Once the analogue is determined, however, the common necessities of the dialectical method begin to operate.

If I understand this correctly, I agree with it: the critic, holding a particular theory and interest in literary art, imposes, with whatever ingenuity he can command (both Crane and Hirsch testify to the facility of the game), a relatively total classificatory scheme for his range of specimens. The distinctions of genres, periods, styles, and other familiar historical categories are never found, but only invented to service a *given* critical interest; they are never inductively confirmed, but they exhibit a certain systematic usefulness and are replaceable by alternative schemes, perspectives, and interests. Once a system of categories is provided with methods for confirming particular claims, we pronounce with confidence that, for instance, this is Baroque and that is an epic—within the system servicing these or those interests (cf. Guillén [1968]; also Lévi-Strauss [1966]).

It is easy to be misled here. Two distinct theorems are at stake. First, there is no formulable respect in which *any* system of fundamental categories can be said to be discovered—as if nature (or art as a special division within nature), contacted without the benefit or prejudice of language, might nevertheless exhibit certain essential or "natural cuts" by which to confirm (whatever that might mean) the correspondence between linguistic distinctions and the inherent structure of nature. This issue is one of the most profound concerns of earlier twentieth-century philosophy, notably central in the work of Ludwig Wittgenstein [1953]. The import of this on our issue is elementary: no distinction of genres, periods, art forms, styles and the like can be supposed to be discovered in any sense which some suitably selected alternative but nonequivalent system of categories could not properly displace (cf. Quine [1960]; Putnam [1975a]).

The second theorem is even more important: the proposal of any classificatory system (including historically oriented systems) can be made only with respect to a range of items independently identified against the background of categories embedded in a given language, and can be justified only in terms of some governing interest or purpose. For purposes of certain sorts—but not for others—it is possible to test classificatory proposals (or, alternatively, the classificatory judgments they subtend) as true or false. For example, *if* one attempts to classify living organisms in a way that is in accord with evolutionary and genetic theory, then the judgment that a whale is a fish (or the proposal to classify whales as fish) is false or inappropriate. The purpose of classifying in the biological domain is to bring descriptive categories into agreement with our causal explanations of relevant phenomena. The single most important difference between such classificatory proposals and those affecting literary criticism is simply that the underlying interest in criticism is *not* causal in any comparable sense, that is, it is not tied to certain predictive and causally explanatory accounts. In fact, it is extremely difficult to say *what* the governing purpose is in the context of criticism—which is why so many *meta*critical disputes are utterly idle and worthless: there is no straightforward sense in which competing classificatory schemes may be shown to be truer, more correct, or more fitting for the *purpose* critics share; the pretension that there is such a sense is simply a form of circular confidence (cf. Margolis [1975c]).

The nature and importance of the problem may be readily seen by scanning some well-known views of Northrop Frye [1957]:

> It occurs to me that literary criticism is now in such a state of naive induction as we find in a primitive science. Its materials, the masterpieces of literature, are not yet regarded as phenomena to be explained in terms of a conceptual framework which criticism alone possesses. They are still regarded as somehow constituting the framework or structure of criticism as well. I suggest that it is time for criticism to leap to a new ground from which it can discover what the organizing or containing forms of its conceptual framework are.

Frye speaks of a "first postulate of this inductive leap [as] the same as that of any science: the assumption of total coherence." In particular, speaking of science, Frye emphasizes "the causal," "the systematic," and whatever may safeguard "the integrity of [the] subject from external invasion"; the implication is that the classificatory schemes of literary criticism may develop conformably. He speaks approvingly of Aristotle's approaching poetry "as a biologist would approach a system of organisms, picking out its genera and species, formulating the broad laws of literary experience." Although the critical theorist must "remov[e] all external goals from literature, thus postulating a self-contained literary universe," Frye claims, without explanation, that "one of the tasks of criticism is that of the recovery of function, not of course the restoration of an original function, which is out of the question, but the *recreation of function in a new context*" [italics added]. Frye assumes that there *are* identifiable literary "organisms," not just literary texts, that may be sorted once one adopts the aesthetic point of view—which presumably yields an ideal classification (along "functional" lines) in the service of some causal theory somehow akin to biological theories. Speaking frankly, this is complete nonsense. There is no logical connection between critical classification (the details of Frye's monomyth) and any theory of critical explanation that would justify *testing the truth* of particular proposals analogously with testing classificatory hypotheses in biology. For one thing, there is no clear sense, as we have seen, in which artworks *are* proper analogues of physical objects. For another, there is no assignable purpose that an insistence on the "aesthetic point of view" isolates, in terms of which *any* classificatory proposal could be tested; arguments about such a purpose are merely camouflaged arguments about *what* literary criticism is concerned to discuss. Nothing is clarified by Frye's insisting that "removing all external goals from literature" preserves some distinctively aesthetic point of view; or by claiming, on the contrary, that F.R. Leavis [1948] has captured it properly in speaking of "the major novelists who count in the same way as the major poets, in the sense that they not only change the possibilities of the art for practitioners and readers, but they are significant in terms of the human awareness they promote; awareness of the possibilities of life." (A similar objection applies, with even more force, against the views of the structuralists; for they assume, ignoring the contingencies of historically generated artworks, that there is some timelessly exhaustive scheme of genres, styles, art forms, or the like to which particular artworks must converge. But they explain neither how such a scheme can be justified without reference to cultural contingencies nor what it would mean to formulate an exhaustive and relevant system of critical categories without attention to the particular, shifting, and variable interests of historically focused criticism; cf. Culler [1975]; Lévi-Strauss [1969a].)

There is, in fact, a certain irony (and convergence) underlying the accounts of Frye and Leavis. Frye admits that he "takes certain literary values for granted, as fully established by critical experience," though "not a shred of systematic criticism" depends on value judgments, which are merely "subjective." Apart from the naiveté of his theory of values, Frye relies on the so-called aesthetic point of view to identify the total range of literary works (unified by a Jungian monomyth *manqué*), with respect to which his "inductive" techniques are supposed to find the governing laws. He actually believes that his system constitutes an initial induction that subsequent critical *science* will refine and confirm (cf. Wimsatt [1966]; Fletcher [1966]). On the other hand, Leavis frankly admits that, as a critic, he is chiefly devoted to clarifying what he calls "the great tradition": that "there *is*—and this is the point—an English tradition, and these great classics of English fiction [his preferences] belong to it; a tradition that, in the talk about 'creating characters' and 'creating worlds,' and the appreciation of Trollope and Mrs. Gaskell and Thackeray and Meredith and Hardy and Virginia Woolf, appears to go unrecognized." In this respect, not unlike Tolstoy, Leavis's own taste and historical perspective dictate his systematic appreciation of fiction: his confidence in the objectivity with which one ranks an artist's "awareness of the possibilities of life" (the "discovery" of the tradition itself) assures him that his own distinctions (despite his opposition to abstract critical categories) are rooted in an objective order of art. Of course, the critical practices of both Frye and Leavis may be preserved as alternative ways of describing and interpreting texts as literature—in the service of alternative tastes and alternative systematic interests. But neither has discovered the true system of genres. It is only the persistence of certain systematic interests that creates the illusion of the inevitability of distinct categories, which (to borrow from Lévi-Strauss) have "made it" socially (cf. Gardner [1959]). As Wellek and Warren [1954] have observed, some genres—for instance William Empson's formulation of the "pastoral" [1935]—do not even have a distinct or dense historical continuity in their favor, but only a certain utility in making comparative studies. They also acknowledge that "period" concepts may be expanded into concepts of psychological and artistic types and are "detachable from [their] historical context"; that "an individual work of art is not an instance of a class, but a part which, together with . . . other works, makes up the concept of a period . . . thus itself modif[ying] the concept of the whole" (cf. Schapiro [1973]).

This is not to say, however, that causal laws of historical change are conceptually impossible. They may be possible, though there is good reason to believe that, in the cultural disciplines, "covering institutions" rather than covering laws may be the best that we can expect (cf. Margolis [1978a], [1978b]). The Marxist account is perhaps the most obvious candidate, though, in my opinion, it is impossible to distinguish its pretended confirmation of detailed social hypotheses and its exhibition, by reference to social events, of the coherence and scope of its own values. The dialectical laws of historical change are simply nonsense, though the doctrine of economic determinism is not (Popper [1957]).

If such a theory were relatively well-confirmed, a classificatory hypothesis about literature might be confirmable also, as congruent with the governing causal theory—in the sense in which the binomial classification of plants and animals is made congruent with developing genetic and evolutionary theory. On the other hand, *if* literary works cannot be treated as organisms, and *if* our aesthetic interest in them is not primarily causal, then, although the categories of Marxist explanation may well enrich the repertory with which critics examine particular works, the favored divisions of cultural history could not be expected to determine the objective categories of criticism—as if to say that the study of the causes of cultural history were equivalent to a study of the causes for an artwork's being the kind of entity it is and exhibiting the kind of aesthetic value it does. Lukács [1964] illustrates these dual tendencies most clearly. For, though he insists that "Marxism has a grasp of the main lines of human development and recognizes its laws," he also says that "the central aesthetic problem of realism is the adequate presentation of the complete human personality." By this, he means that

> the central category and criterion of realist literature is the type . . . in [which] all the humanly and socially essential determinants are present on their highest level of development, in the ultimate unfolding of the possibilities latent in them, in extreme presentation of their extremes, rendering concrete the peaks and limits of men and epochs.

Here, an initially causal theory of social history is (understandably) transformed into a moral criticism of literature (cf. Weimann [1964]).

There is a sense of "interpret" that should at least be mentioned in this account, in which a critic interprets a work in the Freudian or Marxist manner (cf. Arvon [1973]; *Art and Society* [1968]; Zis [1977]; Hauser [1963]) or in the manner of an historian of culture. There is an important ambivalence here. A Freudian might, for instance, function well as a literary critic, arguing ingeniously for an interpretation of *Alice in Wonderland* (Empson [1935]). But he might also use his interpretation, together with other biographical materials, to psychoanalyze Lewis Carroll. The sense of "interpret" appropriate to his second effort is not aesthetically relevant, on any reasonable view; the first has already been provided for. The second supposes that an adequate account of the work has been given; the first contributes to such an account. Freud, it may be recalled, was much exercised to learn whether Wilhelm Jensen, author of *Gradiva,* was an amateur psychoanalyst or a possible client [1917]. But Freud does offer a psychoanalytic interpretation of Jensen's story. On the other hand, his interpretation of Leonardo da Vinci [1947] is, even with the advantage of biographical materials, flatly unacceptable on *critical* grounds, however ingenious and compelling it may appear from the psychoanalytic point of view (Schapiro [1956]; cf. Kris [1952]).

There remains, nevertheless, the possibility that interpretations of a work are, at the same time, interpretations of what an artist has done in producing his work. We have provided for this possibility by rejecting the theory that artworks are primarily perceptual objects and by favoring their status as culturally emergent entities. Also, if we think of art as an artist's effort, of what in a sense he has "uttered," we cannot fail to see that conflating the two senses of "interpret" just considered obscures the relevance of biographical and historical materials in rendering an "aesthetic" account of a given work. This is especially pertinent when we speak of a work's expressing an artist's convictions and beliefs (cf. Sircello [1972]; Casey [1966]). But, for the moment, we may note that, as far as interpretation is concerned, the usual disjunction between the aesthetic and the moral (cf. Hampshire [1954]) is both pointless and indefensible—if not offensive.

7. The Logic of Interpretation

It is difficult to decide what is admissible in interpretation. We surely do not wish to admit every reverie or outburst, but antecedent restrictions are very nearly impossible to agree upon. Suppose, for example, I interpret Voltaire's *Candide* by relating the action of the tale not merely to the superficial and obviously intended correspondences with Leibniz's philosophy, but also to the introspective enterprises of Descartes, of the Reformers, or of Hamlet; suppose I claim it to be aesthetically instructive to compare the plan of the tale with *Genesis* and with the *Odyssey*; or suppose I find it helpful to consider its theme in comparison with *Gulliver's Travels* and with the French and American Revolutions. When will my comments be irrelevant, with respect to providing a critical account of the work? Suppose I happen to read Plotinus just before I reread Wallace Stevens's *Sunday Morning* and find the poem considerably illuminated by the specific philosophical imagery of the *Enneads,* though I have not the slightest idea whether or not Stevens had the work in mind. (Clearly, purely descriptive predications, such as matters of style, may be valid "whether or not the artist . . . is even aware of them" [Goodman ([1975])].) Are my comments that depend on these juxtapositions irrelevant?

Let us be clear about the question. It is easily confused with that concerning perceptual aspects, discussed in Wittgenstein's well-known account [1953] of "seeing as," of the "dawning" of an aspect of a thing perceived. (I can imagine that one might say that the analysis of Matisse's *The Piano Lesson* is concerned with the "dawning" of an aspect of the painting. Still, "interpretation," here, is not to be taken in Wittgenstein's sense.) "You only 'see the duck and rabbit aspects,' " he says, "if you are already conversant with the shapes of these two animals. There is no analogous condition for seeing the aspects [of the 'double' cross—which may be seen as a white cross on a black ground and as a black cross on a white ground]." I should not deny that Tchelichew's *Hide and Seek* and Picasso's *Three Musicians* exploit both these kinds of illusions, which are close to what Heinrich Wölfflin [1929] has in mind, in discussing painterly and linear styles (cf. Arnheim [1974]). For instance, Wölfflin says that if one paints a turning wheel, "only when the wheel has been made indistinct does it begin to turn." But if, having seen the *solution* of a picture-*puzzle,* we must say that one has *to interpret* the branches of a tree as a human shape—Wittgenstein's term is *deuten*—we should still fall short of stating the problem in question. Again, Wittgenstein says, "It is possible to take the duck-rabbit simply for the picture of a rabbit, the double cross simply for the picture of a black cross, but not to take the bare triangular figure for the picture of an object that has fallen over. To see this aspect of the triangle demands imagination." Imagination is an advance; but the point is that, in Wittgenstein's illustration, it is *gratuitous.* It is concerned more with: "Imagine that triangle as . . ." (a child, for instance, imagines a chest to be a house) than with: "Would it be plausible to construe this painting thus?"

Wittgenstein is primarily interested in a certain *clicking-into-place* of perception; so the remark becomes relevant: "I can't see it as a . . . *yet.*" The question here is rather: "Could you defend this way of seeing it?" Wittgenstein concludes, "Aspect blindness will be *akin* to the lack of a 'musical ear' " (*see* Scruton [1974]; Ishiguro [1967]; Sartre [1963]). His emphasis is always on an ordinary ability, or familiar incapacity, to spot aspects of things. The issue rests on "the mastery of a technique"; one may say, "You are looking at it *wrong*" [italics added]. So, whereas Wittgensein speaks of getting someone to see something in a certain way, here the emphasis is rather on whether a certain way of seeing something is critically defensible. For Wittgenstein, you may be *doing* something wrong if you are not able to see what is required; here, your *account* of a particular work may be inadmissible. For him, it is basically a perceptual question; here, it is a question of evidence and justification—applying as much to literature as to the visual arts. Also, of course, *if* an interpretation is defensible, there is no reason why the sort of imagination Wittgenstein has in mind cannot be called into play (cf. Tilghman [1966]; Kivy [1973]).

There are other cautions worth repeating. For one thing, we need not suppose that the critic's remarks are solely occupied with describing or interpreting (or evaluating) artworks. When he is analyzing symbols or giving the meaning of an expression, the critic cannot be doing anything that could be simply characterized as describing or interpreting; also, normally, when he refers to his experience of a larger body of art in order to illuminate a particular passage, the critic's work will elude the simpler epithets (cf. Reichert [1977]). Secondly, we must remember that the nature of an artwork does not, on the argument already advanced, permit us to draw a formal demarcation line between what is *in* a work and what is *outside it,* what may be descriptively true of it and what may be imputed to it only interpretively. So it is quite idle to charge, as John Reichert [1977] does, that "To regard criticism as aiming not just at true statements about, but at new perceptions of a literary work, is to admit among the others [other tests of critical accuracy] a purely pragmatic test for its success—with all the tangles that purely pragmatic tests ordinarily entail." Reichert goes on to say, very much in the spirit of Hirsch's thesis [1967]: "One is right . . . to counter the purely pragmatic criterion with the claim that the function of criticism is not merely to let us see the work in some new way, but to let us see it *as it really is,*" to avoid seeing "something in a text that *isn't there.*" "Pragmatic" license is evidently construed as a critical abuse of Wittgenstein's notion of seeing aspects, but Reichert never supplies an operative criterion for determining just when pragmatic license is actually called into play. I should add that to decide that a given comment about a particular work is defensible belongs to the community of practicing critics; I am not here concerned with that. Also, the assignable merit of particular works is logically dependent on the kind of decision I cannot attempt here. I wish to discuss only the sense—and the logical consequences of admitting the sense—in which interpretive statements are taken to be relevant and justifiably included in an effort to clarify the aesthetic design of a particular artwork.

Some of the oddities of critical interpretation may be made clear by the following case in point. William Empson [1935] has sketched very skillfully an ingenious and fairly orthodox Freudian interpretation of *Alice in Wonderland,* an account which has been called (Hyman [1948]) "probably the most completely successful brief Freudian analysis of literature yet written." The first thing to observe is that, writing in 1865, Lewis Carroll was not familiar with Freud's theories and could not have used them deliberately. The second is that a first-rate critic like Empson is not especially bothered by the apparent anachronism (viewing Freudian psychology in a scientifically neutral sense) and, when criticized by his colleagues, is not necessarily criticized for this fault (cf. Daiches [1956]; Olsen [1978]). The third thing to observe, in a way the most interesting, is that the scientific validity of Freudian analysis is never really in question, and that the relevance of Empson's analysis of *Alice* seems to be independent of the scientific issue. That is, bluntly, even if Freudian psychoanalysis were scrapped as false science, even if Empson had wrongly assumed it was true, it would not lose its possible relevance for the interpretation of works of art (*contra* Fraiberg [1960]; cf. Margolis

[1972]). We might, conceivably, devalue an artwork whose design relied on a false theory originally presumed true (though this does not appear to have counted, say, in the evaluation of French pointillism); we might, also, still be able to give a critical account of some work in terms of that theory (though this could not be properly done with the *kind* of theory to which the pointillists were apparently committed). This tolerance strikes us as odd.

The clue to the puzzle is that, though Freudian psychology claims respectable scientific status, the imagery of psychoanalysis is not at all restricted to the boundaries of the accompanying science; on the contrary, it is so much a part of our general culture that the imagination both of artists and of semi-educated persons is saturated with it. We think, see, and imagine in terms of Freudian symbols, not merely because (on the canonical view) our subconscious selves employ them for ulterior ends—a debatable thesis in the science of psychology—but because our conscious selves have assimilated the fascinating perspectives and fictions that Freud invented (cf. Bruner [1956]; Kazin [1959]; Hoffman [1945]; Kris [1952]; W. Phillips [1957]).

This defense of a Freudian interpretation gains some strength if we recognize that it relies on an influential "myth," just as does Jacques Maritain's not uninstructive analysis [1953] of the poetry of Baudelaire and Rimbaud. Maritain would insist on the truth of the Catholic vision. Critics may be inspired by his claim, but the truth of the Catholic "myth" need not be presupposed in the critical effort to interpret a work in accord with the perspective of that "myth." We should otherwise have to give up Dante's *Commedia* if we were at once practicing literary critics and anti-Catholics in a broader intellectual arena. The same argument may be used to support such quasi-scientific doctrines as Marxism and Jungian analytic psychology. These are powerful systems of ideas which, on the one hand, claim to be true about an important sector of the world and which, on the other, have effectively captured a substantial part of society's habits of thinking and seeing. Our aim here is to be hospitable to ideologically divergent views without committing ourselves, in the context of aesthetic concern, to the correctness of any particular ideology—and without precluding, as a matter of personal commitment, a preference for one ideology rather than another. In a sense, our aim is to permit agreement with Karl Marx's emphasis on the historical nature of cultural life without making it necessary to subscribe to the tenets of dialectical materialism. Marx himself [1962] says: "Men make their own history, but they do not make it just as they please; they do not make it under circumstances chosen by themselves but under circumstances directly encountered, given and transmitted from the past." David Horowitz [1969], who cites the passage, construes it as supporting a kind of "conditional determinism." But it is as reasonable to construe Marx's remark as acknowledging the effective role of ideological orientation and, therefore, as providing an unintended basis for defending plural, non-converging interpretations of art (and cultural events) *within certain minimal constraints* (cf. Morawski [1972]). Discount the scientific (and exclusive) pretensions of Marxism (or of any similar system): plural interpretations cannot be avoided. This is emphatically *not* to espouse radical relativism, cognitive nihilism, radical sociology of knowledge, "cognitive atheism" (Hirsch [1976]) or anything of the kind. The theory of interpretation does not preclude the possibility of objective knowledge; on the contrary, it specifies the conditions of a particular (logically quite weak) form of knowledge. It cannot, therefore, be assimilated (*contra* Hirsch) to the conceptual incoherence of radical relativism (cf. Feyerabend [1975]; Kuhn [1970]; Mannheim [1966]). It relies, rather, on the homely truth that cultural phenomena are not only intentionally overdetermined but possess an historical career in which they are seen to favor or assimilate contingent intentional currents. Thus, for example, the perception of West African masks came, with Picasso's *Demoiselles,* to be particularly informed first by the themes of an emerging cubism; but by this time, such associations have either receded or have been entirely dissolved as far as the appreciation of West African art is concerned.

We should expect someone educated in a Buddhist society to construe the design of Western artworks in terms of the "myths" that guide his own imagination. In a way it is inevitable, an admission that may serve perhaps to soften the force of Maritain's quite extraordinary and otherwise perplexingly arrogant comment [1930], which I cannot resist quoting:

> Consider . . . that wherever art, Egyptian, Greek or Chinese, has attained a certain degree of grandeur and purity, it is already Christian, Christian in hope, because every spiritual splendor is a promise and a symbol of the divine harmonies of the Gospel.

Corresponding statements, of course, can be located in the papers of orthodox Freudians and Marxists. Furthermore, the most powerful of these "myths" must affect the very perception and use of cultural traditions. Hence, the prospect of plural, non-converging interpretations is conceptually linked to the barest concession regarding the nature of ar-

tistic media, the changing and variably perceived representational and
symbolic conventions sustained within diverse and shifting cultures. We
cannot, therefore, contrast, with the confidence of Roland Barthes
[1966], "external" and "immanent" criticism: Marxist and Freudian accounts may prove as convincing and as "immanentist" as accounts formulated in terms of a putative existentialist project. Barthes's general
thesis is, however, obviously congenial: the "disposition of a work
toward openness" (*"une disposition de l'oeuvre à l'ouverture"*), that is,
toward plural interpretations, does not depend on the weakness of
readers but on the structure of the work itself. The key issues, often in-
adequately pursued (cf. the dispute between Barthes and Picard [1965]),
remain the following: (i) that the validity of interpretation is conceptually linked to the theory of the nature and determinable boundaries of artworks; (ii) that relativism is not in principle incompatible with a cognitive
conception of interpretation; (iii) that the defense of plural, non-
converging interpretations is not, on cognitive grounds, incoherent.
More fundamentally, of course, the issues must include the following as
well: (iv) that the intentional properties of artworks (and other cultural
phenomena) cannot be restricted to what may be recovered regarding the
psychological states of their creators; (v) that artworks, enduring
through the shifting currents of human history, tend to become linked or
open to being linked to contingent cultural (intentional) themes; (vi) that
the cultural concerns (ideologies and traditions) of earlier societies, or of
earlier phases of our own society, or of societies other than our
own—concerns that inform their work in intentionally pertinent
respects—are themselves identified in accord with the diachronically
shifting intentional distinctions of our own society.

It must not be supposed that criticism is altogether without rigor. I
mean to stress here the tolerance of the professional world of criticism
for a variety of interpretations (cf. Weitz [1964]), though particular
critics characteristically favor exclusive accounts. I am not speaking of
the testing of particular interpretations, though I may at least cite Meyer
Schapiro's masterful sifting [1956] of the defensible and indefensible in
Freud's classic study of Leonardo da Vinci [1947]: Schapiro entertains
the Freudian proposal as initially eligible and tests its competence in the
light of Leonardo's actual work and the art tradition in which it was produced; as a critic, he disqualifies Freud's particular interpretations
without challenging at all the appropriateness of approaching painting
from a Freudian point of view. The point at issue is this: because our
habits of seeing paintings are susceptible to the Freudian perspective—among others—we cannot *a priori* dismiss a Freudian effort to
construe the design of particular paintings in its own characteristic terms;

but when we examine Freud's comments on the *Mona Lisa* or the *Madonna and St. Anne,* the art-critic can claim no professional privileges from the psychoanalyst. The first wishes to demonstrate only that one can "perceive" the design of these paintings through Freudian habits of thought; the second, that important portions of actual human behavior, including the activity of making fine art, may be correctly analyzed by Freudian science. Thus, the sustained museum display of paintings for a population whose sensibilities are known and expected to change substantially with time (and historically qualified experience) confirms the propriety of a generous view of interpretively imputed designs—where, that is, there is in principle no satisfactory demarcation between what is internal and external to particular artworks. Also, artists cannot fail to be aware of the historical variety and contingency of the interpretive traditions through which their work is bound to move. Should we say, then, that their intentions are probably colored by that sensibility?

I submit that, if critical tolerance is such as I have sketched, one can hardly resist the proposition that, in principle, plural, non-converging, even incompatible hypotheses may be defended as interpretations of a given artwork. If it were adopted, of course, it would force us to review the truth status of critical interpretations—which, on the usual model provided for statements of fact, would in some instances have to be taken as contraries. Notice that the thesis does *not* require that no interpretive effort may be construed as descriptive—in the sense that what is *hidden in* a work may be disclosed by some exercise of critical virtuosity, and that what is thus disclosed may be truly ascribed to that work (Beardsley [1970b]); nor does it require that every artwork *must* be interpreted—in the strong sense, namely, exceeding mere description; and it does not require that if a work invites interpretation, it will *always* support plural, equally plausible, non-converging, and incompatible interpretations. It is enough to concede that some artworks support such interpretations, that the nature of art entails the possibility, and that extremely important artworks interest us in just this way. A not unreasonable way of putting the point is this: subject to minimal constraints, interpretation may be ideologically or doctrinally variable.

I have labelled the Freudian thesis, like the Catholic and the Marxist, a "myth" with respect to its relevance for criticism. Though I set no store by the particular term "myth," use of this label is central to my argument and requires some explanation. Other expressions might have been substituted. A related term, for instance, is "archetype"; but though it has been relatively liberated from Jungian psychology, it applies largely to the kind of symbolic image Jung himself originally explored (cf. Frye [1957]; Jung [1928]; Bodkin [1934]; Campbell [1956]). The Marxist notion of "ideology" is similarly restricted (cf. Caudwell [1937]; Thomson [1941]). In context, Hirsch [1976] favors the term "fiction." In the sense intended, even were it in some fair respect scientifically confirmed, the modern atomic theory of matter could provide a myth for criticism. I take it, for instance, that the body of the new Renaissance science generated, in this sense, a myth illuminating part of the design of John Donne's *Anniversary* poems. As I am using the term, a myth is a schema of the imagination which, independently of the scientific status of the propositions it may subtend, is capable of effectively organizing our way of viewing portions of the external world in accord with its distinctions. It goes without saying, therefore, that myth can organize our daydreams and reveries—our private imagination—as well. We know a myth to be objective for criticism, though it may not be so for science, when the habits of thought, perception, and imagination of a society or substantial sub-population—including of course productive artists—are educable in its terms, and when their responses to appropriate stimuli are generally predictable or congruent with such myths. Systematic traditions of belief may serve as our paradigms here. Once such schemata are specified, we may liberalize the range within which competing interpretations may be provided (by conceding the eligibility of more idiosyncratic views). Also, non-doctrinal considerations (already broached), such as of diachronic meaning changes, the incompleteness of musical notation, artists' intentions, overdetermined historical currents and even relatively indeterminate (that is, yet to be determined) intentional trends—within which artists work—cannot but confirm the reasonableness of divergent interpretations.

The issue of divergent interpretations is sometimes posed in terms of the role of imagination in "perceiving" art, rather than in terms of interpretive judgments. This alternative provides an instructive detour. Roger Scruton [1974] offers the following suggestion:

> . . . the relation between "seeing as" and perception mirrors the relation between imagination and belief. "Seeing as" is like an "unasserted" visual experience: it is the embodiment of a thought which, if "asserted," would amount to a genuine perception, just as imagination, if "asserted," amounts to genuine belief.

Imagining, which in the aesthetic context involves "seeing as," will for that reason have "an irreducibly sensuous character" that is *sui generis.*

In fact, Scruton believes, "the 'unasserted' nature of 'seeing as' dictates the structure of aesthetic experience." For our present purpose, we may note especially that (what Scruton calls) "analogical interpretations . . . are subject to the kind of reasoning that produces double aspects. One man can see a work of art as tragic, another as ironical (*Death in Venice*, say), both be able to justify their judgments to each other, and both refer to the same first-order features in doing so." In our own idiom, what this means is that, given the clearly describable features of a work, appreciation may involve attention to properties that must be interpretively imputed to it but cannot be straightforwardly found "in" it, and may in fact involve the defensible ascription of what, on a model of factual truth, would have to be construed as incompatible properties. Scruton adds that the "seeing-as" phenomenon *"accompanies* the hearing or seeing of the work of art . . . is indeed not truly separable from that seeing or hearing." To concede this, however, is emphatically not to agree with Scruton that aesthetic judgments and aesthetic claims do not have a "propositional form." Obviously, Scruton's reason for denying that aesthetic judgments have a propositional form rests with the difficulty he has in sustaining a tolerant view of imagination (or interpretation) consistently with a cognitive model of some sort. Hence, his defense becomes unnecessarily extravagant and he favors some sort of analogue of R. M. Hare's well-known prescriptivism [1952]. Thus he says:

> The affective theory of aesthetic description argues that the acceptance condition of an aesthetic description may not be a belief but may rather be some other mental state which more effectively explains the point of aesthetic description. To agree to an aesthetic description is to 'see its point,' and this 'seeing the point' is to be elucidated in terms of some response or experience that has yet to be described. Hence aesthetic descriptions need not have truth conditions in the strong sense, and to justify them may be to justify an experience and not a belief. This does not mean that aesthetic descriptions are merely arbitrary or 'subjective,' . . . we must separate the concept of objectivity from that of truth . . . .

First of all, one must distinguish the analysis of imagination and "seeing-as" from the analysis of descriptive and interpretive judgments. Secondly, the logical properties of interpretive judgments depend on the conditions under which relevant predicates (imputing properties) are actually employed. Thirdly, that judgments do not take the values "true" and "false" does not entail that such judgments lack a propositional form or are unable to take substitute values of a suitable kind. Scruton's extreme measures, therefore, dramatize the importance of our issue but are hardly inescapable. More recently, Scruton [unpublished] has, in the setting of a somewhat Hegelian account of what is fitting or appropriate, attempted to defend the objectivity of perceiving *gestalt,* intentional, or tertiary properties in architecture. But whether, for instance, Albert Speer's (cf. Speer [1970]) Nazi halls exhibit "grandeur" or only "mock-grandeur," are "exalted" or only "hollow" seems difficult to decide on the basis of an objective or ideologically neutral historical sensibility. Also, the very point of Scruton's thesis requires that *if* such a sensibility obtained then it would be possible to formulate a corresponding judgment capable of being objectively confirmed.

To return to our central theme, the Freudian, the Marxist, and the Catholic myths pervade our experience. Whatever the scientific description of objects and events may be, things appear in the imaginative dimension of experience to be loaded with associations, symbolic import, and even to suffer distortions in characteristic ways. Insofar as these and similar features become clarified and systematic, we may speak of an independent myth, the power of which is seen in its applicability to novel experiences. The strength of these myths is undoubtedly fed by the conviction that they subtend true accounts of some sector of the world, that is, that they are capable of being formulated as a science. They themselves, however, are merely persistent habits of imagination capable of being described by an independent science. In themselves, they presume to be accounts of the human condition; in critical practice, they are merely imaginative schemata of the human condition.

Of course, all myths need not be as elaborate and as large-scale as the Freudian, Marxist, or Catholic visions (cf. Wellek and Warren [1956]). They may be merely formulable convictions that the artist holds. Considered without regard to their truth or falsity, adequacy or inadequacy, in the hands of the critic they may enable us to impute a coherent design to works otherwise defective or puzzling. For example, Gustav Glück [1936] holds that "Brueghel's habit of concealing the real object of a picture and letting it disappear in the surrounding masses may be explained by his opinion of the World, which he considered to be topsy-turvy and wrong-headed, blind to the importance of the most momentous occurrences." There is a clue here, by the way, to the nature of symbolic art. A symbol need not, as Cleanth Brooks and Robert Penn Warren [1950] assert, be "a metaphor from which the first term has been omitted." A symbol works by way of association and, on a convention, quite literally "stands for" something, however metaphoric the *source* of the symbol (*see* Goodman [1968]). Unlike metaphor, it may appear in any of the arts; also, it is specifically invoked by critics to explain certain sorts of otherwise seemingly defective or puzzling designs of works of art, hence, characteristically, it is used in an interpretive context (cf. Sircello [1972]). Metaphor, on the other hand, is (primarily) a form of figurative speech, a literary device, involving a departure from "literal" sense. The difference, then, is not quantitative, as Wellek and Warren suggest; it turns on a difference in logical use. We think of symbols in terms of what they represent; and we think of metaphors in terms of what they mean or how they play with meanings. In the first, we ask what their particular sign function actually is; and in the second, having already conceded words to be signs, we ask only about their particular sense (*see* Hungerland [1958]). In a word, we construe symbols more syntactically; metaphor, more semantically.

Biographical and historical research may make it likely that Brueghel held the view in question; but the adequacy of basing an interpretation of particular paintings upon such a view depends on altogether different considerations. We might conceivably restrict the sources from which eligible interpretations may be drawn, so that a thesis not congruent, say, with the letters of Brueghel would be excluded (cf. Olsen [1978]); but having defined the eligible sources, we have not yet succeeded in providing a justifiable interpretation of any painting based on those sources. We may always, of course, as in the unending body of *Hamlet* criticism (*see* Weitz [1964]), invite interpretations as much dependent on current myths as on those taken to be prevalent during Shakespeare's own day: hence, the eligibility of Ernest Jones's Freudian interpretation of *Hamlet* [1949]. We need not be at a loss to prescribe a measure of rigor in confirming such hypotheses, because, for one thing, every interpretation will have to be compatible with the minimally describable properties of the work in question and because, for another, the most plausible designs will conform to stable, familiar myths or to such as are antecedently rendered eligible on biographical or historical grounds. Isabel Hungerland [1955] suggests (having considered the propriety of historically oriented criticism) that if one's interest centers on aesthetic or artistic excellence, the relevant rule would be to accept "that interpretation which does the best for the work, i.e., which results in the highest rating in the order of worth" (cf. Olsen [1978]). We need only note that such a selection must be made from among interpretations that are otherwise critically adequate, and possibly mutually incompatible; it logically depends, then, on a subsidiary but obviously familiar rule, rather like that of restricting interpretations to the artist's intention. What needs always to be emphasized, of course, is that, in attempting to fix the most reasonable interpretation of a *given* work, we are bound to be speaking of an object that we identify by ascribing elements of a coherent design (intentional elements) *to* something embodied *in* a physical medium. The artwork exists only in a cultural "space"; and in that space, no straightforwa.d analogy obtains by which, as with physical objects, to demarcate what is and what is not "in" a particular artwork. Authorial intent (cf. Hirsch [1967]) cannot be clearly confined to independently specified psychological states, cannot fail to be elastically construed, is normally both overdetermined and relatively indeterminate, may be circularly assigned on the basis of independently validated interpretations, or may correspond to a preferred constraint imposed on otherwise defensible interpretations. By parity of reasoning, what holds for "authorial intent" holds, with equal force, for "historical accuracy."

In effect, what we are conceding is the inclusion of criticism within the larger enterprise of understanding cultural phenomena. In this regard, we are bound to come to grips with at least two of the central themes of philosophical hermeneutics (*see* Dilthey [1913-1967]; Gadamer [1975]; Habermas [1971]): (i) whether the disciplines concerned with the meaning of texts, human behavior, human work and expression are methodologically similar to the natural sciences; and (ii) whether, given that human beings act to recover the meaning and significance of cultural phenomena—under the condition that both they and what they seek to understand are "historically situated" (Gadamer [1975])—they can determine the uniquely correct meaning of what they are interpreting (Hirsch [1967]), or they can determine the inclusive system of rules for the interpretation of any and every relevant phenomenon (Lévi-Strauss [1969b]). The two themes are conceptually linked; for, once the intentional nature of the cultural (and the human) is conceded—which precludes physicalism and similarly reductive programs (*see* Margolis [1978a])—either the accessibility of authorial intent (Hirsch) or the confirmability of a relatively invariant developmental sequence or order of cultural transformations (cf. Piaget [1971]; Barthes [1967b]) strongly supports a revised account of the unity of science.

Philosophically, the most interesting feature of critical interpretation is its tolerance of alternative and seemingly contrary hypotheses. We should not allow incompatible descriptions of any physical object to stand: at least one would require correction, else we should find the disparities due to the different purposes the descriptions were to serve or the different circumstances under which they were rendered. But given the goal of interpretation—the imputation of a coherent design under conditions descriptively insufficient for that purpose—we do not understand that an admissible account necessarily precludes all others incompatible with itself. Although, Stephen Pepper [1955] has always insisted that there is some ideal object of criticism toward which all relevant experiences of a given work converge (cf. Henze [1955], [1957]). Advancing a view similar to that of Monroe Beardsley [1958], more recent writers—Hirsch [1967]; Olsen [1978]; Reichert [1977]—have, in a variety of ways, also favored exclusively correct and comprehensive interpretations; but no one has *shown* why non-converging interpretations cannot be legitimately defended. Olsen [1978] inadvertently provides a useful clue about this lacuna. "To deal with a text as a literary work," he says, "the reader need not attribute any further intentions to the author, for example intentions concerning the 'meaning' of a work. It is one of the rules of the game that the literary work is autonomous in the sense that the understanding of it is independent of the author's interpretation of his own production. The author's literary intentions are expressed in the work." Nevertheless, (i) rather in the manner of Wimsatt's concession previously considered [1954], Olsen is bound to admit that the author's interpretation *is* relevant *if* it may be construed as already expressed in the work; (ii) there is no satisfactory way, as we have seen in examining Hirsch's strong claims [1967], of fixing authorial intent within a work so as to exclude the relevance of changing interpretive schemata; (iii) there is no logical reason why, even if authorial intent may be validly ascribed, that a work may not support plural, non-converging interpretations consistently with such intent; and (iv) there is, as against Wellek [1965] and Wimsatt [1954], no operative sense in which a work is "autonomous," like a "monument" or physical object, so that what is internal and external to, or descriptive and interpretive of, a particular work may, for all ascriptions, be formally distinguished. Essentially, the issue is a conceptual one. There is no doubt that individual critics tend to favor their own interpretations as exclusively correct; they also seem to believe that canons could be formulated, acceptable to the profession, that would vindicate *some* exclusively correct interpretation. But the collective practice of critics shows a distributed tolerance for competing canons—without any loss of rigor.

I should like to suggest an analogue of this curious tolerance in the physical sciences. One sometimes asks, "How was our solar system created?" "How was the moon formed?" "How did life originate?" "Are all the races of man descended from a common stock?" At the present stage of our researches, these questions must be adjusted. For "How was our solar system created?" we substitute "How could it have been created?" For "Are all the races of man descended from a common stock?" we substitute "Is it conceivable that they originated from different evolutionary lines, or, alternatively, from the same evolutionary line?" Questions of this sort do not involve contrary-to-fact conditions. The answers afforded are such that the consequent of our conditional is true (the facts about the present solar system); and the antecedent is meaningful but, under present circumstances, incapable of being verified. We imagine a set of initial conditions, compatible with known laws of nature and operating in accord with selected suitable laws, by means of which we explain certain features of our present world. Some such accounts, like Buffon's hypothesis or the Kant-Laplace hypothesis, may be demonstrably false; the correct account may be unavailable; and in its absence, alternative hypotheses may be entertained in accord with alternatively preferred causal models, without violating any relevant facts. Peirce [1940] has characterized the process as "abduction." The important point is that interpretive judgments applied where, in principle, we cannot say with certainty what is or is not "in" a given work cannot be confirmed in the strong sense in which, normally, causal claims can be. We are restricted there to appraisals of reasonableness or plausibility, which, though relevant as well to a distinct scientific interest (to, say, how to confine research to the most promising lines of inquiry—cf. Polanyi [1962]), do not represent the strongest logical claims that science can relevantly make.

Now, disregarding the possibility of verifying, at some future time, a given hypothesis about the origin of the solar system, we are in a position, at present, to assess the *plausibility* of such a hypothesis; it is even possible to gauge to some extent the degree of plausibility of alternative hypotheses. We have, then, a procedure for determining the plausibility of causal hypotheses that is logically distinct from that of determining their truth. Not altogether dissimilarly, we are able to assign probabilities to contrary propositions, without contradiction; all that we need remember is that, in epistemic contexts, we cannot detach such probabilized propositions from the evidence relative to which they are said to be probable (*see* Hempel [1965]). In aesthetic criticism, correspondingly, we may determine the truth of statements entering into our description of an artwork and we may determine the plausibility of interpretive statements. Just as a hypothesis about the origin of the solar system must accord with known laws and facts of the system, would-be interpretations must accord with the description of a given work and with admissible myths or schemes of imagination. It is emphatically not necessary to hold, for instance with Monroe Beardsley [1970b], that *if* relevant supporting reasons can justify a judgment, that judgment must be such that it "can be true or false." Beardsley concedes as much, though he does not pursue the matter, for he notes that "there might be reasons for making a certain judgment that are not reasons for saying it is true, if it should be the case that judgments cannot be true or false." He mentions P. H. Nowell-Smith's account [1965], purporting to show that even verdictives (in J. L. Austin's sense [1962]), such as estimates, though not usually said to be true or false, nevertheless "surely involve a claim to truth, which may be allowed or disallowed." But he considers no other possibilities. Beardsley's own conviction, obviously, is that interpretations and evaluations *must* be true or false, but he does not show why this must be so. If one insists that all cognitive claims "involve a claim to truth," we actually do meet that condition by conceding that interpretive claims must be compatible with what is (minimally) descriptively true of a given work. That every judgment—taken distributively—must be true or false is an unfounded superstition that Austin for one [1962] (whom Beardsley professes to follow) has effectively exploded. A trim way of pressing the point is this: falsity is opposed not only to truth but to plausibility; there is an epistemic asymmetry in assessing claims of truth and falsity.

The following provide the principal distinctions between the "true" and the "plausible." (i) We invoke plausibility only when we cannot actually determine truth. (ii) No plausible account may be incompatible with an admittedly true statement. (iii) Neither true nor false statements may be viewed as merely plausible or implausible, and neither plausible nor implausible statements are logically precluded from being judged true or false. (iv) Where the statements "P is true" and "Q is true" are contraries, the statements "P is plausible" and "Q is plausible" are not contraries. (v) Statements are judged plausible or implausible in virtue of their use of preferred explanatory models in any given domain. Where such models may be weighted for preferability, and the features of what is to be accounted for also weighted for priority and importance in explanation, the plausibility of the corresponding statements may also be graded. In science, for example, we may be asked to account plausibly for the origin of the moon without assuming the gravitational activity of any body outside our present solar system, but in accord with the density, size, and composition of the moon itself. Correspondingly, in criticism, we may be asked to interpret an artwork in accord with some well-defined myth in a way that gives due prominence to preferred features of the work itself. For example, an interpretation of *Hamlet* must provide an account of Hamlet's "indecision" and must be pitted, dialectically, against the corpus of accumulated interpretations that are themselves considered relatively plausible. Needless to say, explanation in interpretive contexts is normally not construed in causal terms.

Though they are always marginal to the main effort of science, considerations of plausibility are more nearly central to aesthetic criticism. In fact, scientific speculations of the sort illustrated are treated in terms of plausibility only because of a technical inability to gain the desired information; critical interpretations, on the other hand, are logically weak in principle. It is this weakness, probably, that gives the appearance of lack of rigor to critical pronouncements. But to construe the logical weakness of judgments as a lack of rigor in a given discipline is, at the very least, to be unsympathetic to the special interests of that discipline. Furthermore, the reason these judgments are weak depends, as we have argued, on the very nature of an artwork and on the impossibility of providing a principle for demarcating what is and what is not *in* a particular work. If one concedes the point, it becomes quite impossible to show that interpretive judgments *can* be true.

This tolerance does not entail that any artwork can convincingly support plural, non-converging interpretations. It means only that we cannot logically preclude the eligibility of such accounts. In practice, it may well be that only works of certain sorts will support divergent interpretations: possibly T. S. Eliot's poetry can and Ezra Pound's cannot. At any rate, we cannot ask for more precision than the subject will allow.

Critical interpretations, then, are noticeably weaker than statements of fact. But they are weaker logically, not methodologically. There is absolutely no difference in conceptual rigor in defending divergent interpretations and in confirming exclusive physical facts. What is more important, the methods and procedures associated with deciding the latter are flatly inadequate in resolving questions about the former. There is no reason why, granting that criticism proceeds in an orderly way, practices cannot be sustained in which aesthetic designs are rigorously *imputed* to particular works when they cannot be determinately *found in* them. Also, if they may be imputed rather than found, there is no reason why incompatible designs cannot be jointly defended.

It takes little imagination to see that admitting that judgments which are incompatible on the model of assigning truth-values (true and false) may be jointly defended in terms of the assignment of other values is tantamount to the adoption of a *form* of relativism. The entailment is indifferent to context; hence, if defensible, relativism may be extended in every domain of inquiry. For example, it may be extended to evaluative disputes. More ambitiously, it may be extended to moral and ontological disputes, to the interpretation of human history itself, or to theories of explanatory adequacy. It is important to appreciate the generality of the issue, even though the argument is couched here in terms of the special concerns of aesthetic appreciation.

But relativism is a suspect doctrine (cf. Hirsch [1976]). There seems, in fact, to be a simple way to refute it. Construe it as a conservative thesis: that, for some set of judgments, it is not the case that no judgments of that set can in principle be valid (skepticism), or that judgments can be validly defended on one principle only (what Richard Henson [unpublished] has recently termed "universalism"). Assign truth-values, then, to judgments on relativistic grounds and assume that, in relevantly significant disputes, the correct assignment of incompatible truth-values depends on the use of competing (relativistic) "principles." There is no need to attempt to individuate such principles. The point of the exercise is that, on the hypothesis, relativism leads to contradiction, since judgments would then be able to be validly shown to be both true and false.

The argument is impeccable but indecisive—for an elementary reason. Grant only that a putatively relativistic set of judgments lacks truth-values (true and false) but takes values of other sorts, or takes "truth-values" other than true and false. This, of course, is precisely the maneuver we have adopted. It is also possible to hold that judgments are relativized in the sense that every validating "principle" is said to subtend its own sector of judgments and that no two principles have intersecting sectors. This, roughly, is the theme of conventionalism and of subjectivism in values. I. C. Jarvie [1967] treats relativism as entailed by subjectivism, but he does not consider other forms of relativism—though he does distinguish "diversity of evaluation" from "failure to settle disputes," and though he resists inferring subjectivism from such "diversity." But, although conventionalism is a possible strategy, it is quite uninteresting. It fails to admit a range of *competing* claims, by not admitting minimal grounds justifying the joint application of competing principles. It fails, therefore, to admit not only incompatible judgments relative to a particular principle but also "incongruent" judgments—judgments that, construed in terms of truth and falsity, would be incompatible, that are actually not incompatible, and that involve the use of predicates jointly accessible to competing principles. The weaker or conventionalist form of relativism is uninteresting whether truth itself be thought to be relativized to a particular language (*see* Tarski [1944]; Quine [1960]; Davidson [1967]) or whether a restricted range of judgments be thought to be defensible only in terms of some particular convention or "implicit agreement" (Harman [1975]; cf. Trigg [1973]). I suggest that what we want instead is a form of moderate or "robust" relativism. Actually, the requirements of the coherence of interlinguistic communication entail the inadequacy of relativized accounts of truth. Even if ascriptions of "truth" were relativized, we would require a conception of truth that is not language-relative even if what is true can only be formulated in a way subject to the local features of particular languages, and even if the system of beliefs of a society (including its beliefs about the meanings of what may be said) changes diachronically. Radical relativism regarding truth, meaning, consistency, and knowledge cannot but be incoherent (*contra* Feyerabend [1975]; cf. Lukes [1974]); for, wherever alternative doctrines, theories, claims, or judgments are construed as debatable, we implicitly commit ourselves to their joint intelligibility and testability. In this sense, we cannot relativize meaning and truth, even if our actual criteria and procedures for determining particular meanings and particular truths are open to revision. But the indefensibility of radical relativism does not entail the indefensibility of all forms of relativism; and the denial that a particular kind of judgment (for instance, interpretive judgments) can be flatly true or false, or reliably known to be true or false, does not at all entail radical relativism (*contra* Hirsch [1976]). On the contrary, interpretive (also: appreciative, evaluative, ideological) judgments are conceptually dependent on a range of considerations that cannot be relativized in the same way.

The distinction of a robust relativism, then, includes the following necessary constraints: (1) the rejection of skepticism and universalism for a given set of judgments; (2) the provision that such a set of judgments takes values other than truth and falsity and includes incongruent judgments; (3) the rejection of cognitivism—entailed by (2) in any case—that we possess a matching cognitive faculty (perception or intuition for instance) the normal exercise of which enables us to make veridical discriminations of the presence or absence of the properties designated (cf. Margolis [1975b]); (4) the admission of the joint relevance of competing principles in validating the ascriptions or appraisals in question, that is, the admission of some theory explaining such tolerance—entailed by (2). On reflection, these four conditions appear to be sufficient as well as necessary. They are, in any case, jointly compatible and undercut what may fairly be taken to be the least specialized attack on relativism. Of course, it is not entailed by the above that *all* judgments (taken collectively) be defensibly construed as behaving relativistically. That would require construing truth relativistically and would be tantamount to retreating to a radical version of the weaker sense of relativism. But it may be insisted that a further condition (5) should be appended, namely, that relativistic sets of judgments presuppose some range of non-relativistic judgments, or that relativistic judgments are dependent on there being some viable range of non-relativistic judgments. I take (5) to be entailed by (1); still, the provision precludes the possible embarrassment of conceding that we may say that it is *true* that relativistic judgments ("incongruent" in the sense supplied) do have the values (other than true and false) that they are said to have. It may also be claimed that genuinely relativistic theories should be distinguished sharply from theories that merely admit that the validity of any range of judgments is relative to the supporting evidence, or to the supporting considerations on which that is said to depend. So a further condition (6) may be required, namely, that a set of judgments is relativistic if their validation is determined by considerations bearing on the sensibilities or epistemic states of those who relevantly judge. (This may in fact be the fair sense of the relativistic interpretation of Protagoras's dictum.) But (6) appears to be entailed by (2). Hence, a robust relativism need not reduce to subjectivism, since not only can supporting reasons be supplied and demanded, but also the validity of relevant judgments may actually be confirmed. I am, therefore, proposing a middle ground between skepticism, conventionalism, and subjectivism, on the one hand, and universalism, cognitivism, and absolutism, on the other (cf. Peter Winch [1970] and I. C. Jarvie [1970]). What I am calling a robust relativism entails that there be certain minimal constraints—in terms of what is simply true and false—that relativistic judgments must accommodate. To put the issue this way shows that it is quite insufficient to say merely that interpretation is "indeterminate" (as not being true or false). The fact is that epistemic values of some sort can be assigned interpretations. It is true that interpretive judgments exhibit, as Robert Matthews argues [1977], "epistemic weakness" (cf. Dutton [1977]); but to be "indeterminate" with respect to truth and falsity is not to be epistemically indeterminate. On the contrary, it is in virtue of our theory of artworks that we disallow ascriptions of truth and falsity to particular claims *and* require that interpretations meet criteria of critical plausibility—which entail (a) compatibility with the describable features of given artworks and (b) conformability with relativized canons of interpretation that themselves fall within the tolerance of an historically continuous tradition of interpretation.

A final word about "incompatible" and "plausible" may be in order. Incompatibles cannot be jointly true. There is, however, nothing logically odd about admitting, relative to a certain body of evidence that "In six months, Nixon will be president" and "In six months, Nixon won't be president" are both plausible though they cannot both be true. In context, this means that *the states of affairs* that would make either true cannot jointly obtain, though the *evidence* or *supporting reasons* available for each (which is the only relevant consideration bearing on plausibility—or probability) validates the judgment. Considerations of plausibility and probability, then, concern epistemic constraints on propositions; considerations of truth do not. Here, incidentally, is a strong reason for not treating the statement "In six months, Nixon will be president" as equivalent either to "It is true that, in six months, Nixon will be president" or to "It is plausible that, in six months, Nixon will be president." Though the plausibility of each of the pair of statements about Nixon may be affected by the plausibility of the other, they may be *jointly* plausible—though it is obviously not plausible (it is impossible) to maintain the *conjunction* of those statements. Our proposal, therefore, does not violate any of the usual logical constraints. Thus, musical interpretations A and B of Brahms's *Fourth Symphony* or literary interpretations A and B of *Hamlet* are incompatible in the straightforward sense that there is no interpretation C in which A and B can be combined. But *that* is not to say that A and B cannot both be plausible. (The equivocation on "A" and "B" is benign enough.) When, therefore, I say that "we allow seemingly incompatible accounts of a given work . . . to stand as confirmed," I mean to draw attention (*contra* Barnes [1976]) to the fact that the accounts in question would be incompatible construed in terms of a model of truth and falsity, but are *not* incompatible construed in terms of plausibility. We have, then, succeeded in showing the coherence of a critical practice that tolerates the joint defensibility of interpretive judgments that, on a model of truth and falsity, would be incompatibles. And we have shown both that such a model is favored by independent considerations regarding the very nature of artworks and that there are no compelling counterproposals among its best-known opponents.

8. The Intention of the Artist

"Is the meaning of a poem the meaning the poet intended it to have?" (Redpath [1957]). We ask this sort of question in a variety of ways about all the arts. One of its targets is the loose-jointed interpretation of artworks that seems otherwise in luck of failing to be challenged. The question also points to elaborate conceptions about the artist's creative life, including philosophical theories of the artistic moment (cf. Croce [1922]; Collingwood [1938]; Maritain [1953]; Nahm [1956]). Sometimes, the issue is rendered platonistically. For instance, Carl Hausman [1975] holds that "An object that has Novelty Proper instances a different structure and Form. It exhibits a new structure which newly exemplifies a Form . . . Novelty Proper appears with the first exemplification of a Form." But creativity has also been managed in an empiricist spirit (cf. Scruton [1974]) and, in particular, in psychoanalytic terms (cf. Bergler [1950]; Baudouin [1924]; Kris [1952]; Trilling [1950b]; Caudwell [1937]). I must ignore creativity here as being of more psychological than philosophical interest. The chief aesthetic issue it raises concerns the problem of expression already briefly remarked. In a larger context, it suggests the general problem of universals, of the creativity involved in extending the application of categories to cases beyond whatever may have originally served as their paradigms (*see* Strawson [1970]; cf. Margolis [forthcoming]). This is a vexed issue, not narrowly illuminated by the problem of artistic creation and not likely to bear in a pointed way on the critical relevance of artists' intentions.

I can recall, to offer an instance by which to fix our question, attempting to retail a very ingenious interpretation of Tennessee Williams's *A Streetcar Named Desire,* suggested by a friend, to the effect that the play involved an inversion of Plato's Myth of the Cave. The streetcar's name, the locale (a district called Elysian Fields), the division of Stella Kowalski's apartment—particularly the interior bath—the names Stella and Blanche themselves, the glaring electric light in the outer room and the colored light of the interior room, the presence of a second story that only Stella ascends to, the remembered plantation Belle Reve, a blind woman selling artificial flowers for the dead, the emphasis on make-believe, and a thousand other such details all fall into place convincingly with this superstructure provided. My audience was incredulous, taking a very dim view of Williams's classical interests. (Since that time, Williams wrote a play specifically titled *Orpheus Descending*. Does our effort to see an artist's entire production as thematically unified constitute a sort of intentionalistic criticism? Cf. Stevenson [1962]; Reichert [1977].) I was urged to send the account to Williams himself to "settle the matter"—not, however, without some misgivings among the company, since it appeared possible that Williams might only too happily seize upon the interpretation as according with his own intention. The point is that my audience had to concede that Williams might have intended his play to be taken in the way in which I was interpreting it, and they were prepared to allow it or disallow it on suitable evidence concerning Williams's actual intention; that is, they had satisfied themselves that the interpretation was otherwise plausible (cf. Hirsch [1976]; *contra* Reichert [1977]); they were now raising an additional requirement: a correct interpretation must also accord with the artist's intention.

Other related possibilities come to mind. Suppose I had offered my friends an interpretation of *Beowulf*, based on certain similarities between it and the Biblical tales of the angels' visitation to Lot and the trial of Jonah, or even based on certain similarities between it and the remarkable Japanese motion picture *Ugetsu* (whose sources I know nothing whatever about). I should have been willing to concede that the author of *Beowulf* did not intend or, even, could not have intended, his poem to be construed in these ways. I can very well imagine that, though my audience might have had misgivings about entertaining any interpretation for which the intent of the artist was antecedently ruled out, they would nevertheless have been willing to assess my account on more modest canons of plausibility. We might, in short, have agreed to assess alternative interpretations without appeal to the alleged intentions of the artist.

Artists, we may note, are quite frequently prepared to consider the plausibility of interpretations not necessarily in accord with their intentions, that is, with what they take to have been their explicit intentions (cf. Eliot [1956]; Kris [1952]). Herman Melville (Tindall [1955]), for instance, writing about *Moby Dick* to Mrs. Nathaniel Hawthorne, remarks:

Your allusion for example to the "Spirit Spout" first showed to me that there was a subtle significance in that thing—but I did not, in that case, *mean* it. I had some vague idea while writing it, that the whole book was susceptible of an allegoric construction and also that *parts* of it were—but the specificity of many of the particular subordinate allegories were first revealed to me, after reading Mr. Hawthorne's letter, which without citing any particular examples, yet intimated the part-&-parcel allegoricalness of the whole.

Wellek and Warren [1956], it may be remembered, maintain that "The meaning of a work of art is not exhausted by, or even equivalent to, its intention. As a system of values, it leads an independent life." Suppose, however, I had just discovered certain of Chekhov's letters in which the dramatist tells us quite clearly what his intentions regarding the production of several of his plays were—that he wanted to have them played as comedies and that Stanislavski quite willfully directed them as tragedies (*see* Margashak [1952], [1950]). I think we should be interested, but we should undoubtedly ask ourselves, "Could these plays actually be mounted as comedies (or tragedies)?" That is, we should be asking whether there were reasons internal to a given play that would have made a comic (or tragic) interpretation improbable, impossible, or puzzling. For example, suppose that in one of the plays there was a particularly brutal murder that could not conceivably be softened by any reading of the text or by following any of Chekhov's suggestions for a comic staging. We should be asking whether the comic interpretation, though perhaps not improbable, would incline us to devalue the play.

Even if we should have clear evidence of the artist's intention, in the sense, say, of an *independent* document or independent testimony, we should assess the plausibility of a given interpretation by appeal to critical canons not bound to that intention; hence, the criterion of the artist's intention *in this sense* would be supplementary at best. For example, we might conclude that Chekhov's interpretations of his own plays "trivialized" them, though Stanislavski's were not "accurate." But this does *not* mean that the initially decisive canons would or could be restricted to what may straightforwardly be found "in" the work. Reference to an independent document *is* reference to external evidence. But reference to an artist's intention *in* an actually produced work requires locating that work in the wider intentional life of a culture: merely to ascribe an intention to a work—for instance, merely to ascribe meaning, symbolic import, expressiveness, or representational function—is to construe a certain physical object or medium as embodying an object (an artwork) that organizes a set of purposive (intentional) "strokes" into an articulate design. There is no other way to posit the work itself. There is, then, no way in which an "autonomous" object—the artwork—can be antecedently identified, so that evidence of authorial intentions can somehow be found directly *in it.* The point is obscured, for instance, in Wimsatt's relatively recent review of the issue [1968]:

> To speak broadly and to avoid the simplicity of one-word labels (or to defer the economy of such labels), let us say that an art work is something which emerges from the private, individual, dynamic, and intentionalistic realm of its maker's mind and personality; it is in a sense (and this is especially true of the verbal work of art) made of intentions or intentionalistic material. But at the same time, in the moment it emerges, it enters a public and in a certain clear sense an objective realm; it claims and gets attention from an audience; it invites and receives discussion, about its meaning and value, in an idiom of inter-subjectivity and conceptualization. If the art work has emerged at all from the artist's private world, it has emerged into some kind of universal world.

Against this way of speaking, we may note the following: (i) the "private" world of the artist must be continuous with and informed by the "public" world his work "enters"; (ii) if it is "made" (privately) of "intentionalistic material," a work cannot fail to be examined (publicly) in terms of that material; (iii) making and appreciating art requires complementary efforts regarding how intentional materials can be embodied in some physical medium; hence (iv) there is not, and cannot be, a fundamental methodological difference between the grounds on which the intentional materials of a particular work, and those of the *artist's* intentions or intentional life, can be specified. What clarifies the intentional attributes of a given work remains a fair question; but the resolution of that question cannot possibly be managed in terms of a demarcation between what is intentionally "internal" and "external" to that work. Wimsatt rejects this as the "Genetic Fallacy"; but he fails to see that the issue rests not with the public and private aspects of an artist's intentions, but with the peculiar properties of an artwork, with the conditions on which it is posited or recognized. He does acknowledge that "verbal compositions do not subsist metaphysically, by or in themselves, as visual words on paper. The difference between 'inside' the poem and 'outside' the poem . . . is not like the difference between the printed words and the margin of the page. But neither are verbal compositions merely passing acts or moments of the human spirit, sounds heard then or now but not again.'' True enough, but how, one may ask, does this show that ''extratextual'' materials (cf. Reichert [1977]; Culler [1975]) may not, for the interval in which a poet actually writes, inform us of what we judge to be ''in'' the work—in a way that could not be independently and exclusively otherwise discerned?

Let me put all of this a little more pointedly. If we are interested in knowing how a given work may be plausibly interpreted, then the importance and relevance of what we call the artist's intention depend jointly on (i) how generously ''intention'' and the manifestations of the artist's intentions are construed, and (ii) the actual properties that interpretations are to accommodate. There are properties of artworks that are intentional in the straightforward sense in which representational, symbolic, and semantic properties are intentional; but to discriminate such properties may, on a theory, be tantamount to determining the artist's intention, *and then,* independent evidence regarding the artist's intention (his probable psychological states—including his probable attitude regarding meanings, symbols and the like) may pertinently inform our grasp of such properties (cf. Hermerén [1977]; Black [1972]). For example, ''intention'' may be so broadly construed that to consult the art tradition in which a work is produced entails consulting the artist's intention. It is hardly possible that any serious conception of a critic's work would dismiss the relevance of the ''art-historical'' context in which a particular artwork was produced; but if so, then certain well-known quarrels about the artist's intention are bound to be quite pointless. In particular, what is critically vindicated will be taken to be ''internal'' to the work: what is ''internal'' will not be independently accessible. If an ''independent'' document clarifies a favored interpretation, its contribution will be caught up in the history that is supposed to yield ''internal'' evidence (cf. Wimsatt and Beardsley [1954a]). Similarly, ''intention'' may be so construed that to consult the meaning of some literary passage entails consulting the artist's intention in a psychological sense otherwise thought to yield ''external'' evidence (cf. Grice [1957]; also, Hungerland [1955]; Kaplan and Kris [1948]; Panofsky [1938]; MacIntyre [1958]). There are also said to be expressive properties, especially those ascribable to artworks that cannot be understood except in terms of what the artist expressed about his own convictions and feelings in producing his work (*see* Sircello [1972]); if so, then the critical elucidation of such properties (involving ''external'' evidence of the artist's intention) cannot be denied relevance, on pain of failing to accommodate an artwork's actual properties.

It is possible that the only quarrelsome use of the artist's intention concerns appealing to *independent* evidence of his intention in order to *reduce* the number of otherwise eligible interpretations (even those that inherently involve the artist's intention in the senses already sketched); for, *if* intentional properties of the sorts mentioned are conceded, then the critic's reference to independent evidence bearing on *certain* of the artist's intentions, those that involve fixing the properties in question, cannot possibly be disallowed. The implications for a theory of aesthetic perception and of the nature of a work of art are obvious. On the other hand, if we are appraising artworks already plausibly interpreted, the merit of the work may conceivably vary with the interpretations admitted, but in a way that is completely indifferent to the choice or source of criteria by which they are admitted (*a fortiori,* completely indifferent to their being admitted on grounds of the artist's intention). The only conceivable use for appeal to the artist's intention—when that intention is fixed *altogether independently* of the work in question—is in assessing what may be called "accurate," "historically correct," or "the original" conceptions of particular works of art (cf. Hungerland [1955]; Panofsky [1938]; Wellek and Warren [1956]). There are, however, cases in which the artist's intention is fixed only *partially* by consulting his work; in such cases, independent evidence bears on characterizing the properties of the work to be appraised.

These qualifications suggest an important enlargement of our account. Appeal to the artist's intention is made not only in deciding questions of interpretation—in a sense appropriate to non-performing arts; one may also ask, for instance, what Shakespeare's intention was regarding the staging of *Henry V.* I think this question can only mean, under the circumstances, how was or how could *Henry V* have been staged in Shakespeare's time? On the other hand, if one asks what was George Bernard Shaw's intention regarding the staging of *Major Barbara,* part of the answer will be given in terms of what Shaw *wrote* in the way of stage instructions in the actual text.

We begin to see that the bearing of the artist's intention may vary considerably with the different arts. Music is in a special position. The composer typically bequeaths us a score, which provides not only his notation (notes, key, time, and so forth), but also more detailed directions for the performance of his piece (*dim., ff.,* ped., and so forth). Clearly, the difference between the musical notation and instructions may be open to considerable quarrel. Elements that, on one view, count as part of the score may, on another, be judged part of the instructions that merely accompany the score. Because he construes a score as serving essentially to identify a musical work from performance to performance, Nelson Goodman [1968], as we have already observed, holds that "tempo words cannot be parts of a score [that is, cannot be notational]." But if (as we have also seen) the identity of a musical composition is manageable without adhering to Goodman's severe view of notationality, *and* if one holds that compliance with the composer's instructions is a necessary condition of correct performance, then even seemingly casual instructions would have to be construed as notational: the artist's externally accessible intentions would then become aesthetically critical to the work in question in spite of the fact that scores are not artworks. We need not hold so strict a view. But there is no doubt that the appraisal of a musical performance is regularly made with an eye to the composer's intention—in a sense in which the "internal"/"external" distinction seems particularly inapt; the admission of notations and scores entails the impossibility of excluding altogether the aesthetic relevance of "external" evidence of intentions. Any theory of language and literature that stresses speakers' intentions in utterance and speech act is bound to lead to a related conclusion. Also, by an easy analogy, a painting or sculpture may, at least sometimes, be construed as an (expressive) "utterance," or an object produced by an "uttering" act (cf. Casey [1966]; Abrams [1972]). (This, of course, is the essential theme of the romantic theory of art.) If so, questions of the artist's intention will inevitably intrude. The complexity of this question may be illustrated by citing the following examples provided by Guy Sircello [1972]:

(1) In the unfinished Rondantini Pietà, Michelangelo expressed his final judgment about man and his condition, namely, that he is a helpless creature utterly dependent upon God.

(2) The Eve panel in the Uffizi expresses Cranach's idea of the essence of woman, i.e., that she is a beguilingly beautiful temptress and seductress.

(3) In *Dr. Faustus* Thomas Mann expresses his view of the German national character, to wit, that it is torn by a tragic tension between the humane and orderly, on the one hand, and the demonic, on the other.

(4) Praxiteles expresses in his Hermes the classic Greek notion that man is a beautiful and dignified creature.

(a) *La Belle Jardinière* is calm and serene partly because Raphael *views* his subject calmly and quietly.

(b) *The Rape of the Sabine Women* is aloof and detached because Poussin calmly *observes* the violent scene and *paints* it in an aloof, detached way.

   (c) *Wedding Dance in the Open Air* is an ironic painting because Breughel *treats* the gaiety of the wedding scene ironically.

   (d) *We are Seven* is a sentimental poem because Wordsworth *treats* his subject matter sentimentally.

   (e) *The Dungeon* is an angry poem because in it the poet angrily *inveighs* against the institution of imprisonment.

   (f) *The Lovesong of J. Alfred Prufrock* is a compassionate poem because the poet compassionately *portrays* the plight of his "hero."

   (g) Prokoviev's Grandfather theme is witty because the composer wittily *comments* on the character in his ballet.

   (h) Cage's *Variations II* is impersonal because the composer *presents* his noise-like sounds in an impersonal, uninvolved way.

If examples of either or both of these sorts be conceded (expressions or expressive properties of a propositional and non-propositional nature), then of course we shall have to be very careful about what we take to be the relevance of artists' intentions. For instance, if, as Sircello argues, these intentional ascriptions cannot properly be defended without reference to independent information about the artist who produced the works in question, the denial of "external" evidence would effectively reduce the range of otherwise aesthetically relevant attributions. But if, on the other hand, these intentional formulations were merely a *façon de parler,* expressive qualities would not constitute a distinctive puzzle for the theory of criticism (cf. Tormey [1971]). Whether poetry can be assimilated to fiction (cf. Beardsley [1970b]; Reichert [1977]), however, will, as we shall soon see, substantially affect the dispute.

Familiar quarrels, as is well known, have been touched off by the appearance of an article by William Wimsatt and Monroe Beardsley, "The Intentional Fallacy" [1954a]. They explain that, in the context of literature, the "intention" of the artist:

corresponds to *what he intended* in a formula which more or less explicitly has had wide acceptance. "In order to judge the poet's performance, we must know *what he intended.*" Intention is design or plan in the author's mind. Intention has obvious affinities for the author's attitude toward his work, the way he felt, what made him write.

It must be said at once that their explanatory remarks are noticeably vague and run the risk of making debate about their thesis entirely idle (for example, "plan in the author's mind") or of confusing a number of psychological categories (for example, "attitude toward his work, the way he felt, what made him write") that fail to distinguish between expressive and merely causal considerations. Two further preliminary observations are in order. In the first place, Wimsatt and Beardsley are obliged—attempting to make credible their rejection of "the design or intention as a standard by which the critic is to judge the worth of the poet's performance"—to *decide* that

> whereas notes tend to seem to justify themselves as external indexes to the author's *intention,* yet they *ought* to be judged like any other parts of a composition (verbal arrangement special to a particular context), and when so judged their reality as parts of the poem, or their imaginative integration with the rest of the poem, may come into question. [F. O.] Matthiessen, for instance, sees that [T. S.] Eliot's titles for poems and his epigraphs are informative apparatus, like the notes. But while he is worried by some of the notes and thinks that Eliot "appears to be mocking himself for writing the note at the same time that he wants to convey something by it," Matthiessen believes that the "device" of epigraphs "is not at all open to the objection of not being sufficiently structural." "The *intention,*" he says, "is to enable the poet to secure a condensed expression in the poem itself." "In each case the epigraph is designed to form an integral part of the effect of the poem."

I have italicized the word "ought" because the seeming controversy about the relevance of the artist's intention is surely trivialized in part by this verbal maneuver, however reasonable it may be. If so-called intentionalists had *meant* to point to the aesthetic relevance of notes, epigraphs, and the like, they would be fully supported by Wimsatt and Beardsley. One may almost suppose that the aesthetic relevance or irrelevance of such notes as Eliot has included with *The Waste Land* is, to avoid the Fallacy, determined exclusively on typographical grounds. If the notes had been published separately, would an appeal to them illustrate the Fallacy? And what would Wimsatt and Beardsley say about musical scores? The point is that both the inclusion and exclusion of these sorts of apparatus attest to the common ground on which questions of whether intentions are "internal" or "external" may be decided. Eliot, for instance, is known to have wavered on the question of notes (cf. Matthiessen [1947]). Is publishing the notes *together with The*

Wasteland methodologically different from publishing the notes *as part of* the poem? And is the evidence that supports this, evidence of "internal" or "external" intentions? Other difficulties arise, for instance those bearing on accidental conditions of publication, authorial uncertainty, editors' "collaboration," dawning innovations, and the like (cf. Fowler [1976]; Cioffi [1963-1964]; Hough [1976]).

In the second place, our authors are fully prepared to admit that "the use of biographical evidence need not involve intentionalism, because while it may be evidence of what the author intended, it may also be evidence of the meaning of his words and the dramatic character of his utterance." If I understand this rightly, Wimsatt and Beardsley are simply insisting that, if we do use interpretive clues derived from the independent evidence of the artist's intention, it is our proper concern as critics to decide whether the interpretation may be admitted on critical canons not bound to the artist's intention (so discerned). As I have already argued, no one would wish to deny this. The upshot of their position, then, is that evidence regarding the artist's intention may be critically useful not because it instructs us about the artist's intention, but because it happens independently to provide for a plausible interpretation of the artist's actual work; however (contrary to Wimsatt and Beardsley's intent), it may serve this latter function *by* instructing us about the artist's intention—since, in so doing, it may instruct us (recall Sircello's cases) about properties of the work not otherwise accessible. In this respect, Wimsatt and Beardsley are (oddly) in agreement with their would-be opponents: the contribution may not, on antecedent grounds, be shown to invoke exclusively internal evidence or to have appealed to external evidence.

In fact, Beardsley [1970b] avails himself of the account of illocutionary acts proposed by J.L. Austin [1962] and developed further by William Alston [1964] (cf. Vendler [1972]), precisely in order to clarify the way in which the interpretation of a literary text is managed. But *if* a speech-act analysis of literature is to be sustained, then the artist's intention (in particular, independent contextual evidence regarding the artist's intention) cannot be disqualified as aesthetically irrelevant—either with respect to the artist's *uttering* the work in the first place, or with respect to the *voices* within the work that perform their own intentionally assigned speech acts (cf. Grice [1957]; Sircello [1972]). Beardsley falls back to the thesis that the conditions on the performance of illocutionary acts are to be construed "as so many rules that are tacitly recognized by the speech community in which these illocutionary acts are performed." But there is considerable doubt about the specificity of such putative rules and, in any case, what is at stake is *which* speech act is being performed (think for instance of the impossibility of separating the act of reference from the speaker's intention) rather than what is entailed in performing any speech act correctly (cf. Searle [1969]; Margolis [1973a]; Loewenberg [1975]). Hence, symptomatically, Beardsley analyzes the act of promising with respect to what that must entail rather than with respect to what informs us, in relevant cases, whether that was the act performed. Some theory of intentions and of the relevance of independent ("external") evidence is required here. It should also be noted that *this* point is not in the least affected by Beardsley's treatment of poetry's use of language as "not an illocutionary act [but] the creation of a fictional character performing a fictional illocutionary act."

It may, in fact, be fairly claimed that "The Intentional Fallacy" conflates and confuses what Dilthey originally distinguished as the psychological and hermeneutic conceptions of intentions. The distinction is also essential to the conservative position that E.D. Hirsch [1967] adopts, for Hirsch avowedly follows Dilthey in avoiding all forms of psychologism. What Dilthey meant by a hermeneutic understanding of intentions was an interpretation of texts, actions, and expressive behavior in terms of the public intentional structures of the cultural life of an historical community, not the putatively private, inchoate, or inaccessible psychological states of particular persons (Dilthey [1913-1967]; *see* Habermas [1971]). Wittgenstein's [1953] "forms of life" and rejection of the possibility of a private language serve very neatly as a kind of loose, impressionistic approximation of Dilthey's theory. The point is that, on a hermeneutic view of intentions, it is actually contradictory to deny that documents, texts, historical encounters, and the like (*including* the actions and autobiographical remains of an artist) are pertinent to the interpretation of a given artwork. In this sense, the various arguments that Wimsatt and Beardsley offer against the relevance of intentional considerations falsely represent the distinction between "internal" and "external" evidence as a distinction between non-intentional and intentional evidence. What they really object to are arbitrary and utterly idiosyncratic interpretations; what they claim to oppose are intentional considerations.

If we construe artworks as culturally and historically emergent phenomena, then it is quite impossible to specify the "internal" features of a work without attention to the "external" culture which supplies the very context in which an artwork exists. Nevertheless, Dilthey and his followers appear to have overstated the distinction between the psychological and the hermeneutic—as, perhaps, the development of psychoanalysis and psychoanalytic criticism demonstrates (cf. Habermas [1971])—in the sense that (a) the psychological cannot be restricted to the utterly private, and (b) there is (*contra* Hirsch) no fixed range of discernible genres, cultural types, or the like in terms of which the historically and personally shifting intentions of particular artists can be completely analyzed. So seen, psychologically described intentions cannot be aesthetically irrelevant if hermeneutically described intentions are relevant, and they are neither ineffable nor specifiable solely in terms of essential genres. This criticism of the so-called "objectivist" strain of hermeneutic theory accords, of course, with the major thrust of the so-called "historicist" strain—influenced particularly by Heidegger [1962]—which psychologizes hermeneutics. But it also serves both to provide a basis for resisting the anarchic, ultimately incoherent, claims of the extreme "historicists" (Derrida [1973]; Bloom [1973]) and to reconcile the psychological and hermeneutic dimensions of intentionality.

Here, then, we have a pretty irony. For Beardsley undermines, by his own proposals, his opposition to intentionalistic criticism. First, as already remarked, it is quite impossible to construe literature on a speech-act model without conceding the relevance of a speaker's intention in determining the meaning of what is "said"—in a way that (on Wimsatt and Beardsley's own usage) must either be external to the work, or preclude the division between internal and external evidence regarding it. Secondly, either a poem constitutes, on occasion, a poet's own speech act—in which case intentionalistic considerations are critically eligible; or else a poem employs a fictional voice as a result of the poet's distinctive speech act—in which case, intentionalistic considerations are pertinent again.

Beardsley actually holds that it is the generic essence of poems to be "imitations of illocutionary acts"; but, he admits poems like Lucretius's *De rerum natura* and Milton's *Paradise Lost* to be counterinstances, and he mistakenly believes that the imitation thesis will accommodate lyric poems at least. Reichert [1977], for one, argues convincingly that Robert Frost's "Nothing Gold Can Stay" can hardly be shown to be fictive, and also cites Cleanth Brooks's useful emphasis [1947] on the "dramatic" rather than the "fictional" aspect of poetry. Beardsley's thesis, here, seems singularly arbitrary. Again, the very idea of *imitating* illocutionary acts entails the relevance of the artist's intentions. Also, Beardsley fails to distinguish between an imitation of an illocutionary act (what, after all, is that?) and the assignment of an illocutionary act to a fictitious "voice" (as often in lyric songs): a fictional character performing an illocutionary act is not the rendering of an *imitation* of an illocutionary act; and a poet *creating* a lyric poem in which a character (or the poet himself) speaks is not a poet imitating an illocutionary act (cf. also, Winters [1957], [1960]; Casey [1966]).

But Wimsatt and Beardsley also wish to insist that the critic never uses intention as a "standard" by which to judge the "worth of the poet's performance." Here I am at a loss to understand the force of their argument. They simply disallow the effort to match the poem created with the poem intended. Thus Wimsatt and Beardsley remark:

> How is [the critic] to find out what the poet tried to do? If the poet succeeded in doing it, then the poem itself shows what he was trying to do. And if the poet did not succeed, then the poem is not adequate evidence, and the critic must go outside the poem—for evidence of an intention that did not become effective in the poem.

Again,

> There is a sense in which an author, by revision, may better achieve his original intention. But it is a very abstract sense. He intended to write a better work, or a better work of a certain kind, and now has done it. But it follows that his further concrete intention was not his intention.

These assertions surely depart from our ordinary use of "intention" for the sort of case specified. It is not a question merely of an author's failing to accomplish what, in a purely private and psychological sense, he intended to accomplish (Wimsatt and Beardsley's view of the matter), but rather of an author's failing to accomplish—relative to the historical tradition within which he is recognizably working—what he intended to accomplish.

Not without justice, therefore, Theodore Redpath [1957] criticizes their view on the grounds that the artist's intention and his failure to fulfill it may even be discerned *within* the work itself (cf. Savile [1968-1969]). Redpath's claim is supported in good part by Sircello's illustrations—somewhat contrary to Sircello's own purpose—for Sircello believes that "express" (in the relevant sense) is an achievement verb (in Ryle's sense [1949]) and so does not quite allow for failure. Of course, the discrepancy between what is intended and what is achieved in art need not always be construed in terms of failure. Lukács [1964], for instance, discussing Balzac's *The Peasants,* has the following to say:

> In this novel, the most important of his maturity, Balzac wanted to write the tragedy of the doomed landed aristocracy of France. It was intended to be the keystone of the series in which Balzac described the destruction of French aristocratic culture by the growth of capitalism. . . . Yet, for all his painstaking preparation and careful planning, what Balzac really did in this novel was the exact opposite of what he had set out to do: what he depicted was not the tragedy of the aristocratic estate but of the peasant smallholding. It is precisely this discrepancy between intention and performance, between Balzac the political thinker and Balzac the author of *La Comédie Humaine* that constitutes Balzac's historical greatness.

The strategy of contrasting intention and achievement is quite characteristic of Lukács's method (cf. Lukács [1962]; Nichols [1968]). The issue of intention and failure arises, of course, in all arts—for instance, in the dispute toward the end of the last century regarding the hieratic style of ancient Egyptian sculpture (cf. Worringer [1953]).

On the whole, the range of expressive (as well as representational) properties provides important counterinstances to Wimsatt and Beardsley's position. Sircello holds, for instance, that at least some works of art (he is not proposing a comprehensive theory of art) have expressive qualities and that, among these, are some in which the "anthropomorphic [the expressive] term can be applied either adverbially to 'acts' or adjectivally to 'things' without a difference in the sense of the term or of the sentences in which it is used . . . Thus one may, without change of meaning, say either that Eliot's *Prufrock* is a compassionate poem or that Eliot portrays Prufrock compassionately, in his poem; that Poussin paints his violent scene in an aloof, detached way or that the Sabine picture is an aloof, detached painting." His point is both that the ascription of the adjective is justified "only in virtue of an artistic act [that is, in virtue of 'what the artist *does* in that work']" *and* that "the description of artistic acts in anthropomorphic terms . . . presuppose[s] something about the artist which cannot be known *simply* by attending to his art." Consequently, Sircello rejects what he terms "the Canonical Position" (cf. Bouwsma [1950]), in which, wherever expressive qualities of the relevant sort are involved, it is thought possible to replace "descriptions of artistic acts in favor of 'logically equivalent' descriptions of formal elements and/or represented subject matter" (cf. Beardsley [1958]). Sircello's sensible thesis then is this: artworks may sometimes be viewed as the utterances or expressions of artists in the same sense (though with an enormous increase in freedom and variety) in which we speak of the expression of one's feelings, convictions, or ideas.

Sircello's account is, however, complicated by a platonizing tendency, an imprecision regarding causal connections (though he favors a causal account), and a preference for the "romantic mind." He rejects what he calls an "intentionalistic" account (against Richard Wollheim [1967] and Susanne Langer [1957])—that is, formally matching the features of an artwork and one's "feelings," or intentionally "bringing about . . . something [that could serve as an expression] insofar as it fell under a certain description so that it would be an expression of one's feelings or the like." Langer holds that "An expressive form is any perceptible or imaginable whole that exhibits relationships of parts, or points, or even qualities or aspects with the whole, so that it may be taken to represent some other whole whose elements have analogous relations." This strongly suggests either that, as Sircello claims, she is mistaken or that, in spite of her use of the term "expressive," she intends to speak of (intentional) representation. Wollheim [1968], on the other hand, seems to conflate the notion of "natural expression" (borrowed largely from Wittgenstein [1953]), with the notion of expression as "correspondence," which, as he says, does not involve "any stipulation about its genesis." But he also claims that, "though these two notions are logically distinct, in practice they are bound to interact: indeed, it is arguable that it goes beyond the limit of legitimate abstraction to imagine one without the other. We can see this by considering the appropriateness, or fittingness, conceived as a relation holding between expression and expressed." The linking of the two notions seems quite mistaken, since even a smile (feigned in a play) may have an expressive quality without expressing anyone's actual feelings. Correspondence, also, seems much too general and vague to serve to distinguish expressiveness—apart from the fact that Wollheim has confused the putative grounds for regarding a property as an expressive property and that property itself.

The critical point is that *if*, by comparison with our sense of one's use of language in speech acts and one's use of the body to express feelings non-verbally—even if propositionally (cf. Margolis [1978a])—artworks are construed as expressive, it becomes impossible to preclude considerations of the artist's intention in the "external" sense. These may, as in Longinus and Artistotle, relate to certain affective properties (cf. Elliott [1966-1967]; Meager [1964]; Gombrich [1962]; *contra* Wimsatt and

Beardsley [1954b]). But the notion does not in the least preclude the possibility that a work may also exhibit expressive properties that do *not* express the artist's feelings, convictions, ideas, or the like (cf. Urmson [1973]). The point is central, for instance, to Alan Tormey's correct insistence [1971] that "the particular mistake [of the "Expression theorist," that is, of such theorists as John Dewey, Curt Ducasse, R.G. Collingwood, E.F. Carritt, D.W. Gotshalk, George Santayana, Leo Tolstoy, Eugène Véron—for which Tormey provides an Appendix of apposite citations] arises from assuming that the existence of *expressive qualities* in a work of art implies a prior act of *expression*." There need be no "necessary link between the qualities of the art work and certain [internal psychological] states of the artist"; this, in effect, undermines romanticism (cf. also Hermerén [1969]). If I understand Tormey correctly, he holds (i) that, sometimes, but not invariably, attributions of expression are correctly made of persons on the basis of their putative states of mind; and (ii) that attributions of expressive qualities to artworks are never justifiably based on the artist's state of mind, and are testable solely by reference to the work itself:

> Normal imputations of expression *are* falsifiable, and the assertion that a person's behavior constitutes an expression of something is defeated when it can be shown that the imputed inference is unwarranted. But statements about the expressive qualities of an art work remain . . . statements *about* the work, and any revision or rejection of such statements can be supported only by referring to the work itself.

But Sircello's illustrations and the conceptual difficulties of Wimsatt and Beardsley's thesis show that expressive qualities cannot always be disjunctively assigned to persons and artworks and do not support a clear demarcation between what is "internal" and "external" to an artwork. Tormey also maintains that artworks are "ambiguously self-expressive objects," which, in context, seems to approximate to the correction just given.

I cannot admit that intentional criticism (that is, criticism that is appraisive in intentional terms) is altogether improper in aesthetic quarters (cf. Ducasse [1929]). I think of Picasso's deliberate virtuosity, of a novelist's open concern with accuracy of detail. Also, when questions of historical verisimilitude or deliberate license arise, one sees at once how the appeal to the "rules" of historical fiction may merely be a covert way of appealing to the artist's intention (cf. Olsen [1978]; Culler [1975]). Obviously, in the performing arts, appraisal in intentional terms cannot but be relevant. Among the non-performing arts, I suppose the most famous instance in which intentional judgment would have been pointedly relevant was Gainsborough's *Blue Boy*—which bears, incidentally, on Stuart Hampshire's altogether too sharp distinction [1954] between the aesthetic and the moral, as in problem-solving.

Colin Lyas [1973] makes a particularly convincing argument about the relevance of "personal qualities" which "critics attribute to works of art which do presuppose knowledge of and reference to artists and their intention"; he concedes that "possession of such qualities may not be sufficient to make something art, but that these are qualities for which art is praised cannot . . . be denied." The list of "merit and demerit qualities of works of art," once supplied, renders indisputable at least the thesis about the relevance of the artist's intention; it has the additional merit, as Lyas himself realizes, of precluding works of art from the class of "natural objects." The list includes the following qualities:

> responsible, mature, intelligent, sensitive, perceptive, discriminating, witty, poised, precise, self-aware, ironic, controlled, courageous;

> simple-minded, shallow, diffuse, vulgar, immature, self-indulgent, uncomprehending, heavy-handed, gauche, glib, smug.

An important qualification is required, however. Lyas says that the ascription of such personal qualities *presupposes* knowlege of and reference to the artist and his intention. Certainly, this sometimes obtains—but not always. It shows the aesthetic relevance of biographical and intentional considerations; but, sometimes, an inspection of a given work supports their *ascription*—from which, therefore, we may draw inferences regarding the artist. This, as it happens, is one of Alan Tormey's [1971] central claims regarding the distinctive use of locutions like "expression of *X*." The schema Tormey wishes to defend is this:

> If *A*'s behavior *B* is an *expression* of *X,* then there is a warrantable inference from *B* to an intentional state of *A,* such that it would be true to say that *A* has (or is in state) *S*; and where *S* and *X* are identical.

There is no need to favor one direction only. Lyas's own specimen case, F.R. Leavis's discussion of *Emma* [1948], shows, in context, that antecedent knowledge of the author justifies ascriptions of personal qualities to the novel, and that qualities discriminated in the novel justify inferences regarding the mind and character of the author. Mention of Lyas's point that the list of usual ascriptions entails precluding works of art from the class of natural objects cannot but suggest the conceptual weakness of one of Goodman's key claims. Goodman [1968] holds that artworks possess expressive qualities metaphorically, on the strength of which thesis he concludes that artworks must, *qua* art, function to exemplify the expressive qualities they possess. Clearly, the likeliest grounds for so arguing are that artworks are physical objects that, in some context of discourse, are *assigned* an expressive function *and* that that assignment depends on borrowing metaphorically from human expression. But if artworks are not physical objects (in the same sense in which words and sentences are not mere physical inscriptions or inscriptions to which symbolic functions are specifically assigned) but culturally emergent entities of some sort, then the way is prepared for conceding that artworks literally possess expressive qualities—in the cultural contexts in which they exist—and that expressiveness or expression in art and in human behavior need not be construed univocally or linked merely by way of metaphor.

Another telling sort of case is that of forgery (cf. Goodman [1968]). If forgery (there are many different kinds) is sometimes not perceptually discernible and if what is perceptually discernible is not discernible *qua* forgery, then, granting the aesthetic relevance of a judgment of forgery, it is quite impossible to deny the relevance of intentionalistic appraisal.

I should like to mention an intriguing case regarding intention and interpretation. John Wain [1955] has provided an interesting interpretation of W.B. Yeats's *Among School Children*. Having offered his own view of a given stanza, he cites the following note by Yeats on the very same passage:

> I have taken the "honey of generation" from Porphyry's essay on *The Cave of the Nymphs,* but find no warrant in it for considering it the "drug" that destroys the "recollection" of prenatal freedom. He blamed a cup of oblivion given in the zodiacal sign of Cancer.

Wain remarks:

> Here we come head-on against the huge recurrent problem that faces the reader of Yeats. It is, briefly, the problem of how much notice to take of Yeats's personal fandango of mysticism and superstition. To many readers it will seem intolerably arrogant if I

say that I propose simply to brush aside his reading of his own words. Obviously, they will say, if the poet himself tells us that it is the "shape" who is "betrayed"—it is the child who loses the remembrance of his ideal pre-natal existence by having the practical joke of birth played on him—then that is all; away with his obstinate insistence that it is the "mother" who was betrayed by the pleasure of generation.

Yeats's own reading (his "intention"), Wain continues,

> is an affair of solemn childishness, a product of the side of his nature which found it necessary to construct a system of beliefs in order to write poetry at all . . . the lines could take that interpretation. . . . If this reading is valid, it is valid simply as a piece of Yeats's familiar pessimism, to document which we need not go outside his verse.

His own reading, he claims, renders the stanza "absolutely clear; it relates logically to the rest of the poem; it develops the argument; it is intelligible, compassionate, and human." I think we cannot discount resistance to Wain's interpretation, no matter how ingenious it is or how much grander it makes the poem, on the putative grounds that Yeats's clear intention is aesthetically irrelevant. Wain himself is obviously uneasy about the matter. We may, of course, honor both interpretations on different grounds (say, "accuracy" and "significance").

Wimsatt and Beardsley must, therefore, be mistaken in holding "that the design or intention of the author is neither available nor desirable as a standard for judging the success of a work of literary art." Nor does the Intentional Fallacy fare better in application to the other arts, particularly where notations or analogies of speech acts are of critical importance. Further, when the issues are sorted out, it appears (following a time-honored pattern), that, on the questions our authors are primarily interested in, no one is likely to dispute the impertinence of intentions *qua* intentions; and that, in those matters in which intentions *qua* intentions are taken to be relevant by others, our authors are inclined either to refuse to call the relevant comments intentionalistic or to disallow the appropriate labels of distinction (in particular, the labels "literary criticism" and "aesthetic"). The truth is that the Intentional Fallacy is the obverse side of a doubtful theory about the nature and properties of artworks and can only be exposed by reference to that theory.

Beardsley [1958] has more recently held, challenging Redpath's discussion of the Intentional Fallacy, that "the main question . . . is not whether we can have reason to think that a work falls short of some intention, but whether we can get sufficient evidence of what the specific intention was to determine where, and how far, the work falls short of it; it is this evidence that I think is practically never available." Given the earlier article, this both concedes too much and obliges us to take too literally such phrases as "in the author's mind." At any rate, the objection is no longer a theoretical one and forfeits, therefore, its philosophical status. That is, the issue is no longer (*contra* Wimsatt [1968]) concerned with an account of the nature and autonomy of the artwork, and of what is aesthetically relevant to an appreciation of it. I can see no other conclusion than that Beardsley has, by his latest rebuttal, repudiated the genuinely challenging thesis of the original paper (cf. Aschenbrenner [1950]).

Having said this much in support of intentional criticism, I must admit that there have been excessively large claims made about determining artists' intentions and about their importance in critical interpretation. E.D. Hirsch [1967], as we have already noted, maintains that "the only compelling normative principle that has ever been brought forward [for the valid interpretation of literary texts] is the old-fashioned ideal of rightly understanding what the author meant"; quite simply, he insists on "viewing interpretation [of literary texts] as a re-cognition of the author's meaning." *If* it were genuinely possible to determine "what the author meant" in his text and *if* to determine this would exhaust the work of interpretation, a great many of the ingenious efforts of literary commentators would simply be irrelevant to an *understanding* of a text, however suggestive they may be in the context of a *criticism* of it. Hirsch is quite explicit about the "rigid separation of meaning and significance with respect to textual commentary": by "understanding," he means "a perception or construction of the author's verbal meaning, nothing more, nothing less"; and by "judgment" ("commentary," "criticism," and "evaluation" serve limited clarificatory functions), he means the judging or assessing of the significance of a work whose meaning is already correctly construed. As Hirsch says, "In the first instance [understanding or re-cognitive interpretation] one submits to another [the author]—literally, one stands under him. In the second, one acts independently—by one's own authority—like a judge" (but *see* Hirsch [1976]). He offers some remarks on Hamlet criticism, in order to exemplify his view:

We have posited [this is purely hypothetical, for the sake of an illustration] that Shakespeare did not mean that Hamlet wished to sleep with his mother. We confront an interpretation which states that Hamlet did wish to sleep with his mother. If we assert, as I have done, that only a re-cognitive interpretation is a valid interpretation, then we must, on the basis of our assumed premise about the play, say that the Freudian interpretation is invalid. It does not correspond to the author's meaning; it is an implication that cannot be subsumed under the type of meaning that Shakespeare (under our arbitrary supposition) willed. It is irrelevant that the play permits such an interpretation. The variability of possible implications is the very fact that requires a theory of interpretation and validity.

Consider that Hirsch does not actually deny that "the Freudian argument [respecting *Hamlet*] *could* be valid." In fact, he holds explicitly that "for some genres of texts [literature and law, for instance] the author submits to the convention that his willed implications must go far beyond what he explicitly knows"; a valid interpretation might well be "strange and foreign to the original author." Hirsch seems, here, to be holding fast to the fiction of an author's will in order to assimilate to his model historically emergent and compelling interpretations that, on more normal grounds, would be construed as exceeding the author's intentions—whatever they may be supposed to be. The issue is somewhat confused because it is difficult to construe the author's intent exclusively in either psychological or hermeneutic terms. Hirsch, of course, follows Dilthey here, and means to avoid a purely psychological account of authorial meaning. But even hermeneutically construed, it seems *ad hoc* to claim that an author intends what, given historical orientation, he could not possibly know or even understand.

Hirsch himself is aware of the charge and he has an answer ready: "The human author's willed meaning can always go beyond what he consciously intended so long as it remains within his willed type." But, of course, the reply attenuates the force of his original thesis; for, it indicates that we are not merely to interpret a given work in accord with "what the author meant," since the author may be said to have meant his work to be understood in ways in which, by hypothesis, *he could not* (in an obvious sense of "meant") *have meant* his work to be taken. We may accept Hirsch's adjustment; but we must see that the quarrel between him and theorists who reject "authorial meaning" as the sole norm of valid interpretation is completely altered and even, perhaps, now quite pointless. The objection is conditional, of course, and depends on the

status of the author's "willed type." Even so, Hirsch's view is paradoxical since, on the thesis, novel interpretations of a literary text may be
said to disclose meanings "in the work itself" in spite of the fact that
such meanings cannot be part of what the author knowingly
"willed"—which, paradigmatically, is supposed to determine what is in
the work.

Hirsch is, of course, aware of the paradox, and attempts to resolve it
by reference to his theory of implication and intrinsic genres. "The logic
of implication," he says, "is always . . . a genre logic, as common sense
tells every interpreter. Whether an implication is present depends upon
the kind of meaning that is being interpreted." Disputes about interpretations usually concern a "disagreement about genre"; that is,
"understanding can occur only if the interpreter proceeds under the same
system of expectations [as the speaker or writer], and this shared generic
conception, constitutive both of meaning and of understanding, is the intrinsic genre of the utterance." So a grasp of the "intrinsic genre" of any
utterance (read, "literary text") is a necessary condition of understanding both what an author is saying and what, in the generous sense required, he may be said to "imply." Hirsch thus conflates the intentionality of speech and language and the determinate intentions of particular speakers on particular occasions. One instance may serve to exemplify the equivocation: "That discriminating force [which causes the
meaning to be *this* instead of *that* or *that* or *that*] must involve an act of
will, since unless one particular complex of meaning is *willed* (no matter
how 'rich' and 'various' it may be), there would be no distinction between what an author does mean by a word sequence and what he could
mean by it. Determinacy of verbal meaning requires an act of will." But
of course, as long as a determinate speech act has occurred, we must construe the meaning of an utterance in accord with the rules of language,
even if we must also attend to what the author intended by what he said.

The equivocation affects Hirsch's linking of the concepts of "implication" and "intrinsic genres." He holds "that the implications of an utterance are determined by its intrinsic genre." But he also holds both that
"a genre conception is constitutive of speaking as well as of
interpreting" (which diminishes the role of the author's will in favor of
public rules of linguistic usage) and that "the purpose of a genre is the
communicable purpose of a particular speaker, nothing more nor less"
(which tends rather to favor the author's deliberate will and intention). It
is also true that, following August Boeckh, Hirsch dabbles with the notion that *"Zweck* must be an entelechy, a goal-seeking force that
animates a particular kind of utterance." Yet he hedges on the reality of

so-called intrinsic genres, employs Wittgenstein's notion of family resemblances to avoid (properly) holding to strict classes, and is ultimately reduced to insisting (without supporting evidence) that "there emphatically is such a thing as the intrinsic interpretation of a text"—that is, interpretation in terms of intrinsic genres. It is not in the least clear whether we should ultimately assimilate interpretations to what is "embraced by the author's will," by appeal to our antecedent genres (whose mode of determination is now an utter mystery), or whether we should assess our interpretations in accord with heuristically proposed genres by attention to "what the author meant" (*really* meant—which is another mystery).

Hirsch himself raises the most serious methodological difficulty against his own thesis, namely, the self-confirming nature of interpretations, the "inevitable circularity" of every interpreter's effort by which "all his internal evidence tends to support his hypothesis because much of it was constituted by his hypothesis." Indeed, he goes so far as to say that the "tendency of interpretations to be self-contained and incommensurable is . . . the principal handicap that will always plague the discipline of interpretations." In general, what these reflections point to is the "probable unverifiability of form," in the strong sense favored by intentionalists and structuralists (cf. A. Moore [1973]; Culler [1975]) and opposed by those, like Wimsatt and Beardsley, who believe that artworks are "autonomous" entities with well-formed boundaries.

In the light of these concessions and Hirsch's remarks about the probabilism of interpretation, it is difficult to see how Hirsch could—or why he would—hold that, with respect to a given text, "two disparate interpretations cannot both be correct." Hirsch is actually driven to admit the indecisiveness of evidence primarily because of the so-called "hermeneutic circle" (cf. Hirsch [1976]). Ultimately, he denies the sufficiency of "internal evidence" and insists on "a consideration of all the known relevant data," external evidence regarding "date, authorship, milieu, and so on." The adjustment, however, favors coherence and plausibility rather than fidelity to the author's intention restricted to *a particular work*. On his own view, Hirsch cannot defend his critical thesis—that "genuinely intrinsic judgment is founded entirely on the author's aims and norms"—and he cannot defend a clear demarcation between internal and external criticism. But then, he *cannot* show that interpretations are, in principle, more than plausible or that "disparate" interpretations cannot jointly be confirmed ("validated"), not merely allowed to stand for want of deciding evidence.

One final and extremely telling example is provided by Göran Hermerén [1969]. Erwin Panofsky had apparently held, of Dürer's engraving *Melancholia I,* that the flowers in the woman's wreath were watercress and water ranunculus. But Hermerén reports that Lottlisa Behling, in an article on Dürer's flowers, argued that the flowers were actually the herb lovage. Behling reasons that the flower represented "resembles more than anything else the very old herb lovage (Levisticum officinale Koch), known already in Carolingian days"—which Hermerén glosses, "resembles more than anything else *known to the artist.*" The issue bears on an interpretation of Dürer's symbolism, "since lovage is [already] recommended in Hieronymus Bock's book of herbs as a cure for black melancholy." Behling's argument depends on the fact that Dürer is said to have been "sharp-eyed" and hence "would certainly have noticed" the characteristic features of ranunculus and watercress (which she supplies); but these, she remarks, appear "neither . . . in the engraving nor in the woodcut."

Now, resemblance, on any relevant theory, may well tolerate considerable divergences consistent with representation; in fact, there is in principle no way to restrict representation in terms of the constraints of, say, visual resemblance (cf. Goodman [1968]). (This goes contrary to Beardsley's theory of representation [1958], incidentally, in which similarity or resemblance is essential and in which intentional considerations are notably avoided—a theory that Hermerén effectively challenges. Beardsley's account of symbolism is also affected, since, on Beardsley's view, if a painting of a cross is symbolic, then "[(1)] the painting represents a cross, and [(2)] the cross symbolizes Christianity." But both "represents" and "symbolizes" must be construed intentionally—in ways that cannot effectively exclude "external" evidence. It is quite impossible to ascribe representational properties to an artwork without implicating the artist's intentions; and if a purely "objectivist" hermeneutic interpretation of an art tradition cannot be defended [as the internal weakness of Hirsch's argument confirms], then it is also impossible to deny the critical relevance of the artist's intentions construed psychologically. Both hermeneutic and psychological evidence, however, preclude a clear demarcation between the "internal" and the "external.") In short, there is no way to understand Behling's correction—that is, Behling's *interpretation* construed as a disclosure of what is "hidden" in the engraving, and therefore describable—except in terms of independent biographical and intentional considerations. Even if it were true that a great many representational elements—symbols and motifs for instance—may, because they are clichés, be analyzed in terms of their "meaning" without reference to the artist's intention (in Beardssley's sense), they would remain intentional and would (in the hermeneutic sense) convey the artist's intention nevertheless; *but,* to admit such elements is, effectively, to admit others (like expressive and illustrative properties) that cannot be understood without independent reference to biographical and psychological evidence. To admit intentional properties *and* to reject the conservative version of hermeneutic analysis entail psychologizing the interpretation of such properties; for then, the very system of public genres, traditions, styles, symbols, meanings, and the like—employed in interpretive criticism—cannot but depend conceptually on the shifting historical regularities which the behavior and work of the actual members of particular societies are thought to exhibit.

9. Characteristic Qualities of Works of Art

Apart from the puzzles of interpretation, critical judgments of artworks combine descriptive, appreciative, and evaluative elements in a variety of ways. There is very little agreement about how to sort or account for these elements, although prominent views are quite emphatic about the nature of particular properties and their bearing on the validity of our responses. For example, if one supposes, as Roger Scruton does [1974], that a particular range of properties attributed to a work depends on a certain use of imagination—not perception proper but the important activity of "seeing as"—it would follow that the properties in question cannot validly be asserted to have been found "in" the work. Others, for instance Stephen Pepper [1937], seem to confuse the possible emotional intensity with which we perceive an artwork and the actual qualities we discriminate in it. Pepper alleges that

> We slip back and forth from a more emotional to a more analytical attitude towards the work before us. The realization of the work is increased by these changing attitudes. But if we have lost the capacity for "seizure," for rich emotional fusion and ecstasy in a work, we have lost something precious. We have lost the power of full realization.

He oscillates thus between the thesis that emotional involvement is a moral value of some sort, however perceptually irrelevant, and the thesis that the actual qualities of a work of art depend on "seizure" or "emotional fusion and ecstasy" on our part. The temptation to mix the two derives chiefly, though not entirely, from our habit, in characterizing artworks, of using terms normally applied to emotional states and states of feeling. Music, for instance, is regularly said to be "joyous," "sad," "melancholy," "nervous," "tense," "relaxed," "gay," "brooding," "cheerful." But surely neither the composer nor his audience need be, or need be even disposed to be, in any of the corresponding states in order to detect such qualities (Tormey [1971]).

The existence of these qualities is sometimes thought to be difficult to admit because artworks lack psychological states. Hence, their ascription may be thought to be metaphoric (Goodman [1968]), though the only possible reason for supposing that they are requires (i) that expressive terms designate inherently psychological states, or are applicable only by a metaphoric extension of the psychological; and/or (ii) that the ontological nature of an artwork precludes the literal ascription of expressive qualities even where the sense of expressive terms is not restricted as in (i). One may, for instance, hold that a certain smile is literally sad because it is *characteristically* associated with or induced by a certain sadness (even if it is coolly posed, say, by Sarah Bernhardt). But if such ascriptions are conceded, no conceptual barrier remains against the literal ascription of expressive qualities to artworks (*contra* Goodman). One need not confuse the origin of a term with the conditions of its valid use. To acknowledge the ontic distinction of artworks—for instance, as culturally informed utterances—suggests the rationale for the literal ascription of expressive qualities. Hence, attributing such properties to artworks—however they may be grounded upon sensory qualities in the narrow sense—presupposes (a) a generous reading of "perception," "experience," "imagination," and the like to accommodate relevant cognitive claims, and (b) provision for culturally prepared criteria of recognition in virtue of which sensory qualities, physical marks, and the like may be taken to justify the ascription of the properties in question. In this sense (*contra* Beardsley [1958]) either artworks and "aesthetic objects" are not merely "perceptual objects," or the admission that they are must be qualified along the lines of (a) and (b) (cf. Goodman [1968]; Rudner [1972]; Tomas [1959]; Sibley [1959a]; M. Cohen [1959], [1965]; Beardsley [1969]; Dickie [1965]). "Perception," then, signifies no more than "cognition" or "appreciation"—which is to say that the properties of artworks cannot be restricted to whatever is, in the narrowest sense, accessible to sensory perception. We may for instance "see" a fugal form, the tragic quality of an action, that there is "a reconciliation scene in the fifth act," or that a painting "lacks balance." This means only that we take the associated judgments to be open to objective defense *in some sense*: it says nothing about the cognitive capacity on which a given judgment rests, nor about the logical features of the properties discerned, nor even about whether such properties are to be found "in" the work or merely justifiably imputed to it.

On the other hand, without denying that we respond to art in characteristic emotional ways, one need not subscribe to the extreme view expressed by C.J. Ducasse [1929]:

> . . . feeling is used in these pages, so that by "the feeling of cerulean blue" is not here meant the *color,* cerulean blue, but the

emotion of which we become conscious when, attending to that color, we take towards it the attitude which we have called the aesthetically contemplative. That emotion or feeling is a fact distinct from and additional to the mere blueness, for at least in the case of so trivial a content of attention as a mere patch of color, no noticeable feeling arises unless we deliberately "listen" for it, i.e., unless we take the aesthetic attitude towards the blue attended to.

Ducasse states that he uses "feeling" "to denote only states of the nature of emotion." His example, however, is somewhat artificial; one supposes the "feeling" of cerulean blue, if at all significant, must appear in some more specific or ramified context than he here supplies (think for instance of the "air" or "mood" or "feeling" of the colors of Edward Hopper's paintings). Ducasse seems bent on assigning a distinct "feeling" to every single color; but the thesis is extravagant. Pepper, too, regularly substitutes the notion of emotions produced by attending to works of art for that of "emotional" qualities actually perceived in them (cf. Tsugawa [1961]; Hospers [1959]). The reason perhaps is to save, in a Kantian-like spirit, the putative universality of aesthetically relevant subjective responses. But there are a number of obviously dubious claims involved. For one thing, Pepper and Ducasse hold that there is a distinct perceptual or perception-like discrimination that depends necessarily on adopting the aesthetic attitude. Secondly, both hold, in rather different ways, that there is an emotional quality assignable to qualities perceptible in the sensory sense. Thirdly, again in different ways, both allege that aesthetic experience does not properly obtain unless the discrimination of emotional features also obtains. But there is no reason to think that "the aesthetic attitude" controls any cognitively privileged range of discriminations (cf. Dickie [1974]), even if it is the case that some aesthetic percipients are more discriminating or sensitive than others (cf. Sibley [1959a]). Also, there is no reason to suppose (*contra* Ducasse) that what is distinctly pertinent in aesthetic perception is the discrimination of feelings or emotional qualities of any sort (as opposed, say, to the discrimination of meanings).

The most systematic and extreme theory segregating aesthetic perception in a narrow sense is undoubtedly the one proposed by Virgil Aldrich. Aldrich [1958] contrasts aesthetic perception with scientific perception ("basic imagination" and "observation"), treating both as basic categorial "aspects" (*per* Wittgenstein [1953]) of perceiving what is said to be originally "simply noticed in the neutral field." He thus makes the aesthetic a "mode of perception" and is able to speak of specifically "aesthetic objects" in contrast to "physical objects" (cf. Beardsley [1958]). Apart from the question of whether Aldrich would classify particular perceptions as aesthetic or non-aesthetic, or whether he would permit the apparently perceptual distinction to be reduced to an attitudinal one, one may notice a somewhat more specialized difficulty—that of the propriety of using Wittgenstein's concept of "aspects" to cover an alternation between putative "modes" of perceiving. Wittgenstein's analysis [1953] of the duck-rabbit picture requires distinct "aspects" of a thing for the same "mode" of perception; Aldrich treats the "modes" themselves as distinct categorial "aspects" of some "neutral noticing."

The concept of a "mode" of perception is puzzling in itself. In a more recent discussion, Aldrich [1963] mentions "a categorial option at the base of experience—the phenomenon of categorial aspection." The point of speaking thus is to reinforce the objectivity and distinction of aesthetic perception ("prehension"): we are to suppose that there is "an aspect of the thing that is there in aesthetic space for perception in the mode of prehension." Here, Aldrich explicitly avoids the usual subjectivist-objectivist distinctions based on an observational model suited for science, and he avoids as well a phenomenalism, like Beardsley's [1958], that trades on such a model:

> Take for example a dark city and a pale western sky at dusk, meeting at the sky line. In the purely prehensive or aesthetic view of this, the light sky area just above the jagged sky protrudes toward the point of view. The sky is closer to the viewer than the dark areas of buildings. This is the disposition of these material things in aesthetic space with respect to their medium alone. It is precisely the medium in this sense that is discounted both in the observational view of them and in the plain, nonspecial view. Thus prehension is, if you like, an "impressionistic" way of looking, but still a mode of perception, with the impressions objectively animating the material things—*there* to be prehended.

Two sorts of difficulty remain, however. First, the perception of the "protruding toward the point of view" requires that objects like the city and the sky be discriminated in the same perceptual context as the "protruding." This suggests that, even in aesthetic perception, we cannot possibly be faced with a disjunction between two "modes" of perception. Secondly, Aldrich stresses the "ways in which things may be seen," that is, a kind of aspection that requires imagination in Wittgenstein's sense. But if so, then "aesthetic" qualities need not actually be "there" to be seen. Aldrich thus fails to show us how to determine whether, say, the physiognomic or intentional directionality of the light (in his own illustration) may be confirmed as genuinely perceptible or merely as imputed to what is perceivable in accord with some established practice of imagination. What is required is a theory of how—against the backdrop of culturally informed experience—the presence of sensory qualities, physical marks, and the like (perceivable in accord with the strictest view of sensory perception—what Aldrich perhaps means by scientific "observation") may justify and even confirm the claim that more unusual properties (expressive, intentional, physiognomic, affective, symbolic, representational) are present as well.

What needs to be emphasized is (i) that what is "perceptual" in the full-blooded sensory sense must be construed in terms of an entire battery of various sorts of background information (cf. Dretske [1969]; Gregory [1966])—explicit beliefs, biologically relevant invariances below the level of consciousness, interpretive schemata favored by the percipient, and the like; and (ii) that "aesthetic perception" need not be restricted to, or even primarily focused on, what is accessible in some minimal sensory sense (most notably in literature, cf. Zink [1945]), so that reference to the artist's intentions and craft, imaginative associations, representational and symbolic import, historical influences, uses of tradition, and the like will not be disallowed because of a narrow reading of the category.

In a sense, this is the central theme of E.H. Gombrich's study of naturalism in painting [1960], though Gombrich's thesis is flawed by a decisive but instructive equivocation. Gombrich rejects Ruskin's thesis [1903-1912] of the "innocent eye" as "a myth"; he presses instead the claim that "all seeing is interpreting." Part of his thesis is caught by the following:

Can we . . . compare "the image on the retina" with the "image in the mind?" Such speculations easily lead into a morass of unprovables. Take the image on the artist's retina. It sounds scientific enough, but actually there never was *one* such image which we could single out for comparison with either photograph or painting. What there was was an endless succession of innumerable images as the painter scanned the landscape in front of him, and these images sent a complex pattern of impulses through the optic nerves to his brain. Even the artist knew nothing of these events, and we know even less.

So perception is to be taken, in some sense, as an interpretation of informational input that the interpreter is unaware of. However, following somewhat J.J. Gibson's theories [1950], [1966], Gombrich is prepared to say also that "we are born with the capacity to interpret our visual impressions in terms of a possible world, that is, in terms of space and light" (cf. Popper [1959]). But this entails that we are aware of our visual impressions first and then interpret them. "Interpret" cannot have a univocal sense in these two contexts. In addition, Gombrich presses a third doctrine, namely, that "the artist, no less than the writer, needs a vocabulary before he can embark on a 'copy of reality' ":

> All representations are grounded on schemata which the artist learns to use. But we may now see more clearly why he is so dependent on tradition. The injunction to "copy appearances" is really meaningless unless the artist is first given something which is to be made like something else . . . He is the man who has learned to look critically, to probe his perceptions by trying alternative interpretations both in play and in earnest.

Here, the artist is concerned to *represent* in his painting (the obverse of the percipient's attempt to interpret) what one can perceive (in the second sense noted). He looks for schematic relationships, capturing which he can minimize informational loss and distortion regarding the perceivable world (cf. Berlyne [1974]; Brothwell [1976]; Moles [1966]; Eco [1976]). Interpretation, in this third sense, signifies the "legibility" of a painting; there is, therefore, a multiple equivocation on "interpret" in Gombrich's theory. Yet, almost because of its conceptual inadequacy, the theory highlights the complexity of the notion of aesthetic perception even in the context of the visual. What is said to be objectively perceived, on Gombrich's view, is a function of a theory that at once specifies the nature of the perceivable world and informs our perceptual powers. Hence, it is no more than an extension of this notion—however much open to dispute—to adjust our account of aesthetic perception to our theories about the nature and properties of artworks.

This is not the place to attempt a general account of sensory perception. But there is a critical feature of perception curiously overlooked in attempts to bring the relevant work of psychology to bear on the discrimination of artworks, namely, that the cognition of perceptual forms is informed by, and depends upon, culturally contingent background beliefs. The theme is noticeably missing or slighted in two of the principal discussions of the perception of paintings, for instance in Rudolf Arnheim's [1974] attempt to account for the perception of visual art in terms favored by Gestalt psychology. When Arnheim declares that

> . . . the life of a percept—its expression and meaning—derives en-
> tirely from the activity of the perceptual forces. Any line drawn on
> a sheet of paper, the simplest form modeled from a piece of clay, is
> like a stone thrown into a pond. It upsets response, it mobilizes
> space. Seeing is the perception of action,

we are to suppose that "perceptual forces" are "assumed to be real . . .
as both psychological and physical forces." Here, Arnheim relies, at
least vestigially, on Wolfgang Köhler's original thesis [1947] of an
isomorphism between perceptual *Gestalten* and neurophysiological patterns; hence, he holds that, in being perceptually drawn in accord with
the law of *Prägnanz* (toward the "good" *Gestalt*), we are drawn in a way
almost literally similar to the exertions of physical forces. The result is
that, although he emphasizes the activity of a percipient agent and even
the high intelligence that is involved in perceptual recognition, Arnheim
tends to favor the innate organizational powers of the brain and misses
the conceptual distinction of culturally informed perceptual forms
(*Gestalten,* if one may so speak). This is particularly clear, for instance,
in one of Arnheim's own illustrations, a discussion of a fifteenth-century
painting representing St. Michael weighing souls. Arnheim notes that
"one frail little nude outweighs four big devils plus two millstones" in
St. Michael's scales. But since prayer alone "provides no visual pull,"
the painter adds a palpable dark patch in the folds of the angel's robe
below the pale nude in order to create the weight to offset the dark forms
of the devils. The fact remains, however, that the *need* for the visual
balancing arises only in the context of understanding the symbolic import of the representation; there *is* no operative perceptual pull at the
purely visual level *below* our conception of the symbolism. There is no
law of purely sensory perception operative here. The patch is *not* required in the sense in which Arnheim holds perceptual forces to be
"real"; it is required only to strengthen the intended *sense* of the painting. Actually, Arnheim is obliged to adopt a platonistic view of perceptual forms (cf. J. Hochberg [1957]; Arnheim [1969]); for, otherwise, the
adequacy of "objective" Gestalt explanations of *culturally* favored
forms would remain completely implausible (cf. Kolers [1972]; Goodman [1978b]).

J.J. Gibson's theory of ecological perception [1966] fails for counterpart reasons. Gibson discounts the role of the cognitive agent,

claiming that optic information is objectively present in an external array (as of ambient light). Hence, for Gibson, cognitive agents pick up information passively; they are, in effect, internally organized (probably for reasons of biological survival) to respond to the informational invariants of an external optic array. However, Gibson has no conceivable way of specifying *what* ecologically relevant information could possibly be provided by *two*-dimensional—particularly non-representational—paintings (Gibson [1960], [1978]). To hold that some information or other, normally conveyed within the three-dimensional world, is somehow preserved in the static "illusions" of paintings cannot but be vacuous; and to admit that the perception of paintings requires a grasp of the visual conventions of some tradition cannot but undermine Gibson's original theory. In effect, there can be no perceptual station or stations that passively yield ecological information about small, movable, two-dimensional objects produced in accord with variable conventions. In fact, there is in Gibson's comprehensive theory no recognition of the perceptual relevance of the cognitive activity and culturally contingent orientation of the perceptual agent (cf. Gregory [1966]; Tormey and Tormey [forthcoming]; Segall [1966], [1967]).

To return to the question of aesthetic properties, expressive qualities need to be sharply contrasted with those that involve affective responses on our part, or at least our disposition to such responses. Thus we say a dramatic situation is "tragic," a scene "comic," a melody "stirring," a red "glaring," a joke "funny, " colors "restful," a poem "sublime." We are sometimes *moved* in a certain way by such objects. But more important, we take it that we are disposed to be, and that it is appropriate to be, moved thus (cf. Nowell-Smith [1954]). There is no need to deny that we sometimes characterize artworks in ways that directly depend on our emotions and emotional dispositions. Such "affective" qualities are, however, altogether distinct from "expressive" qualities, although neither have a merely autobiographical or statistical use.

We sometimes mark the contrast by speaking, say, of music or literature as *expressing* and *evoking* sadness. There is a possible misconception even here because, sometimes, the "evoked" feeling is aesthetically irrelevant (as when music accidentally "makes" us sad) and yet at other times, it is quite relevant (as in the amusement aroused by a genuinely funny joke). Hence, against the charge of the Affective Fallacy (Wimsatt and Beardsley [1954b]; Beardsley [1958]), affective responses need not be aesthetically or critically irrelevant; affective terms are sometimes rightly employed with gerundive force. In fact, R.K. Elliott has rather recently [1966-1967], in an extremely suggestive way, extended the theory of evoked emotion explored by Aristotle and Longinus:

> the emotion that I feel in experiencing a work of art from within (and that which I feel as another person's in real life) may be present in me without being predicable of me. It is present in me because I do not merely recognize that the poet is expressing, for example, sadness, but actually feel this sadness; yet the emotion I feel is not predicable of me, i.e., it would be false to say that I *am* sad or even, unqualifiedly, that I feel sad. . . . The emotion expressed in a lyric poem may be "there for me in the speaker of the poem," even if the speaker is a fiction and even if the emotion was never experienced by the historical poet.

Of course, some terms—"gaiety" with respect to music—may signify either an expressive or an affective quality or a quality of a mixed sort. Also, *what* may be said to be perceived or imaginatively experienced in a valid way becomes increasingly difficult to systematize. The fact is that there is no generally adopted theory of perception (or of "experience" or imaginatively informed experience) in terms of which the kinds of properties here being considered may be straightforwardly said to be objectively confirmed. But it is part of Elliott's thesis that the sadness "expressed" in a lyric poem may, on a suitable theory, be (i) discernible "in" the poem; (ii) discernible by means of an appropriate affective response on the reader's part; (iii) discernible, therefore, by means of a culturally informed imagination the exercise of which may be taken to support a certain range of objective claims (cf. Stein [1964]). Hence, Elliott obliges us, at one and the same time, to adjust our theory of affective responses and to concede the variety of cognitive capacities that are called into play when we speak univocally of "experiencing" or "seeing" all the properties of artworks.

On the other hand, Vincent Tomas [1952] correctly tags Bosanquet's "central problem of the aesthetic attitude" [1915]—"how a feeling can get into an object"—a pseudo-problem, since human emotions and the "emotions" of a work of art are different sorts of things; he also fixes the inadequacy of T.S. Eliot's view of the "objective correlative":

> According to Eliot, works of art are expressive in the sense that they are "such that when the external facts, which must terminate in sensory experience, are given, the emotion is immediately evoked" [*Selected Essays: 1917-1932* (New York, 1932), p. 125]. But just as a person may give vent to grief without expressing grief, so, too, a work of art may *evoke* grief without expressing it.

Still, we must be careful not to conflate emotional or affective qualities with expressive ones (cf. Morgan [1952]; Casey [1966]; Bouwsma [1954]; Hospers [1959]). Roughly, the first must be construed relationally, in terms of the capacity to affect (allowing for Elliott's refinement); the second, monadically, on the perceptual model. The first has gerundive force; the second does not. The contrast has been challenged, however; Otto Baensch [1958], for one, construes "emotional" qualities quite differently. They are, he insists, "objective feelings . . . qualities built into the structure of the world as dependent parts or characteristics of objects." They are not, he assures us, confined to states of mind; but he nowhere tells us how such qualities are detected or what assures us that they are "there" to be detected; he says only that they cannot be perceived as sensory qualities. His positive comments are also unhelpful, since they stress only the effect of these independent qualities on the emotional states of human percipients (cf. Santayana [1896]; C. Pratt [1931], [1954]; L. Meyer [1956]).

Theories of the sorts canvassed obviously prize in rather different ways some kind of aesthetic acuity. Often, as we have seen, they link acuity to doubtful or unsupported claims about unusual properties, or unusual cognitive capacities said to be controlled by "the aesthetic attitude." The nature of artworks, the variety of properties ascribed to them, and the near vacuity of terms like "the aesthetic attitude" strongly disconfirm such claims—and the need for them. Still, the range of eligible properties testifies to the relevance of aesthetic acuity even if it alerts us as well to the absence of any sustained account of the relationship between such properties and whatever is open to sensory perception in the narrowest sense. Once we segregate these two issues—the alleged cognitive privilege of the aesthetic attitude and the distinctive acuity that the relevant properties of artworks invoke—we may find ourselves tempted to construe the latter in terms of allegedly uniform features of whatever may be thus discriminated. Otherwise, one wonders how the aesthetic context may be distinguished at all (cf. Urmson [1957]).

Frank Sibley's theory of aesthetic concepts [1959a] is undoubtedly the most important contemporary venture of this sort. Sibley frees the question of acuity from the extravagances we have just been surveying. But, in a very unKantian way, he remains committed to the Kantian thesis that aesthetic judgments exhibit some distinctive logical uniformity. His position requires—and repays—the closest attention. We shall, however, question whether there is *any* significant uniformity that can be assigned to aesthetic perception. In a sense, therefore, we shall attempt to undermine completely the strong Kantian cast of twentieth-century aesthetics.

Many different kinds of judgments are required in the aesthetic context, but, as we shall see, they are neither logically uniform among themselves nor peculiar to aesthetics.

Consider, then, Sibley's thesis:

> We say that a novel has a great number of characters and deals with life in a manufacturing town; that a painting uses pale colors, predominantly blues and greens, and has kneeling figures in the foreground; that the theme in a fugue is inverted at such a point and that there is a stretto at the close; that the action of a play takes place in the span of one day and that there is a reconciliation scene in the fifth act. Such remarks may be made by, and such features pointed out to, anyone with normal eyes, ears, and intelligence. On the other hand, we also say that a poem is tightly-knit or deeply moving; that a picture lacks balance, or has a certain serenity and repose, or that the grouping of the figures sets up an exciting tension; or that the characters in a novel never really come to life, or that a certain episode strikes a false note. It would be neutral enough to say that the making of such judgments as these requires the exercise of taste, perceptiveness, or sensitivity, of aesthetic discrimination or appreciation; one would not say this of my first group. Accordingly, when a word or expression is such that taste or perceptiveness is required in order to apply it, I shall call it an *aesthetic* term or expression, and I shall, correspondingly, speak of *aesthetic* concepts or *taste* concepts.

> It is with an ability to *notice* or *see* or *tell* that things have certain qualities that I am concerned.

The intended contrast is easily misunderstood. Sibley preempts the term "aesthetic" for remarks of his second sort, remarks that call for "the exercise of taste, perceptiveness, or sensitivity." This is not to say that remarks of his first sort are aesthetically irrelevant. On the contrary, he holds that

> aesthetic terms always ultimately apply because of, and aesthetic qualities always ultimately depend upon, the presence of features which, like curving or angular lines, color contrasts, placing of masses, or speed of movement, are visible, audible, or otherwise discernible without any exercise of taste or sensibility.

We normally explain the application of an aesthetic term by reference to appropriate "non-aesthetic features" (cf. Schwyzer [1963]; Sibley [1963]). But it is not altogether clear whether the discrimination of both sorts of features is perceptual in the same sense. Sibley says that the one involves "taste" and the other does not; this may suggest to some readers that distinct kinds of perception are involved. On the other hand, he says that the one involves "perceptiveness" or "sensitivity" and the other does not (in the relevant sense); and this may suggest that a certain level of perceptual acuity, rather than a distinct kind of perception, is involved. The latter reading seems the better one. Aesthetic perception is the perception of features whose concepts are said to behave in a logically distinctive way (cf. Beardsley [1973]; T. Cohen [1973]; Hermerén [1973]; Mitchells [1966-1967]; Freedman [1968]; Logan [1967]; Broiles [1964]). The trouble is that the various features Sibley wishes to account for hardly lend themselves to any familiar theory of purely perceptual competence. Their lack of homogeneity (apart from the claim in question) leads Peter Kivy [1973], for instance, to counter that "one might very well want to maintain that ['aesthetic terms' and 'taste-terms,' those that call for 'the exercise of taste, perceptiveness, or sensitivity'] are not coextensive; that in a perfectly reasonable and philosophically interesting sense of 'aesthetic' and 'non-aesthetic,' not all taste-terms are aesthetic terms and not all non-taste-terms non-aesthetic terms." Kivy also remarks that if aesthetic terms are "non-condition-governed," we may well forfeit the contrast (in the relevant respect) between "actually" and only "seeming" to possess the properties in question. In effect, Kivy argues that if Sibley's analysis of the logical properties of aesthetic concepts holds, then it is unlikely that a genuinely perceptual reading of all aesthetic features can be maintained. Either we save the perceptual thesis by making aesthetic concepts condition-governed, or we seek another model to the extent that we cannot use the "is"/"appears" contrast in a perceptually disciplined way. (One may of course argue that there is not the slightest reason to suppose that aesthetic acuity, aesthetic properties, and aesthetic "perception" are uniform in any theoretically significant way.)

Sibley's thesis, then, is this: "There are no non-aesthetic features which serve in *any* circumstances as logically *sufficient* conditions for applying aesthetic terms. Aesthetic or taste concepts are not in *this* respect condition-governed at all." Virgil Aldrich [1963] takes Sibley's remarks to point to just the kind of perception ("prehension") Aldrich himself is "trying to isolate and characterize." Sibley, however, nowhere characterizes what he means by "perceptiveness" in terms of fundamental perceptual abilities or even "modes" of perception. Still, Aldrich's interpretation draws attention to an important difficulty in Sibley's account. Concede, for instance, that discovering the fugal form in a complex musical composition requires perceptiveness, an ability "to notice or see" what people "with normal eyes, ears, and intelligence" may fail to notice or may learn only with some difficulty. As Kivy suggests, therefore, there may be qualities important in the aesthetic context (not "aesthetic" qualities, on Sibley's usage) that call for a distinct sensitivity though not for what Sibley calls "taste." The apparent equivalence of the terms "taste, perceptiveness, or sensitivity" may, then, be entirely misleading. In fact, on reflection, it seems difficult to explain why a distinct measure of perceptual acuity (construing "perception" generously) *should* conform only to a certain non-condition-governed set of discriminable features. Since the properties in question require "taste," there can be no nonquestionbegging way of forming a consensus regarding their actual presence; hence, to the extent that their discrimination is said to be perceptual and objective, we seem driven to concede a distinct kind of perception, not merely a distinct measure of acuity with respect to a common perceptual ability.

Perceptiveness and sensitivity, one may argue, obtain whenever one points to a feature of an artwork that "dawns" on others only after it is pointed out; if so, its presence cannot insure Sibley's logical thesis. The events of a play, for instance, may take some "perceptual" talent to be seen as a reconciliation scene, but that feature is condition-governed. Again, to judge from *Grove's Dictionary* [1954], the fugue may be assigned necessary conditions and even sufficient conditions; but this does not mean that the perception of the fugal form may not require a certain sensibility. Admittedly, it is not a feature quite like those Sibley emphasizes. But how is its perception relevantly different from that of a reconciliation scene or of a painting's balance? Sibley does not say: all the more reason for resisting the thesis that "there are no *non-aesthetic* features which serve . . . for applying aesthetic terms." Sibley does concede that "taste concepts may be governed *negatively* by conditions." His point, however, is that it is never possible to provide sufficient conditions for the application of one of his "taste concepts." Here, he simply neglects to explain the conditions under which the properties he samples are discernible at all. The fact that they are primarily culturally informed properties, whose use presupposes familiarity with a range of admissible paradigms, argues that they must be condition-governed in some positive sense. Otherwise (against his own intention), Sibley must appear to favor a perceptual ability that behaves rather like a form of intuition. Nevertheless, the variety of properties already reviewed strongly suggests that there can be no uniform cognitive way in which they are discerned and that they cannot all exhibit the logical peculiarity Sibley adduces.

Another complication arises. Imagine, for example, contesting the claim that an Ensor painting (in which brilliantly colored skeletons and witches are crowded into a corner of the canvas) "lacks balance." Here, of course, we find ourselves on the borderline between descriptive and valuational discourse. It cannot be quite enough, therefore, to say (with Sibley) that the application of taste concepts supposes "an ability to notice or see or tell that things have certain qualities": (i) because the qualities alleged may, without contradiction, be denied by another; and (ii) because it may not be possible simply to find or see that the Ensor does or does not "lack balance." In fact, "non-aesthetic" distinctions regarding the Ensor may even be made to support conflicting "taste concepts" ("balance" and "lack of balance," for instance). Here, then, Sibley faces a dilemma. Construe "taste" equivocally: (a) signifying a certain acutely developed perceptual ability; (b) signifying the bias of one's appreciative dispositions. If Sibley interprets "taste concepts" in the sense of (a), he cannot, under the circumstances, avoid a kind of intuitionism. If, on the other hand, he interprets "taste concepts"—at least some taste concepts—in the sense of (b), he cannot maintain his logical thesis uniformly for all aesthetically relevant properties and he cannot construe them (all) on a perceptual model.

Notice, also, that the characterizing expressions we employ range all the way from terms like "red" to terms like "fine," that is, from terms that are purely descriptive to terms that are value-laden and have little or no descriptive power. Sibley [1963] wishes, as he says, to avoid the "evaluative-descriptive antithesis," but that is not sufficient to accommodate a spectrum of varying value-laden terms. It makes obvious sense to say (we possess a reasonable theory explaining how) we "see" or "notice" the red tones of a given painting; challenges can be only of a very restricted sort. The sense in which we say we "see" the balance of a painting, or "see" that a play is tightly-knit, can only be more uncertain and more controversial *once* we concede that we "see" red tones. It would be much less misleading to say we *claim* the painting is balanced, or we *find* the poem well-knit, because, after the claim or finding is defended, the use of "see" can no longer suggest a univocal perceptual sense. If, understanding the reasons you advance in support of the claim that Ensor's painting "lacks balance," I deny the charge and offer a reasonable defense (since I appreciate it differently) you and I simply cannot be said to "see" it in the same way. The question whether the Ensor *is* "balanced" may not be open any further. It *could* not be open, in fact, if both appreciative remarks were fairly supported. We cannot rely, therefore, on an alleged "ability to notice or see," if these terms relevantly signify alternative ways of appreciating things.

Now, Sibley's specimen locutions are actually weighted in favor of appreciative differences: only to the extent, then, that taste becomes official (not, for that reason, available to the man "with normal eyes, ears, and intelligence") could we pertinently speak of "an ability to notice or see or tell." Addressing the same issue, Isabel Hungerland [1968] says that "there are no criteria for [aesthetic concepts], though they have . . . pre-conditions and . . . truth-conditions." She adds that there is no contrasted use for "really is" and "only looks" in the ascription of aesthetic qualities as there is for the usual perceptual qualities; and she construes "correct" descriptions in terms of "common sympathies, snobberies, outlook, personal history, training in certain arts" (cf. Kivy [1973]; T. Cohen [1973]). Her intention is to revise an earlier formula [1963] favoring Sibley by fixing an important weakness in his account. The new account runs as follows: "The 'A's' [i.e., aesthetic terms] are terms invented to describe how N-featured things [i.e., things characterized non-aesthetically], or events, may, *under certain circumstances, look to us from a certain perceptual viewpoint.*" Here, Hungerland means to replace the Sibleyan thesis with an adjusted sense of P.F. Strawson's concept of "presupposition" [1952]. The new alternative is also overstated, however, since it fails to account for appreciative and valuational differences among pertinently valid judgments.

For the sake of accuracy, we may soften the argument. There are appreciative differences that do not entail valuational differences. Aldrich [1963] offers the following instance (always, of course, in the context of his own perceptual theory):

> Suppose . . . that the structural solidity of the Cézanne composition—which spawned the later cubism—dawns on you as you look . . . at the picture. You get the impression, and report it in words. Your companion says that the realistic fruit by Chardin or Fantin-Latour is more obviously solid, adding that Huysmans was right about there being some defect in Cézanne's vision. Your problem then is to show him what you mean by the solidity realized through sculpting with color, not by representational realism . . . In short, you are trying to convey an objective impression in an expressive portrayal.

He remarks that such an exchange often has an instructional aspect: for instance, it may involve gesturing to imitate the way the artist worked (as one sees it) as well as comparing the craft of other artists; it may lead one's companion in the exchange eventually to exclaim, "Now I get it!" Such an exchange, we may say, concerns appreciation though not necessarily taste, in the sense in which it need not involve preferential values. In fact, the widest range of appreciatively oriented but non-value-laden terms includes those associated with a certain comparison of styles—as in the remark that Lehmbruck's *Kneeling Woman* is "rather Maillolesque, though it has perhaps a certain Gothic mien." Of course, such judgments will not involve taste in Sibley's perceptual sense and will not (*contra* Aldrich) require the prehensional model.

One of Sibley's lists [1959a] of relevant terms (*"unified, balanced, integrated, lifeless, serene, somber, dynamic, powerful, vivid, delicate, moving, trite, sentimental, tragic"*) is clearly of a mixed sort, including at least "somber," possibly others like "delicate," that signify appreciative differences without entailing evaluations or verdicts of any kind. Others are clearly value-laden—"tightly-knit," "balanced," "sets up an exciting tension," or "strikes a false note." Still others, possibly including some of these, oblige us to construe the sense of "seeing" interpretively or in terms of the phenomenon of "seeing as" rather than as narrowly sensory. But where appreciative differences obtain—in the relatively value-neutral sense (for instance, when "slimness, lightness, lack of intensity of color, and so on, count only towards, not against, delicacy")—precisely because such qualities can count "only *typically* or *characteristically* towards delicacy," no one can ever be decisively shown to be wrong in affirming or denying delicacy, once we pass beyond "typical" conditions. Only a perceptual analogue of intuitionism could save Sibley's thesis here.

Sibley [1968] makes another telling concession. He admits that ascriptions like *graceful, dainty, moving, plaintive, balanced, lacking in unity,* and the like—what he sometimes calls "tertiary or *Gestalt* properties, among others"—may merely be "*apt* rather than *true.*" He claims that "the relation between the nonexpressive and the expressive properties of an art work is one of ambiguous constituency"; but this simply raises anew the question of objectivity (cf. Tormey [1971]; Stahl [1971]). Nevertheless, he does favor the objectivity of such qualities on the basis of considerations that fail to exclude the appreciative alternative. He notices [1959a] that simple qualities like color admit of "ultimate proof" (that is, proof that they are present) only in the way in which that proof is "tied to an overlap of agreement in sorting, distinguishing and much else which links people present and past . . . where different sets of people agree amongst themselves thus (e.g., groups of similarly color-blind people), it is reference to the set with the most detailed discrimination that we treat as conclusive." He continues in the following way:

> When I say the only ultimate test or proof, I mean that, since colors are simple properties in the sense that no other visible feature makes something the color it is, one cannot appeal to other features of an object in virtue of possessing which, by some rule of meaning, it can be said to be red or blue, as one can with such properties as triangular, etc. With colors there is no such intermediate appeal; only directly an appeal to agreement. But *if* there are aesthetic properties—the supposition under investigation—they will, despite dissimilarities, be like colors in this respect. For though, unlike colors, they will be dependent on other properties of things, they cannot, since they are not entailed by the properties responsible for them, be ascribed by virtue of the presence of other properties and some rule of meaning. Hence a proof will again make no intermediate appeal to other properties of the thing, but directly to agreement.

He also remarks that "this agreement is not easy to describe. Not any agreement will do; the fact that some of us, here and now, make identical discriminations need not settle the color of things."

Clearly, Sibley believes the "perception" of aesthetic or tertiary qualities is not essentially different from the perception of colors: the agreement involved is an agreement about perceived (though dependent) qualities. But then, he needs a *theory* of perception and perceptual qualities to justify construing aesthetic qualities as genuinely perceptual—not such that it would be merely *apt* rather than *true* to say that this poem or sculpture "has" them. Recall that Sibley insists [1965] that "aesthetics deals with a kind of perception," and compares the defective aesthetic percipient with the color-blind man. He also says that "if a work is graceful there will be reasons why it is, and this will be so whether anyone ever knows, or thinks, or has any reason for thinking it so or not." Nevertheless, Hungerland's "is/appears" contrast is decisive: we utterly lack a theory that would justify invoking that contrast in contexts in which most of Sibley's terms would apply. And, in spite of his insistence that "some aesthetic judgments may be characterized as right, wrong, true, false, undeniable," Sibley's own development of the issue actually favors the alternative theory. In fact, he concedes that, even for his own cases, "for some ranges of judgments we prefer terms like 'reasonable,' 'admissible,' 'understandable' or 'eccentric' to 'right' and 'wrong.' "

The question remains whether the concession extends to the rest of Sibley's specimen concepts, or whether some of these reduce to condition-governed concepts. For example, Kivy convincingly construes "unity" in music as conditioned-governed. "Monothematic structure [that can be heard]," he remarks, "is a necessary-and-sufficient condition for the ascription of musical unity, [in one common and relevant sense of 'unity']." And monothematic structure itself is condition-governed in rather the same way as is intelligence (that is, an open-ended set of sufficient conditions can be supplied). Kivy also observes that "unified" has a clearly perceptual, non-value-laden use in music—as in contrasting the unity of Beethoven's *Eroica* (puzzling in its early reception) and the merely "apparent unity" of Verdi's *Stabat Mater* (cf. Grove [1962]). Erwin Panofsky [1953] provides another instructive instance. Speaking of the influence on the Master of Flémalle of Franco-Flemish miniatures of what he calls "the Italianizing kind," Panofsky remarks that "a close similarity has been observed between the Dijon 'Nativity' and the miniatures in the 'Brussels Hours' by Jacquemart de Hesdin. With them it shares a taste for cool, pearly colors (purplish brown, white shaded with blue or mauve, and a neutral gray) which merge into an admirable, silvery tone by virtue of the Master's command of the *nouvelle pratique.*" Göran Hermerén [1975] observes about this passage that, with the exception of "the value-loaded term 'admirable,' " the similarities observed "are relatively uncomplicated and simple, in the sense that it is rather easy to test the statement that there are [the] similarities [noted] between the . . . works [and that] such a test need not presuppose any specific aesthetic sensitivity [*sic*] in Panofsky or his readers." The challenge to Sibley is plain.

Such terms are actually used over and over again, so that though they lack professionally fixed specimens, they come to be associated more or less reliably with recognizable instances. That we cannot formulate logically sufficient conditions for their use and that particular things are said to have the qualities in question on the strength of their quite specific ("non-aesthetic") qualities argues that particular claims cannot be flatly true or false (or, conceding the asymmetry Sibley affirms, cannot at least be flatly true): they may be said to be "reasonable," "fair," "not extreme," "apt," and so on. The result is that, where more or less clear-cut instances are identifiable, predicating any of the sort of quality in question is a matter of fair debate. We need not agree, therefore, with John Hospers [1959], who asserts that a work of art's having a certain emotional quality (the argument is extended to non-emotional qualities) is, at bottom, a matter of "conviction," that defending claims of this sort is at best a dubious business. Henry Aiken [1945] draws a similar conclusion, though this seems in part due to his concern with certain expressive qualities—treated as emotional effects "located *in us* rather than in the object itself." "Conviction," in fact—Hospers' term—sounds very much like "a matter of taste"; but it may be argued that even where divergent tastes are involved, supporting reasons may properly be requested.

The concepts of the great historical styles (the Baroque and the Gothic, for instance) differ markedly from the informal vocabulary we have been examining; they are normally formulated professionally for a predetermined temporal and geographical extension, and with an eye to necessary and sufficient or characteristic conditions (cf. Wölfflin [1929]; Schapiro [1953]). It is interesting to note that Sibley does not consider such concepts, that they are unavoidable in aesthetic criticism, that they require "sensitivity," and that they cannot possibly be construed as non-condition-governed.

There is, also, as has been remarked, a vocabulary parasitic on that of period styles which reflects the informal use of language. Expressions like "Gothicized," "Rembrantesque," "Mozartian"—used to indicate that something is merely *like* some standard instance (in what respect and in what degree is a fair question)—show that in using a large number of characterizing epithets, we are not so much interested in whether a given object *is* (and in that sense capable of being "seen" to be) "Gothicized" or "Mozartian" as we are interested in the *right* to speak thus. Defense of an attenuated sort is, however, still required and possible. I am reminded of a friend who regularly discovered "Matisse women" in the New York subway. Obviously, the theme applies to the relationship between art and nature as well (cf. Forge [1973]; Hepburn [1973]) and becomes increasingly pertinent as characterizing expressions become more and more informal, whether they are value-laden or not. In fact, they all seem to fall under the general rubric of "seeing as," more in the sense of reasoned appreciation than of an arbitrary child's game (cf. Wittgenstein [1953]). Also, these ascriptions mark our inability to say with precision what the demarcation line is between what is and what is not to be found "in" a particular artwork. Hence, the very status of descriptive criticism is affected by our theory of the nature and ontic status of artworks; and a certain measure of relativism—in the appreciative range of our judgments—is unavoidable.

This recalls, of course, the observation that "the true" is opposed not only to "the false" but to "the plausible." Here, then, characterizing expressions verging toward individual appreciative tendencies and individual taste behave logically very much like critical interpretations. Isabel Hungerland's point [1968] about the inapplicability of a contrasting use of "is" and "appears" (in the strict sense required for sensory perception—not in the sense in which we merely voice our own convictions against another's) is obviously crucial: it exposes a certain attenuated, theoretically altered sense of "see" or "perceive" favored (but not sufficiently analyzed) in such accounts as Sibley's. In fact, the extended use may even involve considerations of causal influence that accompany or inform perceptual affinities that cannot themselves be counted as perceptual in the sense usually intended. Appreciative tolerance obtains even here, constrained of course by the details of actual causal connections. Two specimen remarks will make this clear:

> Superficially this painting *Eiffel Tower* has something in common with certain Cubist landscapes by Picasso and Braque. . . . and it seems likely that in these paintings Delaunay had again been directly influenced by what he saw at Kahnweiler's gallery (Golding [1959]).

> Perhaps also during this decade, Caroselli began working in a second Caravaggesque style, derived from Honthorst rather than directly from Caravaggio. . . . Surely the sharp contrasts of light and dark on their figures, and the formal clarity which Briganti notes in their art [that is, in the work of certain artists like Caroselli], were distantly derivative from Caravaggio through his followers (Moir [1967]).

Göran Hermerén [1975], discussing these and similar observations, presses what he calls the "Visibility Requirement" for "all kinds of influence in the wide sense": "If X influenced the creation of Y in some respect, then traces of the influence from X should be manifest (visible or recognizable) in Y." But of course "traces" of influence will be visible *qua* traces only on a theory that correctly construes *what* is visible as a trace. These examples show, by the way, how natural it is to consider causal influences aesthetically (*contra* Beardsley [1958]).

In summary, then, we have established the following: (i) that the aesthetic attitude provides no cognitive privilege and generates no distinctive properties of artworks; (ii) that the descriptive and characterizing concepts used in aesthetic appreciation and criticism are not and cannot possibly be of any logically uniform sort; (iii) that epithets like "perceive" and "experience" signify, in the aesthetic context, cognitively eligible claims without reference to the nature of the contributing faculty, without restricting eligible properties to what may be perceivable in any narrow sense, and without implication as to whether particular properties are or are not to be found "in" any given work; (iv) that it is impossible to deny that aesthetic concepts are condition-governed, in the sense that their use depends on background information and culturally provided criteria in terms of which one may construe what is perceivable in the narrow sensory sense as confirming the presence of the aesthetic qualities in question; (v) that there are certain aesthetic concepts for which necessary, sufficient, or characteristic conditions may be supplied; (vi) that there are certain aesthetic concepts for which the "is"/"appears" contrast does not (relevantly) obtain, as it must in genuinely perceptual contexts; (vii) that the divergent use of appreciative concepts may be defended, whether lacking or possessing valuational import; and (viii) that there is an ineliminable measure of relativism in critical discourse at the putatively descriptive and appreciative level.

10. Evaluating and Appreciating Works of Art

Aesthetic evaluations or valuations are bewilderingly varied. It is quite natural, therefore, that one should attempt to distinguish them either in terms of the purpose they are to serve, or the logical features that mark them off from value judgments of other kinds (cf. Urmson [1957]). The usual effort of the first sort contrasts aesthetic and moral concerns (cf. Hampshire [1954]); the second tends to risk the distinction of aesthetic judgments altogether, but we may anticipate failure along both lines. Consequently, a decisive difficulty looms for those who favor, however vestigially, a Kantian account of aesthetic judgment. Kant [1952] sharply distinguished moral and aesthetic judgments in terms of the relation of such judgments to our behavior and interests, and in terms of their own distinctive logic (cf. Santayana [1896]; also, Kitaro [1973]). If we collect instances of either sort of judgment (moral and aesthetic), we shall find, however, that we cannot segregate them easily on either count—use and purpose, or logic. Still, the Kantian theme is remarkably resilient.

For instance, it is quite generally assumed that moral judgments function to "guide conduct" and that aesthetic judgments never do. Thus Stuart Hampshire [1954] remarks: ". . . aesthetic judgments are not comparable in purpose with moral judgments, and there are no problems of aesthetics comparable with the problems of ethics." He goes on to say:

> A work of art is gratuitous. It is not essentially the answer to a question or the solution of a presented problem. . . . Compare the subject-matter and situation of moral judgment. Throughout any day of one's life, and from the moment of waking, one is confronted with situations which demand action. Even to omit to do anything positive, and to remain passive, is to adopt a policy . . . it always makes sense to ask for the reasons behind any practical decision. . . . But if something is made or done gratuitously, and not in response to a problem posed, there can be no question of preferring one solution to another; judgment of the work done does not involve a choice, and there is no need to find grounds of preference.

His view, in this regard, is rather close to R.M. Hare's [1952]:

> The reason why actions are in a peculiar way revelatory of moral
> principles is that the function of moral principles is to guide con-
> duct. The language of morals is one sort of prescriptive language
> . . . though it is no part of my purpose to "reduce" moral language
> to imperatives . . .

But we may judge actions in the remote past, in fiction, in hypothetical
cases, or regarding what should have been done (now impossible to correct) without supposing that comparable situations will confront us (and,
surely, independent of whether they do confront us): we may, that is,
judge appreciatively without an eye to guiding our own actions—even if
it is the case that "moral consistency" requires a certain conformity if
and when related decisions do confront us. We may even judge regarding
what is still obligatory though now impossible to do. These sorts of considerations raise grave difficulties for Hare's thesis that moral language
is prescriptive of action and similar in logical respects to imperatival
language (cf. Margolis [1971]). Also, against Hampshire as well, it may
be remarked that not every moral appraisal concerns situations that *"demand* action" (cf. Zemach [1971]). Hare himself quite revealingly
asserts:

> . . . if I admit that the life of St. Francis was morally better than
> mine, and really mean this as an evaluation, there is nothing for it
> but to try to be more like St. Francis, which is arduous. That is why
> most of our "moral judgments" about the saints are merely con-
> ventional—we never intend them to be a guide in determining our
> own conduct.

In effect, this is to admit (against Hare's own purpose) the possibility of
moral appreciation where the agent judging cannot choose or act conformably. Similar difficulties confront Hare's strenuous effort [1963] to
resolve the problem of *akrasia,* for the admission of genuine weakness of
will utterly undermines prescriptivism.

We may judge conduct and character also in terms that are jointly
moral and aesthetic; for example, someone's conduct may be said to be
"kindly," "tactful," "generous," "discreet," "gracious," "lordly,"
"foul," "heinous." Here, we judge appreciatively rather than to guide
conduct. No logical distinctions need yet be called into play. But where

value judgments concern grading rather than ranking (as in the use of the predicates cited), it is either false to hold that particular moral judgments are action-guiding (judgments of "goodness" or "rightness," for instance, as opposed to judgments of "duty" or "obligation"), or utterly vacuous. Certainly, knowing that something has a certain measure of value does not "pragmatically" entail, even in context, that, conceding that fact, one straightway acts; and if it is claimed still to have some action-guiding force (for instance, influencing the rationality of one's behavior), then there are absolutely no distinctions that are not action-guiding (*see* Margolis [1971], [1976c]).

But if this is so—*if* the moral appreciation of character is admissible *and if* there are no essential logical distinctions between moral and aesthetic judgments—then in principle we cannot deny the aesthetic relevance of the moral appreciation and appraisal of artworks. This is a rather unexpected benefit. For, it is quite clear that, in clarifying certain properties of artworks, commentators regularly remark on the morally, culturally, politically, and religiously qualified sensibilities of the artist himself and, in doing so, often appraise both artist and work in doctrinally variable ways (*see* Girvetz and Ross [1971]). The complexity of such appraisals casts doubt on the putative moral neutrality of critics and theorists who insist on confining criticism to "the aesthetic object," or to what is (in the aesthetic sense) straightforwardly "internal" to artworks (cf. Beardsley [1970b]; Hirsch [1976]; Frye [1968]; Krieger [1968]). Also, doubt is inevitably cast on the objectivity with which the sensibilities of artists are allegedly appraised. The following comment by Lukács [1964] makes this clear (cf. Leavis [1948]; also, Sircello [1972]):

Paradoxically, Scott's greatness is closely linked with his often narrow conservatism. He seeks the "middle way" between the extremes and endeavors to demonstrate artistically the historical reality of this way by means of his portrayal of the great crises in English history. This basic tendency finds immediate expression in the way he constructs his plot and selects his central figure. The "hero" of a Scott novel is always a more or less mediocre, average English gentleman. He generally possesses a certain, though never outstanding, degree of practical intelligence, a certain moral fortitude and decency which even rises to a capacity for self-sacrifice, but which never grows into a sweeping human passion, is never the enraptured devotion to a great cause. Not only are the Waverleys, Mortons, Osbaldistons, and so on correct, decent, average representatives of the English aristocracy of this kind, but so, too, is Ivanhoe, the "romantic" knight of the Middle Ages. In later criticism this choice of hero was sharply criticized, for example by [Hippolyte] Taine. Such later critics saw here a symptom of Scott's own mediocrity as an artist. Precisely the opposite is true. That he builds his novels round a "middling," merely correct and never heroic "hero" is the clearest proof of Scott's exceptional and revolutionary epic gifts, although from a psychological-biographical point of view, no doubt his own personal, petty aristocratic-conservative prejudices did play an important part in the choice of these heroes. What is expressed here, above all, is a renunciation of Romanticism, a conquest of Romanticism, a higher development of the realist literary traditions of the Enlightenment in keeping with the new times.

On the other hand, even aesthetic criticism sometimes recommends improvement and is not restricted to mere appreciation. Hampshire makes the following counterclaim:

> One may, as a spectator, prefer one work to another, but there is no *necessity* to decide between them . . . A critical judgment is in this sense non-committal and makes no recommendation; the critic may reject the work done without being required to show what the artist ought to have done in place of the work rejected. But the moralist who condemns an action must indicate what ought to have been done in its place; for something had to be done, some choice between relative evils made.

But in moral dilemmas no question of what ought (exclusively) to have been done arises—the evil is unavoidable; moral judgment becomes appreciative again. Certainly, in such cases, there is no "necessity" to decide between alternatives, in the sense of choosing what is required. Hampshire misleads us in suggesting that moral criticism (which he wrongly conflates with condemnation) entails that it was believed that there was something that *ought* to have been done. Also, if—as he sometimes does—a critic judges a particular work to be faulty, he must, (particularly if he thinks the work recoverable—the parallel to the usual moral situation), be able to *recommend* the appropriate changes. He will say "what ought to have been done." We say, for instance, that the right arm of Maillol's *The Mediterranean* is too fat and clumsy for the body; that the stride of Rodin's *John the Baptist* is not correctly balanced for a realistic figure; and that, as Ezra Pound [1950] advised T.S. Eliot, the original draft of *The Waste Land* should be considerably cut and begin with the line "April is the cruellest month."

Moral judgments, then, may well be appreciative rather than prescriptive, and aesthetic judgments may recommend alternative courses of action for artists. In short, moral and aesthetic judgments may be somewhat different in purpose; but they are not, in this respect, two entirely separate species within a common genus. The moral centers more on the general prudential interests of the species (cf. Margolis [1971]); the aesthetic, on certain variable interests regarding which rational advice and direction (including moral direction) is still possible and relevant.

Hampshire has been misled by his insistence that works of art are "gratuitous"; he seems to have drawn the mistaken conclusion that one can never discern the artistic problem of a given work and criticize its solution on internal grounds—which, interestingly enough, would have been fully compatible with Kant's notion of "purposiveness without purpose" (cf. Ecker [1963]; Reynolds [1975]: Discourse VIII). Gombrich [1960], for example, compellingly interprets the entire tradition of naturalistic painting in terms of the gradual solution of certain technical problems of representation (cf. Goodman [1960]; Wartofsky [1972]; Maynard [1972]). It is perhaps pointless to quarrel with Hampshire over whether an artwork is *"essentially* . . . the solution of a presented problem."* But the very idea that it is a work involving the intelligent use of a craft, that it is informed by the cultural sensibilities of an historical society, and that it is an "utterance" of some sort, confirms the strong, central sense in which artworks are almost always viewed by artists, historians, and critics of the arts as involving the solution of technical problems, and answers to questions with moral, political, religious, and intellectual relevance. So the objection to Hampshire's thesis is based not merely on the technical aspects of art but also on the unavoidable bearing of the entire cultural milieu on the production of art—including, prominently, moral considerations.

To say that a work of art is "gratuitous" implies, in context, that there are radical differences between moral and aesthetic judgments, and moral and aesthetic concerns. In fact, the naive and potentially irresponsible thesis of the "gratuitous" nature of art—seemingly subtle when formulated in terms of the Kantian heritage—leads one to express pointed agreement with the otherwise rather bald and dubious pretentions of Soviet aesthetics. For example, in what appears to be a recent textbook of aesthetics, Avner Zis [1977] states very early:

> With reference to the Leninist theory of reflection and the
> materialist interpretation of history, Marxist-Leninist aesthetics
> sees art as a manifestation of social consciousness and man's
> practical-cum-cultural apprehension of the world. These important
> tenets of Marxist-Leninist aesthetics were formulated on the basis
> of dialectical-materialist analysis of art, and in partaicular its social
> essence. Today when aesthetics is the arena of a fierce battle of
> ideas, the significance of these tenets is particularly great. They
> provide a reliable orientation, arm us against idealist conceptions
> according to which art is a separate, self-contained world of artistic
> reality, determined in no way by socio-historical circumstances . . .
> The founders of Marxism-Leninism approached art as a form of
> man's active, practical and energetic relationship to the world
> around him . . . as a specific type of thinking, as artistic cognition
> of the world, as a complex and distinctive form of social con-
> sciousness, as ideology.

Zis's general thesis is obviously more sensible than Hampshire's in providing for the range of critically relevant observations, regardless of the
"scientific" status of Marxist-Leninist claims.

It is a further common assumption, also inherited from Kant, that
aesthetic judgments are judgments of taste—about which it is said there
is no disputing. This assumption involves a misleading way of speaking:
when we think of taste in terms of liking, enjoying, preferring—that is,
when we think of taste merely in terms of our responses to things—we
are not interested characteristically in judgments, but in reports or
manifestations, of taste. On the other hand, when we speak of judgments
we cannot but be interested in the claims critics advance and the grounds
on which these may be justified (cf. Baier [1958]). There may be no more
than a contingent relationship, therefore, between aesthetic judgments
and the attitudes and responses that we associate with our actual tastes.
It is quite possible that one likes what one judges to be of poor quality or
fails to appreciate what one believes to be excellent. Think, for example,
of adults reading childish comic strips or of someone apologizing for his
inability to enjoy Mozart's chamber music. In fact, it is even conceivable
that one judges in accord with the standards of another (cf. Knight
[1954]; Edwards [1955]; Ziff [1960]). But the contingency has only
restricted application.

If I judge a particular work to be good (express the judgment
publicly), I would, on demand, normally attempt to supply justifying

reasons; I have not yet supplied them in issuing the judgment. Yet I have not failed to judge even if I fail to supply the justifying reasons. But *if* the justifying reasons are admitted to be true and relevantly sufficient for the finding or judgment in question, one cannot withhold the finding (cf. Sircello [1968]). The finding or judgment (or verdict) is not an expression of taste, and is only contingently related to our actual taste. Arnold Isenberg [1949b], for one, has made a serious error on this matter. Quite correctly, he says first, "There is not in all the world's criticism a single purely descriptive statement concerning which one is prepared to say beforehand, 'If it is true, I shall *like* that work so much the better.' . . ." He is right in this, of course (though the thesis is emphatically not Sibley's [1959a]). But he goes on to say, *"The truth of R* [the justifying reasons] *never adds the slightest weight to V* [the value judgment or verdict], because *R* does not designate any quality the perception of which might induce me to *assent* to *V"* (cf. Tormey [1973]). Liking, however, is neither a verdict nor a reason for a verdict, and the reasons that would *support* a verdict cannot be said (logically) to support our liking, though they may (contingently) affect our liking. Contrary to Isenberg's view, the justification of a judgment is and must be possible, though the justification of a judgment is hardly the same as the explanation of one's taste (a difference Isenberg seems to concede elsewhere). The apparent plausibility of his claim—apart from conflating judgment and pleasure—rests entirely on the undefended assumption (i) that aesthetic judgments are all of one sort and (ii) that they never allow for more or less adequately defended verdicts. But (i) may be shown to be false, and (ii) is utterly preposterous. In rather different ways, the views of Isenberg, Hampshire, Sibley, Tormey, and Scruton [1974] merely confirm the ubiquity of Kant's protean influence without confirming the validity of the Kantian thesis.

To speak of value judgments as justifiable is to pronounce a tautology. But confirming a value judgment is not, as such, revealing one's taste. Margaret Macdonald [1954a] seems to hold that a critic's verdict calls for justification; but she goes on to suggest that the justification is rather like the sort we supply for "our affections and antipathies"—in short, for our tastes. She draws the conclusion: "Criticism is . . . an indefinite set of devices for 'presenting' not 'proving' the merits of works of art," which, in all fairness, is quite close to the position Isenberg advances (as well as Tormey [1973]). This is a very attractive and subtle point, possibly somewhat too strong in eliminating findings or verdicts, but surely close to the truth. It would be somewhat more convincing, however, if it were associated with matters of *appreciation* (with reasoned preferences) rather than with matters of *taste* (with mere likes and dislikes). We do not justify "our affections and antipathies," but we do justify judgments (possibly expressed in our affections) that presuppose our taste (cf. Clegg [1963]).

"Taste," of course, is distinctly equivocal: signifying (a) the bare fact of someone's or some aggregate's likes, dislikes, and preferences—usually expressed in the plural ("tastes"); or (b) a valuation conforming with, and presupposing, tastes in sense (a)—a judgment, in short, or behavior or disposition implying such judgment, that is not justifiable (that is incapable of being justified merely) in terms of tastes in sense (a) (cf. Ziff [1960]). Sense (a) concerns facts *about* how particular persons value things, and cannot appropriately call for defense; (b) concerns particular valuations *by* persons, and cannot but call for defense. In effect, this is to distinguish (with Kant [1952]: "Dialectic of the Aesthetic Judgment") the alternative senses of "*de gustibus . . .*". A sociologist is likely to take "taste" in sense (a) and hence, to explain it causally—for example, as in the studies of Levin Schücking [1944] (though Schücking admits a difference between taste so considered and merit). A philosopher is likely to take "taste" in sense (b); hence, to seek "reasons for," rather than the "causes of," one's taste, that is, to seek justifications rather than explanations—for example, as in the studies of Bernard C. Heyl [1946]. Another philosopher, George Boas [1937], is in the anomalous position of insisting on the adequacy of sense (a) for the entire range of relevant use. The result is a certain cynical tone, at the price of ignoring an important range of judgments.

Some value judgments cannot be made unless our taste happens to be such and such. Consider Isenberg's illustration, "The expression on her face was delightful." Ordinarily, one says this sort of thing only if the expression has qualities that are apt to delight one (cf. Nowell-Smith [1954]). One need not actually be delighted (think of a tired drama critic who can, without responding, notice what is "charming" or "lovely" or "stirring" or "horrible"). The relevant reasons will *presuppose* but not *include* our tastes. And the predicates ("fascinating," "delicious," "impressive," "beautiful," "sublime," "comic," "ridiculous") *may* be used in such a way that the taste of others rather than one's own is relevant, though such a use ordinarily requires a special context and alters the logic of the judgment (cf. Edwards [1955]). The latter practice has a wide application—for example, in the field of fashion. But if judgments depend on prevailing taste (which may include one's own taste) rather than on one's own personal taste, they would (as we shall say) be "findings" (or "verdicts") rather than "appreciative judgments."

Helen Knight [1954] misleads us then in saying (correctly), "my liking a picture is never a criterion of its goodness," if, as she also insists, " 'Good' is exactly the same kind of word as 'piquant' and 'beautiful,' but its use is far wider" (cf. Meager [1958-1959]; Mothersill [1961]). She is, of course, wrong about "good"; in its commending use (*see* Nowell-Smith [1954]; Hare [1952]), for instance, we can draw from its meaning no characteristic criteria for its application, as we can for "piquant." Nothing could be judged to be *piquant* unless it were supposed to have properties that, under relevant circumstances, tended to arouse a certain sensitive response in the judge *or* in some indicated population. The use of the predicate "piquant" presupposes tastes, though it may enter either an appreciative judgment or a finding. "Good" need not have any affective import at all; its range of uses must be specified through other means. But there is a more serious issue. Knight correctly observes that one's tastes cannot as such supply justifying reasons (though subjectivism consistently construes one's tastes as decisive criteria). She tends, however, to treat all value judgments as being logically rather like what we have been calling findings (or verdicts). Isenberg, on the other hand, tends to construe all value judgments as appreciative judgments, except that he also confuses the two senses of "taste." Both views are overly simple and both are misleading. Sometimes, we defend a judgment (that depends on, or presupposes, our tastes) without it being supposed that another, acknowledging the adequacy of our reasons, is thereby committed to sharing the judgment. And sometimes, we defend judgments that enter a dispute as disjunctive claims, but for which in principle decisive evidence may be collected—evidence that does not depend on personal tastes, though it may well depend on prevailing tastes. Liking, therefore, is not a criterion of goodness, but to judge in accord with one's taste is not to judge arbitrarily; reasons are always relevant.

Macdonald [1954a] asserts categorically that "no one, as Wordsworth said, can be *argued* into a favorable verdict on the *Lyrical Ballads*." But this is a confusion. If we are to arrive at a verdict (in at least one eligible sense of the term), we must be evaluating the *Ballads* according to criteria that are decisive (even if they require consulting prevailing tastes). So it must be possible to be *argued* into a verdict. To demur when the evidence is available is either to construe the judgment appreciatively or to retreat merely to expressing one's taste (cf. Clegg [1963]).

These alternatives help to clarify the fundamental difference between appreciative judgments and findings. The model for findings appears in the legal and medical context: reference to one's taste is logically irrelevant. On the other hand, in appreciative judgments, reference to one's taste is logically implied in advancing supporting evidence, though personal taste does not supply a justifying reason for such judgments. Also, the defense of appreciative judgments must be conceded to be compatible with the obvious fact that we appreciate things differently. Hence, in assessing appreciative judgments, we look for reasons that would justify someone's *saying,* for example, that a painting is beautiful rather than reasons that count as *proving* a painting to be beautiful. This is the upshot of Macdonald's distinction between "presenting" and "proving" the merit of a work of art, though her own formulation is noticeably weaker: we look for reasons that would support an appreciative remark rather than reasons that would show that an object judged actually *has* the qualities ascribed to it. Ordinarily, in non-value-laden exchanges, the contrast is pointless, though (as J.L. Austin has shown [1962]), it is sometimes apt (as in deliberate exaggeration). In appreciative exchanges, it is crucial. We should also notice that not only terms like "sublime," "ridiculous," "horrible," "tragic," and "comic," but also terms like "lovely," "thrilling," "exciting," "charming," and "moving"—which ordinarily have a much greater tolerance for idiosyncratic taste—may have gerundive force (*see* Nowell-Smith [1954]).

Still, some refinements are needed. If findings (or verdicts) are justifiable, one may argue about values and convince another that a given object has or has not an assignable value. To be sure, we cannot *argue* another into enjoying or liking that object. But to evaluate, in the sense of reaching a finding, is to judge in accord with criteria that are logically indifferent to one's appreciative bias. Methodologically, there is no difference between factual judgments and (such) judgments of value; findings are distinguished by their predicates (*see* Margolis [1971]; cf. Baier [1958]). Furthermore, verdictive predicates tend to be antecedently marked as disjunctively eligible. One sees this for instance in judging health and sickness, guilt and innocence, or lying and cheating. In the aesthetic domain, findings (and, more narrowly, verdicts) appear chiefly in professional or academic criticism, that is, wherever a sense of order, tradition, and established values—somewhat like those of medicine or the law—obtains. Professionalization is not essential, however, as can be seen in the moral domain, where judgments of duty or obligation, as distinct from judgments of happiness, behave more or less verdictively, rest on criteria indifferent to personal preferences, and usually resemble logically non-valuational judgments of fact. Verdicts, as in fashion and beauty shows, accord with prevailing taste; but often, such judgments contrast (in different ways) with appreciative judgments and with findings proper.

Put very briefly, the difference between value judgments and those that are not lies exclusively with their predicates, whereas the difference (in a purely formal sense) between factual judgments and those that are not depends on the ascribability of truth values (Margolis [1971]). Valuational, value-laden, or normative predicates are those whose meaning cannot be explicated without reference to determinate norms of worth —with regard to which we either grade or rank the members of eligible sets of things. Where the use of such predicates is publicly fixed and does not depend on personal tastes, relevant judgments are what I am calling *findings* (or evaluative judgments); where the use of such predicates falls within a range of tolerable linguistic usage and is intended to accord with or presuppose one's personal likes and dislikes, relevant judgments are what I am calling *appreciative judgments.* The first are capable (on a convention) of being found true or false and behave in precisely the same way as do (non-valuational) factual judgments. Whether they are objectively valid in the same sense as such factual judgments depends on the prospects of what has come to be called cognitivism (*see* Margolis [1975c])—an altogether independent matter. But appreciative judgments cannot behave that way, though they exhibit their own characteristic rigor. Hence, we see that the fact/value dichotomy is quite misleading (cf. Sibley [1959a]): the division rests on a mixed classification, since being factual (in the purely formal sense) concerns the ascribability of truth and falsity to *judgments,* and being valuational concerns the semantic properties of *predicates.*

Furthermore, as we have already seen (at least implicitly), appreciative judgments fail to provide for the usual "is"/"appears" contrast. The central use of that contrast bears on the confirmability of the actual properties of an object: wherever properties are taken to be descriptively assigned, the contrast is entailed. Hence, findings obtain where some set of the actual properties of an object are, on a theory, taken to be sufficient for the ascription of a certain value; the informality with which such properties may be specified does not affect the logical status of findings. But appreciative judgments obtain where, precisely, the actual (the minimally describable) properties of an object are "filtered" through the personal tastes and sensibilities of the agent judging; there, no set of the actual properties of an object are sufficient to justify the ascription of the relevant value. Hence, on an appropriate theory, we say that an object *has* a certain value (findings) or that one is justified only in *ascribing* a certain value to that object (appreciative judgments). So the "is"/"appears" contrast obtains at two moments of a finding: an object has (as opposed to merely appearing to have) certain non-value-laden properties; having such properties, it also has (as opposed to merely appearing to have) a certain value. For example, if X really did act in such and such a way, then, on a theory, X really did murder Y. Personal tastes are, formally, irrelevant. In appreciative judgments, on the other hand, the properties that an object actually *has* are favored or disfavored in a personal way; no question properly arises, therefore, about its *having,* independently of one's likes and dislikes, properties or qualities that are imputed to it. For example, one *speaks* of the "radiance" of a Bach cantata because of the way in which one appreciates—filters through one's tastes—the (minimally) describable properties the cantata actually has. Supporting remarks here normally range through value-laden and non-value-laden appreciative observations; perhaps the singing voices are "seen-as" ("heard-as") "drenched with piety"—which (presupposing a favorable response on the auditor's part) is taken to justify *saying* that (construing) the cantata as "radiant." The distinction provides, therefore, a full replacement for Sibley's thesis [1959a] (cf. Hermerén [1977]): wherever Sibley maintains that aesthetic qualities are non-condition-governed, we may reasonably suspect that appreciative differences and appreciative judgments are involved. Effectively, this is to admit that Sibley is wrong in assimilating what he distinguishes as perception in accord with "aesthetic concepts" to an extension (*via* "taste") of standard sensory perception. Two closely related reasons may be given: (a) the "is"/"appears" contrast of standard perception no longer applies; (b) aesthetic perception (in Sibley's cases) entails conformity with the variable values of one culture or another.

Appreciative matters dominate, of course, in the aesthetic domain—witness the views of Isenberg, Hospers, Macdonald. Also, it is noticeably easy to escape verdicts or findings there, on the legitimate grounds that one "appreciates things differently" (cf. Hospers [1959]). It is also possible, as in the appraisal of wines, diamonds, Ming vases, and fashions, that a certain prevailing taste becomes academically or professionally enshrined. Then, stock specimens of relevant excellence may be cited; to that extent, much as with legal and medical findings, some range of aesthetic findings will obtain (cf. Urmson [1950]; Nowell-Smith [1954]; Margolis [1976b]). Hence, what I have termed a "robust relativism" may be imputed where both findings and appreciative judgments are affirmed. Appreciative judgments are, of course, inherently relativistic, in the sense supplied. And findings, both because they are defined in purely formal terms and because, substantively, they may depend on the shifting but relatively stable currents of prevailing taste, cannot possibly fail to confirm at least a limited range of relativized judgments.

There are those who implicitly resist both possibilities. David Hume [1874-1875], for example, characteristically bases his account of taste on "the common sentiments of human nature" that enable us to judge "of . . . catholic and universal beauty," on "certain general principles of approbation or blame," on there being "a sound and a defective state in every creature," though "the former alone can be supposed to afford us a true standard of taste and sentiment," a "proper sentiment of beauty," "delicacy of taste." But there is little hope of discovering any natural basis for preferences adequate to resolving the entire range of disputes about taste (*contra* Sibley [1959b]; Morawski [1974]; Sircello [1975]; cf. Kivy [1973]; Brunius [1952]; Brooks [1947]). Admit that persons themselves are culturally emergent and culturally groomed (*see* Margolis [1978a]) and their taste decisively fashioned by the contingencies of their cultural heritage: there remains no way of specifying (non-vacuously) a universal range of taste.

Mark Sagoff [1978] has recently advanced what appears to be a stronger constraint, viz. "that authenticity is a necessary condition of aesthetic value." In effect, on Sagoff's view, something like a connoisseur's sense of accuracy is the *sine qua non* of valid judgments of value. However, read one way, the thesis is tautological; and read another, inconclusive. In the former sense, aesthetic values must (on pain of irrelevance) be ascribed to particular works correctly identified as the very works they are—that is, as this or that particular work; errors then signify that an ascription has been wrongly assigned. In the latter sense, the values that an artwork has or may have imputed to it presuppose that it is an authentic work, not a forgery or a reproduction *or* an object so altered from the original that it no longer is that particular work. Certainly, Van Meegeren's Vermeer forgeries (which were not meant as copies but as "new" works) lose the high value imputed to them in virtue of having been taken to be authentic; but, even as admitted forgeries, they possess or may justifiably have imputed to them (and may even acquire) aesthetic values of an interesting but more modest and reduced range (cf. Kilbracken [1967]). Sagoff is wrong, therefore, in claiming that "the process of making a forgery is the reverse of creative"; he himself concedes that "a forgery, considered as a work of art, is trivial, *except in special cases*" [italics added]. He is right to emphasize that a forgery "is the product of a different process" from that of authentic art—which reminds us once again both that aesthetic properties include nonperceptual ones and that the concept of an artwork is the concept of a distinctively intentional object.

Sagoff takes too strong a stand, for example, on the issue of the "integral" *versus* the "pure" restoration of artworks (that is, on the issue of restoring by "adding new pieces to restore the appearance of a damaged work of art" *versus* restoring by "cleaning works of art and . . . attaching original pieces that may have fallen . . . [where] substitutions [must] avoid any pretense of authenticity"). Sagoff implicitly commits the connoisseur to pure restoration, in committing him to authenticity. But *if* what is deemed authentic is the artist's original design, or the "strokes" in virtue of which a design may be imputed to the work—*not* the particular physical materials that contingently embody the work—*and if* the type/token distinction may be invoked in so-called autographic art (Goodman [1968]) in virtue of restorative intent, then Sagoff cannot have shown that integral restoration is inauthentic in any sense similar to that in which forgery is inauthentic. He claims, for instance, that the "undamaged and restored *Pietà* [Michelangelo], although spatially and temporally continuous under the sortal 'statue,' are not so under the sortal 'Michelangelo'—for the repaired statue, after the *n*th repair, is a De Campos [Reding De Campos: the restorer of the *Pietà*], or something, and not a Michelangelo." But once again, *if* restoring the *original* conveys authenticity to what is chiefly autographic art, *and if* the restoration conforms to the kind of type/token distinctions tolerated, say, among etchings, then the (integrally) restored *Pietà* may fairly be taken not only to be continuous with the undamaged statue but actually identical with it. Sagoff merely affirms that, on Goodman's demonstration, "no notation decides whether two paintings or sculptures are instances of the same work." But, as we have already seen, Goodman's argument is less than conclusive on both autographic and allographic grounds; also, even if one disputed the claim of identity, autographic considerations would still serve to support the claim that the restored *Pietà* was an authentic token of the same type (Michelangelo) as the originally undamaged token. Hence, it is quite reasonable to accept Sagoff's claim that authenticity is a necessary condition of merit while effectively defusing it: (a) because authenticity does not indisputably preclude such things as integral restoration; and (b) because, once disclosed, forgeries (or what may have been characterized as forgery—work done, say, "in the manner of") may begin a new career as "authentic" pieces of some diminished kind (cf. Hermerén [1975]).

The phenomenon of the connoisseur is instructive, here. The connoisseur's most striking feature is his advocacy of a distinct system of preferences. Characteristically, he either ranks recognizably important artworks differently from the tradition, or he appraises these works on different grounds. It is possible, as in judging wines, that one is merely exercising a certain accuracy; if he only judges vintage year and *châteaux* of origin, then, however extraordinary his ability, one's performance is substantially restricted. In the art world, it is less often thus. A connoisseur may be called on to authenticate a work, but establishing its merit is quite another—more important—matter. In observing the connoisseur at work, we are almost spectators of the formation and transformation of prevailing or official taste. Inevitably, there will be divergent appreciative systems at work. A Picasso grotesque may be said to have little aesthetic merit, on the basis of Bernard Berenson's [1948] so-called "tactile values." But on the strength of criteria oriented more toward the so-called "abstractive values" of Wilhelm Worringer [1953], it may well be rated very high. Critics of either sort may provide impeccable analyses of the non-valuational features of the work in question, and they may explain systematically the nature of, and the reasons for, their departure from judgments accepted within the tradition of connoisseurship. They will, in effect, have earned their rank as connoisseurs. (Obviously, we also grade and rank the *informed* taste, the informed appreciation, of would-be connoisseurs.) But it is important to see that we are primarily interested in the power and fluency of their divergent appreciative schemes and not in the correctness of their findings. The mark of the connoisseur is the making of fresh discriminations within the bounds of critical and descriptive accuracy, formed as a coherent, comprehensive *appreciative* system. His work, therefore, exhibits a logical weakness very much like what we have observed in interpretation: alternative systems of appreciation may well be reasonable or compelling; they cannot be straightforwardly valid or correct.

Beardsley [1970b] holds the opposite opinion. The reasons a critic supplies to justify his evaluation, he maintains, conform to the " 'ordinary' sense" of reasons; they "have a bearing on the *truth* of the judgments." But he concedes that "our first question is [should be] whether in fact critical judgments have a truth-value—i.e., are either true or false." Here, he opposes the thesis that critical reasoning is impossible. Michael Scriven [1966], who advances it, holds that "it must be possible for us to know that the reason is true, and also to know that it *is* a reason for the conclusion, *before* knowing that the conclusion is true" (the "independence requirement"). Scriven argues that that condition is not satisfied by aesthetic evaluations. Beardsley believes that the refutation of Scriven's thesis somehow entails his own—that critical judgments (in particular, estimates of "the greatest amount of artistic goodness that [e.g.,] the poem allows of actualizing in any one encounter with it") have truth-value. Against Scriven, he argues:

> But *if,* as I claim, these judgments are estimates, then some reasons *must* be used by the critics in arriving at them, and *therefore* there must be some basic features of literary works that are always merits or defects . . .

This begs the original question, however. For, if supporting reasons may be provided for utterances that lack truth-value, then it cannot be shown that if judgments are estimates and if estimates call for supporting reasons, then judgments have truth-value. Beardsley must show that estimates (or comparable value judgments) require that what is estimated actually have, or fail to have, the properties they are alleged to have *and* that the relevant estimates are entailed by given sets of such properties. He must, in other words, show that estimates cannot but be findings. This he has not done.

A diametrically opposed view is ingeniously developed by Alan Tormey [1973]. It mingles a number of themes but seems to be primarily directed to salvaging, as open to "corroborative" but not "confirmative tests," the appreciative judgments of connoisseurs and others with informed taste (cf. Macdonald [1954a]; Scruton [1974]). If I understand him correctly, I agree with part of Tormey's conclusion but not—for important reasons—either with his sustaining argument or with the full import of its formulation. He wishes to hold that "although critical judgments can be subsumed as instances of neither knowledge nor belief, they can, and should, be regarded as testable claims about phenomenally public objects. The latter contention rescues critical judgments from radical subjectivism; the former prevents their forcible conscription by an uncompromising cognitivism." Tormey's argument rests on attempting to show that "critical judgments . . . are essentially first-person affairs, and consequently, non-transmissible." By "non-transmissible," he intends Hintikka's sense [1962], illustrated by the fact that "*KaKbp ⊃ Kap*" is valid (that is, "if *a* knows that *b* knows that *p,* then *a* knows that *p*"—knowledge is transmissible from *b* to *a*), but that "*Ka Jbq ⊃ Jaq*" is invalid (that is "if *a* knows that *b* judges that *q,* then *a* judges that q "—judgment is not transmissible in the way knowledge is). Though certainly correct, the argument cannot support Tormey's conclusion, for a very simple reason: "judgment" and "claim" are notoriously equivocal, designating both the act and the propositional content of a relevant act; the second sense cannot coherently be preferred in context, and the first shows the irrelevance of Tormey's move. That is, whenever b acts, it cannot be concluded that a acts simply because a knows about b's act; this holds for all contexts—not merely the aesthetic. But that has nothing to do with the possibility that, in judging, a knows that b knows (by having judged). Hence, it is quite possible that aesthetic or critical judgments yield knowledge, in spite of what Tormey claims. In fact, it is quite difficult to see what Tormey could possibly mean by denying that critical judgments altogether lack a cognitive role or function. (To reject cognitivism, with Tormey, is emphatically not to reject the cognitive role of critical judgments.) Judgments are inherently cognitive in requiring supporting reasons. Since, however, appreciative judgments presuppose personal taste, cognitivism and normal questions of truth and falsity must be precluded. But this hardly leads to an emotivist or expression theory of judgment or to some other sort of merely causal account of utterances called critical judgments.

Still, Tormey is right in emphasizing that "in art, unlike the law, we do not admit judgments in the absence of direct or immediate experience of the object of the judgment [or suitable surrogate]." He is also right, I believe, in holding that critical judgments are at least characteristically not open to "confirmative tests," though he must be mistaken in holding that they "are immune from anything as threatening as disconfirmation": *any* judgment that rests on errors of a descriptive sort may be disconfirmed. But he has not noticed sufficiently that the "false" may be opposed not only to the "true" but to the "plausible" (or to other cognate predicates). His conclusion, therefore, is excessively strong:

> The implications of the preceding arguments then constitute a direct challenge to the view that criticism is essentially or even centrally occupied with the rating or grading of art works or with the bestowal of aesthetic merit badges. Moreover, if critical judgments are epistemically non-transmissible, then the critic who hopes to canonize his pronouncements is destined to failure, for there can be neither logically compelling reasons for accepting them nor indirect means of transmitting them. And even universal corroboration of a

critical judgment is not so much the *acknowledgement* of its propriety as the *establishment* of it.

We may round out our account further by remarking that a verdict may be rendered without supporting reasons (*see* Austin [1962]; Vendler [1972]). Apart from applying academic canons, evaluating artworks is characteristically informal; normally, one cannot say in advance what the appropriate *set* of criteria is for evaluating this or that object. If we are appraising pekingese in a show, the marks of merit are known in advance and one may even prepare for a high score. In the context of art, however, we draw upon criteria that are normally relevant, not arbitrarily selected, and yet not formally agreed upon. Disputes are important; findings and verdicts are energetically sought, disputed and defended; but disputants may not know in advance what set of considerations is likely to be decisive (cf. Nowell-Smith [1954]). In a competition, for instance, we frequently find that, "in the opinion of the judges," a particular artist deserves First Prize. Normally, the judges cannot be supposed to have arrived at a common verdict on the application of public criteria. The implication is that verdicts need not follow explicit evaluations. The mere preference of the judges may be decisive.

Helen Knight's [1954] discussion of "good" suffers for related reasons. She speaks of "good" as being "used with this *set* of criteria and with *that*; and so on through an extremely wide range of overlapping sets. On any *one* occasion it is used with one set only, but on this occasion with this set, on that occasion with that, and so on." She observes, "The goodness of [such] things [as tennis players, knitters, pekingese, steaks] depends on their satisfying the criteria of goodness for things of their kind." But those of her own illustrations that are drawn from the arts show that she herself senses a greater informality than her account would allow. She seems, therefore, not to have realized that there may not be any assignable set of criteria for judging the merit of things of every distinct kind (*see* Margolis [1963]).

For such reasons, we speak less of verdicts than of appraisal, and less of appraisal than of appreciation (cf. Ziff [1966]). The truth is that, in evaluation, we proceed more by reference to specimen works that indisputably (that is, relative to an established tradition) exhibit particular merit ("grandeur," "elegance," "tragic power," "sublimity," "delicacy," "subtlety") than by laying out the necessary and sufficient conditions on which we should say any work had such merit. J.A. Passmore [1954] seems to hold a similar view: "Admittedly, we do not usually formulate an explicit list of good books; but, still, if we pick a book, and read it in the expectation of its being good literature, we judge its claims out of our experience of Shakespeare, the great novelists and great poets. . . .'' In combating the ''dreariness of aesthetics,'' however—the tendency, for instance, to ''develop a general theory of 'wrongness' in art''—Passmore urges us to determine the ''principles of literary criticism, principles of musical criticism, etc.'' (cf. Kennick [1958]).

The difference between findings and appreciative judgments remains. The informality with which reasons may be tendered is irrelevant; it is only the nature of the argument that counts. In defending an appreciative judgment, I do not merely provide *my* reasons for the judgment (*see* Ziff [1966]). The reasons I provide are my reasons, in the sense that they accord with my tastes; but my tastes never relevantly serve as supporting reasons. On the other hand, the reasons provided must engage the describable features or eligible interpretations of the object, that is, elements that might conceivably count as reasons for another. Such judgments can be challenged by, for instance, showing incompatibilities with other relevant appreciative judgments, or by showing that they rest on false or indefensible descriptions, analyses, comparisons, interpretations. But if they are vindicated, they can only be shown to be fair or reasonable, never true, because the very effort to defend them presupposes that we may all appreciate things differently. Our appreciative vocabulary has its characteristic stability so that, though tastes may vary, our judgments may be tested nevertheless.

In certain respects, findings will differ from what usually counts as the rendering of verdicts. In the first, we usually seek the qualification appropriate to a given work, whereas, in the second, we apply predicates provided in advance. ''What merit do you find in this work?'' we ask; but ''Do you find for the plaintiff or for the defendant?'' In the one, we collect qualities and attempt to place a proper value upon them. In the other, we construe the given features of an action or object as supporting antecedently prepared, exclusive and exhaustive, verdicts. For these reasons, the use of predicates like ''good,'' ''fine,'' ''beautiful''—which most resembles the rendering of verdicts—is usually given up or restricted within the aesthetic domain; that is, we are under no obligation to render a verdict. We may of course conclude: ''It's an extraordinarily fine piece''; ''On the whole, a very good work''; ''Truly beautiful.'' But in such circumstances, the omnibus judgment is ordinarily a summation of the drift of antecedent evaluative and appreciative remarks, rather than a verdict in the stricter sense (cf. Hungerland [1958]). In the one, we search for the *mot juste;* and in the other, for a kind of justice. It is extremely doubtful (*contra* Beardsley [1958], [1970a]; Sibley [1959a]; Sircello [1975]) that a defensible sense can be formulated in which such evaluative judgments may be shown not only to be true or false by reference to alternative and changing conventions, traditions, or practices, but may be so shown by means of some cognitively independent discovery of the inherent beauty or worth of objects—in such a way, that is, that a robust relativism could be entirely precluded (cf. also Hampshire [1972]; Nielsen [1974]; Lukes [1974]). Also, if we admit the viability and scope of appreciative judgments—conceding that artworks are entities whose cultural properties cannot be discerned in the manner of sensory perception—we see that it is quite impossible to segregate aesthetic and moral interests and to deny that moral (and other cultural) considerations legitimately inform both our findings and our appreciative judgments.

PART THREE

The Literary Arts

11. Literature and Speech Acts

The literary arts have always been particularly difficult to accommodate within classical aesthetics, simply because they are so obviously concerned with more than what may be discriminated by the restricted resources of sensory perception. Attention to meanings and the possibilities of imagination centered on more than sensory images defies philosophical efforts to make the etymology of the term a criterion of legitimate *aesthetic* interests (*see* Beardsley [1958]).

Furthermore, the trivial truth that literature employs language has been fastened on regularly and repeatedly to spawn a remarkable variety of misconceptions. Most famously, it has, as we have seen, led to the untenable thesis that all art is language (Langer [1942], [1953]) and to the more pointed claim that artworks somehow affirm propositions that may be linguistically expressed and straightforwardly judged true or false (Greene [1940]). It has also embarrassed a good deal of theorizing about the nature of aesthetic experience and the aesthetic orientation, and has led to preposterous views about the aesthetic status of the literary arts and about the mistakenly exaggerated importance of words in literature (cf. Bell [1914]; Urmson [1957]). Under the pressure of these curious contingencies, Sidney Zink [1945] was actually led to maintain:

> I think there is a simple way out of the dilemma of the poem's immediate aesthetic value and the symbolic nature of its medium. This is to recognize that linguistic meanings are, like colors and sounds, themselves particular qualities.

One might, more reasonably, have rejected the perceptual model as inadequate (*contra* Prall [1936]). Certainly, if any of the arts appeared to suit the perceptual model, it was patently impossible (*contra* Beardsley [1958]) that the literary arts should do so. Even imagination, one must realize, cannot be satisfactorily analyzed solely in terms of concrete sensory images or their use; over the centuries, the profound, ongoing debate between rationalism and empiricism constantly reconfirms the point. These developments are reasonably well known, party because they form a venerable portion of the history of aesthetics, and partly because the doctrines at stake take so many apparently persuasive guises—even in our own time.

There are other views, however, also largely based on the example of literature, that are at once useful—because they are corrective of other abuses—and in their turn prone to newer mistakes. One such ambivalent corrective is the thesis that an artwork is an utterance of some sort, an intentional act, culturally formed and culturally significant. In effect, this simple thesis exposes at a stroke the distortion that results from pretending to address art relevantly solely in terms of the palpable properties of some "autonomous" or free-standing object or product—more or less on the model of examining a perceptually accessible physical object (*contra* Wellek [1965]; Wimsatt [1954]). On the theory, attention must be directed to the act or agency of the artist by which the work is "uttered," in a sense quite close to that in which a forger is said to "utter" a bad check; by this simple strategem, we are led to see that biographical, historical, and intentional considerations are instructive in an essential way, and that the properties of an artwork cannot possibly be restricted to its merely sensory features—if, admitting conceptual art, a particular work need have such features at all (cf. Binkley [1977]). The proposal, therefore, is at least heuristically useful. Whether it ought also to be enshrined as definitional of art is another question altogether, qualified partly by its being entirely possible to save the corrections without the thesis, and partly by the debatable nature of definitions.

A rather specialized but utterly misleading and unpromising version of the utterance theory maintains that literature as such—as well as such particularly important distinctions within literature as fiction, poetry, and metaphor—may be perspicuously defined or distinguished in terms of a speech-act model. We must be careful here. The general thesis that the phenomenon of language cannot be adequately analyzed apart from contextual considerations bearing on speakers' intentions, assumptions and background beliefs shared by speakers and hearers, the actual history of conversations, and the like, has now been abundantly confirmed by a variety of theorists—including, prominently, J. L. Austin [1962], P. F. Strawson [1950], [1963], H. P. Grice [1957], [1968], [1969], John Searle [1965], [1969], Keith Donnellan [1966], [1970], George Lakoff [1971] (also, Gordon and Lakoff [1975]), and Zeno Vendler [1972]. Still, the general concession that familiar syntactic and semantic studies of the phenomenon of language omit an entire dimension of language, as Austin so ably demonstrated, has rather little to say about the distinctions normally debated in the context of literary theory. (This may well seem paradoxical.) But since the application of the speech-act model to literary analysis shows some tendency to attract advocates, it may be useful to draw explicit attention here to the inherent limitations and difficulties of the enterprise.

Precisely how restricted a general speech-act model is—that is, one not restricted just to literature—can be seen at a stroke simply by noting that the meaning of sentences (i) cannot be equated with what speakers mean in using sentences in the performance of a speech act; (ii) cannot be directly derived from what speakers mean in performing thus; and (iii) itself provides the antecedent basis on which what speakers mean in thus performing can actually be specified (*see* Margolis [1973a]). The most persistent effort to reverse this relationship, to make the meaning of sentences depend on speakers' intentions in uttering sentences, undoubtedly is that made by H.P. Grice [1957] (cf. Schiffer [1972]). But although the meanings of standard sentences, and of the words that compose them, are idealized in some way from a large set of utterances in typical speech-act contexts, the meanings of particular utterances cannot be straightforwardly derived from a particular speaker's intention on the occasion of a particular utterance. Such a view would lead to a kind of linguistic solipsism. On the contrary, to say that speakers mean thus and such by their utterances is normally to say that their intentions conform with whatever can be independently said about the standard meanings of the words and sentences that they have used. The result is that there must be semantic and syntactic dimensions of linguistic use that cannot be dependent on the application of a speech-act model (of any familiar sort), in spite of the fact that normal linguistic use cannot be freed from a speech-act context. Alternatively put, speakers' intentions equivocally (a) determine what speakers *mean* in addition to what they *say* (and to what they say means) or (b) collapse into what such utterances mean (or into what, as we might say, standard speakers *would* mean or intend by such utterances). In effect, reference to speakers' intentions is often an alternative way of designating semantic and syntactic regularities, or of designating the standard functions of discourse. Symptomatically, Grice oscillates between a personal or biographical sense of speakers' intentions, and a social or conventional sense of such intentions (paralleling in a way the "historicist" and "objectivist" alternatives of the hermeneutic theory of intentions). The upshot is that although the concept of a speech act provides a reasonably complete sense of the setting in which language and linguistic communication obtain, a very large part of the analysis of linguistic phenomena cannot be directly pursued in terms of the details of the speech-act model. *A fortiori,* there is good reason to believe that the subtle features of literary discourse—even granting that literature *is* discourse—will not yield in a productive way to a speech-act analysis. (The difficulties of the speech-act model of meaning are, it may be noted, analogues of difficulties, already aired, in expression theory.)

Furthermore, to correct and confine the function of Grice's model is not to suppose that what utterances mean can be fixed straightforwardly by the application of well-formed, comprehensive, independent, reasonably familiar and undisputed rules of sense (*see* Ziff [1960]; Putnam [1975c]; Patton and Stampe [1969]). Theorists have tended to oscillate (Hirsch [1967]) between the conviction that there is a relatively stable way of fixing authorial intent regarding linguistic utterances, and a relatively stable way of fixing the normal meaning of utterances to which authors must subscribe. Both extremes are rendered doubtful by a single and simple consideration: the meanings of human utterances are assignable only in a culturally pertinent context; but such contexts are historically and biographically variable, open, emergent, inventive, informally and provisionally identified, and incapable of being relevantly reduced to a finite set of fixed forms and their variously generated transformations (*contra* Culler [1975]; cf. Margolis [1978a]). This is of course not to deny communication, but only to affirm that an intentional model of the psychological sort (Grice's) cannot but be conceptually dependent on another, and that an explicitly rule-governed model of independent speech-act genres (Searle's) cannot but be invalid and misleading.

Two additional aspects of the general speech-act model may be mentioned. In the first place, there is no clear principle on which an array of distinct—reasonably detailed, recognizable, relatively independent, inclusive—speech acts has ever been specified, relative to which the appropriate *rules* or *maxims* of use can be laid out (*see* Searle [1969]; Vendler [1972]). In the second place, the specimen rules or maxims that have been assigned to the performance of putative speech acts threaten to be hopelessly arbitrary, vague, or downright faulty. Austin's classification of speech acts—verdictives, exercitives, and the rest—are clearly quite provisional and, on his own view, somewhat miscellaneous, not altogether clear, impressionistically sorted, and not entirely differentiable. But more than this, there is no apparent sense in which if an agent, S, uses language in performing an act, it is clear that S is thereby performing a speech act of some determinate sort to which suitable, independently formulable, and relatively specific rules or maxims can be correctly assigned. The issue is rather complicated.

No one has successfully formulated non-circular criteria by means of which to determine precisely what kind of speech act has been performed *and,* consequently, which rules of use apply. Beardsley [1970b], who follows Alston's [1964] version of the speech-act account of meaning, confines his attention solely to what may be known or inferred regarding the specification of meaning to an utterance—once it is known that a speech act of this or that sort obtains. He says nothing about initially detecting which speech act has actually been enacted, and assumes merely that that matter may be decided without significant difficulty. But of course the critical bearing of speakers' intentions, valid but divergent interpretations, the uncertain specificity of styles and genres, and the like depend entirely on the resolution of this problem. Consequently, there is a crucial lacuna in Beardsley's well-known and influential theory.

In adopting the speech-act model, Beardsley wishes of course to minimize—or eliminate altogether—the kind of intentionalism associated with Grice's view. But the objective seems impossible. First of all, as we have seen (*contra* Hirsch [1967]; cf. Culler [1975]) genres are largely heuristic or provisional classificatory distinctions, not independent "entities" determinately fixed in any sense at all, and not entirely freed from authorial intent (in a relatively narrow psychological sense). Secondly, Alston's particular use of the speech-act model confuses type and token unacceptably: clearly two tokens of the same speech-act type may differ in meaning; and whether they do differ in meaning cannot be determined by *independently* determining the speech-act "potential" of those tokens—for, either the "potential" is determined by determining the meaning of distinct (token) utterances or it is just that meaning. At best, then, the account is circular. In any case, there is no viable way in which Alston's model can serve to determine the meaning of utterances in the sense Beardsley requires, because it cannot eliminate intentions. Beardsley also apparently wishes to support his non-Gricean-like model by adopting Alvin Goldman's criterion for individuating actions [1970]. But, apart from the internal difficulties of Goldman's conception (*see* Margolis [1974b]), the criterion cannot but be unhelpful. First of all, Goldman holds that every act is individuated solely in terms of instantiating an essential type-predicate; and secondly, he provides no clue at all as to what might be aesthetically relevant to the individuation *and description* of literary utterances. The first claim is both unusual and doubtful, since (i) in every other context of discourse, we are obviously able to identify and reidentify particulars under a variety of descriptions; and since (ii) Goldman fails to explain what ontic relationship holds between actions individuated in accord with his thesis, and physical movements. The application of Goldman's thesis, therefore, leaves indeterminate precisely what is descriptively true of (found "in" or not "in") a particular poem or novel. Searle [1969], also opposing Grice's intentionalism, formulates rules for speech acts that, on his own admission, hold only ideally. He offers no clues about how to determine (by the application of comparably close-grained criteria) just which speech acts are being, or have been, performed. He also concedes, damagingly, that acts provisionally similar to particular speech-act paradigms may, *in context,* not be such at all; this is true even where so-called performative verbs, such as "promise," are used. Hence, what appear to provide the best candidates for sufficient criteria of recognition prove insufficient even in the clearest range of cases.

Grice [1975] (cf. also, [1978]) has made a fresh effort to advance the theory. Speaking of "conversational implicatures," he offers an example of meiosis: "Of a man known to have broken up all the furniture, one says *He was a little intoxicated.*" Conversational implicatures are taken by Grice to be "nonconventional," that is, they cannot be determined by "the conventional meaning of the words used," but rather will depend on speakers' intentions with regard to "certain general features of discourse" or conversation. 'Implicature' is a term of art designating the determinable form of a family of relations including implication, entailment, pragmatic or contextual implication, and the like. Now, it seems quite impossible to suppose that there is a distinctive kind of speech act instanced by the utterance *He was a little intoxicated*—say, of the sort codified by Austin or Searle—that would yield explicit rules or maxims. Searle's rules are simply too general. Furthermore, it is not in the least clear that a more ramified set of acts (and their appropriate rules) could properly be expected to count as being merely a more detailed (including parasitic and complex) species within the principal and already correctly discerned genera of speech behavior. It is extremely difficult to say precisely what *kind* of speech act was performed by uttering *He was a little intoxicated*; it is correspondingly difficult to say in a nonquestionbegging way what rules or maxims rightly govern our interpretation of the meaning of what was said. Grice himself treats the example as one in which "the first maxim of Quality is flouted"; by this, he means that a speaker "may BLATANTLY fail to fulfill" the maxim, "Do not say what you believe to be false." This is tied to a general concern for conversational efficiency and effectiveness, for which Grice provides a "rough general principle": "Make your conversational contribution such as is required, at the stage at which it occurs, by the accepted purpose or direction of the talk exchange in which you are engaged" (the COOPERATION PRINCIPLE, or CP).

With respect to the difficulty of Grice's undertaking, CP is hopelessly vague: *what* is *required* at *what stage* of any conversation?

What is the *accepted* purpose of an exchange? It is altogether too easy to construct maxims that particular conversational exchanges may be said to satisfy if they are reasonably successful, or even if they are intended by a given speaker to take a certain recognizable form. In context, there are no maxims or rules for conversational cooperation that are not ultimately circular or vacuous. Assume, for instance, that the remark offered is guided by a need to soften a blow, or to avoid merely frontal assertions of what is the case: *it will then have "flouted" no maxim at all.* How could one possibly say (how could Grice himself say) what maxims there are or which ones are "violated," which ones one has "opted out" of, which ones involve a "clash" of maxims, or which ones one has "flouted"? To know the answer to these questions is (on a variety of speech-act theories) to know either the sufficient *personal* intentions of speakers, or the sufficient *conventional* purposes particular speakers are bound by: yet both possibilities can only undermine Grice's sanguine illustrations if we do not know (as we do not) what the entire system of speech acts is like, and how member kinds of speech acts actually are constrained. For instance, *what* constraint could CP possibly yield regarding Blake's line *I sought to tell my love, love that never told can be* (one of Grice's own examples)? What could CP require? And how should we decide?

Further, Grice's illustrations are not particularly closely linked to the usual account of speech acts, even though speech acts are doubtless involved. Meiosis is not a speech act in the usual sense; nor, more pointedly, is metaphor. Regarding metaphor, Grice offers another illustration in which he claims "the first maxim of Quality is flouted": *You are the cream in my coffee.* We cannot provide the full argument here, but it needs to be stressed that metaphor is not a speech act *of any kind*: it concerns a use primarily of words rather than of sentences in the manner of a speech act. (We shall return to the issue.)

Finally, Grice has noticeable difficulty in specifying cases of "generalized conversational implicature" in contrast to "particularized conversational implicature"—that is, cases where special features of the context indicate implicatures that are not "NORMALLY carried by saying that *p.*" But even the "generalized" cases seem doubtful and question-begging. For example, Grice holds that "Anyone who uses a sentence of the form *X is meeting a woman this evening* would normally implicate that the person to be met was someone other than X's wife, mother, sister, or perhaps even close platonic friend." But it is very easy to suppose that "anyone" using the sentence merely intended to withhold the identity of the woman (or person), or intended to be deliberately mysterious, or had other reasons of this sort. It is not clear that such intentions are "generalized" or "particularized." Also, it seems reasonable to hold that *any* sense of the appropriate implicature would require background—specifically, nonlinguistic—information of what could be plausibly taken to be *contextually* implied; if so, the distinction between generalized and particularized implicature seems quite pointless.

I have pursued Grice's account in detail because recent attempts to apply the speech-act model to literature directly depend on it. But to bring the argument effectively to bear on the theory of literature will require some further orienting remarks. Before providing these, however, I must add several observations about Grice's view. For one thing, Grice's maxims are extraordinarily vacant or unqualified. Here is a set of them: *Do not say what you believe to be false. Do not say that for which you lack adequate evidence. Avoid obscurity of expression. Avoid ambiguity. Be brief (avoid unnecessary prolixity). Be orderly. Be relevant. Make your contribution as informative as is required (for the current purposes of the exchange). Do not make your contribution more informative than is required.* Not only is it difficult to believe that these maxims could be refined in some nonquestionbegging way, but it is not in the least clear how it may be supposed that the usual forms of literature are in any sense bound to favor them. To hold that, in *special* circumstances, one is not bound thus, but rather by alternative maxims, is simply to confirm the pointlessness of the entire exercise. Clearly, *in some sense,* discourse must favor such maxims as Grice has listed. But there is no sense in which, nontrivially, particular maxims may be said to be binding in particular contexts. This is simply to say that there is only a pretended rigor in the enumeration of conversational maxims: for every instance in which a maxim is allegedly violated, flouted, or the like, one could provide—both in literary and in conversational settings—alternative maxims that particular utterances actually instantiate. This is due in part to the absence of a settled scheme of speech acts: characterize an act suitably and the appropriate maxims will follow—for the most part, trivially. It is also partly due to the ease with which the putative purpose of any particular discourse may be construed as entailing a departure from whatever allegedly "general" maxims are said to require of us; and it is also probably due to the rather questionable assumption that, because linguistic exchanges are generally successful, they *must* be guided by some finite, antecedently shared, explicitly formulable, public set of maxims.

Secondly, Grice's maxims are not narrowly linguistic at all; indeed, Grice offers non-verbal analogues of the constraints he has in mind (for instance, as in the stranded-motorist case, when a passing driver shows a particular interest in helping out another). But the most general doubt about Grice's venture is that his maxims seem to be attenuated versions of moral maxims, or at least, of favored forms of conversational etiquette. Apparently, the specification of these maxims prompted Robin Lakoff to characterize Grice's maxims as "a subset of the rules of politeness" (M. Pratt [1977]; cf. R. Lakoff [1977]). There is no question that CP is a normative formulation; the trouble is that the very notion of a speech act is impossible to restrict in purely linguistic terms. Regarding Searle's account, it may also be noted that whereas Grice contents himself with formulating regulative maxims, Searle [1969] insists on rules constitutively governing different types of illocutionary acts. Furthermore, Searle's rules explicitly include ethical constraints and are not adjusted in the least for the subtleties of an entire spectrum of putative speech acts. For example, Searle claims that there is a sincerity rule governing assertions and the like (Austin's expositives). So, if S asserts p, then S fulfills the sincerity rule—S believes p. Similarly, Searle maintains that, in making such an assertion, the speaker must conform to the preparatory rule that "S has evidence (reasons, etc.) for the truth of p" and that "it is not obvious to both S and H [the hearer] that H knows (does not need to be reminded of, etc.) p." But these are preposterous constraints on what it is to be an expositive—though, doubtless, no society could function if the sincerity constraint did not obtain with some significant frequency; also, the redundancy of repeating what everyone knows might well become a bore. A good many of Searle's rules are of these sorts; the others are pretty nearly negligible as far as linguistic details are concerned. We cannot fail to see here the close convergence of Grice's and Searle's accounts. But since Searle puts his own in terms of rules *and* does so in terms of necessary and sufficient conditions (even granting that these require a measure of idealization), it is impossible to fail to conclude that neither Grice nor Searle (nor Austin for that matter, though Austin insists on the point himself) has supplied us with a viable scheme of speech acts, on the basis of which we can say with any confidence which rules or maxims must obtain if discourse is to proceed felicitously. Grice's thesis is especially weakened by its conceptual dependence on a speech-act theory that Grice himself does not supply. For, since Grice's maxims are intended to regulate actual utterances, his account must provide for the constitutive criteria of particular speech acts. Lacking these, Grice can offer no basis for assuring us of the relevance of the detailed application of alternative maxims. Their general applicability merely signifies the general intent of speakers to be rational and coherent. But it is impossible to show that all or most apparent violations entail incoherence or irrationality. In effect, our actual linguistic competence—pragmatic as well as syntactic and semantic—*may* be heuristically described in ways that favor Grice's maxims; but that is no reason for supposing that the maxims themselves serve, or can possibly serve, as operational criteria for determining the actual conformity of particular utterances to contextually pertinent requirements of felicitous speech (cf. Hancher [1977], [1978]).

Regarding the application of the speech-act model to the philosophy of literature, broadly speaking, two distinct lines of argument have been pursued. One, deriving from the Russian Formalists and the Prague Circle (*see* Matejka and Pomorsky [1971]), is that literature and/or poetry is *sui generis* and, as such, exhibits distinctive linguistic properties—now, distinctive speech-act properties. The other, opposing the Formalist tradition, argues that literature and/or poetry fall within the general compass of discourse and conform to the constraints to which ordinary speech acts conform. The Formalists included, or have influenced, a number of important writers in literary theory, aesthetics, and linguistics. The more familiar include Roman Jakobson [1971], René Wellek, Roman Ingarden, Roland Barthes, Boris Ejxenbaum, and Viktor Sklovskij. The core of their view is pretty well caught in the 1929 Theses of the Prague Linguistic Circle (*Travaux du Cercle Linguistique de Prague* [1929]):

> In its social role, language [*le langage*] must be specified [*distinguer*] according to its relation to extralinguistic reality. It has either a communicative function, that is, it is directed toward the signified, or a poetic function, that is, it is directed toward the sign itself.   (Translated in Pratt [1977])

Most recently, the Formalist theory, adjusted to the speech-act model, has appeared in the views of Richard Ohmann [1971], [1974] and Monroe Beardsley [1970b]. Thus transcribed, the somewhat "isolationist" social and political features of the original Formalist account have become muted, though the search for essential differences between literature and non-literature continues. (It should perhaps be added at once that current structuralist theories of the analysis of literature— notably Roland Barthes's [1967a]; [1970]; [1972]; [1973]—resemble speech-act theories in important respects and betray comparable weaknesses. They are, however, primarily intended as fairly strict analogues of structural linguistics. Barthes specifically intends to define "a number of non-linguistic 'languages' " [1972], ranging for instance over the worlds of fashion and the novel. But his most systematic effort—to determine the functional rules of fashion [1967b]—betrays the inherently contextual and historically contingent nature of fashion regularities and, by its failure, suggests the unlikelihood of discovering the "deep structure" of the world of literature; cf. Culler [1975].)

Ohmann [1971] offers as "a first approximation of a definition" of literature:

> a literary work is a discourse abstracted, or detached, from the circumstances and conditions which make illocutionary acts possible; hence it is a discourse without illocutionary force.

He supplements this as follows:

> A literary work is a discourse whose sentences lack the illocutionary forces that would normally attach to them. Its illocutionary force is mimetic.

Beardsley holds a quite similar view about poetry: "What is a poem? A poem is an imitation of a compound illocutionary act." (By "a compound illocutionary act" Beardsley intends that an entire poem be construed "as a single act, made up of several: the compound act of its fictional speaker.") Ohmann supports his contention in a rather telltale way. For instance, he claims that "the writer *pretends* to report discourse, and the reader accepts the pretence." Again, he says that "a literary work *purportedly imitates* (or reports) a series of speech acts, which in fact have no other existence." Finally, he says outright that "the only speech-act he [that is the reader] is directly participating in is the one I have called 'mimesis'."

Now, there are a number of substantial confusions here. First of all, mimesis is not, on any familiar grounds, a distinct speech act of any sort. Both speech acts and non-speech acts may be mimetic or imitative. For example, a parrot may mimic speech without producing speech; and a child may mimic another's inflection, choice of words, style of speech, and the like. The first sort of case is irrelevant, though it reflects a normal sense in which speech is mimicked or imitated; in the second sort of case, it is precisely because the child performs a speech act of some sort that *that* act is characterizable as imitative. In short, either mimicking does not involve a speech act at all (the parrot case), or else mimicking is an adverbial qualification of a speech act (the child case). Speaking mimickingly is, therefore, best compared with speaking jokingly, speakirg ironically, and the like. But in those sorts of cases, the adverbial qualification is made of a speech act of some sort.

Secondly, Ohmann pretends to know what a speaker or writer of poetry or literature must intend when he "utters" his discourse—viz., that he intends to imitate or mimic some speech act or kind of speech act. But Lucretius wrote his *De rerum natura* both as poetry and as science. (This, incidentally, is a strong counterinstance to Beardsley's mimetic thesis—which he acknowledges.) There is no reason to think that all writers of literature, fiction, poetry, and the like intend to utter speech acts mimickingly. *And, contra* Ohmann and Beardsley, there is no reason to think that all forms of poetry are forms of mimesis: lyric poetry, didactic poetry, science, narrative, theology, and a thousand other kinds and uses of poetry may reasonably be viewed as the utterances of the author in his own right (*see* Reichert [1977]). These considerations lead to the strong conclusion that poetry, narrative, and other literary distinctions are primarily occupied with *styles* or genres of language, rather than with distinct speech acts. The charge counts heavily against I. A. Richards's well-known contrast [1935] between science and poetry (cf. Levin [1962]).

Thirdly, the effort to formulate an essential "illocutionary definition" of *literature* as such is doomed if it is the case that mimesis is not a speech act, that is, if poetry and narrative, and even dramatization are concerned with alternative styles and genres of art rather than with speech acts. Ohmann's contrast, for instance, between literature and *belles lettres* is at best *ad hoc* and procrustean; at worst, vacuous or circular.

Fourthly, and significantly, Ohmann confuses the differences among speaking poetically, imagining someone speaking, and imitating a speech act. Here, referring to Richard Eberhart's lines:

> In June, amid the golden fields,
> I saw a groundhog lying dead,

Ohmann attempts to apply Austin's criteria for the felicity of illocutionary acts. He wonders, following Austin's suggestion that "the particular persons and circumstances in a given case must be appropriate for the invocation of the particular procedure invoked," whether Eberhart could have been "an appropriate person to attempt the statement."

Ohmann clearly confuses Austin's linguistic conception of "felicity" with a notion having to do with the poetic appropriateness of Eberhart's having organized the images in the way he has (*see* Fish [1976]). He concludes that "something has gone wrong. Either Richard Eberhart is not to be taken as the speaker, or the usual rules for felicity do not apply, or both." Similar considerations, particularly of "faulty reference" (*where* are "the golden fields?"), lead Ohmann to conclude that "the person Eberhart reports is imaginary, and one cannot ask about his qualifications and intentions as if they had any existence outside the poem." But there is absolutely no reason to suppose that it is not Eberhart who is speaking, albeit poetically. If so, then the proprieties that obtain are distinctively connected with the relevant intentions and the poetic custom employed. There is also no reason to suppose that Eberhart is *reporting* anything about a speaker, imaginary or not imaginary, himself or another: he is simply speaking, though not necessarily speaking simply.

Here, there is no doubt that Ohmann conflates reporting what an imaginary speaker "has said" (granting the fiction) and creating a poem in which an imaginary speaker speaks. Fiction, in the logical sense— whether narrative, poetry, or drama—involves a double use of language: speaking fictively, one imagines a world to exist that never did and never can exist; and doing so, one imagines that world peopled with persons who speak with one another. And in creating the fictional world by imagining it to exist, one does not perform a distinct speech act: one performs the distinct act of imagining a certain world to exist, and in doing so creates the setting within which the usual speech acts may be imagined to be performed. *Telling a story* or relating a narrative may, very loosely, be treated as a distinct speech act (but if so, what constraints obtain?). Notice that "narrative" signifies nothing about fiction or nonfiction. The conceptual or logical problem of fiction concerns exclusively the problem of accounting for the apparent reference to non-existent entities. This is a genuine issue, concerning the analysis of the conditions under which names, definite descriptions, and the like may be used in apparently referential ways. From this perspective, we may say that the "naturing" or creative aspect of speaking fictionally is a "presiding" or "executive" feature: it points to the admission of an imaginary world, the world of the fiction, within which certain creatures are taken to exist and to speak.

This actually accords quite closely with the (frankly misleading) views of fictional reference developed by Searle [1969] and Strawson [1959], except that one may dispute their thesis that one cannot refer to what does not exist and that, in referring to fictional entities, one concedes that they do exist but only "exist-in-fiction" (cf. Margolis [1977]). Actually, Searle [1975] has pretty well given up his adherence to the thesis that we cannot refer to what does not exist—or at least qualifies it to the extent that we cannot distinguish, except in terms of speakers' intentions, between reference and pretended reference: "to the extent that we share in the pretense [of a fiction], we will also pretend [speaking of a novel by Iris Murdoch—*The Red and The Green*] that there is a lieutenant named Andrew Chase-White living in Dublin in 1916. It is the pretended reference which creates the fictional character and the shared pretense which enables us to talk about the character." Put very simply, the fictional use of language concerns the *presuppositions* that inform a set of speech acts, not those speech acts themselves; otherwise, granting the fictional world, speech acts are performed by fictional creatures in accord with whatever conventions and practices are to be assumed in imagining the fictional world to exist. In the latter sense, of course, they are not distinctive *qua* speech acts, though they may be distinctive (even unusual) instances of such acts.

In examining Ohmann's theory, we have provided a straightforward sense in which neither literature *tout court,* nor fiction, nor poetry, can be subsumed handily under a speech-act model. We have also considered a sketch of a theory of metaphor, in accord with which that trope also fails to be open to a speech-act analysis. Poetry and literature are conglomerate categories that cannot be expected to exhibit a distinctive or dominant kind of speech act; mimesis is not a speech act of any sort; fiction is either a style of language ("Imagine that Napoleon returned from Elba . . . ") or else is concerned with the referential presuppositions of a set of speech acts.

The second line of argument favoring the speech-act model (opposing the Formalists) has most recently been pursued by Mary Louise Pratt [1977]. Pratt's primary concern is to resist the Formalist distinction between literary and non-literary language (cf. Halliday [1967]; Riffaterre [1962]). But in her constructive development of the speech-act model, Pratt produces a number of additional confusions and, in fact, ultimately mutes the contrast between her own position and that of Ohmann. For one thing, she clearly conflates the matter of the difference between fiction and non-fiction with the fact that narrative may be either fictional or non-fictional. So she says, for instance: "the fiction/nonfiction distinction is neither as clear-cut nor as important as we might think, at least not in the realm of the tellable [that is, the narrative]." But that is because narrative concerns either a style of presentation, or a kind of expositive. Fiction and nonfiction, however, are logically quite different, though the difference cannot be marked in terms of a speech-act model. On the other hand, Pratt criticizes Ohmann's thesis that all literary utterances lack illocutionary force, that they are all mere "quasi-speech acts." But she misplaces the criticism: "It is not the quasiness which gives literature its world-creating capacity. Nonfictional narrative accounts are world-creating in the same sense as are works of literature and, say, accounts of dreams. After all, the actual world *is* a member of the set of all possible worlds." This is a strange argument. She loses the distinction of fictional discourse, fails to see the neutrality of narrative *qua* speech act, and, ultimately, even concedes Ohmann's mimetic thesis. Her objection to Ohmann becomes the somewhat uninteresting one that not all literature is mimetic; still, she agrees that, at least in the "traditional category, 'imaginative literature,' " the theory of "imitation speech acts" is valid.

It remains to provide some specimen instances of Pratt's way of applying the speech-act model, in order to appreciate the weakness of the venture. For one thing, she assimilates to speech-act analysis such genre distinctions as *autobiography* (*Tristram Shandy*), *biography* (Tommaso Landolfi's "Gogol's Wife"), *memoirs* (Machado de Assis's *Dom Casmurro*), and *"natural narrative"* (Jorge Luis Borges's "The Shape of the Sword"). But these categories are not in any clear sense kinds of speech acts, or acts falling under the analyses presented by Austin, Grice, or Searle. What Pratt simply means is that there are "appropriateness conditions" *of some sort* constraining such creations. Again, she insists that there are "appropriateness conditions governing novels and short stories" and "maxims . . . defined for the work's genre" and "for the fictional speaker's utterance"—which, in a curious way, is quite reminiscent of Hirsch [1967]. In effect, what this does is to assimilate *every* linguistic or literary distinction to the speech-act model, without showing either how this is to be managed, or in what sense relevant constraining maxims governing the implicit "conversational context" of literary discourse may be detailed (for Pratt subscribes fully to Grice's account).

Interestingly, Pratt ultimately undermines her own thesis—the applicability of Grice's model—by acknowledging the "anti-novel": that, for example, "rule-breaking can be the point of the utterance," and that literature of a certain sort may require "radically decreasing conformity to the unmarked case for novels [that is, the case where the standard maxims of ordinary conversation obtain] and a concomitant radical increase in the number and difficulty of implicatures." This is an extremely suggestive option, but it is also a *reductio*. Pratt takes note of a perverse kind of Gricean cooperation, namely, "noncooperation" in the game of "verbal jeopardy"—as opposed to "the tellability game of natural narrative." But if this sort of conversational context is admitted, literary criticism cannot but be relatively informal, relativized to admitted genres and practices as well as intentions, and fundamentally retrospective. *No* conversational maxims may be proposed that actually bind discourse, either within or without literature, except the most vacuous: wherever a breach seems to obtain, an adjustment in the alleged intention of a discourse will restore the sense of compliance.

Thus the speech-act model appears to yield no particular advantage to the theory of literature, or to the analysis of particular literary passages. For in the first place, the very conceptions of literature, poetry, fiction, metaphor, and the styles and genres of literature cannot be explicated directly in terms of speech acts. And in the second place, although whatever constraints and distinctive features particular literary works exhibit may well be cast in terms of the speech-act idiom, no such constraints or ordering maxims are actually derivable in a fair sense from the details of speech-act theory. This is not to deny that attention to speech acts may illuminate a particular piece of literature. But the reason would have to be an unusual one. Stanley Fish [1976], for instance, offers a very persuasive interpretation of Shakespeare's *Coriolanus* as a "Speech Act play," that is, as a play that "is about speech acts [in Searle's sense!], the rules of their performance, the price one pays for obeying those rules, the impossibility of ignoring or refusing them and still remaining a member of the community." Fish correctly observes, also, that, normally, a speech-act analysis of literary texts "will . . . be trivial (a mere list of the occurrence or distribution of kinds of acts), because while it is the conditions of intelligibility that make all texts possible, not all texts are *about* those conditions."

One last example speaks for itself. Reviewing the final passage of *Dom Casmurro,* Pratt observes that the sentence

> Well, whatever may be the solution, one thing remains and it is the sum of sums, the rest of the residuum, to wit, that my first love [Capitú] and my greatest friend [Escobar], both so loving me, both so loved, were destined to join together and deceive me . . .

"fails to fulfil [Grice's] second maxim of Quality" (that is, "Do not say that for which you lack adequate evidence"). But, of course, the point of the tale is to prepare us, by a marvellous series of indirect clues, for the developing suspicion—never explicitly confirmed by Capitú, Casmurro's wife—that his son was actually Escobar's natural son. Pratt's observation, therefore, is really a moral not a linguistic comment, confirming the Christian text (given in the tale): "Be not jealous of thy wife lest she set herself to deceive thee with the malice that she learnt from thee."

I have no doubt that "conversational implicatures" of some sort may be drawn from the subtleties of literature, but I cannot see the least possibility of formalizing them in the sense of stating standard conditions of felicity, maxims, or rules in virtue of which the discursive structure of any poem or novel or play may be displayed. The best that we can do—and the only thing that conforms to the nature of conversation as well as literature—is to attend to the shifting practices and conventions of life that are either to be found in actual human societies, or invented in the imagination of authors of talent. But if so, then reference to speech acts cannot be made to yield a descriptive or interpretive *model* for literary criticism; it yields only an appreciation of certain complicating aspects of literary pieces that otherwise might be neglected. The notion of a literary utterance, therefore, catches up very trimly a large set of the puzzles we have already explored—the difficulty of determining what is and what is not in an artwork, the eligibility of non-converging interpretations, the relevance of cultural and contextual considerations of all sorts, the absence of any "natural" classificatory system for the arts, and the pretended discovery of relatively fixed normative constraints on the production and appreciation of artworks.

12. Truth and Reference in Fiction

I take some books down from a shelf and browse. One opens: "Alice was beginning to get very tired of sitting by her sister on the bank, and of having nothing to do . . . ." Another begins: "One day when Pooh Bear had nothing else to do, he thought he would do something, so he went round to Piglet's house to see what Piglet was doing." Another begins: "I am twenty-six inches tall, shapely and well-proportioned, my head perhaps a trifle too large. My hair is not black like the others', but reddish, very stiff and thick, drawn back from the temples and the broad but not especially lofty brow." Still another begins: "It is universally admitted that the family from which the subject of this memoir claims descent is of the greatest antiquity." And still another begins: "In the year 1799, Captain Amasa Delano, of Duxbury, in Massachusetts, commanding a large sealer and general trader, lay at anchor, with a valuable cargo, in the harbour of St. Maria—a small, desert, uninhabited island toward the southern extremity of the long coast of Chile. There he had touched for water."

I begin to get an idea of what these books are about. There is some puzzlement though: I wonder what sort of information I have. They are all stories or novels—there is no question about that—though I see that several are sufficiently plausible to be reports of actual facts. Still, the main thing is that, in reading, I am not concerned to construe the sentences as parts of reports about the world outside the fiction: I wish merely to inform myself about the fictional world of the stories themselves. I can imagine the real Alice asking Lewis Carroll, after he had written *Alice in Wonderland*: "Did Alice have any more adventures?" on which cue, Carroll unfolded *Through the Looking-glass*. So may someone have importuned an ancient teller of tales to tell him the *Second* and *Third* and *Fourth Voyages of Sindbad the Sailor* after he had enjoyed the *First*. And this listener would have known that the Second Voyage was that of the very Sindbad of the *First Voyage*, and we know it to this day. But does the *First Voyage* refer to Sindbad?

Suppose I were to say, "The dwarf said he was twenty-six inches tall, and he thought his head a trifle too large." In context, you would take me to be referring to the dwarf of Lagerkvist's tale; and with this reference settled, you might go on to say that my statement was true as far as the story itself is concerned or, more circumspectly, was in agreement with what we learn from, or are told in, the story. Or suppose I say, "Pooh paid Piglet a visit." Again (grant that I am not telling the story), I am referring to the Pooh of A. A. Milne's story. But does the story, do the sentences of the story, refer to Pooh? Are they used to refer to Pooh?

The problem of referring arises in literature in at least two entirely different ways. One sort of question may be raised about the possible reference of sentences in an admitted fiction to the world outside the fiction. The other question is raised even when we restrict ourselves to the fictional world: do the sentences in a story refer to the unique individuals and events of the story? I do not wish to raise questions about the existence of Alice or Pooh or Flush or Captain Amasa Delano. It is clear enough that they are imaginary creatures: they do not exist, never have, and never shall, and this knowledge guides us in how to use the sentences that tell their stories. This is to agree with W. V. Quine [1950] that: "There is really only one world, and there is not, never was, and never shall be any such thing as Cerberus"; and with R. B. Braithwaite [1933]: "There is no 'universe of discourse' outside the real world in which imaginary objects exist . . . to imagine one of these objects is not to presuppose its existence . . . " Nevertheless (*contra* Quine), to admit this much is *not* yet to affirm or deny that we can refer to fictional entities. Some philosophers are fond of talking about things that exist in "possible worlds" even if not in the actual world (cf. Kripke [1972]; Plantinga [1974]). I shall avoid all such ways of speaking: what "exists" in a possible but not actual world does not exist at all. Hence, imaginary or fictional creatures do not exist in some rarefied world that is either different from the real world or a special enclave "within" it. They necessarily do not exist; that is, it is necessarily true that fictional creatures never, and never can, exist *and* that, *if* we can refer to fictional creatures, they may be ascribed an essential property, viz. non-existence (*see* Margolis [1973b]). Conceivably, actual creatures might exhibit certain of the general properties attributed to fictional creatures (except of course non-existence); but a fictional or imaginary creature cannot be actual. To speak then of a possible world in which an imaginary creature is actual is merely to speak of the conceivability of such a creature in some equally conceivable setting. But it is also to confuse two different senses of "possible world": (a) the sense of what is logically conceivable or logically compossible *simpliciter*; (b) the sense of what is logically (or, under further constraints, causally or similarly) conceivable or compossible *relative to the actual world* (cf. Woods [1974]). In the first sense, mention of the fictitious or the imaginary is irrelevant; and in the second, since reference to the actual world entails provisions for reference to whatever exists in that world, mentioning the fictitious or the imaginary is mentioning what necessarily cannot exist in the actual world, what is therefore not compossible with whatever is actual. It is clear that what is possible in sense (a) may be impossible in sense (b). A possible individual, then, may be an individual "when it is the referent of a consistent singular term" (that is, a term such that what is predicated of the referent in accord with the sense of the term "does not logically imply that the bearer satisfies contradictory predicates") (Routley [1966]; cf. Woods [1974]). But a possible individual in sense (a) may be impossible in sense (b).

I must insist on this point, because it is clear that a great many difficulties arise if it is not conceded. For instance, Alvin Plantinga [1974], pursuing the question of fictional entities, entertains (without accepting) the thesis that "Hamlet and Lear do not in fact exist; but clearly they could have. So there must be possible worlds in which Lear and Hamlet exist; hence they are possible but unactual objects; hence there are some [possible but unactual objects]" (cf. D. Lewis [1978]). The objections to this thesis (Plantinga calls it "the Descriptivist Premiss," the thesis that "we are talking about an object . . . and describing it by predicating of it a property it actually has") are said to be: (i) that sentences like " 'Lear exists' and 'Lear does not exist' express true propositions" (he doesn't really exist though he exists in the play); (ii) that "it seems wrong . . . to say that we just do not happen to *know* whether [say, 'Santa Claus wears a size ten shoe'] is true or false; there seems nothing *to* know here"; and (iii) "such statements as ['Hamlet was ummarried'] and ['Lear had three daughters'] are presumably *contingent* on the Descriptivist View." These are provisional difficulties and may be readily met. Statement (ii) seems quite true; (iii) is not entailed by the view that we can refer to fictional objects—it is possible that Shakespeare could have assigned Lear and Hamlet other relationships but, having assigned these, they are not contingently true of Lear and Hamlet (a fact which has to do more with the nature of fiction than with the "essential natures" of the denizens of possible but unactual worlds); and (i) simply trades on an equivocation. Plantinga then goes on to introduce a deeper objection of

David Kaplan [1973]: apparently, the term "Lear" in "Lear had three daughters" must be taken to be "functioning as a proper name—a name of a possible but unactual object. But how could it be? On the Searlean view of proper names, one who thus uses 'Lear' must be able to produce an identifying description of what he uses it to name. And how could he do that? He starts as follows: Lear is the possible individual who has the properties P_1, P_2, . . . P_n. But why does he suppose that there is just *one* possible individual with the P_1? If there are *any* possible objects that have the P_1 there will be as many as you please." But this simply misses the implication of the difference between the two senses of "possible worlds" given and the consequence of admitting the fictional use of language. For one thing, Lear and Hamlet are *not* possible objects, in sense (b) of "possible worlds"; and for another, in *that* sense, their being impossible objects (objects that could not exist in the actual world) corresponds to our using language fictionally, that is, *to our imagining a particular creature to exist about whom this story is being told.* The problem of many possible individuals having certain general attributes, answering to indefinite descriptions (Quine's well-known problem about "McX" and "Wyman" [1963]) bears only on interpretation (a) of "possible worlds" (cf. Kripke [1972]; Woods [1974]). Interpretation (b) does not preclude (and even accommodates) reference to Lear and Hamlet (who cannot possibly appear in the actual world); such reference (if admissible) would depend on an actual story *intended* to be about a unique (but necessarily non-existent) referent. There simply is no other consideration to invoke: any other imagined creature, imagined to be numerically distinct from Hamlet or Lear, having the properties ascribed to Hamlet or Lear but (necessarily) *not* the property of being the one we are imagining this story to be about, simply does not bear on the peculiarities of fictional discourse. Alternatively put, we may "imagine," in both the (a) and (b) senses of "possible worlds," but we would not be doing the same thing. The critical point which distinguishes Quine's example of the "possible fat man in that doorway" from Hamlet is that there is an actual play *Hamlet* which is intended to be about Hamlet; and that the intended referent (Hamlet) is conceived as necessarily incapable of compossible existence with the things of the actual world. So if we disengage reference from existence, the notion of fictitious referents may still be viable.

Some theorists flirt with the notion that, say, Sherlock Holmes exists-in-fiction though he does not exist (Searle [1969]; cf. Strawson [1950]). But John Woods's [1974] observation is surely telling: "It would be hard to dispute that the intuitive and philosophically unprejudiced gloss upon the proposition that [Sherlock Holmes] exists merely in fiction is that he is merely fictional and hence does not exist. 'Sherlock Holmes exists' requires special pleading; its negation does not." Of course, to *say* that Sherlock Holmes exists-in-fiction is, precisely, to register a certain uneasiness about denying that we can refer to Sherlock Holmes in spite of the fact that he does not exist; that is, it is to raise doubts about the so-called "axiom of existence." On the other hand, the denial (because Sherlock Holmes does not exist) that "Sherlock Holmes lived in Baker Street" is clearly misleading (did he live in Bleeker Street?).

There is also a possible difference to be noted between viewing the sentences of Conan Doyle's story as *referring* to Holmes and as *being about* Holmes. For one thing, reference may fairly be restricted to a certain use to which sentences may be put by a speaker in the performance of a speech act (*see* Searle [1969]; Strawson [1950]); whereas "being about" may merely signify (all or a certain salient part of) the intentional content of a sentence or of a sentence as used in a speech act (cf. Goodman [1961]). For instance, even if we should quarrel about whether the sentence "Holmes lived in Baker Street" can be used to refer to Holmes (since there is, necessarily, no one who exists who is identical with Holmes), we could hardly deny that the sentence is about Holmes or about where Holmes lived. So reference may be *intentional* (as depending on a speaker's intention [*see* Donnellan ([1966]); Kripke ([1973]); Margolis and Fales ([1976])]), but aboutness is merely *intensional* (in being extracted from the sense of a sentence or from the sense of a sentence as used in some speech act).

The two questions I originally posed are different. The first asks about the relation between fiction and reality, and whether the sentences in a fiction may be said to be used to refer to events and persons in the real world external to the fiction. The second asks what is the language of fiction *qua* fiction, and whether, in being used, it is used to refer to fictional entities. A third question—Can *we* refer to fictional or imaginary creatures?—is readily answered, although it may complicate other philosophical issues. The answer is, very clearly, yes, at least prephilosophically speaking. We regularly (appear to) refer to Cerberus, Pegasus, Hamlet, Mr. Pickwick—and not merely to the body of Greek mythology, Shakespeare's plays, or Dickens's novels. We may also say true and false things about any of these imaginary creatures; their not actually existing does not make all statements (apparently) referring to them false. Nevertheless, we could not make reference to them unless there existed actual mythical traditions, plays, and stories which fix their "careers"; and we could not test the truth or falsity of any of our statements about them unless we could appeal to such traditions, plays, and stories—in fact, to the things of the actual world. I wish to emphasize, however, that to refer to fictional creatures is not to refer to the sentences of a story.

Of course, to admit that we can refer to fictional or imaginary creatures entails that the so-called "axiom of existence" must be rejected (*see* Margolis [1977]), that is, the axiom that "whatever is referred to must exist." But John Searle [1969] who enunciates the axiom, following Frege and Strawson [1959], also manages to say that

> if in the fictional mode of discourse I say, "Mrs. Sherlock Holmes wore a deerstalker hat" I fail to refer for there is no fictional Mrs. Sherlock Holmes. Holmes, to speak in the fictional mode, never got married. In short, in the real world talk both "Sherlock Holmes" and "Mrs. Sherlock Holmes" fail of reference because there never existed any such people. In fictional talk "Sherlock Holmes" refers, for such a character really does exist in fiction, but "Mrs. Sherlock Holmes" fails of reference for there is no such fictional character. The axiom of existence holds across the board: in real world talk one can refer only to what exists; in fictional talk one can refer to what exists in fiction (plus such real world things and events as the fictional story incorporates).

Surely, this effectively means that, in the real world, I can refer to what exists and, in the same linguistic context, refer to what is fictional or imaginary; that, "in fictional talk," in referring to what "exists in fiction," I am referring to what does not (and cannot) actually exist; and that, at least implicitly, fictional creatures are sometimes ascribed the capacity to refer not only to other denizens of their "world" but to the creatures of the actual world (cf. Strawson [1950]; Pleydell-Pearce [1967]). Searle himself, therefore, cannot sustain the axiom, falsifying it by his own concession. By the same consideration, to admit reference to fictional or imaginary creatures entails rejecting existential import to whatever is merely canonically rendered in terms of the quantificational prefixes of sentences, for instance as in W.V. Quine's account [1960] (*see* Margolis [1973b]; cf. also H. Hochberg [1957]; Margolis [1968]):

> Insofar as we adhere to this notation [the canonical notation of quantification], the objects we are to be understood to admit [as ex-

isting] are precisely the objects which we reckon to the universe of values over which the bound variables of quantification are considered to range. Such is simply the intended sense of the quantifiers "(x)" and "$(\exists x)$": "every object x is such that," "there is an object x such that." The quantifiers are encapsulations of these specially selected, unequivocally referential idioms of ordinary language. To paraphrase a sentence into the canonical notation of quantification is, first and foremost, to make its ontic content explicit, quantification being a device for talking in general of objects.

Effectively, then, we are bound to treat reference as a grammatical rather than as an ontological distinction; consequently, we need not anticipate that there are special logical constraints on the kinds of speech acts we may perform or sentences we may issue, though the truth value of what we may actually say about fictional or actual entities will obviously be affected. In any case, the axiom of existence leads to paradox, whether formulated in Searle's sense or in Quine's, quite apart from fictional considerations (*see* Margolis [1977]). For, where the ontic *commitment* of speakers rather than the *existence* of putative referents is said to be entailed (Quine's view), existence is not actually required for the success of reference; and where existence is required (Searle's view), uncertainty, doubt, or ignorance of what actually exists (say, in accord with Quine's metaphysical skepticism) undermines reference or knowledge of successful reference. The latter alternative is intolerable; the former concedes the point.

Let us put the matter as clearly as possible. If the axiom of existence or cognate notions are rejected, then we cannot suppose that, in successful reference, we must be referring to what exists; correspondingly, in saying what is true of what we are referring to, we are not necessarily saying something true of what exists. Also, in saying something true of fictional entities, we are not saying something false of the entities of the actual world or something false of the actual world. Considerations neither of truth nor reference dictate that, always or unless suitably qualified, we must be concerned (only) with the features of the actual world. The canonical view of quantifiers and (in effect) of reference (cf. Quine [1960]) holds that the use of the relevant features of our discourse entails ontic commitment, that is, that what we are speaking about we take to exist. On the interpretation of so-called free logics (cf. Leonard [1956];

Lambert [1963]; Hintikka [1959]; Heintz [forthcoming]), we may speak of individual fictional entities as such, and say what is true of them, but we cannot infer that whatever befell a particular fictional entity befell *someone*; the inference from a singular statement (employing the name of a fictional entity) to its counterpart existential generalization (employing the existential quantifier) becomes invalid—which is itself anomalous. If, however, we deny ontic import to quantifiers and treat reference merely grammatically (to speak of what belongs to our "universe" or "domain of discourse" is merely to specify what we are referring to or are prepared to refer to in some further remark), normal inferences go through without anomaly. Pressure shifts, however, to the existential presuppositions of our discourse. For example, in ordinary discourse, it is fairly conventional to take it that if one says "Sherlock Holmes had tea with Gladstone," then the context of reference is fictional—it being granted that fictional entities do not exist in a fictional world or at all. But if one says "Gladstone had tea with Sherlock Holmes," then, precisely because Gladstone was an actual person and Holmes, fictional, the use of the sentence is ambiguous with regard to existential presuppositions—were it the actual world, what is stated would be false; were it the fictional "world" (that is, what we merely imagine to exist), what is stated would be true. Where our conventions are not sufficiently reliable, we simply require clearer clues about referential intent. So it is not, here, so much a matter of logic as of speakers' intentions, or not so much a matter of logic as of the interpretation of what we are committed to by purely logical considerations. What is true, then, need not be true of the actual world; and what we are referring to, when we are successful, need not exist in the actual world. If "snow is white" is true if and only if snow is white, then "Hamlet killed Polonius" is true if and only if Hamlet killed Polonius (cf. Tarski [1944]). There is no need to equivocate on truth or reference or existence or even the meaning of our predicates. All that is required is clarity about *what* we are talking about: the *criteria* for deciding what is true or false will doubtless change with changes in our existential presuppositions, but that is just what we should expect. (cf. Parsons [1975]). At any rate (*contra* D. Lewis [1978]), sentences not prefixed by the intensional operator, "In such-and-such fiction . . . ," are not automatically about the actual world—whatever our informal practice; they may merely be insufficiently explicit in this regard.

Woods [1974] offers some interesting distinctions here, though they appear to be connected with a doubtful thesis:

> It hardly wants saying that not every object that does not exist is fictional, for there are the objects of mythology (e.g. Zeus). And

not every assent-worthy statement that nonetheless reports something that did not "really" happen is a statement of fiction, for there are statements about legendary figures (e.g. Paul Bunyan). Mythological figures can be likened to fictional characters at least in the sense that they are reckoned not to exist by whomsoever recognizes their mythologicality or their fictionality. And mythological statements resemble fictional statements at least insofar as neither kind is thought, by those who recognize them to be mythological or fictional, to describe the real world. But there are differences. Mythology tends to be theology and science fallen into disrepute—what began as serious reports of the nature of the world end up as the cherished or tolerated fantasies or fancies of a tribe or a people viewed as benighted, and usually heathen. Fiction, however, pretends no such literal congress with reality; it is make-believe from the beginning. The most singular difference between the legendary, on the one hand, and the fictional and mythological, on the other, is that the classification of a person as legendary does not compel an affirmation of its non-existence. Neither need it be that all assent-worthy statements about legendary figures fail to record what really occurred. Sometimes people become legends because they did, really, do extraordinary things in consequence of which a reputation is born and bestowed upon a gullible world eager to augment it, indeed to exaggerate it out of recognizable shape. Thus, Nero, Billy the Kid, and Orson Welles.

I take these distinctions to confirm the utility and reasonableness of *not* construing reference in terms of the axiom of existence; otherwise, we should be forced, counterintuitively, to view the syntax or grammar of relevant sentences (for instance sentences about King Arthur or Faust) as subject to certain discoveries about the world. Whether King Arthur or Faust ever lived hardly seems to be the right sort of information to decide the logical form of given sentences. Nevertheless, Woods wishes to contrast sentences of these sorts with others that, at least grammatically, also appear to be about non-existent entities—notoriously, the sentence: "The present king of France is bald" (*see* Russell [1905]; Strawson [1950]). Here, I cannot agree with Woods when he says that, "On the naive view [that is, the view that the truth of fictional sentences depends on 'the author's sayso and whatever can legitimately be inferred from statements true in virtue of the author's sayso'] it is not at all clear that we would be right to call fictional objects INTENTIONAL." Woods's language is extremely cautious, but he does appear to construe fictional objects as "non-existent, non-intentional objects." He means to stress that fictional sentences, unlike sentences containing "empty singular terms," are "bet-sensitive"—for instance that, "as between 'The present king of France is bald' and 'The present king of France is vigorously hirsute' there is no rational wager to make"; also, that rational wagers about Holmes's residence can be made. As Woods puts the matter:

> What is striking about fictional objects is that, short of non-existence, they fail this test of intentionality [that is, that 'objects' like the present King of France 'do not fit "the objectificatory apparatus of our language: articles, pronouns and the idioms of identity, plurality and predication." ']. Of Holmes there is no stopping such idioms as 'he who did so and so,' 'the sole solver of the case of the such and such,' 'an unsympathetic personality,' 'one and the same with the man who lived at so and so address in Baker Street,' 'was only one of the persons who attempted to aid the Baskerville family,' and 'is Φ,' 'is Ψ,' 'is X,' . . . for a multitude of everyday predicates Φ, Ψ, and X . . . . By the most reasonable tests, the present king of France might be an intentional object, but not, certainly, in the way Holmes is. For even though Holmes does not exist, we know who he is. He is a non-entity who is a somebody. The present king of France is a nonesuch.

But of course, though the differences that Woods reports do obtain, reference to Holmes depends (as does reference to mythology and legend) on actual stories or traditions in virtue of which such reference can succeed. In that sense, Holmes *is* an intentional object—a matter of very great importance; but, then, perhaps we should say that reference, as a distinct (though dependent) speech act (Searle [1969]), takes a tautologous intentional object (its referent) even though what it refers to may or may not actually exist. In *that* sense, there is no difference between Holmes and the present King of France, except that, since the referent in the second instance is *intended* to be actual, further rational wagers about "his" properties are not "bet-sensitive" (since no such person exists). My recommendation, then, comes to this: treat reference as a grammatical distinction having no ontic import—hence, uniform for actual and fictional entities. The full adjustments required cannot be attempted here. But we should have to divest quantifiers of existential import, construe "existence" as a predicate (Margolis [1973b]), and deny that reference is or entails a relationship unless that be construed in a purely grammatical sense.

Because a fiction is a system of sentences that tells a story (or, elliptically, it is the story told, the world of the story), we are, in viewing fiction as fiction, interested in finding out and understanding what the story is. (We need not concern ourselves at the moment with what it means to *tell* a story.) What needs to be emphasized is that fiction provides us with an account of a world of action that exists, as we say, in the imagination, that is, a world we imagine to exist but which we know does not and never did exist. Since we are party to this quite innocent fraud, it cannot be appropriately described as a lie or a falsehood *about the world.* Margaret Macdonald's arguments [1954b] on this issue are conclusive. Her position rests on the observation that there is a "mutual conspiracy" between author and audience, that "no factual discovery can verify a fictional statement," and that "the expressions of fiction are neither self-contradictory nor nonsensical" (cf. Ayer [1946]). (This may well accord with what, from hearsay, it appears Saul Kripke has suggested in his recent, unpublished Locke Lectures: that in fiction we simply imagine a world of a certain description to be real and then proceed as usual, as far as reference and related speech acts are concerned, in speaking about what obtains "in that world.")

It needs also to be stressed that fictional creatures are not to be treated as a kind of creature—except grammatically, for the purpose of reference and predication; that is, as Kant [1933] demonstrates, real and imaginary hundred dollar bills are not distinct species of hundred dollar bills. If reference is treated grammatically only, and *if* quantification is freed from all ontic import, then no ontic anomalies such as the view attributed to Meinong—that fictional objects are "incomplete objects"—need be conceded (*see* Woods [1974]). It is true that, regarding Hamlet, we may not be able to determine whether the clothes he wore on some occasion (on which it is clear from the text that he wore clothes) were of this or that specific color; but we need treat this limitation only epistemically, not ontologically. Notice that there is a double remove here: (i) no questions about actual existence arise, since we are speaking of a fictional creature; (ii) we may well be necessarily ignorant of certain "matters of fact" regarding the fictional world that we think should otherwise obtain—treating the fictional world analogously to the actual world. But fictional creatures are *not* "incomplete" creatures; they are not actual creatures at all. Hence, regarding what, necessarily, is non-existent, it is entirely plausible that we should, necessarily, be ignorant of information that analogy with the real world suggests would be pertinent. We are ignorant simply because what we claim to know *of* a fictional referent depends exclusively on an actual text or tradition. To speak of an incomplete creature is, in this respect, an ellipsis for speaking of a text that fails to provide sufficient details to support the analogy tendered. Epistemic questions, here, concern only information provided in an actual text or provided by inference or interpretation of that text. So it is not in the least unreasonable to suppose that we may infer—by induction, based on the textual evidence—certain events and traits that are not textually explicit or even logically entailed by what is explicit (cf. Wolterstorff [unpublished]). The non-actual fictional world and the actual world can have no actual causal relations, but in the actual world we may perform the speech act of referring to the things of the fictional world, as well as the act of imagining a world in which fictional creatures make reference to themselves and to our world.

We must remember that fictional worlds are not "possible worlds" in the (b) sense, given above, that is, in the sense of being (with whatever adjustments) compossible with the actual world. In the (b) sense, they are impossible worlds. Now, it is also sometimes thought that, *among* fictional worlds, there may be impossible worlds in the (a) sense, that is, worlds that are not compossible *simpliciter*. So seen, theorists (for instance, Heintz [forthcoming]) are tempted to introduce special relevance logics to restrict the standard consequence that everything will be true in the fictional world imagined. But there are actually three distinct kinds of case that need to be sorted. One, like Wells's *The Time Machine* or Mann's *The Transposed Heads,* simply requires that the apparent impossibility—say, time travel (cf. Horwich [1975])—is imagined to be satisfactorily interpreted on a model—say, space travel—that is known not to be impossible: the events of the story are construed in terms of conventional space travel and then simply read back in terms of the idiom of time travel. A second, as in talking of "time warps" in so much of science fiction, is simply content to leave the apparent anomaly or impossibility uninterpreted; it becomes, then, a sort of *deus ex machina* for connecting parts of the story otherwise difficult to render intelligible—it may of course involve adjustments of the first sort as well. A third simply introduces a flat impossibility. Heintz offers a fine example, Ray Bradbury's "A Sound of Thunder," in which, apparently, a certain character, Keith, is both elected President in 2055 and not elected President in 2055—where the inconsistency is essential to the story. Here, it is just the intended presuppositions of the fictional world about which the story is told that set *interpretive* constraints on what the inconsistency affects. In short, in none of these cases must we construe impossible worlds as requiring a distinctive logic; the issue is normally one of interpretation and is normally settled by the storyteller's intention.

I shall not press any superficial resemblances between fiction and poetry or drama; though there are respects in which these latter arts behave like fiction. I suggest, rather, that fiction is primarily *a use* of language—in the sense intended in speaking of speech acts (*see* Searle [1969]; Alston [1964])—and poetry, a *style* of language (*contra* Beardsley [1970b]; cf. Reichert [1977]). There are, I take it, no logical peculiarities essential to poetry (which is not to say there are none in poetry). This remark, which seems reasonable enough, has rather important consequences. For instance, matters of fact may be stated poetically; therefore, I. A. Richards's well-known thesis [1935], contrasting poetry and science, falls at a stroke.

There is, in fact, an entire nest of puzzles suggested by the distinctions between poetry and fiction. For one thing, though it is linked with the analysis of speech acts, fiction primarily poses the problem of reference to, and predication of, non-existent entities. If we grant that there are no speech acts that obtain in non-fictional discourse that cannot be incorporated in fiction, it becomes clear that the sentences within a fiction cannot be distinguished by way of any speech-act model, that the essential feature of fiction concerns constraints on ranges of putative referents about which we can speak, rather than on the grammatical features of the very act of reference itself. In particular, these concessions suggest the misleading thrust of the popular thesis that fiction—as well as poetry—essentially involves an imitation of speech acts (*see* M. Pratt [1977]; Ohmann [1971]; Beardsley [1970b]). That thesis confuses the difference between imagining a fictional creature performing a speech act (speaking about other characters, for instance) and some actual creature or some machine imitating or mimicking a speech act (a parrot uttering sounds, for instance).

Regarding poetry, not only Richards but also the Russian Formalists and the Prague Circle (*Travaux du Cercle Linguistique de Prague* [1929]) have pressed the distinction of "communicative" (roughly, "factual" or "scientific") and poetic language behaving according to substantially different "laws":

In its social role, language [*le langage*] must be specified according to its relation to extralinguistic reality. It has either a communicative function, that is, it is directed toward the signified, or a poetic function, that is, it is directed toward the sign itself. [Translation in Pratt]

The claim lends itself to putatively syntactic or at least formal differences between poetry and non-poetry, the imitation thesis, the linking of poetry and fiction, and exaggerated emphasis on such variable features as versification (cf. Matejka and Pomorsky [1971]). But to admit that poetry is a mongrel category of some sort, collecting an immense variety of texts that could not conceivably yield to any uniform analysis—quite apart from considering ulterior social and political purposes sometimes alleged to have shaped Formalist doctrine—pretty well negates the plausibility of the claim.

We may also take note of the fact that the structuralist tradition of literary theory (*see* Culler [1975]) has simply generalized the search for "deep" rules of linguistic and literary structure. As Culler puts it, "structuralism effects an important reversal of perspective, granting precedence to the task of formulating a comprehensive theory of literary discourse and assigning a secondary place to the interpretation of individual texts." But if the point of the venture is "a science of the conditions of content, that is to say of forms" (Barthes [1966]), structuralism maintains an extremely implausible thesis (cf. also Frye [1957]; Hirsch [1967]). There is not the slightest evidence that there is, or could be, anything supporting Hjelmslev's thesis [1961], for instance, viz.: "*A priori* it would seem to be a generally valid thesis that for every *process* there is a corresponding *system*, by which the process can be analysed and described by means of a limited number of premises." Actually, the claim could be read equivocally. For, it might mean (a) that, though there may be no such system that actually generates such processes in any causally or psychologically pertinent sense, nevertheless a "generative" system may be retrospectively fitted to any set of processes; or it might mean (b) that an actual system obtains that does generate such processes in the causal sense. It was Chomsky's thesis [1965] that generative grammar is "not a model for a speaker or a hearer" but "assigns" a grammatical description to a sentence. However, Chomsky [1972] also holds that his thesis about generative grammar is actually a thesis about cognitive psychology. Were this not affirmed, the Chomskyan thesis (and any of its structuralist analogues) would have to be construed merely instrumentally or heuristically—which can hardly have been the point of the original theory. For his part, Culler [1975] maintains, curiously, that "literature is a second-order semiotic system."

The principal objections, then, to the implicit innatism (see Margolis [1978a]) or structuralism sketched are as follows: (i) there is no plausible sense in which the use of language in the literary arts is a second-order use, for both literary and non-literary uses (whatever we may mean by that) presuppose an antecedent practice that includes, without reference to such ordering, both literary and non-literary uses; (ii) there is no plausible sense in which an historically reflexive and developing activity, like the invention of literature, could be construed so that its products are actually generated (in sense [(b)]) from some antecedently fixed, finite, complete, comprehensive and ahistorical system of forms; (iii) for any set of literary works for which a system (in sense [(a)]) can be provided, it is in principle possible to provide alternative and incompatible such systems, without its being possible to determine some exclusively correct or valid such system, in sense (b) (cf. Quine [1960]). Apart from these general objections, structuralism has failed to provide evidence of any particular system for the analysis of literature, answering to sense (b), that matches, say, Lévi-Strauss's achievement regarding kinship myths [19679]—ignoring whatever internal difficulties may confront the latter (cf. Culler [1975]). Finally, there appears to be no way to show that particular analyses or interpretations of literary pieces actually favor the structuralist thesis over the non-structuralist.

To return to our original questions about fiction, there is a "voice" in any fiction, that of the implicit or explicit story-teller, that provides us with the story. The exception, of course, is dramatic fiction; dramas are not told but enacted or imagined enacted. The important point about the "voice" is that it is not the author's voice, if we understand the author to be an actual person who may speak about his fiction or about the world independent of his fiction. The "voice" in a fiction is a machine, so to say, that makes the story available to its readers or auditors; the principal (normally the exclusive) thing it can do is provide its story. That we are to imagine such a "voice" to exist is usually a matter-of-fact discovery that we make from all the contextual clues, that enables us to read a story as a story. Even if the "voice" in the story inclines us to suppose that it is only the author's utterance referring to the real world, we must not be misled. Melville's *Benito Cereno* begins as if it were a factual account, somewhat like the entry of a captain's log. The "voice" in Virginia Woolf's *Flush* speaks of the tale as a "memoir," and it is true that, in writing the story, Virginia Woolf availed herself of much information about Elizabeth Barrett Browning and about Flush, her dog; yet, to concede that the "voice" of a fiction is a fictional voice does not preclude the possibility that the story it tells is intended to be in part about the actual world. There is no logical reason why portions of the actual world cannot be imagined to be part of the fictional world. Still, since fictional creatures do not exist at all, they cannot actually tell us about the world.

An additional subtlety needs to be exposed here. "Imagine a man of such-and-such description doing such-and-such act" probably does not involve a fictional *use* of language though it does involve a fictional *style*. That is, if a man merely introduces putative facts this way, he is not to be viewed in the same way as another who invents a story and, by chance, discovers a correspondence with certain actual events. Drama, similarly, may be viewed as a way of presenting things, a *style* of language, whether factual or fictitious—or, indeed, indeterminate in this regard. Clearly, the difference is an intentional one, distinguishing the presuppositions of certain speech acts.

The point at stake may be logically trivial but not philosophically unimportant. Insofar as we regard a story as a fiction, we dismiss the question of its truth or falsity about events and persons in the actual world as altogether ineligible. The reason is that, in order to construe it as verifiable, we must decline to regard it as a story; for, as a story, it is merely imagined to have taken place, or to refer to what is merely imagined to have taken place. For the same reason, it cannot be said to refer to particular events and persons in the actual world. (It may of course be imagined to refer to the actual world.) Now, it is sometimes said that a novel is "about" life in the actual city of London, or that Tolstoy wrote "about" the actual Napoleonic wars (cf. Scriven [1954]; Wolterstorff [unpublished]). Insofar as a work is a fiction, reference within the "world" of the fiction can be (that is, can be imagined to be) reference to the actual world; and novels (as opposed to fictions) may be said to make reference to the actual world—but only insofar as the sentences of the *novel* are construed as the utterances of the *author* rather than as the utterances of a fictional voice. Fictitious creatures cannot actually refer, for they cannot actually do anything. Fiction is a logical distinction concerning the existential presuppositions, or the existential status, of a speaker. The concept of the novel does not as such mark a comparable distinction, though it entails *some* fictional use of language.

Thus Monroe Beardsley [1958] ("simplifying" Strawson's view of the question of referring) quite completely mistakes the philosophical significance of the *refusal*, at times, of law courts to construe certain would-be works of fiction as fiction:

> if you write a novel about a bookie who lives at 1329 West Eighty-
> ninth Street, Manhattan, and has the telephone number BO 7-3927,
> and it turns out by chance that there is such a person with that ad-

dress and number, you have referred to that person, whether you meant to or not, and your story becomes false.

Beardsley explains:

> I want to say that the sentence has truth-value quite independently of any intentions or wishes if the unique referent exists, and does not if it doesn't. And this is borne out by the practice of the courts, for it is possible to libel another unintentionally.

If the novel is a *fiction,* such reference is impossible; the courts merely *decide* not to regard such sentences as fictional. Fictional sentences and libelous sentences do not belong to the same classificatory system. Put another way, reference is inherently intentional: to intend to refer to a *fictional* creature is to intend not to refer to an *actual* creature; attributive compliance of the sort Beardsley considers is simply not enough to convert the one to the other. In fact, if existence is construed predicatively, even such attributive compliance must fail. Beardsley's account betrays at least two weaknesses: one, that the admission of the intentional nature of reference would undermine other of his views about the irrelevance of an author's intention; the other (more important here), that he assumes without argument that a unique referent could be supplied either by an informal use of referentially weighted predicates of the sort he introduces, or else (rather as with Quine [1960]) by the use of a set of general predicates or indefinite descriptions that uniquely sort all individuals. The trouble is that, in creating a fictitious character, an author *cannot* be supposed to have referred to an actual person; and in referring to an actual person, he cannot have been supposed to have created a fictitious character. In that sense, there simply are no sentences *of a fiction that could be true of an actual person.* Beardsley detaches general predicates or indefinite descriptions from the fictional presuppositions of their use and then, assuming an actual referential context drawn from those same fictional presuppositions (or from the normal non-fictional designations of *selected* proper names and the like), entertains the possibility that the sentences of the *novel* might be true of an actual person and that the *author* has referred to such a person in spite of the fact that he had no such intention and perhaps knew nothing at all about such a person. The thesis is unnecessary, counterintuitive, and confuses the categories of fiction and the novel.

A fiction is, so to say, a one-term system; it is whatever it is. We may understand it or enjoy it, but it refers to nothing beyond itself. It is simply the imagined world provided by the sentences of a story; that is, by using the sentences as fiction, we imagine a certain world to exist. We may notice certain resemblances between the fictional world and our own, and we may refer to these. The author may have intended to draw attention to such resemblances; perhaps his letters, prefaces, diaries, and conversations may inform us that he intended his work to refer to something in the real world, and may even facilitate determining what it was. We should express this by saying that he intended by his work to refer to some particular event or person, or that he intended that his work make such reference, or even that he used it to refer (or to represent) something about the world (or even, further, about the fictional world). This last formulation agrees, for instance, with a very sensible view proposed by David Novitz [1975] regarding pictorial representation and its relationship to stories:

> To represent something pictorially . . . is to use a picture to communicate information which pertains to, or is about, what is pictured (or an aspect of what is pictured), where such an act of communication may be performed under a range of descriptions commonly given to illocutionary acts.

> The activity of depicting . . . is an intentional activity; so that a picture of a black horse, like the thought or story of Black Beauty, never requires the existence of the horse in question.

Reference, depicting, and representing are intentional activities and may therefore be used to convey information about either imagined or actual referents. But the author's or artist's intended use of his own speech act or "utterance" (what he "meant"—in a sense more or less captured by Grice's well-known discussion of meaning [1957]) raises ulterior questions. What is in his story (his fiction), as a story (fiction)? Or, what is the story? We must go "outside" the story to provide for the *author's* reference, even if we go to selected sentences printed in the text that provides the story; sentences that are used referentially are, in *this* sense, parts of two-term systems—whether the referents are actual or fictional. We ask what the story is, what is in the story, what the story tells about—all equivalent expressions; but we ask what the author says about that story, and what his remarks refer to. Fictionally used sentences refer (if they refer at all) to what is in the imaginary world conforming to that use (the world we imagine to exist, possibly including portions of the actual world). But this is a matter utterly different from inferring from the evidence of the work itself, or from other "external" evidence, that the author intended to refer to, or to represent, certain features of the actual or an imagined world. As in dealing with certain expressive properties of works of art, it is of course quite possible that the author's intentions are aesthetically essential to an appreciation of the work (*see* Sircello [1972]). But that has nothing to do with the logical features of the fictional use of language. Reference and all other intentional activities may be grammatically *represented* in relational terms, but one cannot have an actual relationship with a fictional character. By parity of reasoning, when one refers to an actual individual, the grammar of one's utterance need not change: one may have an actual relationship with an actual person, but that relationship is not as such *grammatically* represented in referential expressions. (A parallel point affects Goodman's [1968] account of monadic and dyadic representation: the distinction concerns the world represented, not the grammar, so to say, of representation; it is merely Goodman's refusal to countenance intentional distinctions that leads him to the ellipsis.)

What may have misled some theorists is that it is always possible, in imagining a fictional world (as in *War and Peace*), to imagine that it includes an (adjusted) portion of the actual world. To speak here of reference to the actual world is an ellipsis for speaking of reference to a fictional world that includes, say, much of the Napoleonic era. We may draw attention to a resemblance between a story and some particular events in the world; questions of verisimilitude and of the status of the historical and realistic novel are concerned with such resemblance. As a mere story, a story does not assert such a resemblance and does not refer to whatever it does resemble. Notice of such resemblance may enlarge our understanding of the sort of literary achievement that lies behind a story, but the story remains a one-term system, a fictional "world." (Here is what is potentially misleading about a fiction's being said to be "true to" the world—in spite of its not being "true about" it.) Only *we* can decide what comparisons to venture; literary criticism may be interested in such comparisons, and the author may have had such comparisons in mind, but the story as a fiction makes no reference to them. To mistake our interest, or the critic's interest, or the author's purpose, with a story's "voice" is, in effect, to deny the story its status as fiction (cf. Hospers [1958]). This is emphatically *not* to say that an appreciation of the author's achievement—fixed by his inscription of a certain set of sentences—would never justifiably lead us to construe his intention, in composing his story, to refer to, depict, or represent aspects of the actual world (or even his feelings about the fictional world he has created).

To read Aesop's *Fables* or the parables of Jesus as lessons probably requires that, after a story is told and digested, one must deny that it is a mere fiction at bottom and consider instead the lesson *exhibited,* depicted, or represented (which may also perhaps be neatly appended as an explicit moral). The moral and, elliptically, the story (that is, the lesson presented in story *form*) may be judged true or worthwhile with respect to the actual world. Such literature, however, cannot be fiction; and that is analytically true. This explains, for example, the subversive force of Lenin's "Aesopian language." It also resolves a worry that Michael Scriven [1954] raises: "If 'the language of fiction' includes all that lies within a work of fiction, then it appears to include at least some expressions that *do* function as propositions, that can be true or false." Scriven has in mind certain kinds of *novels*, which he somewhat misleadingly assimilates to "work of fiction"; he is chiefly concerned with verisimilitude in the historical and realistic novel. But the issue of verisimilitude cannot be managed in terms of the sense of "language of fiction" Scriven has provided, and his use of "fiction" casts no light at all on the logically distinctive fictional use of language. *Novels* may very possibly combine fictional and non-fictional uses of sentences—I should hardly wish to deny that. But if so, then the historical novel—Tolstoy's *War and Peace* for instance—may require us to oscillate between the utterances of a fictional voice and those of the actual author; or, at the very least, to suppose that the fictional voice is *meant* (by the author) to refer to the details of the actual world, or to predicate what is true of the actual world.

Some literature incorporates fictional elements in logically more involved ways. An ingenious possibility is suggested by a line from Gilbert and Sullivan's *Pirates of Penzance.* The Major-General sings: "I can hum a fugue of which I've heard the music's din afore,/And whistle all the airs from that infernal nonsense, Pinafore." The charm of the line depends absolutely on the ambiguity of supposing that the actual songs of *Pinafore* are known in the fictional world of Penzance or that the creatures of Penzance are, somehow, in touch with the actual world (or the fictional world of *Pinafore*). To return to one of our earlier instances for another illustration, in her Notes to *Flush* (printed with the story), Virginia Woolf refers to the actual Elizabeth Barrett, Robert Browning, Miss Mitford, Mr. Kenyon, Mr. Horne, Mrs. Bridell-Fox, and others. She *invites* us thereby (speaking in her own voice) to consider the *accurate* detail, not the *truth* (an odd expression here) of her fictional memoir. In her Notes, then, she refers to these actual persons; in her story, she creates a fictional world about a Miss Barrett, a Mr. Browning, and others. Though one speaks of the author's creating a fictional world, no such world exists and none is created; one simply imagines a world of a certain description to exist, as did the author. (This is *not* to deny, however, that we refer to fictional entities, or that fictional "voices" may refer to the creatures of the imagined world—a thesis Gilbert Ryle [1933] would not concede.)

In addition to imagining that the fictional world of *Flush* exists, we are invited, in the context of the story and of the Notes, to compare the imaginary Miss Barrett and Mr. Browning with the actual Miss Barrett and Mr. Browning. A close correspondence between fact and fiction will be judged verisimilitude; a divergence, a fictional liberty. Since Virginia Woolf explicitly indicates her own intention, we may reasonably challenge her accuracy; had she not made this clear, we should doubtless still look for a measure of verisimilitude but with considerable (and perhaps indefinite) tolerance. Viewed as a fiction merely, *Flush* does not suggest the question; viewed as a fictional memoir or historical novel, it does, but not in a way to dissolve the fiction. In fact, it is only by regarding the Miss Barrett of the story as a fiction and not as the actual Miss Barrett (that is, as referring to her) that such an issue as verisimilitude can possibly arise.

This suggests another possibility. *Flush* might also be thought of as a fictitious account of certain actual creatures. In such a case, verisimilitude is waived and we concede the author a certain literary license; for here, the fictional use of sentences does not primarily concern reference to *fictional entities,* but rather the use of fictional attributes or *fictionally ascribed attributes to actual entities.* Such a use of language directly involves the counterfactual, which raises questions about reasonable measures of license: the question cannot arise in the same sense wherever reference is made exclusively to fictional entities, and wherever verisimilitude is intended. But it is important to take notice of the fact that the fictional use of language may exhibit a dual form, depending on which intention we ascribe to the use of language—whether, that is, a fictional world or a fictionally altered actual world (that is, a world including at least a certain number of actual individuals) is thought to be presented. Tolstoy's *War and Peace* is either a fictionalized account of the actual world (including fictional relationships between actual and imaginary individuals in the actual world), or else an account of a fictional world *simpliciter.* The first alternative involves counterfactual attributions and reference; the second does not, but permits verisimilitude. Each, therefore, construes the historical novel in logically different ways.

The reason is simply that there can be no actual interaction between fiction and reality. Put another way, on the first view of an historical novel, the *author's* reference to fictional entities is "story-relative" (in the sense given by Strawson [1959], but not for his own purpose); on the second, reference is autonomous, marked by a distinctive use of language. But both require reference to be intentionally specified, which—I am arguing—is just as true of actual entities as of fictional ones.

Verisimilitude, then, is also quite a different matter from that of the truth of fiction. Morris Weitz [1950] asks, "Can art embody truth claims?" He answers affirmatively, with literature chiefly in mind, opposing I. A. Richards's emotivism (Ogden and Richards [1923]) and employing an adjustment of G. E. Moore's well-known use of "implies" (*see* Schilpp [1942]). Nevertheless, even granting his thesis, his remarks are not free of a crucial ambiguity. For example, speaking of Richard Wright's *Native Son,* Weitz says, "The first thing we notice as we read the novel is that it is not *about* an isolated Negro but about all Negroes and group minorities in America" [italics added]. Insofar as it is *about* "an isolated Negro," the account is a fiction; it may also, symbolically and still within the fictional framework, be about "all Negroes"; but if it is to be *about* "all Negroes" in Weitz's sense, it must *refer* to actual Negroes and make assertions, explicit or implied, about them. Weitz does not sort these senses of "about." He adds, however (I shall italicize the words that are ambiguous on the issue at stake): "*Through Bigger* . . . Wright is *claiming* . . .*"* (Weitz himself italicizes "claiming"); "Bigger is more than a *symbol* of exploitation and *represents* all men who . . . "; "Bigger Thomas, the subject of the novel in the course of his experiences, *epitomizes and embodies the truth claim* that individual freedom is still an abortive idea in America . . . " No clarification for any of these terms is provided, nor is it made clear how Weitz might have arrived at his claims or how they may be squared with the fact that *Native Son* is admittedly a work of fiction. "Epitomizes and embodies the truth claim that" is especially instructive, since "epitomizing and embodying" is just right for a certain sort of verisimilitude, without truth claim; and "truth claim" rightly points to the author, without raising any question of verisimilitude. When Weitz says that the novel is *not* about Bigger Thomas, he is in effect denying that *Native Son* is a fiction, or else claiming that it is an account presented in the *style* of a fiction. When he says that Bigger Thomas is a *symbol* of, or *represents,* the plight of actually exploited men, he concedes that *Native Son* is at least a fiction. When he says that Bigger Thomas "embodies the truth claim that . . . ," he is implying that Richard Wright, "uttering" the fiction

Native Son, meant (in Grice's sense) to claim something about the actual world. Furthermore, the question arises whether Weitz's remarks are intended as remarks about the novel or about the author: is *Native Son* a novel in which certain truth claims are made about the condition of man, or does the novel provide us with evidence about the author's convictions? On the first reading, the novel has properties expressive of the author's attitudes and feelings; on the second, the properties of the novel enable us only to infer what those attitudes and feelings may have been (cf. Weitz [1943], [1945]; Sirridge [1975]; Beardsley [1958]).

Moore's use of "implies" is elaborated for fiction in a more careful way by John Hospers [1958], who makes it clear that the fictional use of sentences is not to be disturbed:

> works of literature may provide us with evidence about the author's beliefs, attitudes, and intentions, thus entitling us to infer these propositions; and . . . quite apart from any reference to their authors, these works may suggest or intimate (say without saying) numerous propositions which are not about the author but about the world, about the subject-matter of the work itself. And since some of these suggested propositions are doubtless true, we have here, surely, an important sense of truth in literature, and one which it seems to me that many critics who have made claims for truth in literature have had in mind without being fully aware of it.

Hospers's formulation, however, is not without its difficulties. Hospers fails to distinguish clearly between inferring certain truths about the author from the evidence of his work, and the work's *implying* (in a sense akin to Moore's) certain propositions (cf. Hospers [1960]; Brooks [1947]; Hungerland [1960]). I may, for example, infer from a novel that its author is naive; but this is not to say that the novel implies any particular propositions. That Hospers confuses, at times, the very distinction he wishes to introduce may be seen from the following remark:

> There are countless clues in [Dreiser's] novels themselves that we could cite as evidence for the author's beliefs. (Not for the truth of the beliefs, but for the truth of the proposition that the author entertained them.) And there are no contrary clues. From observing all this, we can say with considerable confidence that the work implies that the author had these beliefs.

Here, the sense of "implies" does not correspond with Moore's sense and does not bear on Hospers's own topic of "implied truths in literature" (Hospers [1966]; cf. Margolis [1966]). Its sense is akin, rather, to the sense of "implies" that fits such expressions as "dark clouds imply rain." But the ease of shifting from the one sense to the other, and the difficulties of providing even informal criteria for the required sort of contextual implication (in fiction), suggest how modest a gain the thesis provides.

A much more convincing way of capturing the claim intended depends on construing the literary piece (or other artwork, for that matter) as the artist's "utterance," that is, as behavior expressive of the artist's convictions, feelings, moods, and the like, *in virtue of which* the work itself is endowed with certain expressive properties (*see* Sircello [1972]) or certain "implicatures" (*see* Grice [1975]; M. Pratt [1977]). By such devices, even fiction could be said to preserve "artistic truths." Obviously, the reason for so speaking lies in the interest we take in comparing fictitious and actual persons, and developing a comprehensive battery of distinctions for understanding not only the actual lives we encounter but also the possibilities that are open to such lives. Julian Mitchell [1973] expressly holds that

> The purpose of reading literature, which is a complex imaginative process, seems to me the same whether we're reading history, autobiography or fiction. We read to gain new information about life. And we do this by imagining ourselves into situations we haven't been present at, or which have never taken place at all, and by imagining ourselves to be people other than ourselves, real or fictional. It makes very little difference to us, I believe, whether we're concerned with real or fictional situations and people: the value lies in the imaginative process.

He does not succeed, however, in explaining what he means by "truth," "knowledge," and "imagination": he is content, for instance, with merely pointing out that "we *can* call true a book which we know perfectly well is neither true nor false." The commensurability of fact and fiction in understanding the features and possibilities of actual lives must be responsible for the extended sense of "true"—and for the sense that, preeminently, literature has a moral function (cf. Beardsmore [1973]; D. Phillips [1973]; Girvetz and Ross [1971]).

I suggest that one way in which both (the deviant sense of) truth and moral function are reasonably invoked concerns a certain use of the notion, associated with Aristotle, of "fidelity to human nature." In praising a character in the relevant way, we assimilate actual human beings *to the type of the character*. We do not praise Hamlet by searching for flesh-and-blood Hamlets; we praise him by noticing that certain human beings appear to approach the fictional character we know so well. This man is a Hamlet; that one, a Quixote. This is what we ordinarily mean in saying that a character is "true to life": truth concerns a certain excellence that we assign to invented characters in terms of whose lives we offer a certain appreciation or appraisal of the lives and events of the actual world (cf. Casey [1966]; Margolis [1966]). Thus we treat actual lives as if they were token instances of the same type for which some author has provided the paradigm (token).

To judge the verisimilitude of a fiction is precisely to *compare* a fiction with the actual world; hence, questions of truth and falsity are ineligible. To make the judgment is not to imagine a new fiction or to disturb the old one. Ryle's remarks [1933] about *Pickwick Papers* being somehow accidentally true of some person are, therefore, quite misleading. Taken literally by G. E. Moore [1933] and soundly criticized, these remarks do not entirely fit with Ryle's insistence that the propositions of *Pickwick Papers* are "only a pseudo-designation." Ryle sometimes speaks as if *Pickwick Papers* were merely "one big composite predicate." On his own view, however, it must also be *imagined* to refer to someone—it must be taken as fiction, as not referring to any actual person. I do not believe Ryle has satisfactorily met this additional constraint. Attributions to fictional entities are not merely pseudo-attributions; they are merely not attributions to actual entities.

To turn to the second of our original questions, suppose we read in Lagerkvist's *The Dwarf* [1945]: "When the wrestling match was arranged between Jehoshaphat and myself I forced him onto his back after twenty minutes and strangled him. Since then I have been the only dwarf at this court." Must we not suppose that the dwarf refers to Jehoshaphat and a particular wrestling match, and to a particular princely court that flourished at some time and place? I believe we must. The persons and events that the dwarf refers to, in relating his own story, are themselves items in the fictional world of the story itself. That is, the way in which the dwarf refers to the events and persons of his fictional world is grammatically the same as the way in which we make reference. The reason we say so is simply that *they* are "confined" within their world and *we* are committed to imagining that world to exist.

Still, this says nothing about the use of language in fiction. On the contrary, it neutralizes the difference between fiction and actuality by pointing out that language may be used to refer to events in fiction as well as in the actual world, and in precisely the same way. Notice, of course, that we must refer to Jehoshaphat as an imaginary person in an actual story, while the dwarf cannot refer to him as fictional at all. It is because we imagine the fictional world to exist that the creatures within the fiction are imagined to regard one another and themselves as really existing. Therefore, we imagine them also to refer to one another.

The question remains: What is the nature of the specifically fictional use of language? Here I think of an analogy from classical philosophy (Spinoza for instance)—that of the relation of nature naturing and nature natured. A fictional world must first be created in order for reference to obtain within it—that is, not actually constructed but imagined: such a world is "created" by the "naturing" power of language. The fictional use of language, then, cannot be a referring use because it initially creates the world of creatures and events that some language may later be used to refer to. To say that the dwarf refers to Jehoshaphat is to imagine that the dwarf and Jehoshaphat exist.

The language of fiction functions in two ways, therefore. In one, used appropriately, the sentences of a fiction "body forth" a particular imaginary world—producing Jehoshaphat, who is referred to, as well as the dwarf, who makes reference to him; in another, the "voice" of the dwarf, collapsed into the "voice" of the fiction (since the story is told in the first person), is imagined to refer to Jehoshaphat. Hence, the referring use of language occurs in fiction only insofar as the world of the fiction is already assumed to exist; but it is then, precisely, that the distinction between fiction and reality is no longer critical. Where the fictional use of language is paramount—where one first "tells a story," first releases the "voice" of the fiction, uses the sentences of a story fictionally—the referring use of language (our reference to fictional creatures, their reference to themselves) is as yet impossible since the world, so to say, has not yet been created. The primary use of fictional language *cannot* then include a referring use; it is a *sui generis* use that first makes reference possible.

A standard thesis about speech acts (Searle [1969]) holds that reference is a dependent speech act. But the quarrels about reference to what does not exist normally neglect to notice that the very possibility of fiction insures the possibility of fictional reference. We cannot imagine a world to exist that we know does not exist, except against the backdrop of discourse about the actual world. But *if* we admit that *we can imagine a world to exist that we know does not exist,* then we cannot deny that we can refer to things within that imagined world. For even if we imagine that something instantiates a certain predicate, we shall, for grammatical reasons, need to make reference to that imagined instance. The critical question is not whether we can refer to what does not exist, but whether we can imagine things to exist that do not and cannot exist: those who deny that we can refer to what does not exist must be denying that we can imagine things to exist that do not and cannot exist—which is plainly untenable. All disputants admit that we can at least imagine a fictional world to exist. But to do so, though it is not as such to refer to the imagined members of that world, nevertheless necessarily provides for such reference. It makes no sense to say that I can imagine Sherlock Holmes to exist unless it makes sense to say that I can refer to the very Sherlock Holmes that I have imagined to exist. This is why the intentional nature of reference is crucial: because, even in the context of the actual world, I must intend, by what I say, to refer to something of that world. Reference does not succeed because what I purportedly refer to exists; it succeeds because, near misses aside (*see* Donnellan [1966]; Margolis and Fales [1976]), I refer to what I intended to refer to. No actual world, however dense, can insure the success of reference (*see* Strawson [1950]). Why then, *if* it is admitted that we can imagine a world to exist, should the success of reference to *what we have imagined to exist* be denied?

The *Second Voyage of Sindbad* refers to Sindbad, but only because it is imagined to be an additional narrative about the world the *First Voyage* has already created. The same is true of the second chapter of any novel. But notice that it is not the actual author, but only the fictional narrator, who refers to Sindbad. In speaking of fiction, we regularly shift from such expressions as "X told us (related) a story," "Father, tell us a story" to such expressions as "we are told in the story." It makes all the difference in the world whether we are speaking of an actual person telling us a story or of a certain fictional dwarf telling us a story, because the first way of speaking bears on the fictional use of language, and the second bears on the uses of language internal to the fictional world we have imagined to exist by the fiat of the first way of speaking. "Once upon a time" is both a contextual clue to the fictional use to which sentences that follow are to be put and an expression used by a fictional "voice" to refer to the events of a world imagined to exist (cf. Wellek and Warren [1956]).

The fictional use of sentences is a "presiding" or "executive" use. It indicates only, by presupposition, the "world" *in* which the sentences given are issued—an imagined world rather than the actual world. Sentences cannot be merely fictionally used, just as they cannot be used merely to refer—though for different reasons. The referring use must always be joined to some other primary speech act, such as affirming, denying commanding (*see* Searle [1960]). The fictional use of sentences merely supplies a special referential context within which sentences used in the usual speech acts are understood to apply; adhering to the presuppositions of fiction, questions of truth, accuracy, exactitude, and the like, which properly apply to the actual world, are necessarily rendered irrelevant. (The admission of "free logics" of course [cf. Woods ([1974])], in which terms may denote non-actual individuals, supports the viability of our thesis.) "Nonfiction" is an odd expression unless we see it as a necessary warning against "switching back" to the actual world while reading a fiction—which tends to confirm that there are no essential grammatical differences between fiction and nonfiction.

If we should say that statements in *Pickwick Papers* are about Mr. Pickwick, we should mean that either one of his associates, or the "voice" of the fiction, referred to Mr. Pickwick in the course of the story; or that, by using *Pickwick Papers* fictionally, Mr. Pickwick is imagined to exist; or that Dickens wrote *Pickwick Papers,* which is "about" Mr. Pickwick in the sense just mentioned. We may refer to Mr. Pickwick, but only by virtue of the actual *Pickwick Papers*; although referring to Mr. Pickwick is not referring to *Pickwick Papers.* It is worth noting that G. E. Moore [1933] does not provide any clarification of the "natural sense of the word 'about' " in which statements that Dickens "makes in *Pickwick Papers*" are "about Mr. Pickwick," except, perhaps, when he states that Dickens thought of Mr. Pickwick as

> a man having certain well-known characteristics, which had already been assigned to him in the story (different ones, no doubt, on different occasions when he wrote the name), and in addition, always, as *the* man, having the characteristics in question, *about whom I am telling this story.*

But Dickens's "telling the story" merely invites us to imagine Mr. Pickwick to exist: Pickwick's characteristics cannot yet have "already been assigned to him in the story"; the sentences cannot yet be "about" him or used to refer to him. Moore has confused the two aspects of fictional language: that in which one imagines Mr. Pickwick to exist, and that in which speech acts internal to the imagined world obtain. Emphasis should have been placed on "telling this *story*," on the fiction; for if it were merely on *"about whom* I am telling this story," there would be no logical reason why it could not be true or false of some actual person. Hence, Moore does not actually avoid the difficulty he rightly notes in Ryle's account. Emphasis on the story, however, would have rendered the rest of Moore's remark superfluous. Furthermore, speaking of

Dickens's telling the story, Moore is led to conjecture irrelevantly about what Dickens is supposed to have thought.

What we have done, then, in the entire foregoing account is to construct a theory of fiction that coherently permits: (i) a distinction between the fictional and the actual world; (ii) a univocal sense of "exists"; (iii) a uniform theory of reference independent of existential import; (iv) reference to fictional creatures as particulars; (v) a demonstration that the fictional use of language is not a distinct kind of speech act but may be sorted rather in terms of its ontic presuppositions.

The most strenuous objection to the pivotal thesis (iv) is linked to the supposition that if fictional creatures are (or are to be treated as) particulars, then, since they must be "incomplete" particulars, the thesis fails for logical reasons. The most sustained argument of this kind is Wolterstorff's [unpublished], (cf. also, Wolterstorff [1975a]), but it is demonstrably indecisive. Wolterstorff relies on two principles. The first, the Principle of Exemplification, is either tautological or questionbegging: "Everything x is such that for every property P and every time t, x has P at t only if x exists at t." Consider that "has" is equivocal: it may mean (a) "actually possesses"—in which case the Principle of Exemplification is tautological; or it may mean (b) "may have truly predicated of it"—in which case the Principle is not obviously true, unless (the very issue at stake) we simply rule out all predications of fictional entities. Wolterstorff himself notes that the Principle entails that "we cannot refer to what does not exist"—which betrays at a stroke its own bias (the axiom of existence). The second principle, the Principle of Completeness, is either trivially satisfied or inherently faulty: "for everything x and every property P, x either has P or lacks P (has the complement of P)." Here, again, Wolterstorff trades on an equivocation. He argues that "denial of the Principle requires that one also deny certain of the laws (theorems) of first-order logic. For example, one such law is that a disjunction, *either p or q*, is not true unless either p is true or q is true"; and he adds that reference to Sherlock Holmes as a particular fictional entity entails, under the circumstances of Conan Doyle's story, that it is not true that Holmes had a mole on his back and it is also not true that Holmes did not have a mole on his back.

But it is entirely possible to reinterpret these claims without becoming illogical. What needs to be borne in mind is that there are two senses of negation intended here—so-called "internal" and "external" negation. Furthermore, the point of the objection to the second Principle can be formulated only if the first Principle is itself waived; for otherwise, no predications of fictional entities can even be entertained. On the essential strategy, however, the following may be noted. It is certainly false that Sherlock Holmes had a mole, and it is certainly false that Sherlock Holmes did not have a mole (or, that Sherlock Holmes had a non-mole). In saying this, of course, we mean that, relative to the information in Conan Doyle's story, these propositions are false or (perhaps more accurately) indeterminate; furthermore, since Sherlock Holmes admittedly does not exist, it makes no sense to insist that he *must* have or possess properties apart from whatever properties *may be ascribed* to him on the "say-so" of Conan Doyle (cf. Woods [1974]) or on what may be inferred or interpreted on the basis of Conan Doyle's "say-so." There simply are no other sources to canvass. In any event, if the propositions in question are both indeterminate or (relative to our information) both false, nothing yet said vindicates the Principle of Completeness. For consider that we assume Holmes lacks property P (having a mole). Then does he have "the complement of P?" Well, he does have a violin! And, from a logical point of view, having a violin constitutes a possible specification within the "complement" of P. But surely, Wolterstorff could not have meant that: he meant that Holmes must have had a mole on his back, or had a smooth back or had a back marked in such and such a way, or. . . . That it is false (external negation) that Holmes had a mole on his back and that it is false that Holmes lacked a mole on his back cannot be made straightforwardly to yield the denial of the Principle of Completeness; for (relative to internal negation) that Principle is either trivially satisfied or inherently faulty. It is trivial if, for instance, it is satisfied when Sherlock Holmes lacks a mole but has a violin; and it is faulty if it requires that, although it makes no sense to say that Sherlock Holmes has the property P or (an appropriate specification of) its complement, Sherlock Holmes must nevertheless have that property or its complement. For example, it makes no sense to say that a stone has or lacks a sense of humor. It is false (by external negation) that a stone has a sense of humor or lacks one. Hence, external negation is simply opaque or uninstructive about whether denials are due to false attributions or to the mere inapplicability of certain sets of attributes. Wolterstorff argues that the rejection of the Principle of Completeness entails adopting the thesis (Meinong's) of incomplete entities; but that is a mistake. The *theory* of fiction entails that it is improper to ascribe properties to fictional entities that exceed what may be inferred or interpreted about them on the basis of the author's "say-so."

At least partly for reasons of the sort just considered, Wolterstorff argues that because fictional characters cannot be particulars (since they do not exist), they must instead be *kinds* (which he believes are entities that do exist [see Wolterstorff ([1970])]). One may argue that it is contrary to our ordinary view of fictional reference to hold that we do not treat Hamlet or Holmes as individuals but only as kinds. For instance, one may *admire* Hamlet or *resemble* Holmes. More pertinently, we may say, first of all, that on the counter-argument to Wolterstorff's interpretation of the Principle of Completeness, the thesis that characters are kinds is no longer required—the apparent anomalies having been dissolved; and secondly, that the thesis is anomalous in its own turn—kinds being such that they cannot be created or destroyed. (We may, if we wish, treat characters as tokens-of-a-type: Marlowe's and Goethe's Fausts, then, may be viewed as different tokens of the same type). In any event, thesis (iv) is fully restored, consistently with our larger theory.

13. Figurative Language

We are all forewarned against taking poetic figures literally, though we often find them puzzling and inquire about their sense. The effort to explicate them tends to be roundabout. Indeed, we should find it a curious suggestion that they could be simply defined or synonymously replaced. For one thing, figurative language is characteristically inventive and novel; for another, it quite deliberately departs from the standard uses of such expressions catalogued in dictionaries and lexicons. Figurative language is not, therefore, language incorrectly used; on the contrary, one supposes the poet knows very well how language is ordinarily used in non-figurative ways, and trades on such knowledge (cf. Hungerland [1958]).

I do not wish to suggest, however, that figurative language is exclusive to poetry. Some poetry is non-figurative, and much non-poetry is figurative. Figurative language and incorrect usage both depend on the standard uses of words and phrases, but their relations to such uses are different. Incorrect usage is simply the failure to use language correctly, whereas figurative language is a deliberate departure from language usage that is determinably standard; we make reference to standard usage to clarify poetic figures; but if we judge them, we must do so on grounds other than that of deviation from the standard uses of the expressions in question. The concession is important because, for one thing, it forces us to attend to the irreducibly intentional nature of figurative language (cf. Grice [1957]); and for another, it exposes the logical oddity of supposing that language is or could be inherently metaphoric in nature. The latter thesis seems to have been somewhat theatrically defended by Nietzsche [1964]: "A nerve-stimulus, first transformed into a percept! First metaphor! The percept again copied into a sound! Second metaphor. And each time he [that is, man] leaps completely out of one sphere right into the midst of an entirely different one." Of course, the relationship between language and non-language cannot be metaphorical if metaphor entails a departure from literal sense. Also, the distinction between figurative and non-figurative language cannot be the same as the distinction between earlier and later phases of the formation of language (cf. Barfield [1973]).

The intelligibility of figurative language depends on our grasp of the ways in which it is intended to upset certain standard rule-like ways of speaking; hence, the provision of would-be rules for the explication of metaphor may well involve grasping the poet's intention (or a fairly ascribed intention) to replace the semantic regularities that obtain in literal speech with others parasitic upon them. It is useful to observe that language is *not* figurative or metaphoric merely because it is used to speak about, and to make linguistic distinctions regarding, a world that is, in some important sense, pre-linguistically given: figurative speech can be distinguished as such only by way of contrast with language that is not figurative. Still, to say that figurative language is parasitic on literal discourse is emphatically *not* to say that natural languages are actually stratified as such by some straightforward procedure. If that were so, then the apparent "deviance" of metaphor could be confined in a relatively straightforward way. In fact, the very notion of there being standard rule-like regularities holding for the literal use of words represents an idealization by which, on a theory, we manage to fix the dictionary entries for words as well as their putative figurative use. But metaphor is as natural to human speech as literal sense; only by introducing favored uniformities in analyzing the flow of actual discourse can either be specified with precision (cf. Ziff [1960]; Putnam [1975c]; somewhat *contra* Alston [1964]). The admission undercuts the pretensions of a formalized semantics for natural language (*contra* Katz [1966]; Davidson [1967]). The crucial point is rather a nice one to press: *if* the rule-like regularities of natural languages are idealizations only, then the very idea of a departure from literal sense also involves an idealization. Hence, the distinction between first-order (literal) usage and second-order (figurative) usage cannot really correspond to recognizably regular and ordered distinctions within the practice of any natural language; this undercuts a great many theories of metaphor which pretend that the contrast is relatively well-marked.

There are many different ways in which we may depart from standard usage. Suppose we have arranged a secret code such that when I telephone you to say, "The blankets have been delivered," you understand that the bombs have been set. We might also, of course, have devised an unfamiliar set of vocables to keep our code secret. All such inventions require that the code expressions be readily translatable into expressions that have standard uses in our language; in fact, the first are to be regarded as exact equivalents of the second. We are left, then, merely with secret equivalents for standard expressions, and we may err in using these in ways equally applicable to their equivalent expressions. Codes are interesting because, for one thing, they cannot be distinguished from standard speech by way of particular speech acts; presumably, whatever speech acts are standardly available are available in the use of a code. Secondly, it is quite possible that the same locution (as the instance given shows) could function either as a code or metaphorically (or even literally). Nevertheless, metaphor and code are distinct uses of language that, once again, depend on speakers' intentions.

Consider another instructive case, that of slang. Quite by chance, I find myself in the company of heroin addicts—I know nothing about their customs or their slang. One turns to another to say, "I've got to get this monkey off my back." I misunderstand him if I take what he says literally, that is, if I assign some standard, non-slang sense to the sentence he has uttered. The slang use of familiar words and phrases is a deviant use in that, like the technical use of equally familiar expressions—as in law, engineering, medicine, or freemasonry—it marks a departure from the usage that obtains when we have no clear cues that quite specialized senses are to be assigned our words. But it is not a deviant use in that, as with the technical use of expressions, it is part of our standard way of using language under determinably restricted circumstances; it is not as such a metaphoric use of language. Consequently, considerations of incorrect usage apply here as well. Still, the code use, the slang use, and the technical use of expressions all point to other ubiquitous uses, so that we may be said to depart at least from the primary standard uses of expressions, without yet speaking figuratively and without necessarily speaking incorrectly. These departures are primarily semantic or perhaps syntactic; they do not in any important way depend on the introduction of novel sorts of speech acts. (I may, however, mention the ingenious, exploratory work of Ted Cohen [1975], which enlarges on Austin's theory of illocutionary acts [1962] to provide an illocutionary analogue of metaphor—for example, "I beg you to get well," which cannot be an instance of begging. Still, metaphor is primarily not a use of sentences in the sense of performing speech acts but rather a use of words.) What remains fundamental to such considerations is just that it is quite impossible, relative to any particular utterance, to determine independently of one another the nature of the speech act performed and the sense of the words used in performing that very act; in particular (*contra* Alston [1964]), we cannot first determine the speech act conveyed by an utterance, and then the sense of particular words by considering how replacements affect the "speech act potential" of the original utterance.

Consider yet another case. I say jokingly to you, "You know, you shouldn't be stealing the company's money." You answer quite seriously, "I've never taken a red cent. Besides, all the other clerks 'borrow' a little and make it up. I never have. And you'd better not go spreading that around." You have taken me literally, that is, mistakenly. Speaking jokingly constitutes a different sort of departure from standard usage than that of codes, slang, and technical usage. The latter have to do specifically with assigning meanings to particular words and expressions departing from primary standard usage; speaking jokingly does not require a specialized vocabulary but has to do, as we say, with the spirit in which anything may be said. A command jokingly given is not intended to be carried out; a question jokingly asked is not expected to be answered; a statement jokingly made is not to be confirmed, investigated, denied, or taken to be true or false. Speaking jokingly is a special way of qualifying some speech act such as commanding, asking, or stating something, a way in which the logical job of such acts is, so to say, waived (cf. Searle [1969]). It is not an independent speech act. It is also to be contrasted with the act of telling a joke (which invites even further distinctions, somewhat like those that would be offered in identifying the act of telling a story). Telling a story is an act using language, but it is not a speech act in the sense in which the term is currently used, because (as we have already seen) it is concerned essentially with the existential presuppositions with which any otherwise *bona fide* speech act is performed. And speaking jokingly is not a speech act, though it is also an act involving the use of language, because it is concerned essentially with altering the standard intentions with which otherwise *bona fide* speech acts are performed. Telling a joke is an act of a less uniform sort, for it is likely to be either a case of telling a story (of a certain sort), or of reviewing the facts (in a certain way). If we know the manner or spirit of a remark, if we know that it was made jokingly or mock-seriously or ironically, we know that certain sorts of responses or judgments, otherwise appropriate, are rendered inappropriate. Also, understanding that what is said is said jokingly, ironically, or in some similar way entails understanding the speaker's intention (what he *meant* in saying what he did).

Speaking loosely and exaggerating are also intentional departures from the standard ways of speaking usually associated with making statements (that way of speaking, say, in which what is said is simply true or false), though they are themselves part of our usual way of speaking. They cannot, however, stand as independent speech acts. If one has exaggerated, it is inappropriate to judge what he has said to be false, though this is indeed the *prima facie* conclusion on which exaggeration trades. Questions of accuracy, exactitude, and understatement are closely related considerations and similarly affect the logical features of what is said (Austin [1962]).

Of all of these peculiarly dependent acts, however, irony is the only one regularly classified as a trope (cf. Henle [1958]). Irony is ordinarily taken to be a somewhat humorous manner of speaking in which the opposite of what is literally said is intended, or at least what is said is tempered in the direction of the opposite. What is praised is intended to be blamed; what is said to be so is to be taken not to be so. Speaking jokingly is a more neutral way of speaking; what seems to be asked is really not asked and what seems to be asserted is not asserted. Speaking jokingly is also simpler than irony, in that the literal sense of what is said remains intact, but the logical use to which it would ordinarily be put is cancelled. Exaggerating is closer to irony, in that we distinguish what is literally said, by way at least of partial negation, from what may be the intended sense of what is said.

We see, therefore, that departures from standard usage of this second sort—irony, speaking jokingly, exaggerating, understatement—are more complex than those of the first sort—codes, slang, and technical jargon. In fact, those of the first sort are not really departures at all; they are special cases of standard usage. The items of the second sort all trade, in a variety of ways, on standard usage. Still, it needs to be emphasized that the very notion of standard usage is itself an idealization that may misleadingly suggest an actually stratified language. In this sense, exaggeration and irony are neither departures nor deviations from "ordinary" usage; they are marked thus only relative to a theory that counts certain favored linguistic regularities as central to normal or literal speech.

That the sort of departure from standard usage marked by the principal tropes—metaphor, synecdoche, and metonymy—is distinct from that just considered is patent, once we admit that expressions using these figures may make no literal sense at all. An example is, "Fold a roseleaf round thy finger's taperness" (Keats)—cited by Stern [1931] for other reasons. Metaphor, synecdoche, and metonymy have to do with the meanings of expressions that are used in sentences, and not with the uses of sentences (such as commands, questions, statements) that we classify as speech acts; in this regard, they are to be sharply distinguished from irony, exaggeration, speaking jokingly, and understatement. The possibility that figurative expressions may be literal nonsense requires a fundamental revision in Monroe Beardsley's Controversion Theory [1958] (cf. Empson [1951]), which describes metaphor as

> a significant attribution that is either indirectly self-contradictory (e.g., to call a man "a fox," to call streets "metaphysical") or obviously false in its context, and in which the modifier connotes characteristics that can be attributed, truly or falsely, to the subject.

By "attribution" Beardsley intends

> any linguistic expression containing at least two words, one of which denotes a class and also characterizes it in some way, and the other of which qualifies or modifies the characterization . . . whether a phrase . . . or a complete sentence.

Two objections may be made against the Controversion Theory. For one, since metaphors, taken literally, may be nonsense, they need not be attributions of any sort—certainly not "indirectly self-contradictory" or "obviously false." For another, even if they make some sort of literal sense, metaphors need not themselves be attributions, no matter how helpful it may be to *consult* possible attributions in order to explicate their meaning. Beardsley tends to construe metaphor in terms of such uses of sentences (speech acts) as making statements (in this sense, "phrase-attributions" are merely implicit "sentence-attributions") (cf. T. Cohen [1975]), whereas metaphor should be construed in terms of using words in a certain way regardless of the uses of sentences. William Charlton [1975] supplies some useful specimens of metaphors not used in assertions or denials (hence, neither true nor false)—for instance, "Unthrifty loveliness, why dost thou spend upon thyself thy beauty's legacy" (Shakespeare), and "Fly envious Time, till thou run out thy race" (Milton) (cf. Warner [1973]). The distinction, limited as it is, is important even if it seems not quite to meet Beardsley's claim, because Beardsley's view leads inevitably to the thesis that metaphor is always paraphrasable so as to recover truth values; the truth is that it is not, and that the recovery of truth value is not essential. If an attribution is *metaphorical,* then it is quite beside the point that some *literal* use of the expression involved is false, contradictory, or nonsensical (cf. Binkley [1974]). (Whether any attribution is intended in a metaphorical utterance is still unresolved.)

In fact, though Beardsley insists that an attribution contains "at least two words" which cofunction in a way that permits us to speak of attributing something to something, it is entirely possible to have a single word (or a word prefaced by the article) function metaphorically; if so, of course, it would be quite impossible to maintain that metaphors are, necessarily, attributions of some sort. Christine Brooke-Rose [1958] gives a very clear instance of what she terms "simple replacement metaphors": Antony says of Cleopatra, in context, "The Witch shall die" (Shakespeare). *Being a witch* is certainly not predicated of Cleopatra in any sense that is at all accessible grammatically; she is simply referred to, as a witch—"the" functioning referentially. There is a certain looseness in Brooke-Rose's characterization of metaphor: "Metaphor . . . is any replacement of one word by another, or any identification of one thing, concept or person with any other," but her illustrations support a firmer theory. In any case, the implication is plain, though she herself feels that metaphors of this sort are "on the whole restricted to the banal, the over-familiar, or to metaphors which are so close in meaning to the proper term that the guessing is hardly conscious, or that they depend much more on the general context than do other types of noun metaphors." Brooke-Rose also considers Old English kennings, which need not meet Beardsley's condition either: for instance, "heaven's candle" (the sun), "the swan-road" (the sea), "the ocean's charger" (a ship), "the sea-stallion" (a ship). She herself views these as instances of what she calls "the Replacing Type of Genitive Link (e.g., sea-stallion = stallion of the sea . . .)." Here again, we have an epithet that cannot be construed in terms of a grammatically distinct form of attribution. These examples illustrate the reason for the quibble between Brooke-Rose's view and Beardsley's. Attribution is, on Beardsley's view, either an explicit or an implicitly intended speech act, an assertion (or the intention or willingness to assert) that such and such is the case. But if a ship is identified or referred to as "the sea-stallion," nothing yet signifies that the speaker literally affirms or is prepared to affirm *that* the ship is a sea-stallion.

Here, a not unimportant quarrel arises regarding the tropes (cf. Jakobson and Halle [1956]; Dubois *et al.* [1970]). "Metonymy" is a term often taken to include the sorts of figures that were, at one time, distinguished more sharply as synecdoche and metonymy; and "metaphor" is a term that often is taken to include all the tropes, though it is sometimes applied more narrowly (and more carefully) to a special range of figures. What is at stake in these terminological shifts is the very adequacy of a theory of metaphor. Synecdoche, narrowly construed, is taken to cover shifts from the literal to the figurative, in which genus is substituted for species, species for genus, part for whole, whole for part, the name of the material for the thing made. Metonymy is taken to cover somewhat looser substitutions like cause for effect, effect for cause, the sign for the thing signified, the container for the thing contained. Metaphor, narrowly taken, is said to cover shifts in sense that depend on resemblance and analogy, possibly accidental and marginal (cf. Wellek and Warren [1956]). Even with this information (and adding what has already been said of irony), it is clear that we cannot have a simple, comprehensive rule for all the tropes. More specifically, there is reason to think that metonymy and synecdoche need not be metaphoric at all, but may be figurative in the merely ornamental sense; that is, if for instance we replace the word for the whole by the word for the part, *meaning to refer to the whole,* we do not have metaphor but we do have synecdoche. The line *What immortal hand or eye/Could frame thy fearful symmetry?* (Blake) may well be read as synecdoche in this sense, at least as far as "hand or eye" (that is, God) is concerned; "frame thy fearful symmetry" may be literal or metaphoric, depending on the sense of "frame." This suggests the stratified models for the replacement of one word by another and shows, incidentally, the weakness of Brooke-Rose's formulation.

It may be somewhat trivial to generalize about metaphor, since the force of the generalization depends merely on reclassifying seeming exceptions. Resemblance or similarity, for instance, is the favorite candidate for the principle of metaphor, but are "giddy brink," "jovial wine," and "daring wound" metaphors? (cited from Lord Kames, by Richards [1936]; cf. Ushenko [1955]). Richards insists that there are grounds for metaphor other than similarity; he distinguishes between "direct resemblance" between two things and "some common attitudes which we may (often through accidental and extraneous reasons) take up towards them both." The distinction suggests that similarity is hopelessly elastic term when it is made out to be the comprehensive pr ciple of metaphor, and that the effort to paraphrase attributions is bound to be misleading (cf. Goodman [1968]). This surely points also to the weakness of Paul Henle's theory of metaphor [1958], which is based on C.S. Peirce's account [1939] of iconic signs—hence on resemblance. If Peirce's semiotic theory must be employed, "jovial wine" would probably have to be treated indexically rather than iconically (Henle takes indexical signs to have no bearing on the present issue). It may also be remarked that Henle takes no notice of Richards' implicit objection to his own theory, though he refers to partial correspondences between some of his distinctions and those of Richards' (cf. Ushenko [1955]).

We might metaphorically call someone a "duck," offers Richards, because of some feeling "of 'tender and amused regard.' " To speak of a resemblance or (iconic) similarity here would be quite misleading—though, I suppose, not absolutely impossible. Gustaf Stern provides a long list of metaphors based on relations other than similarity, though most of these would probably be viewed as instances of metonymy (cf. Empson [1951]). Some of the more interesting, which suggest the questionbegging aspect of separating metaphor and metonymy, include: "peeler" and "bobby" (the London policeman, so-called from the name of the founder of the corps, Sir Robert Peel), "un goddam" (Parisian slang for an Englishman), "I'm for Bedfordshire" ("I want to go to bed"), "to travel by Mr. Foot's horse" (to walk). In any case, in treating metaphor in terms of resemblance, the emphasis is misplaced since the logical question is: What *use* is made of such resemblance, or other relations, in metaphor? The point is strongly pressed by Goodman [1968], though as a nominalist [1966] he fails to account satisfactorily for the phenomenon of resemblance itself (cf. Goodman [1970]; Margolis [forthcoming]).

We may gain a better perspective on figurative language by considering a no-man's land between metaphor and literal expression. Imagine someone pointing to the lower shell of a turtle and asking, "What does that look like?" or "What does that remind you of?" or "What would you call that?" (Here, I am taking a liberty with one of Henle's illustrations.) The answer might well be, "A breastplate." It is, technically, now actually called a "plastron" (the name for the metal breastplate worn, in medieval armor, under the hauberk). If the answer is, "It's actually like a breastplate," or "It really resembles a breastplate," it is a literal answer to a literal question. We can always authorize an extension of the literal sense of some term to cover instances with regard to which it could appropriately be employed with "like" (or a suitable substitute) in such sentences as, "It's actually like a breastplate." "Breastplate [or 'plastron'] of a turtle" is not, then, a metaphorical expression when technically used in zoological circles. On the other hand, if, independently of any question of what the lower shell of a turtle actually resembles, and independently of any technical usage, I simply characterize the lower shell of a turtle as a "breastplate" (that is, by deliberately using a term that applies to the metal breastplate worn, in medieval armor, under the hauberk), the expression becomes a metaphor.

The point is that the very same term may be generated by either metaphorical or literal considerations. A principle of resemblance is at work in both cases, which shows at once the inadequacy of distinguishing metaphor merely in this way (cf. Isenberg [1973]). Stern, for one, is careful to distinguish the two sorts of cases mentioned by speaking of "intentional transfer (non-figurative)" and "figures of speech." Max Black [1954-1955] notes the process of catachresis (without derogatory implications), observing neatly, "It is the fate of catachresis to disappear when it is successful" (cf. Srzednicki [1960]; Edie [1963]; Berggren [1962], [1963]). Richards usefully observes that "however stone dead . . . metaphors seem, we can easily wake them up." However, he is inclined at times to overstate his regard for metaphor. "The worst" of Artistotle's assumptions (in *Rhetoric*), he tells us, is "that metaphor is something special and exceptional in the use of language, a deviation from its normal mode of working, instead of the omnipresent principle of all its free action." He opposes the view that it is "a grace or ornament or *added* power of language, not its constitutive form" (cf. Ushenko [1955]). Whatever else it is, metaphor must be an added power, because all figurative language trades on logically prior non-figurative language; we could not otherwise even speak of extending meanings metaphorically, as an eligible thesis (*contra* Foss [1942]; cf. Wimsatt [1954]). But it does not follow that it is a mere ornament or separable stratum of language.

There is a temptation to construct a theory of metaphor solely on instances that behave like the expression "the breastplate of a turtle" (Henle's iconic theory, for example [cf. Hospers ([1960]). The feature of all such expressions is that there is always some readily denotable item that can be described in the required way, no matter how circuitously, without the metaphoric reference. The metaphor manages to decay conveniently into a literal expression for the reason that it serves economically to fix what we otherwise lack a name for, or describe only by rather roundabout methods. This thesis leads directly to the paraphrasability theory. Here, too, possibly, is the root notion behind the view that metaphor and simile are either essentially the same or isomorphically related (cf. Buchanan [1929]; Beardsley [1958]; Brooke-Rose [1958]). Certainly, many expressions in our language must be decayed metaphors, lending plausibility to the view that metaphors are implied comparisons or that metaphor is the original step in filling the gaps of our descriptive vocabulary. If this were so, then the process would also involve freely coining inessential expressions as well, as in slang: for instance, "inkslinger" (writer), "sawbones" (surgeon), "trotters" (feet), "peepers" (eyes)—all of which are provided by Stern [1931].

Nevertheless, many metaphoric expressions, notably employed in poetry, show no tendency to decay. They may decline, in the sense in which they tend to become standard or trite, or they may be outlandish or dull, but they do not tend to become literal expressions. In these cases it is markedly difficult to hold a metaphor to be an elliptical simile or to hold that it fills gaps in our descriptive vocabulary (at least in the sense plainly appropriate for phrases like "breastplate of a turtle"). Paraphrase becomes increasingly difficult, and we turn instead to explanation; that is, we are disinclined to offer literal equivalents for the metaphor itself, explaining, rather, how the metaphor *works*. In fact, the assurance that, short of providing for their charm and economy, we can provide an adequate literal paraphrase tends to reduce metaphor to a mere ornament of language. But the complex metaphors of poetry defeat such a view and suggest instead that metaphors have a distinctive logical character.

Briefly, paraphrasing a metaphor supposes that a metaphorical expression has a literal connotation, obscured by the ornament of the figure, that the paraphrase supplies. On that view, a metaphor is an expression whose literal sense is suppressed in the form of connotation—to which we are directed, however, by the seeming sense, or lack of it, of the figure taken literally. We are to dismiss the latter (when we paraphrase, though not when we savor, the metaphor) because of certain telltale features, and we are to explicate the former by consulting the clues in the figure itself. Thus Beardsley [1958] writes: "It is the logical absurdity of statements in poems that gives them meaning on the second level." Again: "The speaker or writer utters a statement explicitly but in such a way as to show that he does not believe what he states, and thereby calls attention to something else that he has not explicitly stated." (Beardsley's theory of metaphor, by the way, complements his theory of literary interpretation.) Black [1954-1955], on the other hand, holds that there is a variety of kinds of metaphor, that only what he calls "substitution-metaphors and comparison-metaphors can be replaced by literal translations (with possible exception for the case of catachresis)" and that " 'interaction-metaphors' are not expendable."

The principal objection to views of Beardsley's sort is simply that the departure from the non-figurative standard uses of words and phrases is taken as abortive: the metaphor does depart from standard usage, but we are advised to draw out the literally appropriate connotations hidden in its folds, rather than to appreciate its ingenuity, brilliance, or novelty.

Figurative sense, then, is literal sense in a special and attractive guise. If, however, the figurative sense of a metaphor is not always paraphrasable, though a metaphor may be explained, and though there is a use in providing what we call a paraphrase, we shall have to think along entirely different lines (cf. Wheelwright [1954], [1962]). Beardsley [1962] usefully criticizes the view that metaphor concerns a comparison of objects (as leading to "the unfortunate doctrine of 'appropriateness' "); nevertheless, he holds to the view that "the correct question is what is *meant* by the words—what properties are attributed to" the objects in question "via the marginal meanings of the metaphorical attribute." He holds that a metaphor attributes properties to something; the problem is to find out *which* properties. This clearly calls for paraphrasability.

Apparently, the metaphor must arrest our inclination to take it literally. It may be clearly nonsense (such as "a hyphenated man"), it may concern a blatant impossibility (such as "the clock smiled"), or we may choose to disregard its literal sense (such as, "the leg of a table"—Richards' illustration). Beardsley [1958] holds that the initial arresting is due to the metaphor's being "either indirectly self-contradictory or obviously false in its context." Perhaps he wishes to include the feature of nonsense under the heading of the "indirectly self-contradictory," but his illustrations ("female uncle," "the man is a fox") do not quite provide for it; nor does he make provision for expressions like "the leg of a table," which may in fact not be "obviously false," may make good literal sense, but which we may choose to treat metaphorically (cf. Burke [1941]). Ted Cohen [1975] presses the point effectively. He offers: "No man is an island," "Jesus was a carpenter," and "Moscow is a cold city," as "metaphorical sentences" that are "altogether normal in . . . surface syntax and semantics, and [that] can even be true" (cf. T. Cohen [1976]).

But we cannot always read a metaphor literally; we must seek another account. To state the issue in the most general form: a metaphor often appears literally to attribute something to something. It does not in fact do so, for if we construed it thus (where attribution seems plausible), we should allow no distinction (beyond ornament and device or beyond implicit and explicit attribution) between figurative and literal sense; figurative sense would simply be a sub-distinction within literal sense. This is the outcome of Beardsley's view. If, however, we examine some characteristic poetic figures, we see that we cannot subscribe to it.

Consider John Donne's lines:

> When I dyed last, and, Deare, I dye
> As often as from thee I goe [.]

We have an option here. We may take the lines to be exaggeration, in which case the remark is not to be regarded as false, though they would be false if taken literally. On the other hand, we may take them metaphorically. If we regard them as an exaggeration, we do not have to change the sense of "When I dyed last" and "I dye/As often as from thee I goe"; we should be concerned, rather, with statements that could serve as appropriate reductions of the exaggeration (for instance, "It's always terribly painful to leave you"). The focus then, would be on the use of the exaggerative *sentence* rather than on the sense, or play with the sense, of its constitutive *words*.

But if we treat the lines, "I dye/As often as from thee I goe," metaphorically, our view of a lover leaving his lady is determined by our conception of dying. The context indicates that we are concerned with a lover's leaving his lady; the lines do not quite specify this. Literally construed, they involve a contradiction. We do not ignore the fact, cancel it, suppose it a riddle to be literally deciphered. Rather, we collect (usually, quite informally) the standard senses of "dying"—commonplace associations and beliefs, whether farfetched or not, whether true or false—and whatever else relating to dying the context may suggest; and *we try to construe a lover leaving his lady as dying.* (I take no notice here of any play with the sense of "goe" or the sexual use of "dye.") The crucial point to bear in mind is simply that *if* we read the lines as metaphor, *we construe leaving and dying as substantially different* and, *thereupon,* deform the sense of the terms and our associations with each phenomenon in order that they may be treated as the same, knowing that they are not.

An utterly futile effort that seems to have characterized much of metaphoric theory down through the ages searches for a schematism of natural kinds (of all sorts) by reference to which genuine or appropriate metaphors may be identified (cf. Brooke-Rose [1958]). A particularly vulnerable view of this sort appears in W.M. Urban's theory [1939], where the distinction of metaphor is made to depend on recognizably distinct "universes of discourse." But however suggestive the comparison may be between Urban's thesis and Wittgenstein's conception [1953] of "language games" (cf. Shibles [1971]; Urban [1939]), the relevant distinction between contexts or "universes" cannot be formally drawn. The theory in question is entirely wrong and quite unnecessary. It obviously lies behind paraphrastic theories, however, suggesting as it does how to avoid arbitrariness and how to specify the *correct* sense of a metaphor. But it requires: (a) a language relatively stratified between literal and figurative sense; and (b) what in effect is an ontological basis for marking relatively fixed natural kinds to which (a) may correspond. A more economical view concedes no more than that, in construing expressions metaphorically, we commit ourselves to treating other distinctions and attributions as literal. Thus, by construing a line as metaphor, we confirm the literal inappropriateness of a given identification, characterization, or the like and, precisely by deforming the sense and associations thus provided, we read it *as* appropriate. So metaphor normally requires (i) a semantic inappropriateness in a phrase or sentence literally construed; and (ii) a deformation of the sense of such phrase or sentence, and relevant beliefs about the world, in order to interpret what is semantically inappropriate as if it were appropriate. Requirement (ii), therefore, involves a deliberate game with the sense and associations of words; and (i) may be weakened, as when the literal and metaphoric senses are not too much opposed, or when a so-called dead metaphor is revived.

Normally, our background beliefs and associations about what is designated, and the uniformities of literal speech, do confirm the relative inappropriateness of the expression in question, but this in itself does not entail a theory of natural kinds. Quintilian [1921], for instance, adhering to such a theory, seems to have made much of transposition between the animate and the inanimate in every possible combination (cf. Brooke-Rose [1958]). No doubt, the effectiveness of certain metaphors may be gauged in terms of certain favored contrasts. But such transpositions require no more than certain habits of use: if Scipio is said to have been barked at by Cato, then the metaphoric force of the line depends on construing "barking" as normally reserved for dogs, not men. In a word, both (i) and (ii) must be treated intentionally in terms of the speaker's purpose. The adjustment conforms very neatly to our previous observations about the avoidability of essentialism in definition (cf. Putnam [1975c]). Furthermore, the inappropriateness cannot be captured by any merely grammatical formula. Hence, Beardsley's controversion theory, as well as Brooke-Rose's preference for a grammatical rather than a conceptual account of metaphor, are bound to be defective.

One of the most sustained attempts to construct a theory of metaphor on the basis of natural kinds appears in the recent work of Samuel Levin [1977]. Levin unites T. Cohen's theory [1975] of "illocutionary deviance" with Jerrold Katz's account [1972] of the way in which semantic rules operate on syntactical phrase-markers underlying the sentences of a natural language. Katz's apparatus, though heuristically instructive in exploring the "semantic deviance" of metaphors, is open to serious challenge precisely in terms of its obvious essentialism. For one thing, there is no straightforward way in which to demarcate semantic deviance and unexpected or surprising facts: Is "Cats are robots" semantically deviant (as Katz would maintain) or merely empirically unexpected (cf. Putnam [1975a])? Secondly, there is no straightforward way in which to demarcate the meanings of terms (or the "semantic markers" associated with them) and information about what those terms designate: Is "All lemons are yellow" analytic (as Katz would maintain) or contingently true of a certain population of things (cf. Putnam [1975a])? Without a favorable resolution of such questions—seemingly quite impossible on essentialist terms—Levin's attempt cannot but be undermined. Both issues concern what has been marked as the distinction between "dictionaries" and "encyclopedias" (cf. Wilson [1967]; Katz [1972]). Levin himself merely adopts Katz's model of language—with, it may be noted, a very telling adjustment. Unlike Katz, Levin wishes to permit a grammar to generate deviant or anomalous sentences; if it does, however, then he has precluded the very foundation on which Katz believes the relevant semantic markers for given lexical terms can be provided. But then, the very nature of metaphor remains unclear.

Furthermore, Levin's distinctive proposal suffers from a general confusion between fiction and metaphor—not altogether unlike Beardsley's confusion [1958] between poetry and fiction. As Levin says:

> We have concluded that deviant sentences in poetry are to be taken literally, that, so taken, they have meaning and thus express truth conditions. This conclusion is enabled by a shift in world orientation. Instead of attempting to construe the expression, i.e., make it conform to a sentence that has a truth value in this world, we as it were construe the world—into one in which the deviant sentence is no longer deviant.

Here, Levin construes his solution as the result of "a contract between the poet and the reader"—interpreted more in the idiom of speech acts than in that of their presuppositions. He fails to distinguish between the "world of fiction" and "possible worlds"—sometimes, as in time travel, the fictional is not a possible world; and he fails to distinguish between fictional and metaphoric considerations—the issue of deviance cannot be the same for both. Also, the alleged contract presupposes, but does not provide, a solution to the problem of natural kinds. Again, the very notion of taking deviant sentences of poetry (presumably, metaphoric sentences) *literally* is either anomalous or parasitic on what (in an unexplained way) literally holds in *our* world; what, short of definitional fiat, could possibly be intended by the "natural kinds" of some "possible world"?

Theories of Levin's (*a fortiori,* Katz's) sort may be termed foundationalist, in the sense that they posit a fixed level of meanings in terms of which metaphor may be construed as measurably deviant. Another version of foundationalism is suggested by W.H. Leatherdale [1974]: "There really does seem to be a language which is neutral to theory and which may be regarded as the literal language . . . it is the language of direct perception or of 'ostensivity' . . . experimental or observational phenomena are expressible in this neutral (to theory) or literal language, and the existence of such a language is an essential auxiliary to science, if science is to be corrigible, and capable of qualification, replacement and other forms of progress." Apart from the avoidance of the polar extremes of treating language or the expansion of language as inherently or basically metaphoric (Cassirer [1946]; Richards [1936]) and of treating perceptual language as radically theory-laden (Feyerabend [1962]), the required fixity of literal language seems conceptually impossible to defend.

In addition to its internal difficulties, the application of Katz's theory to metaphor is further strained by the fact that "the properties that count in metaphor are not the actual properties of things denoted by the metaphorical term, but believed properties" (Beardsley [1978a]; cf. Black [1954-1955]; Matthews [1971]; *contra* Cohen and Margalit [1974]; and Bickerton [1969]). Hence, metaphor cannot be construed solely in terms either of purely linguistic regularities or of essentialism. Nevertheless, the adjustment is not sufficient to support Beardsley's version of what he calls a controversion theory: that is, "that when an expression becomes a metaphorical segment [read: word or expression] it acquires a sense different from any of its standard senses." Two preliminary difficulties arise here: first, an expression *used* metaphorically need not acquire a sense different from any of its standard senses; second, as in catachresis (Black [1954-1955]), or by deliberate extension (Putnam [1975c]), an expression may acquire a new sense without acquiring it metaphorically. The first favors the thesis that metaphor is a game with the standard meanings of words; the second counts heavily against Goodman's [1968] brief sketch of a theory of metaphor—which involves transferring labels from the elements of a customary domain to the elements of one that is not customary.

Beardsley's own theory [1978a] is formulated thus:

(A) An expression E is a metaphorical segment of sequence S iff
(i) E is a proper part of S and is a predicate or modifier of part or all of the (literal) remainder of S (S$\overline{\text{E}}$) (note that this allows for metaphors within metaphors);
(ii) the combination of E with S$\overline{\text{E}}$ is barred by a rule;
(iii) some credence-properties of the extension of E (in one of its standard senses) are such that it is possible for them to be properties of members of the extension of (part or all of) S$\overline{\text{E}}$ (in one of its standard senses).
(B) The intension of E in S consists of the set of all credence-properties of the extension of E (in the relevant standard sense) that are not denied of members of the extension of S$\overline{\text{E}}$ (in the relevant standard sense) by the context, verbal or situational, of S.

Now, it is of particular interest that Beardsley does not discuss (ii): "I must set it aside here," he says. But (ii) absolutely requires some form of Katz's theory of terms and (on Beardsley's own account) must give way to the ascription of "credence-properties." But *if* the crucial properties are credence-properties, then it is difficult to understand the force of "possible" in (iii): it cannot be either semantical or factual. Also, (iii) cannot but be vacuous. Suppose the credence-properties include "has been mentioned," "referred to," "discussed," "described," and so on. No clue would then be forthcoming about metaphorical usage. Furthermore, if (A) is thus affected, (B) must be trivialized. The trouble with Beardsley's account, not unlike the vulnerability of accounts that rely on Katz's theory (which Beardsley implicitly opposes), lies with his avoidance of intentional considerations. Emphasis on speakers' intentions entirely obviates the need for a quasi-formal apparatus like Beardsley's, that, precisely because of its abstractness, cannot help but be vulnerable to ready counterinstances or to being trivialized. It also precludes paraphrase.

To paraphrase is to formulate sentences that, more or less, have the sense of the original; to make sense out of a metaphor is *to play a certain game with language,* with *words*: to deform, so to say the sense of a lover's leaving his lady and of dying as if (but not actually) to characterize the one as the other (cf. Brooks [1947]). The question of paraphrase does not arise with respect to metaphor proper, though explanation does, and though the question of paraphrase may arise as a further thought and convenience (cf. Richards [1936]; Black [1954-1955]; Hungerland [1958]). If we are attributing properties to something, no matter how indirectly, it is clear that paraphrase may correctly be required; but if we are not making attributions at all, it is not clear in what sense paraphrasing is initially pertinent. If to understand metaphor is to deform the sense of terms that have literal meanings in standard usage, the purpose of paraphrasing is bypassed. To insist on it is simply to misunderstand the use we make of language in inventing metaphors. (Cleanth Brooks's notion [1939] of "the heresy of paraphrase," we may remark, has very little to do with the theory of metaphor; it is rather more closely related to the problem of appreciation [(cf. also, Brooks and Warren [1950])].)

A warning is in order about Black's theory [1954-1955], which rejects paraphrase in cases covered by the "interaction view of metaphor." Black discounts paraphrase because it results in "a loss of *cognitive* content," because "it fails to give the *insight* that the metaphor did." As he says, "the metaphor selects, emphasizes, suppresses, and organizes features of the principal subject by *implying* statements about it that normally apply to the subsidiary subject." In a word, Black's thesis is that metaphors are or imply statements about things seen "in a special light," through a "filter" or "screen." I am maintaining, on the contrary, that metaphor is not primarily a *cognitive* use of language providing statements which, because of their characteristic distortion, cannot be suitably paraphrased—though I would not deny that rich metaphors may contribute new insight. Metaphor is, rather, what might be called an *effective* use of language, by which we deliberately deform things in the manner characterized. It is not primarily concerned with claims or implied claims; it is more a game in which we play with meanings. Paraphrasing, therefore, is not simply inadequate; it is irrelevant.

The trouble with Black's theory is that it applies solely to some *initial* cognitive discovery: once it is formulated and absorbed (say, in the body of science), it must decay by catachresis or be replaced by some nonfigurative invention. So it cannot be paraphrased by the existing vocabulary, but it eventually obviates the need for paraphrase; or, by further linguistic invention, it becomes as paraphrasable as any other originally literal statement. What Black says seems to be instructive about scientific theory and is used thus by Mary Hesse [1963], who holds that "the deductive model of scientific explanation should be modified and supplemented by a view of theoretical explanation as metaphoric redescription of the domain of the explanandum"—which is not very far from Urban's view (cf. Shibles [1971]). Nevertheless, Hesse draws attention to a fundamental distinction that shows the uncertainty of Black's original thesis. For Black holds (as she rightly notes) that in some cases "it would be more illuminating . . . to say that the metaphor creates the similarity than to say it formulates some similarity antecedently existing." Hesse insists rather that "whatever may be the case for poetic use, the suggestion that *any* scientific model can be imposed a priori on *any* explanandum and function fruitfully in its explanation must be resisted. Such a view would imply that theoretical models are irrefutable. That this is not the case is sufficiently illustrated by the history of the concept of a heat fluid or the classical wave theory of light. Such examples also indicate that no model even gets off the ground unless some antecedent similarity or analogy is discerned between it and the explanandum"—that is, some similarity judged appropriate or promising against the backdrop of actual scientific explanation.

Neither Hesse nor Black adhere to the "comparison" (in effect, the simile) view of metaphor. Hesse holds that "metaphor works by transferring the associated ideas and implications of the secondary to the primary system [that is, two otherwise independent systems, like *man* and *wolf* that are brought together in the metaphor]." If I understand her correctly, "literal expressions" associated with both the primary and secondary systems are altered by the metaphors employed in explanation. In effect, then, metaphor is construed as a *linguistic process by which to alter the literal meanings of given expressions.* This she takes to be "the kernel of the interaction view and . . . Black's major contribution to the analysis of metaphor." She insists on this because it entails that "descriptions and descriptive laws in the domain of the explanandum [cannot] remain empirically acceptable and invariant in meaning to all changes of explanatory theory." But the price for holding this view is Hesse's insisting that "the rules of literal usage and of metaphor, though they are not identical, are nevertheless not independent." This may have a trivial (but not negligible) intent: that literal and figurative usage occur in the same language, but it is probably tantamount rather to the adoption of catachresis. Still, in Black's account, there is the inkling of an entirely different conception of metaphor, whatever may be said about its use in explanatory contexts.

Alternatively put, Black's and Hesse's accounts focus on the search for an increasingly adequate and comprehensive explanatory theory in the body of science; the selection of the best metaphors concerns the formulation of such a theory. In this sense, Black and Hesse are rather more concerned with the uses of metaphor than with its distinctive nature. A powerful and successful new metaphor in science leads to a *change in meaning* of the descriptive idiom treating would-be explananda; hence, the use of such metaphors is cognitive but, once successful, reduces to a kind of catachresis. If metaphors did not thus decay, they would not, in Hesse's terms, be refutable. But metaphor in the poetic sense *is* irrefutable—or better, obviates the issue of refutability altogether. Metaphors may be appraised and appreciated; they may even accidentally illuminate some domain in a cognitive respect; but they need not harbor *claims* of any kind. Poetic metaphors are not arbitrary, in that they must trade on the established uniformities of literal speech, and associated beliefs and connotations. But they often are arbitrary in the sense that their failure to make a cognitive contribution is not in the least a serious constraint on their viability, intrinsic interest, comparative force, or the like. There is, therefore, a certain equivocation in Black's notion of the *filter*: in the context of science, it refers to an explanatory theory and its implicit claims; in the context of the usual poetic or aesthetic concerns, it refers to a schema of imagination in terms of which certain apparently inappropriate locutions (judged against a backdrop of beliefs and associations) are systematically deformed in order to render them appropriate, knowing that (literally construed) they are not.

A metaphor, then, is not a comparison, though it may trade on comparison. Donne's *The Flea* is very nearly an exercise of just this sort:

> Marke but this flea, and marke in this,
> How little that which thou deny'st me is;
> It suck'd me first, and now sucks thee
> And in this flea, our two bloods mingled bee;
> ***
> This flea is you and I, and this
> Our marriage bed, and marriage temple is.

Simile, of course, is figurative also. But where, in metaphor, emphasis is placed upon seeing one thing as another in the manner indicated, in simile, emphasis is upon seeing the resemblance or comparison between one thing and another as adequate (when it is not)—for instance, "errors, like straws, upon the surface flow." The deformation, in metaphor, is of the things or attributes in question; in simile, of the comparison between them (cf. Ushenko [1955]). One feels, therefore, the relative weakness of simile; the difference between a literal comparison and a comparison that does not literally obtain tends to dissolve much more easily than in the metaphoric counterpart.

Our principal finding, then, is that metaphor is not a use of language in the sense appropriate to commands, assertions, or questions; it cannot be true or false, accurate or inaccurate, answered, fulfilled, or the like. It is not a speech act of any sort, though it may, to be sure, appear in sentences used in any of these ways. Furthermore, it does not seem possible to view all metaphors as paraphrasable. To do so is to treat a metaphoric expression as more or less equivalent to some literal expression, hence to treat figurative language as mere embellishment, and metaphoric meaning as merely "hidden." In its most interesting form in literature, metaphor is primarily a non-reducible use of language fairly described as playing a certain game with the sense of words. The game is to view one thing as another, to construe something quite deliberately as another, to conceive things deformed so that, contrary to apparent fact, or belief, they may be identified or properties not or not relevantly attributable to them may be treated as if they were. The game continues by elaborating the respects in which the deformation may be accommodated; and alternative criteria may well be available for the evaluation of different metaphors. In this sense, metaphor is readily contrasted with simple synecdoche and metonymy, for the latter are concerned merely with types of substitutions. A given figure may be construed as both metonymy and metaphor—for instance, read as a metaphor in the context of *Endymion,* the line from Keats cited above makes a very witty line. But a logical difference still remains: synecdoche and metonymy are mere ornaments; metaphor is a distinct, non-reducible use of language affecting meaning. Furthermore, the metaphoric game entitles us merely to "play" with the apparent identities and attributions; metaphor is not itself a covert attribution or identity that we may discover by solving a puzzle. Also, it is a linguistic and parasitic game, not the equivalent of any other standard use of language. What is misleading about metaphor depends on confusing the speech-act context in which metaphor obtains and the special use of language that *is* metaphor. The linguistic context of a speech act or imagined speech act must obtain in order for the game of metaphor to have any point at all. But the game concerns only a certain deformation of objects and properties within such contexts, not those contexts themselves (cf. Turbayne [1962]), and not, as in science, the ulterior use to which fruitful metaphors may be put.

There is the suggestion of a related view in a recent essay by Donald Davidson [1978]. But apart from the extreme vagueness of his account of the use of metaphor, Davidson maintains that metaphor is not a matter of meaning at all but of use. He means by this, first of all, that words have some "primary" or original [or literal] meanings," that "literal meaning and literal truth conditions can be assigned to words and sentences apart from particular contexts of use''; second, that the use of metaphor lies in leading us ''to see something in a new light,'' that ''metaphor makes us see one thing as another by making some literal statement that inspires or prompts the insight.'' The upshot is that, as with our own view, paraphrase misuses metaphor. The trouble, however, remains that only in the context of the meaning of words can the special ''use'' of metaphor be discerned, *and* that it is quite impossible to fix the meaning of words ''apart from particular contexts of use.'' As we have already seen, natural language has no discernible layers of the literal and figurative sort; but on the thesis that words have a metaphoric sense, some idealized account of literal sense must be provided from which, on the interpretation favored, the metaphoric is seen to deviate. All devices for fixing the meaning of words require attention to contextually invoked background beliefs, changing information about the non-verbal world, the tradition of use, the absence of any decisive set of sentence frames in terms of which to establish context-free meanings, and the like. But if this is so, then, contrary to Davidson's proposal, it is impossible to rely on a stable range of literal meanings assignable to words, in virtue of which one may advance the theory that metaphor is a certain non-linguistic use of words. Lacking the one, we cannot depend on the other. We are, then, drawn back to the metaphoric use of words.

REFERENCES

Abrams, M.H. [1972] "What's the Use of Theorizing about the Arts?" in Marvin W. Bloomfield (ed.), *In Search of Literary Theory* (Ithaca: Cornell University Press).

Abrams, M.H. [1976] "The Deconstructive Angel," *Critical Inquiry,* II.

Aiken, Henry David. [1945] "Art as Expression and Surface," *Journal of Aesthetics and Art Criticism,* IV.

Aiken, Henry David. [1955] "The Aesthetic Relevance of Artists' Intentions," *Journal of Philosophy,* LII.

Aldrich, Virgil. [1958] "Picture Space," *Philosophical Review,* LXVIII.

Aldrich, Virgil. [1963] *Philosophy of Art* (Englewood Cliffs: Prentice-Hall).

Alexander, Samuel. [1933] *Beauty and Other Forms of Value* (London: Macmillan).

Alexander, Samuel. [1939] *Philosophical and Literary Pieces* (London: Macmillan).

Alston, William. [1964] *Philosophy of Language* (Englewood Cliffs: Prentice-Hall).

Apel, Willi. [1953] *The Notation of Polyphonic Music 900-1600,* 5th ed. rev. (Cambridge: Harvard University Press).

Apel, Willi. [1969] *Harvard Dictionary of Music,* 2nd ed. (Cambridge: Harvard University Press).

Arnheim, Rudolf. [1969] *Visual Thinking* (London: Faber and Faber).

Arnheim, Rudolf. [1974] *Art and Visual Perception* (The New Version) (Berkeley: University of California Press).

Arnold, Matthew. [1938] *Essays in Criticism,* 2nd series (London: Macmillan).

Art and Society. [1968] trans. from the Russian (Moscow: Progress Publishers).

Arvon, Henri. [1973] *Marxist Esthetics,* trans. Helen Lane (Ithaca: Cornell University Press).

Aschenbrenner, Karl. [1950] "Intention and Understanding," *Meaning and Interpretation* (Berkeley: University of California Press).

Austin, J.L. [1952-1953] "How to Talk," *Proceedings of the Aristotelian Society,* LIII.

Austin, J.L. [1962] *How to do things with words* (Oxford: Clarendon).

Ayer, A.J. [1946] *Language, Truth and Logic,* 2nd ed. (London: Victor Gollancz).

Baensch, Otto. [1958] "Art and Feeling," in Susanne K. Langer (ed.), *Reflections on Art* (Baltimore: Johns Hopkins University Press).

Baier, Kurt. [1958] *The Moral Point of View* (Ithaca: Cornell University Press).

Barfield, Owen. [1973] *Poetic Diction,* 3rd ed. (Middletown: Wesleyan University Press).

Barnes, Annette. [1976] "Half and Hour Before Breakfast," *Journal of Aesthetics and Art Criticism,* XXXIV.

Barrett, Cyril. [1973] "Are Bad Works of Art 'Works of Art?' " in *Philosophy and the Arts* (Royal Institute of Philosophy Lectures, Vol. 6, 1971-1972) (New York: St. Martin's Press).

Barthes, Roland. [1966] *Critique et Vérité* (Paris: Seuil).

Barthes, Roland. [1967a] "Science versus Literature," *The Times Literary Supplement* (September 28).

Barthes, Roland. [1967b] *Système de la mode* (Paris: Seuil).

Barthes, Roland. [1970] *S/Z* (Paris: Seuil).

Barthes, Roland. [1972] *Critical Essays,* trans. Richard Howard (Evanston: Northwestern University Press).

Barthes, Roland. [1973] *Le Plaisir du texte* (Paris: Seuil).

Bateson, F.W. [1950] *English Poetry: A Critical Introduction* (London: Longmans, Green).

Battcock, Gregory (ed.). [1973] *Idea Art* (New York: Dutton).

Baudouin, Charles. [1924] *Psychoanalysis and Aesthetics,* trans. Eden and Cedar Paul (London: George Allen and Urwin).

Beardsley, Monroe C. [1958] *Aesthetics* (New York: Harcourt, Brace).

Beardsley, Monroe C. [1962] "The Metaphorical Twist," *Philosophy and Phenomenological Research,* XXII.

Beardsley, Monroe C. [1969] "Aesthetic Experience Regained," *Journal of Aesthetics and Art Criticism,* XXVIII.

Beardsley, Monroe C. [1970a] "The Aesthetic Point of View," in Howard E. Kiefer and Milton K. Munitz (eds.). *Contemporary Philosophic Thought,* Vol. IV (Albany: State University of New York Press).

Beardsley, Monroe C. [1970b] *The Possibility of Criticism* (Detroit: Wayne State University Press).

Beardsley, Monroe C. [1973] "What is an aesthetic quality?" *Theoria,* XXXIX.

Beardsley, Monroe C. [1976] "Is Art Essentially Institutional?" in Lars Aagaard-Mogensen (ed.), *Culture and Art* (Nyborg and Atlantic Highlands: · F. Løkkes Forlag and Humanities Press).

Beardsley, Monroe C. [1978a] "Metaphorical Senses," *Nous,* XII.

Beardsley, Monroe C. [1978b] "In Defense of Aesthetic Value," Presidential Address, American Philosophical Association, Eastern Division (1978).

Beardsmore, R.W. [1973] "Learning from a Novel," in *Philosophy and the Arts* (Royal Institute of Philosophy Lectures, Vol. 6, 1971-1972) (New York: St. Martin's Press).

Bell, Clive. [1914] *Art* (London: Chatto and Windus).

Bentley, Eric (ed.). [1948] *The Importance of Scrutiny* (New York: G.W. Stewart).

Berenson, Bernard. [1948] *Aesthetics and History in the Visual Arts* (New York: Pantheon).

Berggren, Douglas. [1962] "The Use and Abuse of Metaphor," Part I, *Review of Metaphysics,* XVI.

Berggren, Douglas. [1963] "The Use and Abuse of Metaphor," Part II, *Review of Metaphysics,* XVI.

Bergler, Edmund. [1950] *The Writer and Psychoanalysis* (Garden City: Doubleday).

Berlyne, D.E. (ed.). [1974] *Studies in the New Experimental Aesthetics* (New York: John Wiley).

Bickel, Alexander M. [1975] *The Morality of Consent* (New Haven: Yale University Press).

Bickerton, Derek. [1969] "Prolegomena to a Linguistic Theory of Metaphor," *Foundations of Language,* V.

Binkley, Timothy. [1974] "On the Truth and Probity of Metaphor," *Journal of Aesthetics and Art Criticism,* XXXIII.

Binkley, Timothy. [1975] "Deciding about Art: A Polemic against Aesthetics," in Lars Aagaard-Mogensen (ed.), *Art and Culture* (Nyborg and Atlantic Highlands: F. Løkkes Forlag and Humanities Press).

Binkley, Timothy. [1977] "Piece: Contra Aesthetics," *Journal of Aesthetics and Art Criticism,* XXXV.

Black, Max. [1954-1955] "Metaphor," *Proceedings of the Aristotelian Society,* LV.

Black, Max. [1972] "How Do Pictures Represent?" in Maurice Mandelbaum (ed.), *Art, Perception, and Reality* (Baltimore: Johns Hopkins University Press).

Bloom, Harold. [1973] *The Anxiety of Influence; A Theory of Poetry* (New York: Oxford University Press).

Boas, George. [1937] *A Primer for Critics* (Baltimore: Johns Hopkins University Press).

Bodkin, Maud. [1934] *Archetypal Patterns in Poetry* (Oxford: Clarendon).

Bonner, John Tyler. [1969] "Hormones in Social Amoeba and Mammals," *Scientific American,* CCXX.

Bosanquet, Bernard. [1915] *Three Lectures on Aesthetics* (London: Macmillan).

Bouwsma, O.K. [1950] "The Expression Theory of Art," in Max Black (ed.), *Philosophical Analysis* (Ithaca: Cornell University Press).

Bradley, A.C. [1909] "Poetry for Poetry's Sake," *Oxford Lectures in Poetry,* 2nd ed. (London: Oxford University Press).

Braithwaite, R.B. [1933] "Imaginary Objects," *Proceedings of the Aristotelian Society,* Suppl. Vol. XII.

Brand, Myles. [1968] "Danto on Basic Actions," *Nous,* II.

Brée, Germaine. [1959] *Camus* (New Brunswick: Rutgers University Press).

Brentano, Franz. [1973] "The Distinction between Mental and Physical Phenomena" (1874), in Oskar Kraus (ed.), *Psychology from an Empirical Standpoint;* English edition ed. Linda L. McAlister (London: Routledge and Kegan Paul).

Broiles, R. David. [1964] "Frank Sibley's Aesthetic Concepts," *Journal of Aesthetics and Art Criticism,* XXIII.

Brooke-Rose, Christine. [1958] *A Grammar of Metaphor* (London: Secker and Warburg).

Brooks, Cleanth. [1939] *Modern Poetry and the Tradition* (Chapel Hill: University of North Carolina Press).

Brooks, Cleanth. [1947] *The Well-Wrought Urn* (New York: Harcourt, Brace).

Brooks, Cleanth. [1951] "Irony as a Principle of Structure," in M.D. Zabel (ed.), *Literary Opinion in America,* rev. ed. (New York: Harper and Row).

Brooks, Cleanth and Robert Penn Warren. [1950] *Understanding Poetry,* rev. shortened ed. (New York: Holt).

Brothwell, Don R. (ed.). [1976] *Beyond Aesthetics. Investigations into the Nature of Visual Art* (London: Thames and Hudson).

Bruner, Jerome S. [1956] "Freud and the Image of Man," *Partisan Review,* XXIII.

Brunius, Teddy. [1952] *David Hume on Criticism* (Laocoon: Swedish Studies in Aesthetics, Vol. 4) (Uppsala: Acta Universitatis Upsaliensis).

Buchanan, Scott. [1929] *Poetry and Mathematics* (New York: John Day).

Bultmann, Rudolf. [1955] "The Problem of Hermeneutics," in *Essays Philosophical and Theological,* trans. J.C.G. Greig (London: SCM Press).

Bultmann, Rudolf. [1962] "The Case for Demythologizing," in *Kerygma and Myth,* Vol. 2, ed. Hans Werner Bartsch, trans. Reginald Fuller (London: S.P.C.K.).

Bunge, Mario. [1977a] "Emergence and the Mind," *Neuroscience,* II.

Bunge, Mario. [1977b] "Levels and Reduction," *American Journal of Physiology,* CCIII.

Burke, Kenneth. [1941] "Semantic and Poetic Meaning," *The Philosophy of Literary Form* (Baton Rouge: Louisiana State University Press).

Campbell, Joseph. [1956] *The Hero with a Thousand Faces* (New York: Meridian Books).

Cardoza, Benjamin N. [1921] *The Nature of the Judicial Process* (New Haven: Yale University Press).

Cary, Joyce. [1944] *The Horse's Mouth* (New York: Harper).

Cary, Joyce. [1958] *Art and Reality* (Cambridge: Cambridge University Press).

Casey, John. [1966] *The Language of Criticism* (London: Methuen).

Cassirer, Ernst. [1946] *Language and Myth,* trans. Susanne K. Langer (New York: Harper).

Caudwell, Christopher. [1937] *Illusion and Reality* (London: Macmillan).

Champigny, Robert. [1959] *Sur un héros paien* (Paris: Gallimard).

Charlton, William. [1975] "Living and Dead Metaphors," *British Journal of Aesthetics,* XV.

Chomsky, Noam. [1965] *Aspects of the Theory of Syntax* (Cambridge: MIT Press).

Chomsky, Noam. [1972] *Language and Mind,* enl. ed. (New York: Harcourt Brace Jovanovich).

Cioffi, Frank. [1963-1964] "Intention and Interpretation in Criticism," *Proceedings of the Aristotelian Society,* LXIV.

Clegg, Jerry S. [1963] "Verdicts," *Dialogue,* II.

Cohen, L. Jonathan and Avishai Margalit. [1974] "The Role of Inductive Reasoning in the Interpretation of Metaphor," in Donald Davidson and

Gilbert Harman (eds.), *Semantics of Natural Language* (Dordrecht: D. Reidel).

Cohen, Marshall. [1959] "Appearances and the Aesthetic Attitude," *Journal of Philosophy,* LVI.

Cohen, Marshall. [1965] "Aesthetic Essence," in Max Black (ed.), *Philosophy in America* (Ithaca: Cornell University Press).

Cohen, Ted. [1973] "Aesthetic/Non-aesthetic and the Concept of Taste: a Critique of Sibley's Position," *Theoria,* XXIX.

Cohen, Ted. [1975] "Figurative Speech and Figurative Acts," *Journal of Philosophy,* LXXI.

Cohen, Ted. [1976] "Notes on Metaphor," *Journal of Aesthetics and Art Criticism,* XXXIV.

Collingwood, R.G. [1938] *The Principles of Art* (London: Oxford University Press).

Crane, R.S. [1967] "Critical and Historical Principles of Literary History," *The Idea of the Humanities,* Vol. 2 (Chicago: University of Chicago Press).

Croce, Benedetto. [1922] *Aesthetics,* 2nd ed., trans. Douglas Ainslee (London: Macmillan).

Cruickshank, John. [1959] *Albert Camus and the Literature of Revolt* (London: Oxford University Press).

Culler, Jonathan. [1975] *Structuralist Poetics: Structuralism, Linguistics, and the Study of Literature* (Ithaca, Cornell University Press).

Daiches, David. [1956] *Critical Approaches to Literature* (Englewood Cliffs: Prentice-Hall).

Danto, Arthur C. [1964] "The Artworld," *Journal of Philosophy,* LXI.

Danto, Arthur C. [1973a] *Analytical Philosophy of Action* (Cambridge: Cambridge University Press).

Danto, Arthur C. [1973b] "Art Works and Real Things," *Theoria,* XLIX.

Danto, Arthur C. [1974] "The Transfiguration of the Commonplace," *Journal of Aesthetics and Art Criticism,* XXIII.

Danto, Arthur C. [unpublished] "Pictorial and Artistic Representation," presented in Symposium: "What Is A Painting?" Philadelphia Museum of Art (Behavioral Research Directorate, US Army Human Engineering Laboratory), April 17, 1978.

Davidson, Donald. [1967] "Truth and Meaning," *Synthese,* XVII.

Davidson, Donald. [1971] "Agency," in Robert Binkley *et al.* (eds.), *Agent, Action, and Reason* (Toronto: University of Toronto Press).

Davidson, Donald. [1978] "What Metaphors Mean," *Critical Inquiry,* V.

Dennis, Nigel. [1978] "Portrait of the Artist," *New York Review of Books,* XXV (May 4).

Derrida, Jacques. [1972] *La Dissémination* (Paris: Seuil).

Derrida, Jacques. [1973] *Speech and Phenomena,* trans. David B. Allison (Evanston: Northwestern University Press).

Dewey, John. [1934] *Art as Experience* (New York: Minton, Balch).

Dickie, George. [1965] "Beardsley's Phantom Aesthetic Experience," *Journal of Philosophy,* LXII.

Dickie, George. [1973] "Defining Art II," in Matthew Lipman (ed.), *Contemporary Aesthetics* (Boston: Allyn and Bacon).

Dickie, George. [1974] *Art and the Aesthetic* (Ithaca: Cornell University Press).

Diffey, T.J. [1969] "The Republic of Art," *British Journal of Aesthetics,* IX.

Dilham, Ilham. [1967] "Imagination," *Proceedings of the Aristotelian Society,* Suppl. Vol. XLI.

Dilthey, Wilhelm. [1913-1967] *Gesammelte Schriften,* Vol. 7 (Gottingen: Vandenhoeck and Ruprecht).

Donnellan, Keith S. [1962] "Necessity and Criticism," *Journal of Philosophy,* LIX.

Donnellan, Keith S. [1966] "Reference and Definite Descriptions," *Philosophical Review,* LXXV.

Donnellan, Keith S. [1970] "Proper Names and Identifying Descriptions," *Synthese,* XXI.

Dretske, Fred I. [1969] *Seeing and Knowing* (Chicago: University of Chicago Press).

Dubois, J. *et al.* [1970] *Rhétorique générale* (Paris: Larousse).

Ducasse, C.J. [1929] *The Philosophy of Art* (New York: Dial Press).

Ducasse, C.J. [1948] *Art, the Critics, and You* (New York: Hafner Publishing Co.).

Dufrenne, Mikel. [1973] *The Phenomenology of Aesthetic Experience,* trans. Edward S. Casey *et al.* (Evanston: Northwestern University Press).

Duthie, George. [1949] *Elizabethan Shorthand and the First Quarto of 'King Lear'* (Oxford: Basil Blackwell).

Dutton, Denis. [1977] "Plausibility and Aesthetic Interpretation," *Canadian Journal of Philosophy,* VII.

Ecker, David [1963] "The Artistic Process as Qualitative Problem Solving," *Journal of Aesthetics and Art Criticism,* XXI.

Eco, Umberto. [1976] *A Theory of Semiotics* (Bloomington: Indiana University Press).

Edie, James M. [1963] "Expression and Metaphor," *Philosophy and Phenomenological Research,* XXIII.

Edwards, Paul. [1955] *The Logic of Moral Discourse* (Glencoe: Free Press).

Eliot, T.S. [1932] "The Function of Criticism," *Selected Essays 1917-1932* (New York: Harcourt Brace).

Eliot, T.S. [1956] "The Frontiers of Criticism," *Sewanee Review,* LXIV.

Elliott, R.K. [1966-1967] "Aesthetic Theory and the Experience of Art," *Proceedings of the Aristotelian Society,* LXVII.

Ellis, John M. [1974] *The Theory of Literary Criticism: A Logical Analysis* (Berkeley: University of California Press).

Elton, William. [1953] *A Guide to the New Criticism,* rev. and enl. (Chicago: Modern Poetry Association).

Empson, William. [1935] *Some Versions of Pastoral* (London: Chatto and Windus).

Empson, William. [1951] *The Structure of Complex Words* (London: Chatto and Windus).

Feigl, Herbert. [1967] *The "Mental" and the "Physical"; The Essay and a Postscript* (Minneapolis: University of Minnesota Press).

Feyerabend, Paul (P.K.). [1962] "Explanation, Reduction and Empiricism," in H. Feigl and G. Maxwell (eds.), *Scientific Explanation, Space and Time* (Minnesota Studies in the Philosophy of Science, Vol. III) (Minnesota: University of Minnesota Press).

Feyerabend, Paul (P.K.). [1975] *Against Method* (London: NLB).

Fish, Stanley. [1972] "Literature in the Reader," *Self-Consuming Artifacts; The Experience of Seventeenth-Century Literature* (Los Angeles: University of California Press).

Fish, Stanley E. [1976] "How to Do Things with Austin and Searle: Speech Act Theory and Literary Criticism," *Modern Language Notes,* XCI.

Fletcher, Angus. [1966] "Utopian History and the Anatomy of Criticism," in Murray Krieger (ed.), *Northrop Frye in Modern Criticism* (New York: Columbia University Press).

Fodor, Jerry A. [1968] *Psychological Explanation* (New York: Random House).

Forge, Andrew. [1973] "Art/Nature," in *Philosophy and the Arts* (Royal Institute of Philosophy Lectures, Vol. 6, 1971-1972) (New York: St. Martin's Press).

Foss, Martin. [1942] *Symbol and Metaphor in Human Experience* (Princeton: Princeton University Press).

Foucault, Michel. [1965] *Madness and Civilization,* trans. Richard Howard (New York: Pantheon).

Foucault, Michel. [1972] *The Archeology of Knowledge,* trans. A.M. Sheridan Smith (New York: Pantheon).

Fowler, Alastair. [1976] "Intention Floreat," in D. Newton-De Molina (ed.), *On Literary Intention* (Edinburgh: Edinburgh University Press).

Fraiberg, Louis. [1960] *Psychoanalysis and American Literary Criticism* (Detroit: Wayne State University Press).

Fraser, G.S. [1955] "On the Interpretation of the Difficult Poem," in John Wain (ed.), *Interpretations* (London: Routledge and Kegan Paul).

Freedman, Marcia. [1968] "The Myth of the Aesthetic Predicate," *Journal of Aesthetics and Art Criticism.*

Freud, Sigmund. [1917] *Delusion and Dream,* trans. Helen M. Downey (New York: Moffat, Yard).

Freud, Sigmund. [1947] *Leonardo da Vinci,* trans. A.A. Brill (New York: Random House).

Fry, Roger. [1933] *Art History as an Academic Study* (Cambridge: Cambridge University Press).

Frye, Northrop. [1957] *The Anatomy of Criticism* (Princeton: Princeton University Press).

Frye, Northrop. [1968] "On Value Judgments," in L.S. Dembo (ed.), *Criticism; Speculative and Analytical Essays* (Madison: University of Wisconsin Press).

Gadamer, Hans-Georg. [1975] *Truth and Method,* trans. (from 2nd ed.), Garrett Barden and John Cumming (New York: Seabury Press).

Gadamer, Hans-Georg. [1976] *Philosophical Hermeneutics,* trans. David E. Linge (Berkeley: University of California Press).

Gardner, Helen. [1959] *The Business of Criticism* (London: Oxford University Press).

Geach, Peter. [1956] *Mental Acts* (London: Routledge and Kegan Paul).

Gibson, J.J. [1950] *The Perception of the Visual World* (Boston: Houghton Mifflin).

Gibson, J.J. [1960] "Pictures, Perspective, and Perception," *Daedelus.*

Gibson, J.J. [1966] *The Senses Considered as Perceptual Systems* (Boston: Houghton Mifflin).

Gibson, J.J. [1978] "The Ecological Approach to the Visual Perception of Pictures," *Leonardo,* XI.

Giedion, Siegfried. [1948] *Mechanization Takes Command* (New York: Oxford University Press).

Girvetz, Harry and Ralph Ross (eds.). [1971] *Literature and the Arts: The Moral Issues* (Belmont: Wadsworth Publishing Co.).

Glickman, Jack. [1976] "Creativity in the Arts," in Lars Aagaard Mogensen (ed.), *Culture and Art* (Nyborg and Atlantic Highlands: F. Løkkes Forlag and Humanities Press).

Glück, Gustav. [1936] *Peter Brueghel the Elder,* Trans. E. B. Shaw (London: Commodore).

Golding, John. [1959] *Cubism: A History and an Analysis 1907-1914.* (London: Faber and Faber).

Goldman, Alvin I. [1970] *A Theory of Action* (Englewood Cliffs: Prentice-Hall).

Gombrich, E.H. [1960] *Art and Illusion* (New York: Pantheon).

Gombrich, E.H. [1962] "Art and the Language of Emotions," *Proceedings of the Aristotelian Society,* Suppl. Vol. XXXVI.

Goodman, Nelson. [1960] Review of E.H. Gombrich, *Art and Illusion, Journal of Philosophy,* LVII.

Goodman, Nelson. [1961] "About," *Mind,* LXX.

Goodman, Nelson. [1966] *The Structure of Appearance,* 2nd ed. (Indianapolis: Bobbs-Merrill).

Goodman, Nelson. [1968] *Languages of Art* (Indianapolis: Bobbs-Merrill).

Goodman, Nelson. [1970] "Seven Strictures on Similarity," in Lawrence Foster and J.W. Swanson (eds.), *Experience & Theory* (Amherst: University of Massachusetts Press).

Goodman, Nelson. [1972] *Problems and Projects* (Indianapolis: Bobbs-Merrill).

Goodman, Nelson. [1975] "The Status of Style," *Critical Inquiry,* I.

Goodman, Nelson. [1978a] "When is Art?" in *Ways of Worldmaking* (Indianapolis: Hackett Publishing Co.).

Goodman, Nelson. [1978b] "A Puzzle about Perception," in *Ways of World-making* (Indianapolis: Hackett Publishing Co.).

Gordon, David and George Lakoff. [1975] "Conversational Postulates," in Peter Cole and Jerry L. Morgan (eds.), *Syntax and Semantics,* Vol. 3 (New York: Academic Press).

Graff, Piotr and Slaw Krzemién-Ojak (eds.). [1975] *Roman Ingarden and Contemporary Polish Aesthetics* (Warsaw: Polish Scientific Publishers).

Greene, T.M. [1940] *The Arts and the Art of Criticism* (Princeton: Princeton University Press).

Gregory, R.L. [1966] *Eye and Brain* (New York: McGraw-Hill).

Grice, H.P. [1957] "Meaning," *Philosophical Review,* LXVI.

Grice, H.P. [1968] "Utterer's Meaning, Sentence-meaning, and Word-meaning," *Foundations of Language,* IV.

Grice, H.P. [1969] "Utterer's Meaning and Intentions," *Philosophical Review,* LXVIII.

Grice, H.P. [1975] "Logic and Conversation," in Peter Cole and Jerry L. Morgan (eds.), *Syntax and Semantics,* Vol. 3 (New York: Academic Press).

Grice, H.P. [1978] "Further Notes on Logic and Conversation," in Peter Cole (ed.), *Syntax and Semantics,* Vol. 9 (New York: Academic Press).

Grove, George. [1954] *Dictionary of Music and Musicians,* (ed.) Eric Blom (London: Macmillan).

Grove, George. [1962] *Beethoven and His Nine Symphonies,* 3rd ed. (New York: Dover).

Guillén, Claudio. [1968] "Second Thoughts on Currents and Periods," in Peter Demetz *et al.* (eds.), *The Disciplines of Criticism* (New Haven: Yale University Press).

Habermas, Jürgen. [1971] *Knowledge and Human Interests,* trans. Jeremy J. Shapiro (Boston: Beacon Press).

Hadas, Moses. [1957] Review of Bernard M.W. Knox, *Oedipus at Thebes, New York Times Book Review,* June 16.

Halliday, Michael A.K. [1967] "The Linguistic Study of Literary Texts," in Seymour Chatman and Samuel Levin (eds.), *Essays on the Language of Literature* (Boston: Houghton Mifflin).

Hampshire, Stuart. [1954] "Logic and Appreciation," in William Elton (ed.), *Aesthetics and Language* (Oxford: Basil Blackwell).

Hampshire, Stuart. [1966] "Types of Interpretation," in Sidney Hook (ed.), *Art and Philosophy* (New York: New York University Press).

Hampshire, Stuart. [1972] *Morality and Pessimism* (Cambridge: Cambridge University Press).

Hancher, Michael. [1977] "Beyond a Speech-Act Theory of Literary Discourse," *Modern Language Notes,* XCII.

Hancher, Michael. [1978] "Grice Through the Looking-Glass," presented at the 93rd Annual Convention, Modern Language Association (1978).

Hare, R.M. [1952] *The Language of Morals* (Oxford: Clarendon).

Hare, R.M. [1963] *Freedom and Reason* [Oxford: Clarendon).

Harman, Gilbert. [1975] "Moral Relativism Defended," *Philosophical Review,* LXXXIV.

Hauser, Arnold. [1963] *The Philosophy of Art History* (New York: World Publishing Co.).

Hausman, Carl R. [1975] *A Discourse on Novelty and Creation* (The Hague: Martinis Nijhoff).

Heidegger, Martin. [1962] *Being and Time,* trans. John Macquarrie and Edward Robinson (London: SCM Press).

Heidegger, Martin. [1971] "The Origin of the Work of Art," *Poetry, Language, Thought,* trans. Albert Hofstadter (New York: Harper and Row).

Heintz, John. [forthcoming] "Reference and Inference in Fiction," *Poetics.*

Hempel, Carl. [1965] *Aspects of Scientific Explanation* (New York: Free Press).

Henle, Paul. [1958] "Metaphor," in Paul Henle (ed.), *Language, Thought, and Culture* (Ann Arbor: University of Michigan Press).

Henri, Adrian. [1974] *Total Art: Environments, Happenings, and Performance* (New York: Praeger).

Henze, Donald. [1955] "Is the Work of Art a Construct?" *Journal of Philosophy,* LII.

Henze, Donald. [1957] "The Work of Art," *Journal of Philosophy,* LIV.

Hepburn, R.W. [1973] "Nature in the Light of Art," in *Philosophy and the Arts* (Royal Institute of Philosophy Lectures in Philosophy, Vol. 6, 1971-1972) (New York: St. Martin's Press).

Hermerén, Göran. [1969] *Representation and Meaning in the Arts* (Lund: Scandinavian University Books).

Hermerén, Göran. [1973] "Aesthetic Qualities, Value and Emotive Meaning," *Theoria,* XXXIX.

Hermerén, Göran. [1975] *Influence in Art and Literature* (Princeton: Princeton University Press).

Hermerén, Göran. [1977] "Structure, Intention, and Representation," *Grazer Philosophische Studien,* III.

Hesse, Mary B. [1963] "The Explanatory Function of Metaphor," *Models and Analogies in Science* (London: Sheed and Ward).

Heyl, Bernard C. [1946] "Relativism Again," *Journal of Aesthetics and Art Criticism,* V.

Hintikka, Jaakko. [1959] "Existential Presuppositions and Existential Commitments," *Journal of Philosophy,* LVI.

Hintikka, Jaakko. [1962] *Knowledge and Belief* (Ithaca: Cornell University Press).

Hirsch, Jr., E.D. [1967] *Validity in Interpretation* (New Haven: Yale University Press).

Hirsch, Jr., E.D. [1968] "Literary Evaluation as Knowledge," in L.S. Dembo (ed.), *Criticism; Speculative and Analytical Essays* (Madison: University of Wisconsin Press).

Hirsch, Jr., E.D. [1976] *The Aims of Interpretation* (Chicago: University of Chicago Press).

Hiz̆, Henry. [1977] "The Logical Foundation of Semiotics," in Thomas A. Sebeok (ed.), *A Perfusion of Signs* (Bloomington: Indiana University Press).

Hjelmslev, Louis. [1961] *Prolegomena to a Theory of Language,* rev. (Madison: University of Wisconsin Press).

Hochberg, Herbert. [1957] "On Pegasizing," *Philosophy and Phenomenological Research,* XVII.

Hochberg, Julian E. [1957] "Effects of the Gestalt Revolution: the Cornell Symposium on Perception," *Psychological Review,* LXIV.

Hoffman, Frederick J. [1945] *Freudianism and the Literary Mind* (Baton Rouge: Louisiana State University Press).

Horowitz, David. [1969] *Empire and Revolution* (New York: Random House).

Horwich, Paul. [1975] "On Some Alleged Paradoxes of Time Travel," *Journal of Philosophy,* LXXI.

Hospers, John. [1956] "The Croce-Collingwood Theory of Art," *Philosophy,* XXXI.

Hospers, John. [1958] "Literature and Human Nature," *Journal of Aesthetics and Art Criticism,* XVII.

Hospers, John. [1959] "The Concept of Artistic Expression," in Morris Weitz (ed.), *Problems in Aesthetics* (New York: Macmillan).

Hospers, John. [1960] "Implied Truths in Literature," *Journal of Aesthetics and Art Criticism,* XIX.

Hospers, John. [1966] "Art and Reality," in Sidney Hook (ed.), *Art and Philosophy* (New York: New York University Press).

Hough, Graham. [1976] "An Eighth Type of Ambiguity," in D. Newton-De Molina (ed.), *On Literary Intention* (Edinburgh: Edinburgh University Press).

Hoy, David Couzens. [1978] *The Critical Circle; Literature and History in Contemporary Hermeneutics* (Los Angeles: University of California Press).

Hume, David. [1874-1875] "On the Standard of Taste," *Philosophical Works,* (eds.) T.H. Green and T.H. Grose (London: Longmans, Green).

Hungerland, Isabel C. [1955] "The Concept of Intention in Art Criticism," *Journal of Philosophy,* LII.

Hungerland, Isabel C. [1958] *Poetic Discourse* (Berkeley: University of California Press).

Hungerland, Isabel C. [1960] "Contextual Implication," *Inquiry,* IV.

Hungerland, Isabel C. [1963] "The Logic of Aesthetic Concepts," *Proceedings of the American Philosophical Association,* XXXVI.

Hungerland, Isabel C. [1968] "Once Again, Aesthetic and Non-Aesthetic," *Journal of Aesthetics and Art Criticism,* XXVI.

Hutchinson, Ann. [1954] *Labanotation* (New York: New Directions).

Hyman, Stanley Edgar. [1948] *The Armed Vision* (New York: Knopf).

Ingarden, Roman. [1964] "Artistic and Aesthetic Values," *British Journal of Aesthetics,* IV.

Ingarden, Roman. [1973a] *The Literary Work of Art,* trans. George G. Grabowicz (Evanston: Northwestern University Press).

Ingarden, Roman. [1973b] *The Cognition of the Literary Work of Art,* trans. Ruth Crowley and Kenneth R. Olson (Evanston: Northwestern University Press).

Ingarden, Roman. [1975] "Phenomenological Aesthetics: An Attempt at Defining the Range," *Journal of Aesthetics and Art Criticism,* XXXIII.

Iseminger, Gary. [1973] "The Work of Art as Artifact," *British Journal of Aesthetics,* XIII.

Isenberg, Arnold. [1949a] "Perception, Meaning, and the Subject-Matter of Art," *Journal of Philosophy,* LXI.

Isenberg, Arnold. [1949b] "Critical Communication," *Philosophical Review,* LVIII.

Isenberg, Arnold. [1973] "On Defining Metaphor," in William Callaghan *et al.* (eds.), *Aesthetics and the Theory of Criticism. Selected Essays of Arnold Isenberg* (Chicago: University of Chicago Press).

Ishiguro, Hidé. [1967] "Imagination," *Proceedings of the Aristotelian Society,* Suppl. Vol. XLI.

Jakobson, Roman. [1971] "Closing Statement: Linguistics and Poetics," in Thomas A. Sebeok (ed.), *Style in Language* (Cambridge: MIT Press).

Jakobson, Roman and Morris Halle. [1956] *Fundamentals of Language* (The Hague: Mouton).

Jarvie, I.C. [1967] "The Objectivity of Criticism of the Arts," *Ratio,* IX.

Jarvie, I.C. [1970] "Understanding and Explanation in Sociology and Social Anthropology," in Robert Berger and Frank Cioffi (eds.), *Explanation in the Behavioural Sciences* (Cambridge: Cambridge University Press).

Joad, C.E.M. [1929] *Matter, Life and Value* (London: Oxford University Press).

Jones, Ernest. [1949] *Hamlet and Oedipus* (New York: Norton).

Jung, C.G. [1928] "On the Relation of Analytical Psychology to Poetic Art," *Contributions to Analytical Psychology,* trans. H.G. and C.F. Baynes (London: Routledge and Kegan Paul).

Kahler, Erich. [1959] "What is Art?" in Morris Weitz (ed.), *Problems in Aesthetics* (New York: Macmillan).

Kant, Immanuel. [1933] *Immanuel Kant's Critique of Pure Reason,* 2nd imp. corrected, trans. Norman Kemp Smith (London: Macmillan).

Kant, Immanuel. [1952] *The Critique of Judgment,* trans. James Creed Meredith (Oxford: Clarendon).

Kaplan, Abraham and Ernst Kris. [1948] "Esthetic Ambiguity," *Philosophy and Phenomenological Research,* VIII.

Kaplan, David. [1973] "Bob and Carol and Ted and Alice," in Donald Davidson and Gilbert Harman (eds.), *Semantics of Natural Language* (Dordrecht: D. Reidel).

Katz, Jerrold J. [1966] *The Philosophy of Language* (New York: Harper and Row).

Katz, Jerrold J. [1972] *Semantic Theory* (New York: Harper and Row).

Kazin, Alfred. [1959] "Psychoanalysis and Literary Culture Today," *Partisan Review,* XXVI.

Kennick, William E. [1958] "Does Traditional Aesthetics Rest on a Mistake?" *Mind,* LXVII.

Khatchadourian, Haig. [1961] "Artnames and Aesthetic Judgments," *Philosophy,* XXXVI.

Kilbracken, J.R.G. [1967] *Van Meegeren: Master Forger* (New York: Scribner's).

Kirby, Michael. [1965] *Happenings* (New York: Dutton).

Kitaro, Nishida. [1973] *Art and Morality,* trans. David A. Dilworth and Valdo H. Vighelmo (Honolulu: University of Hawaii Press).

Kivy, Peter. [1973] *Speaking of Art* (The Hague: Martinus Nijhoff).

Knight, Helen. [1954] "The Use of 'Good' in Aesthetic Judgments," in William Elton (ed.), *Aesthetics and Language* (Oxford: Basil Blackwell).

Köhler, Wolfgang. [1947] *Gestalt Psychology* (New York: Liveright).

Kolers, Paul A. [1972] *Aspects of Motion Perception* (Oxford: Pergamon Press).

Krieger, Murray. [1968] "Literary Analysis and Evaluation—and the Ambidextrous Critic," in L.S. Dembo (ed.), *Criticism; Speculative and Analytical Essays* (Madison: University of Wisconsin Press).

Kripke, Saul A. [1972] "Semantical Considerations on Modal Logic," in Leonard Linsky (ed.), *Reference and Modality* (London: Oxford University Press).

Kripke, Saul A. [1973] "Naming and Necessity," in Donald Davidson and Gilbert Harman (eds.), *Semantics of Natural Language* (Dordrecht: D. Reidel).

Kris, Ernst. [1952] *Psychoanalytic Explorations in Art* (New York: International Universities Press).

Kristeller, P.O. [1951] "The Modern System of the Arts: A Study in the History of Aesthetics," Pt. I, *Journal of the History of Ideas,* XII.

Kristeller, P.O. [1952] "The Modern System of the Arts: A Study in the History of Aesthetics," Pt. II, *Journal of the History of Ideas,* XIII.

Kubie, Lawrence S. [1958] *Neurotic Distortion of the Creative Process* (Porter Lectures, Ser. 22) (Lawrence: University of Kansas Press).

Kuhn, Thomas S. [1970] *The Structure of Scientific Revolutions,* 2nd ed. enl. (Chicago: University of Chicago Press).

Lagerkvist, Par. [1945] *The Dwarf,* trans. Alexandra Dick (New York: L.B. Fischer).

Lakoff, George. [1971] "Presupposition and Relative Wellformedness," in Danny D. Steinberg and Leon A. Jakobovits (eds.), *Semantics* (Cambridge: Cambridge University Press).

Lakoff, Robin. [1977] "What You Can Do With Words: Politeness, Pragmatics, and Performatives," in Andy Rogers *et al.* (eds.), *Proceedings of the Texas Conference on Performatives, Presuppositions, and Implicatures* (Arlington, Va.: Center for Applied Linguistics).

Lambert, Karel. [1963] "Existential Import Revisited," *Notre Dame Journal of Formal Logic,* IV.

Langer, Susanne K. [1942] *Philosophy in a New Key* (Cambridge: Harvard University Press).

Langer, Susanne K. [1953] *Feeling and Form* (New York: Charles Scribner's Sons).

Langer, Susanne K. [1957] *Problems of Art* (New York: Charles Scribner's Sons).

Langer, Susanne K. [1962] "On a New Definition of 'Symbol,' " *Philosophical Sketches* (Baltimore: Johns Hopkins University Press).

Leatherdale, W.H. [1974] *The Role of Analogy, Model and Metaphor* (Amsterdam: North-Holland).

Leavis, F.R. [1945] " 'Thought' and Emotional Quality," *Scrutiny,* XIII.

Leavis, F.R. [1948] *The Great Tradition* (London: Chatto and Windus).

Leavis, F.R. (comp.). [1968] *A Selection from Scrutiny,* Vol. I (Cambridge: Cambridge University Press).

Leonard, H.S. [1956] "The Logic of Existence," *Philosophical Studies,* IV.

Lévi-Strauss, Claude. [1966] *The Savage Mind,* trans. (Chicago: University of Chicago Press).

Lévi-Strauss, Claude. [1969a] *The Elementary Structures of Kinship,* rev. ed., trans. J.H. Bell, J.R. von Sturmer, and Rodney Needham (ed.) (Boston: Beacon).

Lévi-Strauss, Claude. [1969b] *The Raw and the Cooked,* trans. John and Doreen Weightman (New York: Harper and Row).

Levin, Samuel R. [1962] *Linguistic Structures in Poetry* (The Hague: Mouton).

Levin, Samuel R. [1977] *The Semantics of Metaphor* (Baltimore: Johns Hopkins University Press).

Lewis, David K. [1966] "An Argument for the Identity Theory," *Journal of Philosophy,* LXIII.

Lewis, David K. [1969] *Convention* (Cambridge: Harvard University Press).

Lewis, David K. [1978] "Truth in Fiction," *American Philosophical Quarterly,* XV.

Lewis, Wyndham. [1952] *The Writer and the Absolute* (London: Methuen).

Lindsay, Kenneth C. and Bernard Huppé. [1956] "Meaning and Method in Brueghel's Painting," *Journal of Aesthetics and Art Criticism,* XIV.

Lippard, Lucy. [1973] *Six Years: The Dematerialization of the Art Object from 1966 to 1972* (New York: Praeger).

Loewenberg, Ina. [1975] "Intentions: The Speaker and the Artist," *British Journal of Aesthetics,* XV.

Logan, J.F. [1967] "More on Aesthetic Concepts," *Journal of Aesthetics and Art Criticism,* XXV.

Lukács, Georg. [1962] *The Historical Novel,* trans. Hannah and Stanley Mitchell (London: Merlin Press).

Lukács, Georg. [1964] *Studies in European Realism,* trans. Edith Bone (New York: Grosset and Dunlap).

Lukes, Steven. [1974] "Relativism: Cognitive and Moral," *Proceedings of the Aristotelian Society,* XLVIII.

Luppé, Robert de. [1960] *Albert Camus,* 6th ed. (Paris: Editions Universitaires).

Lyas, Colin. [1973] "Personal Qualities and the Intentional Fallacy," in *Philosophy and the Arts* (Royal Institute Lectures in Philosophy, Vol. 6, 1971-72) (New York: St. Martin's Press).

Macdonald, Margaret. [1951] Review of Morris Weitz, *Philosophy of the Arts, Mind,* LX.

Macdonald, Margaret. [1952-1953] "Art and Imagination," *Proceedings of the Aristotelian Society,* LIII.

Macdonald, Margaret. [1954a] "Some Distinctive Features of Arguments Used in Criticism of the Arts," in William Elton (ed.), *Aesthetics and Language* (Oxford: Basil Blackwell).

Macdonald, Margaret. [1954b] "The Language of Fiction," *Proceedings of the Aristotelian Society,* Suppl. Vol. XXVIII.

MacIntyre, A.C. [1958] *The Unconscious* (London: Routledge and Kegan Paul).

Mandelbaum, Maurice. [1965] "Family Resemblances and Generalization Concerning the Arts," *American Philosophical Quarterly,* II.

Mannheim, Karl. [1966] *Ideology and Utopia* (London: Routledge and Kegan Paul).

Manns, James W. [1971] "Representation, Relativism and Resemblance," *British Journal of Aesthetics,* XI.

Margarshak, David. [1950] *Stanislavski: A Life* (London: Macgibbon and Kee).

Margarshak, David. [1952] *Chekhov the Dramatist* (London: Faber and Faber).

Margolis, Joseph [1963] "Classification and the Concept of Goodness," *Austalasian Journal of Philosophy,* XLI.

Margolis, Joseph [1965] *The Language of Art and Art Criticism* (Detroit: Wayne State University Press).

Margolis, Joseph [1966] "Three Problems in Aesthetics," in Sidney Hook (ed.), *Art and Philosophy* (New York: New York University Press).

Margolis, Joseph. [1968] "On Names: Sense and Reference," *American Philosophical Quarterly,* V.

Margolis, Joseph. [1971] *Values and Conduct* (Oxford: Clarendon).

Margolis, Joseph. [1972] "The Myths of Psychoanalysis," *The Monist,* LVI.

Margolis, Joseph. [1973a] "Meaning, Speakers' Intentions, and Speech Acts," *Review of Metaphysics,* XXVI.

Margolis, Joseph [1973b] *Knowledge and Existence* (New York: Oxford University Press).

Margolis, Joseph. [1974a] "Works of Art as Physically Embodied and Culturally Emergent Entities," *British Journal of Aesthetics,* XIV.

Margolis, Joseph. [1974b] Review of Alvin I. Goldman, *A Theory of Action,* *Metaphilosophy,* V.

Margolis, Joseph. [1975a] Review of George Dickie, *Art and the Aesthetic,* *Journal of Aesthetics and Art Criticism,* XXXIII.

Margolis, Joseph. [1975b] "Moral Cognitivism," *Ethics,* LXXXV.

Margolis, Joseph. [1975c] *Negativities. The Limits of Life* (Columbus: Charles Merrill).

Margolis, Joseph. [1976a] "The Ontology of Persons," *New Scholasticism,* L.

Margolis, Joseph. [1976b] "The Concept of Disease," *Journal of Medicine and Philosophy,* I.

Margolis, Joseph. [1976c] "G.E. Moore and Intuitionism," *Ethics,* LXXVII.

Margolis, Joseph. [1977] "The Axiom of Existence: Reductio ad Absurdum," *Southern Journal of Philosophy,* XV.

Margolis, Joseph. [1978a] *Persons and Minds* (Dordrecht: D. Reidel).

Margolis, Joseph. [1978b] "Reconciling Freud's *Scientific Project* and Psycho-analysis," in H. Tristram Engelhardt, Jr. and Daniel Callahan (eds.), *Morals, Science, and Sociology* (The Foundations of Ethics and Its Relationship to Science, Vol. 3) (Hastings-on-Hudson: The Hastings Center).

Margolis, Joseph. [forthcoming] "The Problem of Similarity: Realism and Nominalism," *The Monist.*

Margolis, Joseph and Evan Fales. [1976] "Donnellan on Definite Descriptions," *Philosophia,* VI.

Maritain, Jacques. [1930] *Art and Scholasticism,* trans. J.F. Scanlan (New York: Scribner's).

Maritain, Jacques. [1953] *Creative Intuition in Art and Poetry* (New York: Pantheon).

Marsh, Robert. [1967] "Historical Interpretation and the History of Criticism," in Phillip Damon (ed.), *Literary Criticism and Historical Understanding* (New York: Columbia University Press).

Marx, Karl. [1962] "The Eighteenth Brumaire of Louis Napoleon," in *Marx and Engels. Selected Works,* Vol. 1 (Moscow: Foreign Languages Publishing House).

Matejka, Ladislav and Kristyna Pomorsky (eds.). [1971] *Readings in Russian Poetics: Formalist and Structuralist Views* (Cambridge: MIT Press).

Matthews, Robert J. [1971] "Concerning a 'Linguistic Theory' of Metaphor," *Foundations of Language,* VII.

Matthews, Robert J. [1977] "Describing and Interpreting Works of Art," *Journal of Aesthetics and Art Criticism,* XXXVI.

Matthiessen, F.O. [1947] *The Achievement of T.S. Eliot,* 2nd ed. rev. & enl. (New York: Oxford University Press).

Maynard, Patrick. [1972] "Depiction, Vision, and Convention," *American Philosophical Quarterly,* IX.

Panofsky, Erwin. [1938] "The History of Art as a Humanistic Discipline," in Theodore M. Greene (ed.), *The Meaning of the Humanities* (Princeton: Princeton University Press).

Panofsky, Erwin. [1939] *Studies in Iconology* (New York: Oxford University Press).

Panofsky, Erwin. [1953] *Early Netherlandish Painting* (Cambridge: Harvard University Press).

Panofsky, Erwin. [1955] *Meaning in the Visual Arts* (Garden City: Anchor Books).

Parsons, Terence. [1975] "A Meinongian Analysis of Fictional Objects, *Grazer Philosophische Studien,* I.

Passmore, J.A. [1954] "The Dreariness of Aesthetics," in William Elton (ed.), *Aesthetics and Language* (Oxford: Basil Blackwell).

Pater, Walter. [1917] "The School of Giorgione," *The Renaissance* (London: Macmillan).

Patton, T.E. and D.W. Stampe. [1969] "The Rudiments of Meaning: On Ziff on Grice," *Foundations of Language,* V.

Peirce, Charles Sanders, Collected Papers of, Vol. 4 [1939] (eds.) Charles Hartshorne and Paul Weiss (Cambridge: Harvard University Press).

Peirce, Charles Sanders. [1940] "Abduction and Induction," in Justus Buchler (ed.), *The Philosophy of Peirce. Selected Writings* (London: Routledge and Kegan Paul).

Pepper, Stephen. [1937] *Aesthetic Quality* (New York: Scribner's).

Pepper, Stephen. [1952] "Further Considerations of the Aesthetic Work of Art," *Journal of Philosophy,* LXIX.

Pepper, Stephen. [1955] *The Work of Art* (Bloomington: Indiana University Press).

Phillips, D.Z. [1973] "Allegiance and Change in Morality: A Study in Contrasts," in *Philosophy and the Arts* (Royal Institute of Philosophy Lectures, Vol. 6, 1971-1972) (New York: St. Martin's Press).

Phillips, William (ed.). [1957] *Art and Psychoanalysis* (New York: Criterion Books).

Piaget, Jean. [1971] *Structuralism,* trans. Chinanah Maschler (New York: Basic Books).

Picard, Raymond. [1965] *Nouvelle Critique ou Imposture* (Paris: Pauvert).

Plantinga, Alvin. [1974] *The Nature of Necessity* (Oxford: Clarendon).

Pleydell-Pearce, A.G. [1967] "Sense, Reference and Fiction," *British Journal of Aesthetics,* VII.

Polanyi, Michael. [1962] *Personal Knowledge,* corr. ed. (Chicago: University of Chicago Press).

Pole, David. [1973] "Presentational Objects and Their Interpretation," *Philosophy and the Arts* (Royal Institute Lectures in Philosophy, Vol. 6, 1971-1972) (New York: St. Martin's Press).

Popper, Karl R. [1957] *The Poverty of Historicism* (London: Routledge and Kegan Paul).

Popper, Karl R. [1959] *The Logic of Scientific Discovery* (New York: Basic Books).

Pound, Ezra, The Letters of, 1907-1941. [1950] (ed.) D.D. Paige (New York: Harcourt, Brace).

Prall, David. [1936] *Aesthetic Analysis* (New York: Thomas T. Crowell).

Pratt, Carroll C. [1931] *The Meaning of Music* (New York: McGraw-Hill).

Pratt, Carroll C. [1954] "The Design of Music," *Journal of Aesthetics and Art Criticism,* XII.

Pratt, Mary Louise. [1977] *Toward A Speech Act Theory of Literary Discourse* (Bloomington: Indiana University Press).

Putnam, Hilary. [1960] "Minds and Machines," in Sidney Hook (ed.), *Dimensions of Mind* (New York: New York University Press).

Putnam, Hilary. [1962] "It Ain't Necessarily So," *Journal of Philosophy,* LIX.

Putnam, Hilary. [1965] "How Not To Talk about Meaning," in Robert S. Cohen and Marx W. Wartofsky (eds.), *Boston Studies in the Philosophy of Science,* Vol. II (New York: Humanities Press).

Putnam, Hilary. [1966] "The Analytic and the Synthetic," in Herbert Feigl and Grover Maxwell (eds.), *Minnesota Studies in the Philosophy of Science,* Vol. III (Minneapolis: University of Minnesota Press).

Putnam, Hilary. [1975a] "Is Semantics Possible" in *Philosophical Papers,* Vol. 2 (Cambridge: Cambridge University Press).

Putnam, Hilary. [1975b] "The Meaning of 'meaning'," in *Philosophical Papers,* Vol. 2 (Cambridge: Cambridge University Press).

Putnam, Hilary. [1975c] *Philosophical Papers,* Vol. 2 (Cambridge: Cambridge University Press).

Putnam, Hilary. [1978] *Meaning and the Moral Sciences* (London: Routledge and Kegan Paul).

Quine, Willard Van Orman. [1950] *Methods of Logic* (New York: Holt).

Quine, Willard Van Orman. [1960] *Word and Object* (Cambridge: MIT Press).

Quine, Willard Van Orman. [1963] "On What There Is," in *From a Logical Point of View* (Cambridge: Harvard University Press).

Quintilian. [1921] *Institutio Oratoria,* trans. H.W. Butler (Cambridge: Harvard University Press).

Ransom, John Crowe. [1941] *The New Criticism* (Norfolk: New Directions).

Redpath, Theodore. [1957] "Some Problems of Modern Aesthetics," in C.A. Mace (ed.), *British Philosophy in the Mid-Century* (London: George Allen and Unwin).

Reichert, John. [1977] *Making Sense of Literature* (Chicago: University of Chicago Press).

Reynolds, Joshua. [1975] *Discourses on Art,* (ed.) Robert R. Ware (New Haven: Yale University Press).

Richards, I.A. [1935] *Science and Poetry,* rev. (London: K. Paul, Trench, Trufner).

Richards, I.A. [1936] *The Philosophy of Rhetoric* (London: Oxford University Press).

Richards, I.A. [1974] *Poetries: Their Media and Ends* (The Hague: Mouton).

Riffaterre, Michael. [1962] "Criteria for Style Analysis," in Seymour Chatman and Samuel Levin (eds.), *Essays on the Language of Literature* (Boston: Houghton Mifflin).

Riffaterre, Michael. [1970] "Describing Poetic Structures: Two Approaches to Baudelaire's 'les Chats'," in Jacques Ehrmann (ed.), *Structuralism* (Garden City: Anchor Books).

Robertson, D.W. [1969] "Some Observations on Method in Literary Studies," *New Literary History*, I.

Rosenberg, Harold. [1972] *The De-definition of Art: Action Art to Pop to Earthworks* (New York: Horizon Press).

Routley, Richard. [1966] "Some Things Do Not Exist," *Notre Dame Journal of Formal Logic*, VII.

Rudner, Richard. [1958] "The Ontological Status of the Esthetic Object," *Philosophy and Phenomenological Research*, X.

Rudner, Richard. [1972] "On Seeing What We Shall See," in Richard Rudner and Israel Scheffler (eds.), *Logic & Art; Essays in Honor of Nelson Goodman* (Indianapolis: Bobbs-Merrill).

Ruskin, John. [1903-1912] *The Elements of Drawing*, in *The Works of John Ruskin*, (eds.) E.T. Cook and Alexander Wadderburn (London: George Allen).

Russell, Bertrand. [1905] "On Denoting," *Mind*, XIV.

Ryle, Gilbert. [1933] "Imaginary Objects," *Proceedings of the Aristotelian Society*, Suppl. Vol. XII.

Ryle, Gilbert. [1949] *The Concept of Mind* (London: Hutchinson).

Sagoff, Mark. [1978] "On Restoring and Reproducing Art," *Journal of Philosophy*, LXXV.

Said, Edward W. [1978] "The Problem of Textuality," *Critical Inquiry*, IV.

Santayana, George. [1896] *The Sense of Beauty* (New York: Scribner's).

Sartre, Jean-Paul. [1963] *Imagination; a Psychological Critique*, trans. Forrest Williams (Ann Arbor: University of Michigan Press).

Savile, Anthony. [1968-1969] "The Place of Intention in the Concept of Art," *Proceedings of the Aristotelian Society*, LXIX.

Saw, Ruth. [1962] "Art and the Language of Emotions," *Proceedings of the Aristotelian Society*, Suppl. Vol. XXXVI.

Saw, Ruth. [1971] *Aesthetics* (Garden City: Anchor Books).

Schapiro, Meyer. [1953] "Style," in A.L. Kroeber (ed.), *Anthropology Today* (Chicago: University of Chicago Press).

Schapiro, Meyer. [1956] "Leonardo and Freud: An Art-Historical Study," *Journal of the History of Ideas*, XVII.

Schapiro, Meyer. [1973] *Words and Pictures. On the Literal and the Symbolic in the Illustration of a Text* (The Hague: Martinus Nijhoff).

Schiffer, Stephen R. [1972] *Meaning* (Oxford: Clarendon).

Schilpp, P.A. (ed.). [1942] *The Philosophy of G.E. Moore* (Evanston: Northwestern University Press).

Schleiermacher, F.D.E. [1959] *Hermeneutik,* (ed.) Heinz Kimmerle (Heidelberg: Karl Winter); [trans. James Duke and Jack Forstman (American Academy of Religion Texts and Translation Series, No. 1) (Missoula: Scholars Press, 1977)].

Schönberg, Arnold. [1950] "Composition with Twelve Tones," *Style and Idea,* trans. Dika Newlin (New York: Philosophical Library).

Schücking, Levin. [1944] *The Sociology of Literary Taste,* trans. S.W. Dickes (London: Kegan Paul).

Schwyzer, H.R.G. [1963] "Sibley's 'Aesthetic Concepts,' " *Philosophical Review,* LXXII.

Sclafani, Richard J. [1971] " 'Art,' Wittgenstein, and Open-Textured Concepts," *Journal of Aesthetics and Art Criticism,* XXIX.

Scriven, Michael. [1954] "The Language of Fiction," *Proceedings of the Aristotelian Society,* Suppl. Vol. XXVII.

Scriven, Michael. [1966] "The Objectivity of Aesthetic Evaluation," *The Monist,* L.

Scruton, Roger. [1974] *Art and Imagination* (London: Hutchinson).

Scruton, Roger. [unpublished] "Architecture and Morality," presented to the School of Architecture, Princeton University, Fall 1978.

Searle, John. [1965] "What Is a Speech Act?" in Max Black (ed.), *Philosophy in America* (Ithaca: Cornell University Press).

Searle, John. [1969] *Speech Acts* (Cambridge: Cambridge University Press).

Searle, John. [1975] "The Logical Status of Fictional Discourse," *New Literary History,* VI.

Segall, Marshall H. [1976] "Visual Art: Some Perspectives from Cross-Cultural Psychology," in Don Brothwell (ed.), *Beyond Aesthetics* (London: Thames and Hudson).

Segall, Marshall H. *et al.* [1966] *The Influence of Culture on Visual Perception* (Indianapolis: Bobbs-Merrill).

Selfe, Lorna. [1978] *Nadia: A Case of Extraordinary Drawing in an Autistic Child* (New York: Academic Press).

Sellars, Wilfrid. [1963] "Philosophy and the Scientific Image of Man," *Science, Perception, and Reality* (London: Routledge and Kegan Paul).

Sessions, Roger. [1951] *Harmonic Practice* (New York: Harcourt, Brace).

Shafer, Jr., John Jackson. [1971] "Analysis and the Foundations of Esthetics," Ph. D. dissertation (University of Calgary).

Shibles, Warren A. [1971] *An Analysis of Metaphor in the Light of W.M. Urban's Theories* (The Hague: Mouton).

Shwayder, David. [1965] *The Stratification of Behavior* (New York: Humanities Press).

Sibley, Frank (F.N.). [1959a] "Aesthetic Concepts," *Philosophical Review,* LXVIII.

Sibley, Frank (F.N.). [1959b] "Aesthetics and the Looks of Things," *Journal of Philosophy*. LVI.

Sibley, Frank (F.N.). [1960] "Is Art an Open Concept? An Unsettled Question," in *Proceedings of the IVth International Congress of Aesthetics* (Athens).

Sibley, Frank. (F.N.). [1963] "Aesthetic Concepts: A Rejoinder," *Philosophical Review*, LXXII.

Sibley, Frank (F.N.). [1965] "Critical Judgments of Aesthetic Value," *Philosophical Review*, LXXIV.

Sibley, Frank (F.N.). [1968] "Objectivity and Aesthetics," *Proceedings of the Aristotelian Society*, Suppl. Vol. XLII.

Silvers, Anita. [1976] "The Artworld Discarded," *Journal of Aesthetics and Art Criticism*, XXXIV.

Sircello, Guy. [1968] "Subjectivity and Justification in Aesthetic Judgments," *Journal of Aesthetics and Art Criticism*, XXVI.

Sircello, Guy. [1972] *Mind & Art* (Princeton: Princeton University Press).

Sircello, Guy. [1975] *A New Theory of Beauty* (Princeton: Princeton University Press).

Sirridge, M.J. [1975] "Truth from Fiction?" *Philosophy and Phenomenological Research*, XXXV.

Speer, Albert. [1970] *Inside the Third Reich*, trans. Richard and Clara Winston (New York: Macmillan).

Srzednicki, J. [1960] "On Metaphor," *Philosophical Quarterly*, X.

Stahl, Gary. [1971] "Sibley's 'Aesthetic Concepts': An Ontological Mistake," *Journal of Aesthetics and Art Criticism*, XXIX.

Stein, Edith. [1964] *On the Problem of Empathy*, trans. W. Stein (The Hague: Martinus Nijhoff).

Stern, Gustaf. [1931] "Meaning and Change of Meaning," in *Göteborg Högskolas Ârsskrift*, XXXVIII, Part 1 (Göteborg: Wettergren and Kerbers Förlag).

Stevenson, C.L. [1944] *Ethics and Language* (New Haven: Yale University Press).

Stevenson, C.L. [1950] "Interpretation and Evaluation in Aesthetics," in Max Black (ed.), *Philosophical Analysis* (Ithaca: Cornell University Press).

Stevenson, C.L. [1957] "On 'What is a Poem?' " *Philosophical Review*, LXVI.

Stevenson, C.L. [1958] "Symbolism in the Nonrepresentative Arts," in Paul Henle (ed.), *Language, Thought and Culture* (Ann Arbor: University of Michigan Press).

Stevenson, C.L. [1962] "On the Reasons That Can Be Given for the Interpretation of a Poem," in Joseph Margolis (ed.), *Philosophy Looks at the Arts* (New York: Charles Scribner's Sons).

Stolnitz, Jerome. [1960] *Aesthetics and Philosophy of Art Criticism* (Boston: Houghton Mifflin).

Stoutland, Frederick. [1968] "Basic Actions and Causality," *Journal of Philosophy*, LXV.

Strawson, P.F. [1950] "On Referring," *Mind,* LIX.

Strawson, P.F. [1952] *Introduction to Logical Theory* (London: Methuen).

Strawson, P.F. [1959] *Individuals* (London: Methuen).

Strawson, P.F. [1963] "Intention and Convention in Speech Acts," *Philosophical Review,* LXXIII.

Strawson, P.F. [1970] "Imagination and Perception," in Lawrence Foster and J.. Swanson (eds.), *Experience & Theory* (Amherst: University of Massachusetts Press).

Suger (Abbot). [1947] "The Book of Suger, Abbot of St. Denis," in Elizabeth Gilmore Holt (ed.), *Literary Sources of Art History* (Princeton: Princeton University Press).

Tarski, Alfred. [1944] "The Semantic Conception of Truth and the Foundations of Semantics," *Philosophy and Phenomenological Research,* IV.

Tatarkiewicz, Wladyslaw. [1963] "Classification of Arts in Antiquity," *Journal of the History of Ideas,* XXIV.

Tatarkiewicz, Wladyslaw. [1971] "What is Art? The Problem of Definition Today," *British Journal of Aesthetics,* XI.

Taylor, Charles. [1964] *The Explanation of Behaviour* (London: Routledge and Kegan Paul).

Thomson, George. [1941] *Aeschylus and Athens* (London: Lawrence and Wishart).

Tilghman, B.R. [1966] "Aesthetic Perception and the Problem of the 'Aesthetic Object,' " *Mind,* LXXV.

Tindall, William Y. [1955] "The Literary Symbol," in Lyman Bryson *et al.* (eds.), *Symbols and Society: Fourteenth Symposium of the Conference on Science, Philosophy and Religion* (New York: Harpers).

Tolstoy, Leo. [1938] *What is Art?,* trans. Aylmer Maude (London: Oxford University Press).

Tomas, Vincent. [1952] "The Concept of Expression in Art," in *Science, Language, and Human Rights* (American Philosophical Association Proceedings, Vol. 1) Philadelphia: University of Pennsylvania Press).

Tomas, Vincent. [1959] "Aesthetic Vision," *Philosophical Review,* LXVIII.

Tormey, Alan. [1971] *The Concept of Expression* (Princeton: Princeton University Press).

Tormey, Alan. [1973] "Critical Judgments," *Theoria,* XXXIX.

Tormey, Alan and Tormey, Judith. [forthcoming] "Seeing, Believing and Picturing," in Calvin F. Nodine and Daniel F. Fisher (eds.), *Views of Pictorial Representation* (New York: Praeger).

Toulmin, Stephen and Kurt Baier. [1952] "On Describing," *Mind,* LXI.

Travaux du Cercle Linguistique de Prague. [1929] I.

Trigg, Roger. [1973] *Reason and Commitment* (Cambridge: Cambridge University Press).

Trilling, Lionel. [1950a] "The Sense of the Past," *The Liberal Imagination* (New York: Viking).

Trilling, Lionel. [1950b] "Art and Neurosis," *The Liberal Imagination* (New York: Viking).

Tsugawa, Albert. [1961] "The Objectivity of Aesthetic Judgments," *Philosophical Review,* LXX.

Turbayne, Colin. [1962] *The Myth of Metaphor* (New Haven: Yale University Press).

Tuve, Rosemond. [1947] *Elizabethan and Metaphysical Imagery* (Chicago: University of Chicago Press).

Urban, W.M. [1939] *Language and Reality* (London: Allen and Unwin).

Urmson, J.O. [1950] "On Grading," *Mind,* LIX.

Urmson, J.O. [1957] "What Makes a Situation Aesthetic?" *Proceedings of the Aristotelian Society,* Suppl. Vol. XXXI.

Urmson, J.O. [1973] "Representation in Music," in *Philosophy and the Arts* (Royal Institute of Philosophy Lectures, Vol. 6, 1971-1972) (New York: St. Martin's Press).

Ushenko, Andrew. [1955] "Metaphor," *Thought,* XXX.

Vendler, Zeno. [1972] *Res Cogitans* (Ithaca: Cornell University Press).

Vivas, Eliseo. [1955] *Creation and Discovery* (New York: Noonday Press).

Vivas, Eliseo. [1961] "Animadversions on Imitation and Expression," *Journal of Aesthetics and Art Criticism,* XIX.

Vivas, Eliseo. [1963] "The Neo-Aristotelians of Chicago," *The Artistic Transaction* (Columbus: Ohio State University Press).

Wacker, Jeanne. [1960] "Particular Works of Art," *Mind,* LXIX.

Wain, John (ed.). [1955] *Interpretations* (London: Routledge and Kegan Paul).

Walton, Kendall L. [1970] "Categories of Art," *Philosophical Review,* LXXIX.

Walton, Kendall L. [1971] "Pictures and Make-Believe," *Philosophical Review,* LXXX.

Warner, Martin. [1973] "Black's Metaphors," *British Journal of Philosophy,* XIII.

Wartofsky, Marx. [1972] "Pictures, Representation, and the Understanding," in Richard Rudner and Israel Scheffler (eds.), *Logic & Art; Essays in Honor of Nelson Goodman* (Indianapolis: Bobbs-Merrill).

Wartofsky, Marx. [1978] "Rules and Representations: The Virtues of Constancy and Fidelity Put in Perspective," *Erkenntnis,* XII.

Webster, William B. [1971] "Music Is Not a 'Notational System,' " *Journal of Aesthetics and Art Criticism,* XXIX.

Webster, William B. [1974] "A Theory of the Compositional Work of Art," *Journal of Aesthetics and Art Criticism,* XXXIII.

Weimann, Robert. [1964] "The Soul of the Age: Towards a Historical Approach to Shakespeare," in Arnold Kettle (ed.), *Shakespeare in a Changing World* (New York: International Publishers).

Weitz, Morris. [1943] "Does Art Tell the Truth?" *Philosophy and Phenomenological Research,* III.

Weitz, Morris. [1945] "The Logic of Art: A Rejoinder to Dr. Hoekstra," *Philosophy and Phenomenological Research,* V.

Weitz, Morris. [1950] *Philosophy of the Arts* (Cambridge: Harvard University Press).

Weitz, Morris. [1956] "The Role of Theory in Aesthetics," *Journal of Aesthetics and Art Criticism,* XV.

Weitz, Morris. [1964] *"Hamlet" and the Philosophy of Literary Criticism* (Chicago: University of Chicago Press).

Weitz, Morris. [1973] "Wittgenstein's Aesthetics," in Benjamin R. Tilghman (ed.), *Language and Aesthetics* (Lawrence: University of Kansas Press).

Weitz, Morris. [1977] *The Opening Mind* (Chicago: University of Chicago Press).

Wellek, René. [1963] "The Revolt against Positivism in Recent European Literary Scholarship," in Stephen G. Nichols, Jr. (ed.), *Concepts of Criticism* (New Haven: Yale University Press).

Wellek, René. [1965] *Concepts of Criticism* (New Haven: Yale University Press).

Wellek, René and Austin Warren. [1956] "The Mode of Existence of a Literary Work of Art," *Theory of Literature,* 2nd ed. (New York).

Wheelwright, Philip. [1954] The Burning Fountain (Bloomington: Indiana University Press).

Wheelwright, Philip. [1962] *Metaphor and Reality* (Bloomington: Indiana University Press).

Wiggins, David. [1967] *Identity and Spatio-Temporal Continuity* (Oxford: Basil Blackwell).

Wilson, N.L. [1967] "Linguistic Butter and Philosophical Parsnips," *Journal of Philosophy,* LXIV.

Wimsatt, Jr. W.K. [1954] *The Verbal Icon* (Lexington: University of Kentucky Press).

Wimsatt, Jr. W.K. [1963] *What To Say about a Poem* (CEA Chapbook) (Saratoga Springs: Skidmore College).

Wimsatt, Jr. W.K. [1966] "Northrop Frye: Criticism as Myth," in Murray Krieger (ed.), *Northrop Frye in Modern Criticism* (New York: Columbia University Press).

Wimsatt, Jr. W.K. [1968] "Genesis: A Fallacy Revisited," in Peter Demetz *et al.* (eds.), *The Disciplines of Criticism* (New Haven: Yale University Press).

Wimsatt, Jr., William K. and Monroe C. Beardsley. [1954a] "The Intentional Fallacy," in W.K. Wimsatt, Jr., *The Verbal Icon* (Lexington: University of Kentucky Press).

Wimsatt, Jr., William K. and Monroe C. Beardsley. [1954b] "The Affective Fallacy," in W.K. Wimsatt, Jr., *The Verbal Icon* (Lexington: University of Kentucky Press).

Winch, Peter. [1970] "Understanding and Explanation in Sociology and Anthropology," in Robert Borger and Frank Cioffi (eds.), *Explanation in the Behavioural Sciences* (Cambridge: Cambridge University Press).

Winters, Yvor. [1957] *The Function of Criticism* (Denver: A. Swallow).

Winters, Yvor. [1960] *In Defense of Reason* (London: Routledge and K. Paul).

Wittgenstein, Ludwig. [1953] *Philosophical Investigations,* trans. G.E.M. Anscombe (New York: Macmillan).

Wittgenstein, Ludwig. [1956] *Remarks on the Foundations of Mathematics*, trans. G.E.M. Anscombe (Oxford: Basil Blackwell).

Wittgenstein, Ludwig. [1958] *The Blue and Brown Books* (Oxford: Basil Blackwell).

Wölfflin, Heinrich. [1932] *Principles of Art History*, trans. M.D. Hottinger (London: G. Bell).

Wollheim, Richard. [1967] "Expression," in *The Human Agent* (Royal Institute of Philosophy Lectures, Vol. 1) (London: St. Martin's Press).

Wollheim, Richard. [1968] *Art and Its Objects* (New York: Harper and Row).

Wollheim, Richard. [1974] "The Work of Art as Object," *On Art and the Mind* (Cambridge: Harvard University Press).

Wolterstorff, Nicholas. [1970] *On Universals* (Chicago: University of Chicago Press).

Wolterstorff, Nicholas. [1975a] "Worlds of Works of Art," *Journal of Aesthetics and Art Criticism*, XXXV.

Wolterstorff, Nicholas. [1975b] "Toward an Ontology of Art Works," *Nous*, IX.

Wolterstorff, Nicholas. [unpublished] "Characters and Their Names."

Woods, John. [1974] *The Logic of Fiction: A Philosophical Sounding of Deviant Logic* (The Hague: Mouton).

Worringer, Wilhelm. [1953] *Abstraction and Empathy*, trans. Michael Bullock (New York: International Universities Press).

Zemach, Eddy N. [1971] "Thirteen Ways of Looking at the Ethics-Aesthetics Parallelism," *Journal of Aesthetic and Art Criticism*, XXIX.

Ziff, Paul. [1953] "The Task of Defining a Work of Art," *Philosophical Review*, LXIII.

Ziff, Paul. [1954] "Art and the 'Object of Art,' " in William Elton (ed.), *Aesthetics and Language* (Oxford: Basil Blackwell).

Ziff, Paul. [1960] *Semantic Analysis* (Ithaca: Cornell University Press).

Ziff, Paul. [1966] "Reasons in Art Criticism," in Israel Scheffler (ed.), *Philosophy and Education*, 2nd ed. (Boston: Allyn and Bacon).

Zink, Sidney. [1945] "The Poetic Organism," *Journal of Philosophy*, XLII.

Zis, Avner. [1977] *Foundations of Marxist Aesthetics*, trans. Katharine Judelson (Moscow: Progress Publishers).

GENERAL INDEX

INDEX OF REFERENCES